Lecture Notes in Computer Science 7122

Commenced Publication in 1973
Founding and Former Series Editors:
Gerhard Goos, Juris Hartmanis, and Jan van Leeuwen

Joaquin Garcia-Alfaro
Guillermo Navarro-Arribas
Nora Cuppens-Boulahia
Sabrina de Capitani di Vimercati (Eds.)

Data Privacy Management and Autonomous Spontaneus Security

6th International Workshop, DPM 2011, and
4th International Workshop, SETOP 2011
Leuven, Belgium, September 15-16, 2011
Revised Selected Papers

 Springer

Volume Editors

Joaquin Garcia-Alfaro
TELECOM-Bretagne, Campus de Rennes
2, rue de la Châtaigneraie, 35512 Cesson Sévigné Cedex, France
E-mail: joaquin.garcia@telecom-bretagne.eu

Guillermo Navarro-Arribas
Universitat Autonoma de Barcelona
Edifici-Q, Campus UAB, 08193 Bellaterra, Spain
E-mail: gnavarro@deic.uab.cat

Nora Cuppens-Boulahia
TELECOM-Bretagne, Campus de Rennes
2, rue de la Châtaigneraie, 35512 Cesson Sévigné Cedex, France
E-mail: nora.cuppens@telecom-bretagne.eu

Sabrina de Capitani di Vimercati
Università degli Studi di Milano
Dipartimento di Tecnologie dell'Informazione
Via Bramante 65, 26013 Crema, Italy
E-mail: sabrina.decapitani@unimi.it

ISSN 0302-9743   e-ISSN 1611-3349
ISBN 978-3-642-28878-4   ISBN 978-3-642-28879-1 (eBook)
DOI 10.1007/978-3-642-28879-1
Springer Heidelberg Dordrecht London New York

Library of Congress Control Number: 2012933375

CR Subject Classification (1998): K.6.5, E.3, K.4.1, K.4.4, C.2, C.3, D.4.6, H.3.5

LNCS Sublibrary: SL 4 – Security and Cryptology

Typesetting: Camera-ready by author, data conversion by Scientific Publishing Services, Chennai, India

Printed on acid-free paper

Springer is part of Springer Science+Business Media (www.springer.com)

Foreword from the DPM 2011 Program Chairs

The current volume constitutes the proceedings for the 6th Data Privacy Management International Workshop (DPM 2011), which includes revised versions of the papers presented at the workshop. The aim of DPM is to promote and stimulate international collaboration and research exchange on novel data privacy topics. This sixth edition of the workshop was co-located with the ESORICS 2011 symposium in Leuven (Belgium). Previous DPM workshops were: 2010 in Athens (Greece), 2009 in Saint Malo (France), 2007 Istanbul (Turkey), 2006 Atlanta (USA), and 2005 Tokyo (Japan).

The program of this year's workshop consisted of nine full papers and one short paper. The topics of these papers included location privacy, privacy-based metering and billing, record linkage, policy-based privacy, application of data privacy in recommendation systems, and privacy considerations in user profiling, in RFID, in network monitoring, in transaction protocols, in usage control, and customer data.

We would like to acknowledge and thank all the support received from the Program Committee members, external reviewers, and the Organizing Committee of ESORICS 2011. The General Chair of DPM 2011, Joaquin Garcia-Alfaro, and the General Chair of ESORICS 2011, Bart Preneel, are thanked. We would like to thank Saartje Verheyen for all her support and help. In the same vein we thank the sponsors of the workshop for helping with economic, logistic, and technical issues: Technicolor, Institut TELECOM, the Internet Interdisciplinary Institute (IN3) of the Open University of Catalonia (UOC), the Artificial Intelligence Research Institute (IIIA - CSIC), the UNESCO Chair in Data Privacy, the Spanish-funded projects N-KHRONOUS TIN2010-15764, ARES-CONSOLIDER CSD2007-00004 and eAegis TSI2007-65406-C03-01/TSI2007-65406-C03-02, and the DEMONS project FP7-ICT-2009-5 from the European Commission. Last, but definitely not least, we would like to thank all the authors who submitted papers, all the attendees, and the keynote speakers who took part in the workshop: Claudia Diaz, George Danezis, and Gildas Avoine.

November 2011
Nora Cuppens-Boulahia
Guillermo Navarro-Arribas

Foreword from the SETOP 2011 Program Chairs

This volume contains the papers presented at the fourth issue of the SETOP workshop, held in Leuven (Belgium), during September 15–16. The SETOP workshop is a companion event of the ESORICS symposium which presents research results on all aspects related to the security of autonomous and spontaneous networks. These two notions imply that specific communities of nodes, capable of interconnecting, are dynamically created, building on self-configuring mechanisms. In the end, they are expected to become autonomic systems that provide services without external intervention.

The program of this year's workshop consisted of nine full papers and two short papers. These papers were selected after rigorous review and intensive discussion by the Program Committee members and external reviewers. The topics of these papers included access control, policy derivation, requirements engineering, verification of service-oriented architectures, query and data privacy, policy delegation and service orchestration. The workshop was also honored with three distinguished keynote speakers — Claudia Diaz from Katholieke Universiteit Leuven, George Danezis from Microsoft Research Cambridge, and Gildas Avoine from Université Catholique de Louvain. Thank you, Claudia, George and Gildas, for having accepted our invitation.

Many other people also deserve our gratitude. We would like to thank the General Chair of SETOP 2011, Frederic Cuppens; and the General Chair of ESORICS 2011, Bart Preneel. The Organizing Committee from ESORICS 2011 helped with the local organization. We would like to thank Saartje Verheyen for all her support and help; and the sponsors of the workshop for helping with economic, logistic and technical issues: Technicolor, Institut TELECOM, the Internet Interdisciplinary Institute (IN3) of the Open University of Catalonia (UOC), and the Spanish-funded projects N-KHRONOUS TIN2010-15764, ARES-CONSOLIDER CSD2007-00004, and e-Aegis TSI2007-65406-C03-01/TSI2007-65406-C03-02, and the DEMONS project FP7-ICT-2009-5 from the European Commission. We finally thank all authors of submitted papers, as well as the Program Committee members and external reviewers for their help, availability, and commitment.

November 2011
Joaquin Garcia-Alfaro
Sabrina De Capitani di Vimercati

6th International Workshop
on Data Privacy Management – DPM 2011

Program Committee Chairs

Nora Cuppens-Boulahia	TELECOM Bretagne, France
Guillermo Navarro-Arribas	Autonomous University of Barcelona, Spain

Workshop General Chair

Joaquin Garcia-Alfaro	TELECOM Bretagne, France

Program Committee

Diala Abihaidar	Dar Al Hekma College, Saudi Arabia
Anas Abou El Kalam	Toulouse Institute of Computer Science Research, France
Carlos Aguilar Melchor	XLIM Research Institute, France
Mohd Anwar	University of Pittsburgh, USA
Joan Borrell	Autonomous University of Barcelona, Spain
Milan Bradonjic	Los Alamos National Laboratory, USA
Jordi Castella-Roca	Rovira i Virgili University, Spain
Iliano Cervesato	Carnegie Mellon University, Qatar
Valentina Ciriani	Università degli Studi di Milano, Italy
Frederic Cuppens	TELECOM Bretagne, France
Mourad Debbabi	Concordia university, Canada
Josep Domingo Ferrer	Rovira i Virgili University, Spain
David Evans	University of Cambridge, UK
Philip W.L. Fong	University of Calgary, Canada
Sebastien Gambs	Université de Rennes 1, France
Javier Herranz	Universitat Politecnica de Catalunya, Spain
Wei Jiang	Missouri University of Science and Technology, USA
Georgios Lioudakis	National Technical University of Athens, Greece
Javier Lopez	University of Malaga, Spain
Bradley Malin	Vanderbilt University, USA
Jordi Nin	Universitat Politecnica de Catalunya, Spain
Kai Rannenberg	Goethe-Universität, Germany
Yves Roudier	EURECOM Sophia-Antipolis, France
Tomas Sander	Hewlett-Packard Labs, USA
Yucel Saygin	Sabanci University, Turkey

4th SETOP International Workshop on Autonomous and Spontaneous Security – SETOP 2011

Program Committee Chairs

Joaquin Garcia-Alfaro	TELECOM Bretagne, France
Sabrina De Capitani di Vimercati	Università degli Studi di Milano, Italy

Workshop General Chair

Frederic Cuppens	TELECOM Bretagne, France

Program Committee

Gildas Avoine	Catholic University of Louvain, Belgium
Michel Barbeau	Carleton University, Canada
Carlo Blundo	University of Salerno, Italy
Joan Borrell	Autonomous University of Barcelona, Spain
Mike Burmester	Florida State University, USA
Jordi Castella-Roca	Rovira i Virgili University, Spain
Ana Cavalli	TELECOM SudParis, France
Iliano Cervesato	Carnegie Mellon University, Qatar
Frederic Cuppens	TELECOM Bretagne, France
Nora Cuppens-Boulahia	TELECOM Bretagne, France
Vanesa Daza	Universitat Pompeu Fabra, Spain
Sabrina De Capitani di Vimercati	Università degli Studi di Milano, Italy
Josep Domingo-Ferrer	Rovira i Virgili University, Spain
Sara Foresti	Università degli Studi di Milano, Italy
Joaquin Garcia-Alfaro	TELECOM Bretagne, France
Stefanos Gritzalis	University of the Aegean, Greence
Jordi Herrera	Autonomous University of Barcelona, Spain
Wei Jiang	Missouri University of Science and Technology, USA
Krishna Kant	Intel and NSF, USA
Sokratis Katsikas	University of Piraeus, Greece
Evangelos Kranakis	Carleton University, Canada
Pascal Lafourcade	University Joseph Fourier, France
Giovanni Livraga	Università degli Studi di Milano, Italy

Table of Contents

Autonomous and Spontaneous Security

Short Papers

Privacy Challenges in RFID

Gildas Avoine

Université Catholique de Louvain
B-1348 Louvain-la-Neuve, Belgium

Abstract. Privacy in RFID systems is a fruitful research field that emerged a few years ago only, and that is today covered by several hundred scientific publications. This short paper relates the content of the invited talk given by Gildas Avoine on the privacy challenges in RFID. It explains why privacy is an important matter but it also investigates whether the current researches appropriately answer to the real problem.

Keywords: Privacy, Security, Cryptography, RFID.

1 Threat Classification

1.1 Background

Radio Frequency Identification (RFID) is a pervasive technology deployed in various everyday life applications in order to identify objects without line of sight. As illustrated in Fig. 1, an RFID system consists of tags, namely microcircuits with an antenna carried by the object, and readers which can potentially be connected to a back-end system. A major characteristic of such systems is that there is no communication between the tags.

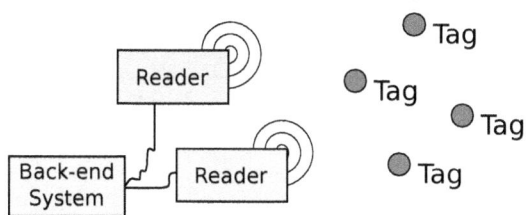

Fig. 1. RFID System Architecture

A common controversial problem is about the frontier between RFID and the other technologies. The question is whether a contactless smartcard is or not an RFID tag. In a recommendation published in 2009, the European Commission considers that RFID *"means the use of electromagnetic radiating waves or reactive field coupling in the radio frequency portion of the spectrum to communicate to or from a tag through a variety of modulation and encoding schemes to*

J. Garcia-Alfaro et al. (Eds.): DPM 2011 and SETOP 2011, LNCS 7122, pp. 1–8, 2012.
© Springer-Verlag Berlin Heidelberg 2012

uniquely read the identity of a radio frequency tag or other data stored on it." [15]
According to this definition, contactless smartcards also belong to RFID. Note
however that there is not only one RFID technology: depending on the considered application, the tag can be designed to fit the needs. Fig. 2 represents
the most relevant tag characteristics, and Fig. 3 and 4 illustrate two typical
configurations in logistics and access control.

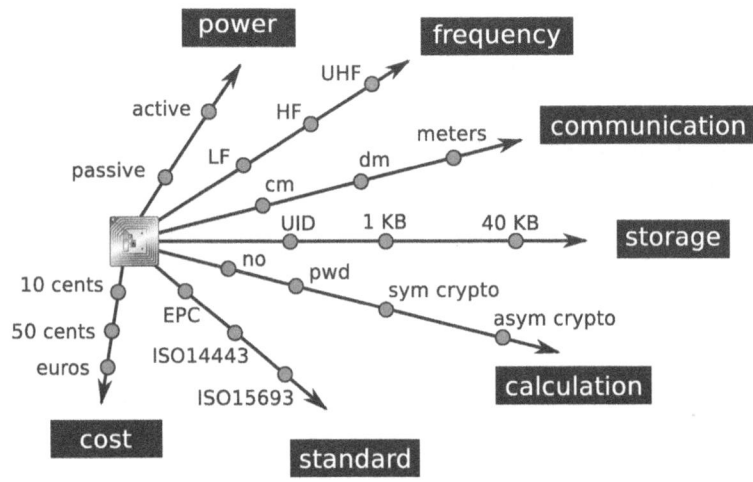

Fig. 2. Tag Characteristics

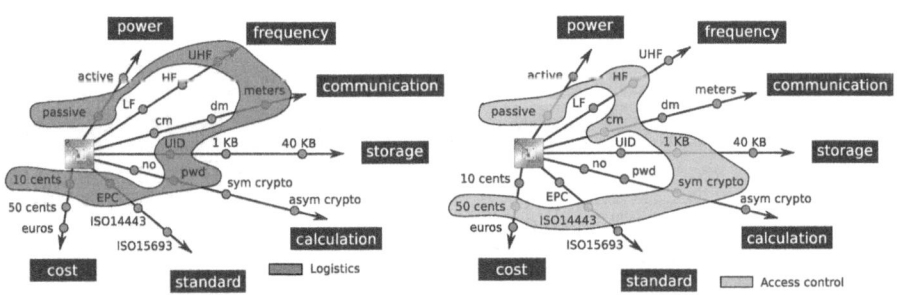

Fig. 3. Supply Chains   **Fig. 4.** Access Control

Visionaries expect a large deployment of the technology in the future. Nevertheless, RFID is already largely deployed in many applications, for example
pet identification, electronic passports, real-time localization, library inventory,
tracking in supply chain, access control especially in mass transportation where
RFID speeds up the customer flow, loyalty cards, etc.

1.2   Security Threats

While RFID has existed for several decades, RFID security and privacy has only recently become a major concern in the information security community. Expertise in security of smartcards was already well-established but the RFID technology has raised new problems, unexplored until then, due to the following specificities: (1) wireless communications are more sensitive to channel manipulations; (2) tags have lower capabilities than contact-based smartcards, and the business model behind RFID still reinforces the pressure to manufacture cheap chips; (3) the ubiquity of the tags clearly magnifies the privacy threat; (4) the wireless property of the communications opens the door to new applications, for example on-the-fly authentication in mass transportation, which still puts more constraints on the cryptographic algorithms, especially requiring them to be very fast. Threats can actually be divided into 4 categories as follows: denial of service, impersonation, information leakage, and malicious traceability. Other threat classifications exist [9], but the one provided here considers the adversary goals, which presents the advantage that the classification does not depend on the capabilities of the tags, and can thus be equally applied to both low-cost tags and powerful contactless smartcards.

Impersonation. This attack consists in being authenticated as someone else without being authorized to do so. This can be achieved by replay attacks, for instance, or any other weakness in the protocol, including those that allow an attacker to acquire knowledge on the secret of a tag (key recovery). The attacker can then disguise an expensive product into a cheap one, or gain access to restricted areas. The attack may have a theoretical impact only against a protocol not yet deployed in the real life, or it can be a practical attack against an existing product. A list of publications related to theoretical and practical *impersonation attacks against RFID protocols* can be found by searching for the keyword "impersonation" on the RFID Security and Privacy Lounge [1].

Denial of service. This attack occurs when an adversary attempts to prevent the application from functioning properly. In the framework of RFID, this can be done using various techniques such as using a blocker tag [12], introducing electromagnetic noise on the channel, etc. Electronic denial of service attacks are extremely difficult to avoid, and are usually not taken into account in the security analyzes of the authentication protocols. Some other types of denial of service attacks are due to weaknesses in the protocol design. For instance, desynchronization attacks in stateful protocols make further authentication of a tag-reader pair impossible. In practice, a denial of service can also be simply the erasing of data on a tag whose memory is not write-protected, which is surprisingly common in the real life.

The first two *security* threats clearly target the system, but do not necessarily aim to harm the customers. Sect. 2 and 3 introduce two *privacy* threats whose goals are precisely to expose the customers. An analysis of the literature [1] shows that more than 600 research papers have been published in the field of RFID security and privacy since 2002. Among them 38% clearly deal with privacy[1] and 18% more specifically focus on design or analysis of privacy-friendly authentication protocols. Only 2% of the whole set of papers focus on privacy models.

2 Privacy: Information Leakage

Information leakage occurs when an adversary obtains private information on a person. People are nowadays more aware of this threat, given the rapid deployment of social network tools like Facebook, LinkedIn, and Picasa to name a few. Nevertheless, RFID is certainly more pernicious than these tools is the sense that it is directly worn by the customers, and comes along with useful applications without alternative for the customers: ePassport, public transportation pass, access control badge, etc. Sect. 2.1 and 2.2 highlight that the personal information may leak from the tag, but it may also leak from the back-end system.

2.1 Information Revealed by the Tag

When the tag carries personal data, it is clear that it may reveal them to any passerby if no suited cryptographic mechanism is implemented. This case is surprisingly very common. For example, electronic passports without basic access control [3] may reveal personal information about its holder, including name, birthday, picture, and digitalized signature. Many other applications store personal data in the tags without any protection, for example the public transportation passes used in Brussels [4].

It is important to underline that an information that is not intrinsically attached to a person is not necessarily harmless. A vivid illustration is the public transportation cards, for example those relying on Calypso [6], an electronic ticketing standard developed by European partners. In this standard, the card does not necessarily contain the name of the holder, and its identity can even not appear printed on the card if the latter is an anonymous one. Nevertheless, the card contains technical data, including information about the three last travels of the customer, and the link between the card and the customer is just trivial because he keeps his card with him for future travels. This points out that the adversary is not necessarily an unlikely passerby, but she can be the customer's wife [2], who wonders why he is late and tries to discreetly find an explanation.

2.2 Information Revealed by the Back-End System

When the tag's answer sent to the reader is meaningless without additional data, the previous problem seems to be solved. It is actually only postponed, because the threat is shifted toward the back-end system. Obviously, protecting the back-end system is much easier that protecting the data on the tag. Nevertheless, it makes sense to mention this issue as it commonly occurs in practice.

---

[1] Papers where the number of occurrences of the word "privacy" is at least 20.

[2] Replace appropriately to suit your case.

To illustrate this statement, an example is the regulations about the pet identification in the Schengen Area. Dogs, cats, and ferrets crossing borders within the Schengen Area are required since July 3rd, 2011, to carry an implanted electronic tag. When a tag is queried by a reader, it simply provides a number that is meaningless for those who do not have access to the pet identification databases. Countries indeed manage national databases that contain information about both the pets and their holders. In some countries, e.g. Belgium, this database is freely available on the Web. Given the UID received from the tag carried by a pet, information about its owner can be retrieved from the database. When an owner announces on a website that he lost his pet, he usually provides some information about the animal, including the UID of its tag, and he also displays his phone number, but keeps confidential his name and address. However, by inserting the UID found in an announcement in the appropriate field of the database, the information about the owner, including name and address, is revealed to anyone. Given that the UIDs in this application are not random but sequential, the attack can even have more important consequences than one may *a priori* expect.

3   Privacy: Malicious Traceability

Malicious traceability has probably less dangerous consequences than information leakage, but no solution to this problem exists yet. Malicious traceability consists in tracing a tag and therefore a customer in space or time. Intuitively, this concept could be defined as follows: given a set of readings between tags and readers, an adversary should not be able to correlate two readings, that is to guess that they have been performed by the same tag. This implies that the response of the tag must change with each session and have negligible correlation with the previous (and future) responses.

3.1   Models and Protocols

Any communication between a reader and a tag starts with an identification or authentication protocol, followed by other protocols depending on the application. Evaluating the privacy compliance of a protocol first requires to precisely catch the concept of privacy. The intuitive definition provided above is clearly not sufficient to rigorously evaluate the privacy of a protocol, but several models have been proposed during the last years, e.g., [2,7,13,18,19].

The large body of literature on RFID security and privacy demonstrates that designing a privacy-friendly protocol is still a challenging task. Indeed, although many protocols have been proposed over the years, none can be deemed as ideal. Researches essentially focus on the following (non-exhaustive) list of topics: protocols whose reader complexity is better than linear, protocols based on public-key cryptography, protocols relaxing the privacy property, and protocols based on non-standard cryptographic primitives.

3.2   A Problem without Solution

Most of the papers published so far focus on authentication or identification protocols, possibly with some variants, for example ownership transfer, yoking-proofs, anti-counterfeiting, etc. However, few of them address the lower layers of the communication. Indeed, Avoine and Oechslin explain in [5] that ensuring privacy requires to ensure this property not only in the application layer, but also in the physical and communication layers. This illustrates the major difference between privacy and the other security properties, namely confidentiality, integrity, and authenticity which, if ensured in a theoretical model, are also ensured in practice, assuming there is no implementation weakness. According to [5], the malicious traceability problem can be solved in the communication layer, namely in the collision-avoidance layer, if the tag has a cryptographically secure pseudo-random number generator. However, Avoine and Oechslin also explain that there is no solution to solve the malicious traceability problem in the physical layer due to, on the one hand the diversity of the standards, on the other hand the electronic fingerprinting of the circuits.

Designing an RFID solution that is privacy-friendly is a dead-end, which is quite a pessimistic conclusion. Attacks in the physical, communication, and application layers are significantly different, though, which means that finding a solution that solves the problem in one layer only makes sense anyway.

4   Research Challenges

4.1   Need of Privacy

The examples provided all along this paper clearly point out major privacy problems in RFID systems. Two solutions can be considered: either finding technical or legal means to fix the problems, or considering that there is no problem. Indeed, while privacy is today something most people take care, it is not clear whether privacy will still be relevant in the far future. Even today, not all the people take care with the same interest about their privacy. A quick search on Internet on a given person usually reveals tons of information: address, phone numbers, pictures, close friends, education, employer, hobbies,... Internet is actually one information source, but many others exist, as every action is today recorded in a database: validating a transportation pass, opening the door of his building, giving a call, accessing an Internet website, even refuelling is recorded at least by the car, the pump, the payment reader and the video surveillance system.

Whatever one may think about privacy, the point is that activists fight RFID and slow down the deployment of this technology. Authorities also take care of the problem and require manufacturers to address it. For example, the European Commission stated in 2009 [15]:

"Because of its potential to be both ubiquitous and practically invisible, particular attention to privacy and data protection issues is required in the deployment of RFID. Consequently, privacy and information security features should be built into RFID applications before their widespread use (principle of security and privacy-by-design)".

Similar initiatives also exist in North America [8,17]. If no one knows what privacy will mean in the far future, it is clear that this problem is real today and must be addressed.

4.2   Security as a Whole

Several works about malicious traceability and information leakage in RFID have been published during the last years. However, most of them target the design of a tag-reader protocol that preserves privacy without considering the remaining elements of the RFID system, especially the readers and the back-end system. Although the protection in terms of privacy of the communications between the tag and the reader is of the utmost importance, privacy models should consider the system as a whole. Indeed, RFID systems usually deal with a large amount of personal information, stored in local or centralized databases. This sensitive information must be treated with the utmost care. In recent years, several cases of data loss have hit the headlines, especially in the EU [11]. Also, most current guidelines about RFID security only focus on external breaches; however the major threats usually come from insiders: according to [16] more than half of information losses are due to both malicious employees and others who have made some kind of "unintentional blunder". This critical aspect is commonly put aside in current analyzes of RFID systems.

4.3   Toward a Privacy Certification

In spite of the large body of literature on RFID privacy, everyday life applications are definitely designed without any privacy requirements. A few exceptions can probably be pointed out, for example the ePassport standardized by the ICAO. The situation comes from the lack of business model related to privacy. Indeed, their is a direct benefit in implementing security measures, namely to avoid frauds, but there is no clear benefit in implementing privacy measures.

While there exist security models, for example the Common Criteria [10], and initiatives to develop quantitative measure of security, for example the US MITRE project [14], the existing work cannot be directly transposed to the privacy problem. A privacy certification may allow the manufacturers and integrators to get an international, undeniable, and transferable proof that their RFID solutions protect the personal information they process.

Such a certification would require to no longer focus on the tag-reader communication only, but to consider RFID privacy with a larger view. The works done so far in RFID privacy are important, but quite narrow. Finally, such a certification could be used as a lever to introduce privacy in the design of forthcoming applications.

References

1. Avoine, G.: RFID Security & Privacy Lounge, http://www.avoine.net/rfid/
2. Avoine, G.: Adversary Model for Radio Frequency Identification. Technical Report LASEC-REPORT-2005-001, Swiss Federal Institute of Technology, EPFL (2005)
3. Avoine, G., Kalach, K., Quisquater, J.-J.: ePassport: Securing International Contacts with Contactless Chips. In: Tsudik, G. (ed.) FC 2008. LNCS, vol. 5143, pp. 141–155. Springer, Heidelberg (2008)
4. Avoine, G., Martin, T., Szikora, J.-P.: Lire son passe navigo en un clin d'œil. Multi-System & Internet Security Cookbook – MISC 48 (March-April 2010)
5. Avoine, G., Oechslin, P.: RFID Traceability: A Multilayer Problem. In: S. Patrick, A., Yung, M. (eds.) FC 2005. LNCS, vol. 3570, pp. 125–140. Springer, Heidelberg (2005)
6. Calypso Networks Association, http://www.calypsonet-asso.org/
7. Canard, S., Coisel, I., Etrog, J., Girault, M.: Privacy-Preserving RFID Systems: Model and Constructions. Cryptology ePrint Archive, Report 2010/405 (2010)
8. Cavioukan, A.: Privacy guidelines for RFID information systems (2006)
9. Chatmon, C., van Le, T., Burmester, M.: Secure Anonymous RFID Authentication Protocols. Technical Report TR-060112, Florida State University (2006)
10. Common Criteria, http://www.commoncriteriaportal.org/
11. ICO. Information commissionner's office, http://www.ico.gov.uk/
12. Juels, A., Rivest, R., Szydlo, M.: The Blocker Tag: Selective Blocking of RFID Tags for Consumer Privacy. In: ACM CCS 2003, pp. 103–111. ACM Press (2003)
13. Juels, A., Weis, S.: Defining Strong Privacy for RFID. In: PerCom 2007, pp. 342–347 (2007)
14. MITRE. Making security measurable, http://measurablesecurity.mitre.org/
15. Reding, V.: Commission recommendation of 12.05.2009 - sec(2009) 585/586, on the implementation of privacy and data protection principles in applications supported by radio-frequency identification (2009)
16. Richardson, R.: 15th annual 2010/2011 computer crime and security survey. Technical report, Computer Security Institute (2011)
17. Simitian, J.: CA Senate Bill No. 682 (2005), http://leginfo.public.ca.gov
18. van Deursen, T., Mauw, S., Radomirović, S.: Untraceability of RFID Protocols. In: Onieva, J.A., Sauveron, D., Chaumette, S., Gollmann, D., Markantonakis, K. (eds.) WISTP 2008. LNCS, vol. 5019, pp. 1–15. Springer, Heidelberg (2008)
19. Vaudenay, S.: On Privacy Models for RFID. In: Kurosawa, K. (ed.) ASIACRYPT 2007. LNCS, vol. 4833, pp. 68–87. Springer, Heidelberg (2007)

Fake Injection Strategies
for Private Phonetic Matching

Alexandros Karakasidis[1], Vassilios S. Verykios[2], and Peter Christen[3]

[1] Department of Computer and Communication Engineering
University of Thessaly
Volos, Greece
akarakasidis@inf.uth.gr
[2] School of Science and Technology
Hellenic Open University
Patras, Greece
verykios@eap.gr
[3] ANU College of Engineering and Computer Science
The Australian National University
Canberra, Australia
peter.christen@anu.edu.au

Abstract. In many aspects of everyday life, from education to health care and from economics to homeland security, information exchange involving companies or government agencies has become a common application. Locating the same real world entities within this information however is not trivial at all due to insufficient identifying information, misspellings, etc. The problem becomes even more complicated when privacy considerations arise. This introduction describes an informal approach to the privacy preserving record linkage problem. In this paper we provide a solution to this problem by examining the alternatives offered by phonetic codes, a range of algorithms which despite their age, are still used for record linkage purposes. The main contribution of our work, as our extensive experimental evaluation indicates, is that our methodology manages to offer privacy guarantees for performing Privacy Preserving Record Linkage without the need of computationally expensive cryptographic methods.

Keywords: Privacy, Record Linkage, Approximate Matching, Phonetic Encoding, Relative Information Gain.

1 Introduction

One of the characteristics of our times is the high dissemination of personal information. Almost every day, all of us fill in either electronic or hard copy forms with information that should not be made publicly available. Consequently, large volumes of data are stored in repositories of distinct organizations. Each organization uses of course its own representation of these data. However, these data would be useful if combined for applications ranging from crime fighting to scientific research. The problem becomes even more complicated considering that not

J. Garcia-Alfaro et al. (Eds.): DPM 2011 and SETOP 2011, LNCS 7122, pp. 9–24, 2012.

rarely, the stored data have low quality, such as discrepancies, misspellings, null values and so on. For many years the field of Record Linkage has been providing solutions towards this direction [9].

But, what happens when it comes to privacy? It is obvious that we would not be very happy if our personal information stored by our health care organization or even by our bank were freely distributed in order to be linked, even for legal or scientific purposes. To make the problem more tangible, we will provide a fairly recent real world example. In the near past, the German authorities in their attempt to fight tax evasion among German citizens bribed a clerk of a Swiss bank to gain access to the bank's database. Of course the problem is not that some people will eventually have to pay their taxes, but the fact that the privacy of many more people has been compromised [20].

The aforementioned example provides a clear justification for the need of privacy preservation regarding sensitive information. At this point however someone would wonder if there could be a legal way to discover tax cheaters without jeopardizing privacy. Inevitably, some more questions are rising. Do classical record linkage techniques provide privacy? If they do, to what extent? Can we enhance them in order to provide privacy? Employing classical record linkage techniques for privacy preserving record linkage has the advantage of using our existing experience in a new variation of the same problem. But is this sufficient or do we need to develop new methods? In other words, can we teach an old dog new tricks? We will try to provide answers to all of these questions examining the paradigm of phonetic encoding.

A phonetic encoding is an algorithm for matching words based on their pronunciation [2]. Phonetic encoding algorithms have been used for decades, therefore they are a good starting point for assessing the privacy provided by an established technique to the private version of the record linkage problem. The main feature of phonetic encoding algorithms is their fault tolerance against typographical errors. Moreover, their complexity is much lower compared to Edit Distance [18] or N-gram based methods [5]. In this work we will attempt to investigate properties that might be suitable for performing private approximate matching.

In this paper we assume Soundex [21] as our phonetic encoding algorithm and examine its statistical properties to assess the amount of privacy it provides. However, our methodology can be easily applied to other phonetic encoding algorithms as well. Our work is motivated by [15] where phonetics-based private matching was originally introduced and fake codes where used to provide privacy. In this paper we assess the impact of different fake injection strategies on privacy and data quality in a phonetics based record matching setup.

Our methodology focuses on studying the effects of different fake data distributions on the original dataset and the impact on the original distribution in terms of statistical privacy preservation. Therefore we compare the results of our study by using Relative Information Gain, an Information Theoretic Metric.

Our contributions may be briefly outlined as follows. First, we propose a new, more practical definition of private record linkage. Next, we propose three fake injection strategies for providing privacy in a phonetics based record linkage setup. Finally, we provide empirical evidence of our claims by extensive experimentation.

The rest of our paper is organized as follows. Section 2 provides work related to ours. In Section 3 we provide a new formulation of the problem, as we see it from our perspective. Section 4 provides the necessary background for understanding our approach. In Section 5 we detail our approaches for privacy preserving record linkage based on phonetic codes. Section 6 provides the experimental evaluation of our work. Section 7 concludes our paper and provides some thoughts for future research directions.

2   Related Work

Record matching (or linkage) is a rather old yet important area of research that aims at consolidating data from heterogeneous sources. These data often exhibit low quality. Towards solving this problem, various methods for performing approximate string matching have been proposed. An overview of all major currently used methods can be found in [9]. Performance has always been an issue as indicated in [4]. The extensive research on the field has led to the development of a variety of approximate record linkage systems such as Tailor [8] and Febrl [3].

We will make special reference to a specific category for approximate string matching algorithms. Phonetics-based methods make use of certain string transformations in order to take advantage of the way words sound for crossing out the effects of various typing and spelling errors. The most well known phonetic encoding is Soundex [21]. Other typical examples of such techniques include Metaphone [22], ONCA [10] and NYSIIS [28].

However, record linkage algorithms were not initially developed for protecting the privacy of the individuals whose data were stored and linked. As a result, Privacy Preserving Record Linkage was developed, a new research field which aimed at performing classical record linkage while maintaining privacy at the same time.

First research directions on this field were provided in [6] stating the needs and problems that rise. State of the art includes the work of Churches et al. [5] who propose deidentifying the Dice coefficient of n-grams using hashing. However approaches relying on [5] suffer from very high complexity. Privacy preservation of distance-based methods performed well only in cases of non-encrypted data as indicated in [30]. Moreover, as detailed in Trepetin's survey [29], some attempts to address the problem of privacy preserving record linkage fall short in providing a sound solution, either because they are very resource demanding or because they are unable to provide both matching accuracy and fault tolerance.

Inan et al. suggest using a hierarchical value generalization blocking scheme either in a hybrid setup with cryptographic functions [12] or in combination with differential privacy [13]. Scannapieco et al. [24] achieve privacy preserving data matching using embedding spaces and schema matching based on a global schema. The privacy properties of k-anonymity on joins explored by Kantar-cioglu et al. can be found in [14]. In an approach proposed by Atallah et al. [1] the edit distance algorithm is modified for providing privacy to genome sequence comparisons. Schnell et al. [25] have recently proposed a method based on a combination of bigrams and Bloom filters while Karakasidis et al. [17] use Bloom filters for private edit distance operations together with a phonetics based blocking scheme. Categorizations of recent approaches can be found in [16,11].

3   The PPRL Problem Formulation

In this Section we provide all the necessary details for describing the new formulation we suggest for the Privacy Preserving Record Linkage Problem (PPRL).

3.1   The PPRL Problem Restatement with Privacy Guarantees

Originally, the PPRL problem was formulated as following: Considering two data sources A and B, we wish to perform record matching between their datasets R_A and R_B in a way that at the end of the process, source A will only know the subset of B's data that match A's data. Equivalently, B will only acquire the subset of A's data that match its own data.

Currently, to the best of our knowledge, all secure record linkage methods provide an alternative representation of the original data in order to be compared and merged. Each alternative representation is always somehow related to the original data in order to maintain certain characteristics that will render it useful for approximate matching. The ability of inferring the original text given the representation used by each method is the factor that offers privacy. In order to measure this quantity, we introduce Definition 1.

Definition 1. *Let μ be a privacy metric for PPRL. Having a plain text database D_{pt} and its ciphered equivalent D_c, μ represents the ability to infer data from D_{pt} using data from D_c.*

According to this definition, higher values of the privacy metric μ result in higher ability of inferring the original text from the encoded text. Using this metric now, we are going to assess the privacy offered by a PPRL method.

Definition 2. *A PPRL method is considered to offer sufficient privacy guarantees, if the value of its privacy metric μ does not exceed a predetermined privacy threshold δ.*

Now using Definitions 1 and 2 we may restate the PPRL problem as follows:

Definition 3. *Considering data sources A, B, we wish to perform record matching between datasets R_A and R_B in a way that at the end of the process the privacy metric for source A, μ_A will not exceed δ_A. Similarly, the privacy metric for source B, μ_B will not exceed δ_B.*

At a first glance this definition may seem to offer a more relaxed version of the problem compared to the original one. However, this is not the case. This definition is more flexible in terms of allowing each participant of the PPRL process to define separate privacy metrics and separate privacy thresholds. Obviously, both A and B may use the same privacy metric $\mu = \mu_A = \mu_B$ and the same privacy threshold $\delta = \delta_A = \delta_B$. As expected, all the implications of the classical record linkage problem still remain with its private equivalent. This means that we still have to deal with non-unique identifiers and low quality data. In this paper our privacy metric μ will be the Relative Information Gain (RIG), as defined by Information Theory.

4 PPRL Building Blocks

In this section we will provide all the necessary elements for building our approach. We will use an existing matching protocol suitable for our approach and present the theoretical background for our technique.

4.1 The Soundex Forge

Soundex [2], based on English language pronunciation, is the oldest (patented in 1918 [21]) and best known phonetic encoding algorithm. It keeps the first letter in a string and converts the rest into numbers according to Table 1.

Table 1. Soundex Conversion Table

a, e, h, i, o, u, w, y	$\to 0$
b, f, p, v	$\to 1$
c, g, j, k, q, s, x, z	$\to 2$
d, t	$\to 3$
l	$\to 4$
m, n	$\to 5$
r	$\to 6$

All zeros (vowels and 'h', 'w' and 'y') are then removed and sequences of the same number are merged to a single one (e.g. '333' is replaced with '3'). The final code is the original first letter and three numbers (longer codes are stripped-off, and shorter codes are padded with zeros). As an example, the Soundex code for 'Peter' is 'P360', while the code for 'Christen' is 'C623'. A major drawback of Soundex is that it maintains the first letter, thus any error or variation at the beginning of a name will result in a different Soundex code. To overcome this problem a common approach is to also use the Soundex encoding of the reversed names.

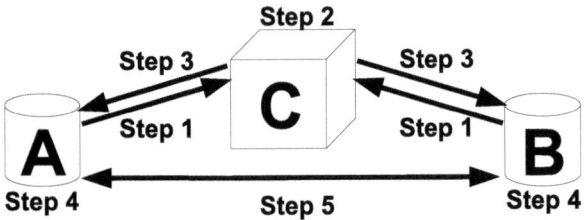

Fig. 1. A Matching Protocol for PPRL

4.2   A Matching Protocol for PPRL

To illustrate the operation of our methodology, we will assume a simple matching protocol similar to the one used by [15], consisting of three parties A, B and C as illustrated in Figure 1. A and B will be the data sources, while C will operate as an intermediate trusted node used to hide some information from A and B. The protocol can be outlined as follows.

Initially, each source generates the Soundex encoding for each record field it wishes to match. Since the most common Soundex code and consequently the most common name class can be inferred using frequency analysis, we inject fake Soundex codes to diminish the probability of undertaking such an attack. All codes are encrypted through a secure hash function e.g. MD5 [23] and randomly scrambled to ensure that C cannot infer which records refer to real world entities.

The first step of our protocol requires both A and B to send their Soundex encoded names to C. This is illustrated in Figure 1 as *Step 1*. At *Step 2* now, C joins the encrypted Soundex codes. C's role is important in this setup, since it refrains either A or B from acquiring information from each other's dataset. Neither of the two dataholders is aware of the others dataset size nor of the data transmitted to C. On the other hand, neither C has full access to information, since it only collects and joins Soundex codes. Some of the codes are fake, while phonetic encoding itself, as we show in Section 6, offers some inherent privacy features.

Then, as indicated by *Step 3*, C returns to the sources the identifiers for which there was a match. At *Step 4* each source processes the results gathered from C. This is an important step, because a party omits from the results the codes which reflect to fake records and those which are very highly distinctive.

Finally, at *Step 5*, each source contacts directly the other transmitting the Soundex codes that were not discarded during *Step 4* asking for the respective data. After receiving the query, each source delivers data for the remaining identifiers after *Step 4*. This does not lead to a privacy breach because the counterpart cannot be sure whether a record is fake or not. Similarly, the party which removed the distinctive record, may not be sure either whether it was matched with a fake or not.

4.3   The Relative Information Gain as a Measure of Privacy

In this section we provide the theoretical background necessary for our approach. We evaluate the privacy of our approach by using the metric of Relative Information Gain (RIG). To understand RIG it is necessary to describe Information Gain first. At this point we have to mention that Information Gain as a measure of privacy for record linkage has also been used in [7]. However, we prefer using Relative Information Gain which was initially referred to as *Inference* in [19], since it provides a normalized measure and is not affected by a dataset's size.

Information Gain is closely related to the Entropy measure, which is the amount of information in a message [26]. The Entropy is a function of the probability distribution over the set of all possible messages. The Entropy of a discrete random variable X is defined as:

$$H(X) = - \sum_{x \in \mathcal{X}} p(x) \log_2 p(x) = \sum_{x \in \mathcal{X}} p(x) \log_2 \frac{1}{p(x)}. \tag{1}$$

Practically speaking, the measure of entropy provides a degree of a set's predictability. Low entropy of X means low uncertainty and as a result, high predictability of X's values. Similarly, the conditional entropy of a discrete random variable Y given the value of the discrete random variable X, $H(Y|X)$ is defined as:

$$H(Y|X) = - \sum_{x \in \mathcal{X}} p(x)H(Y|X = x). \tag{2}$$

Empirically, the notion of conditional entropy aims at quantifying the amount of uncertainty in predicting the value of the discrete random variable Y given X. Information Gain between the discrete random variables Y and X is defined as

$$IG(Y|X) = H(Y) - H(Y|X). \tag{3}$$

Information Gain is a metric for assessing the difficulty of inferring the original text (Y), knowing its enciphered version (X), or in other words, how the knowledge of X's value can reduce the uncertainty of inferring Y. Lower Information Gain means that it is difficult to infer the original text from the cipher. However, Information Gain depends on the size of the measured dataset. Relative Information Gain on the other hand, provides a normalized scale with regard to the Entropy of the original text Y and is defined as:

$$RIG(Y|X) = \frac{IG(Y|X)}{H(Y)}. \tag{4}$$

Using Equations 3 and 4 we are led to the following observations. $RIG(Y|X)$ is a normalized metric. Its marginal values will be $RIG(Y|X) = 0$ when $H(Y) = H(Y|X)$ and $RIG(Y|X) = 1$ when $H(Y|X) = 0$. In the first case, the practical meaning is that given the ciphertext X, no information is gained, regarding the original text Y. As such, the transformation applied to the original text is considered to be absolutely secure. In the second case, using the ciphertext provides us the same amount of information as in the case of only having the original plaintext. It is evident that we aim at creating methods which will reduce the Relative Information Gain of a dataset. As a result the amount of information someone is able to infer about the Surnames when their Soundex codes are given will be reduced.

4.4   An Example Illustrating the RIG Metric

Table 2 holds the data for our sample scenario. In column *Surname* we can see the surnames of some tax payers. We assume that these surnames appear more than once in our database. The probability of a surname appearance in our database is displayed in the *p(Surname)* field. Finally, the *Soundex(Surname)* field provides the Soundex encoding for the Surname of the respective record.

Table 2. Sample Data

RecId	Surname	p(Surname)	Soundex(Surname)
1	Avdill	0.2	A134
2	Abdallah	0.3	A134
3	Apotolas	0.1	A134
4	Saussey	0.3	S200
5	Sawaski	0.1	S200

In this example, by using the data from Table 2, we will illustrate how Relative Information Gain for surnames given a set of Soundex codes is calculated for this specific dataset.

The entropy of the Surname distribution is: $H(Surname) = 0.2 \log_2 (1/0.2) +$ $\ldots + 0.1 \log_2 (1/0.1)$. This results in $H(Surname) \approx 2.17$

The probabilities for Soundex from Table 2 are: $p(A134) = 0.6$ and $p(S200) = 0.4$. The conditional entropy for all surnames will be:

$$H(Surname|Soundex) = p(A134)H(Surname|A134) + p(S200)H(Surname|S200)$$

Since $H(Surname|A134) = 1.45$ and $H(Surname|S200) = 0.097$ the conditional entropy of the Surname given Soundex will be: $H(Surname|Soundex) = 0.6 \cdot 1.45 + 0.4 \cdot 0.097 = 0.9088$. From Equation 3 we have: $IG(Surname|Soundex) = 2.17 - 0.9088 = 1.2612$. As a result, using Equation 4, the Relative Information Gain will be: $RIG(Surname|Soundex) = 1.2612/2.17 \approx 0.58$. Considering that the plaintext's RIG is equal to 1, since from Equation 3 we have $H(Y|X) = 0$, we understand that Soundex does provide inherent privacy preserving characteristics. But, can we do any better?

5   A Faking Phonetic Encoding Methodology

In this section we present three approaches using fake record generation for providing privacy. We will illustrate their theoretical properties and provide formulas for calculating the resulting RIG when possible. We will assume again our example scenario, where our plaintexts consist of Surnames and the ciphertexts consist of Soundex codes. Both the Surnames and the Soundex codes follow different distributions. Our aim is to minimize the RIG metric by altering both of these distributions.

To be consistent with our description, we will employ the following notation. We consider having n distinct surnames which are mapped to m distinct Soundex codes. A Soundex code may refer at most to K distinct Surnames. Also, the maximum number of occurrences for any given Surname in the original plaintext dataset is equal to L. We next describe our three privacy preservation techniques.

5.1   Uniform Ciphertext/Uniform Plaintext

The Uniform Ciphertext/Uniform Plaintext (UCUP) approach derives directly from the observation that in order to reduce RIG, the plaintexts and the ciphertexts should appear an equal number of times. In other words we want to force both of these sets, which in our example are the Surnames and the Soundex codes, to exhibit uniform distributions. To achieve this, we inject fake records in a way that all Soundex codes will map to an equal number of surnames.

Let us assume that each distinct surname appears at most L times. To achieve uniform distribution for the Surnames, the number of occurrences for each of the n distinct Surnames has to be altered such as all of them have to appear an equal number of times, that is L. Each of the m distinct Soundex codes appears at most K times. Consequently, the number of distinct names that contribute to each Soundex code will be equal to K/L. Since we want all Soundex codes to appear an equal number of times, we should have again a total of mK records. However, we originally had Ln records, since we set each name to appear exactly L times. Considering this together with the fact that we have added $mK - Ln$ records to make all Soundex codes appear an equal number of times, the number of distinct fake surnames n' will be:

$$n' = \frac{mK - Ln}{L} \tag{5}$$

After the injection of fakes, the total number of distinct Surnames will be $n+n'$ and the total number of Surnames including fakes equal to $L(n+n')$. From Equation 1, we calculate the entropy H of the dataset we create as following:

$$H(Surname) = (n+n')\frac{L}{L(n+n')} \log_2 \frac{L(n+n')}{L} = \log_2(n+n') \tag{6}$$

Similarly, since each Soundex code reflects to L/K Surnames, the contribution of each of them to its corresponding Soundex code will be K/L. Therefore, the conditional entropy for a specific Soundex code will be:

$$H_{spec}(Surname|Soundex) = \frac{K}{L}\frac{L}{K} \log_2 \frac{K}{L} = \log_2 \frac{K}{L} \tag{7}$$

Because each of the m Soundex codes equally appears $1/m$ times, we finally have:

$$H(Surname|Soundex) = m\frac{1}{m}\log_2\frac{K}{L} = \log_2\frac{K}{L} \qquad (8)$$

Leading to RIG equal to:

$$RIG_{AE}(surname|Soundex) = \frac{\log_2(n + n') - \log_2\frac{K}{L}}{\log_2(n + n')} \qquad (9)$$

This technique offers the advantage of easily calculating the induced Information Gain with simple formulas. However, as we illustrate in Section 6, the number of fake Surname records that has to be inserted is huge compared to the initial dataset.

5.2   Uniform Ciphertexts by Swapping Plaintexts

In order to avoid oversized datasets, we introduce the Uniform Ciphertexts by Swapping Plaintexts (UCSP) strategy. In this approach, we calculate the average number of Surname occurrences for each Soundex code and denote it as $\lceil \bar{K} \rceil$. Next, for each Soundex code with more than $\lceil \bar{K} \rceil$ occurrences, we remove the redundant occurrences of the actual Surnames and add an equal number of fake occurrences for Soundex codes with less than $\lceil \bar{K} \rceil$ appearances, such that at the end each Soundex code appears exactly $\lceil \bar{K} \rceil$ times.

The advantage of the swapping approach is that it is not necessary to create an excessive number of fake records, in order to reduce information gain. However, this method also has a drawback. Each surname that is removed from the dataset in order to be exchanged with a fake one, will not participate in the record linkage process. These records will have to be separately stored and the matching process should initiate from the beginning. The rejected records form a different dataset and the procedure has to be repeated again. In Section 6 we will experimentally illustrate the properties of this strategy both in terms of RIG and data quality.

5.3 k-Anonymous Ciphertexts

It is evident that in many cases we can neither afford the UCUP strategy, nor wish to repeat the matching process as in the UCSP case. Therefore we suggest the k-anonymous Ciphertexts approach (kaC). Similar to the k-anonymity approach as used for anonymous data publishing [27], this approach aims at creating datasets where each Soundex code reflects to at least k Surnames. Since each Soundex code appears k times, it improves privacy. It is evident that this approach is parametric, having k as its tuning parameter. Therefore, for each Soundex code which consists of less than k Surnames, we inject fake surnames. For example, if a Soundex code is created by a single surname, then we will inject $k - 1$ distinct fake surnames in our dataset, all mapping to the specific Soundex code.

This approach does not produce either uniform Ciphertext distributions or uniform Plaintext distributions, but it has the advantage that it is tunable by

Table 3. Distributions of data used in empirical evaluation

Dataset	Distribution	Number of records	K
O	Original	6917514	75087
L	Linear	81867776403	364928606
U	Uniform	404642	1462
Z	Zipf	5443039	410007

means of the k parameter. As such, the required RIG can be adjusted against the fake records added. We will also provide empirical evaluation for this approach both for the achieved RIG and the additional fake records required.

6   Empirical Evaluation

In this section we provide empirical results in order to evaluate our theoretical approach. To achieve this we have used four Plaintext datasets. They are summarized in Table 3 together with the number of Surname records for each one. K, as introduced earlier in Section 5, stands for the maximum number of distinct Surnames a single Soundex code refers to.

All datasets contain the same number of distinct Surnames n in order to compare the results of each method on a standard basis. The Original dataset (O), features the genuine distribution of names found in the Australian online phone book. Each Surname might appear more than once. We also employ three synthetic datasets which derive from the Original dataset. The Linear dataset (L) features a linear distribution of the Surnames. The most frequent Surname has n occurrences. The occurrences for all the other $n-1$ Surnames fall linearly until the last Surname of the dataset which occurs only once. In the Uniform dataset (U) each Surname only occurs once. As a result, the size of the dataset is equal to the number of distinct Surnames n available in the dataset. Finally, in the Zipf dataset (Z) the Surnames follow a Zipf distribution.

For our empirical evaluation, for each record of each dataset, we have calculated the equivalent Soundex code and hashed it using the MD5 hashing function [23]. Hereafter, the term *Soundex Code* will refer to an MD5 hashed Soundex code.

6.1   Soundex Inherent Information Gain

In this set of experiments we aim at quantitatively measuring the inherent reduction in RIG that the Soundex algorithm provides. We calculate the Entropy of the Plaintexts and their Conditional Entropy given their Soundex encodings for all four distributions we employ. The results for this experiment are illustrated in Figure 2. Considering that any Plaintext distribution has $RIG = 1$, we can easily assess from Figure 2(b) how the Plaintext distribution affects the RIG of the Soundex algorithm. It is evident that in all cases Soundex hides information regarding the plaintext. However, better performance is achieved in the cases of

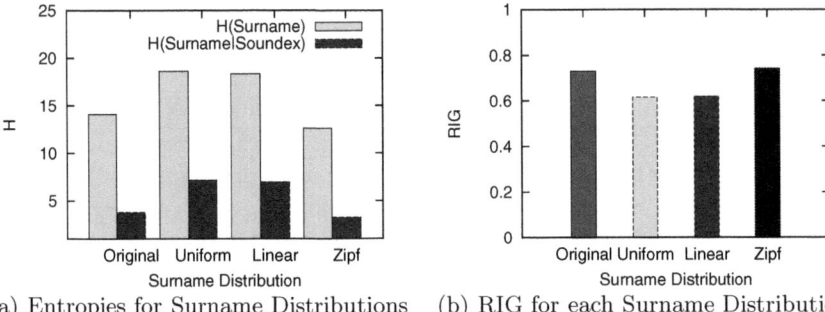

(a) Entropies for Surname Distributions   (b) RIG for each Surname Distribution

Fig. 2. Entropies and RIG for each Surname Distribution without Fake Injection

Uniform and Linear Distribution. This is because in these datasets the Surnames have smoother distributions and as we can see from Figure 2(a) this results in almost doubled Conditional Entropies, compared to the O and Z distributions.

6.2   Higher Privacy by Fake Injection

In this set of experiments we will use fake records in order to further reduce RIG. We will follow the three different approaches we have described in order to determine the impacts of injecting fakes on the RIG. We will illustrate the results of the three fake injection approaches we described earlier, i.e. UCUP, UCSP and kaC for each of the four datasets of Table 3.

In all Figures 3(a) through 3(d) the vertical axes represent the RIG achieved by each method. The horizontal axis should be used as a reference only in the case of kaC to indicate the different parameters of k. These were elected at characteristic values of the dataset. The greatest value of k reflects to the maximum number of names that map to a single Soundex code for the given dataset. These values of K for each distribution are given in Table 3. Regarding the results, it is obvious that no matter of the data distribution used, almost each method follows similar behavior for all datasets.

First, the UCUP approach, provides a standard reduction to the RIG of the initial dataset. Next, the UCSP strategy also manages to reduce the RIG of all datasets. It tends to perform equally or better, compared to UCUP in cases of datasets featuring smooth Plaintext distributions such as U (Figure 3(a)) and L (Figure 3(b)). Last but not least, lies the most promising approach, kaC. As expected, by increasing k, the difficulty of inferring the original plaintext given its Soundex code also increases. The only exception occurs for some values in the marginal case of the Uniform Distribution (Figure 3(a)). These results become even more interesting when combined with our data quality assessment where the number of additional fake records for each method is measured.

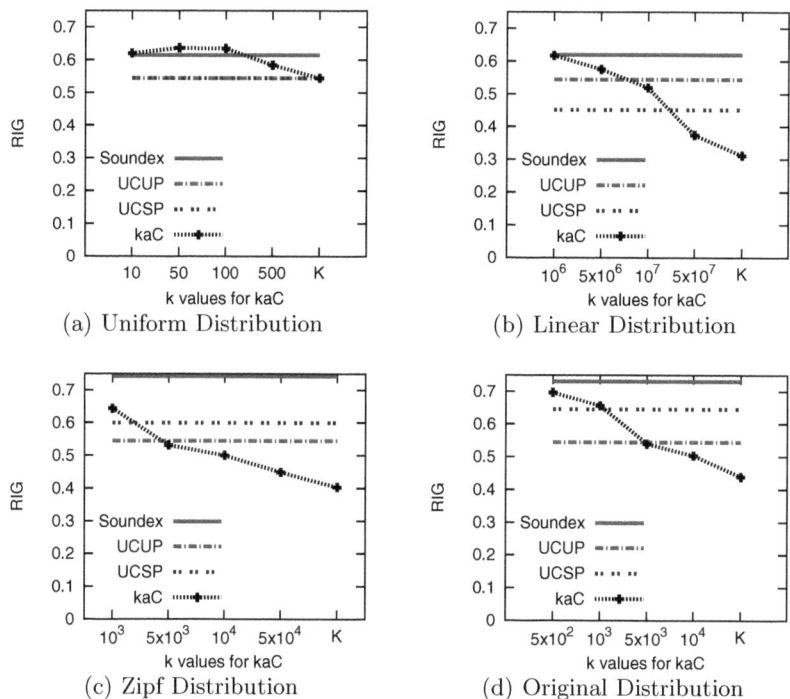

Fig. 3. Relative Information Gain (Lower values are better)

6.3   Impact of Fake Injection on Data Quality

Since our main strategy is to modify the original distribution of the data sets by inserting fake records, it is very interesting to observe how the data quality is affected. Figure 4 illustrates this set of experiments. The vertical axes represent the percentage the original dataset was augmented. The top horizontal axis is used for the kaC in order to assess the number of fake records inserted against k. As expected, the UCUP method vastly increases the size of the initial especially for the most uneven distributions, namely Z (Figure 4(c)) and O (Figure 4(d)). On the contrary, in these cases UCSP performs relatively well. One important observation regarding the UCSP strategy is that, while in these experiments we see the number of fake records added, only for this case, due to the swapping approach, the size of the initial dataset remains the same. Finally, for the kaC approach we can see as already expected from Figure 3, that as more fake records are added, the greater is the drop in RIG.

Combining the results of Figures 3 and 4, it is evident that the naive UCUP approach adds a significant amount of records in order to reduce information gain. On the other hand, the UCSP method seems to achieve a fair performance. It does not add the amount of records UCUP does, while on the other hand it manages to reduce RIG quite well. Finally kaC, offers an adjustable intermediate

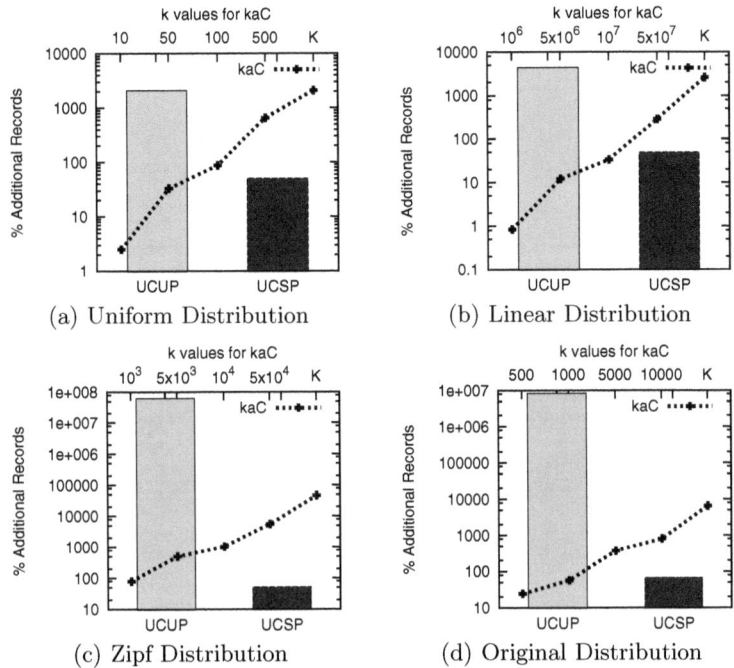

Fig. 4. Additional fake records overhead of suggested algorithms for each distribution (Lower values are better)

way between the two. Depending on the value of k selected, we can select between privacy or data quality. It is easy to deduce that UCUP is not applicable in real world conditions. On the other hand both UCSP and kaC are. The first because it manages to reduce RIG without adding too much burden to the original dataset, while the second since it provides an adjustable knob between privacy and utility.

7   Conclusions and Future Work

In this paper we have shown that using an old fashioned technique such as phonetic encoding may be suitable for dealing with privacy concerns in record linkage systems. We have shown by extensive experimentation that even without using complicated encryption schemes we have managed to obfuscate the original information by adjusting the entropy of our datasets.

Our next step is to proceed to a scalability analysis of our method in order to evaluate its behavior for combinations of more than one matching fields and explore the drawbacks that might occur. One other interesting extension would be to create a probabilistic alternative of Soundex which would map surnames to the correct Soundex code with a given probability p. Moreover we aim at creating a new privacy evaluation metric that will accurately measure privacy compared to data quality.

Finally, we aim at extending this work by comparing the behavior of our approach and other phonetic encoding algorithms such as NYSIIS [28] and ONCA [10] with state of the art PPRL methods.

Acknowledgments. This research is partially supported by the FP7 ICT/FET Project MODAP (Mobility, Data Mining, and Privacy) funded by the European Union. URL: www.modap.org.

References

1. Atallah, M.J., Kerschbaum, F., Du, W.: Secure and private sequence comparisons. In: Proceedings of the 2003 ACM Workshop on Privacy in the Electronic Society, pp. 39–44. ACM, New York (2003)
2. Christen, P.: A comparison of personal name matching: Techniques and practical issues. In: Workshop on Mining Complex Data, held at IEEE ICDM 2006, Hong Kong (2006)
3. Christen, P.: Febrl-: an open source data cleaning, deduplication and record linkage system with a graphical user interface. In: Proceeding of the 14th ACM SIGKDD International Conference on Knowledge Discovery and Data Mining, pp. 1065–1068. ACM (2008)
4. Christen, P.: A survey of indexing techniques for scalable record linkage and deduplication. IEEE Transactions on Knowledge and Data Engineering 99(PrePrints) (2011)
5. Churches, T., Christen, P.: Blind Data Linkage Using n-gram Similarity Comparisons. In: Dai, H., Srikant, R., Zhang, C. (eds.) PAKDD 2004. LNCS (LNAI), vol. 3056, pp. 121–126. Springer, Heidelberg (2004)
6. Clifton, C., Kantarcioglu, M., Doan, A., Schadow, G., Vaidya, J., Elmagarmid, A., Suciu, D.: Privacy-preserving data integration and sharing. In: DMKD 2004: Proceedings of the 9th ACM SIGMOD Workshop on Research Issues in Data Mining and Knowledge Discovery, pp. 19–26. ACM (2004)
7. Durham, E.A., Xue, Y., Kantarcioglu, M., Malin, B.: Quantifying the correctness, computational complexity, and security of privacy-preserving string comparators for record linkage. Information Fusion (in press, 2011)
8. Elfeky, M.G., Elmagarmid, A.K., Verykios, V.S.: Tailor: A record linkage tool box. In: ICDE, pp. 17–28 (2002)
9. Elmagarmid, A.K., Ipeirotis, P.G., Verykios, V.S.: Duplicate record detection: A survey. IEEE Trans. Knowl. Data Eng. 19(1), 1–16 (2007)
10. Gill, L.E.: The Oxford medical record linkage system. In: Int'l Record Linkage Workshop and Exposition, pp. 15–33 (1997)
11. Hall, R., Fienberg, S.E.: Privacy-Preserving Record Linkage. In: Domingo-Ferrer, J., Magkos, E. (eds.) PSD 2010. LNCS, vol. 6344, pp. 269–283. Springer, Heidelberg (2010)
12. Inan, A., Kantarcioglu, M., Bertino, E., Scannapieco, M.: A hybrid approach to private record linkage. In: ICDE, pp. 496–505 (2008)
13. Inan, A., Kantarcioglu, M., Ghinita, G., Bertino, E.: Private record matching using differential privacy. In: Proceedings of the 13th International Conference on Extending Database Technology, EDBT 2010, pp. 123–134. ACM, New York (2010)

14. Kantarcioglu, M., Jiang, W., Malin, B.: A Privacy-Preserving Framework for Integrating Person-Specific Databases. In: Domingo-Ferrer, J., Saygın, Y. (eds.) PSD 2008. LNCS, vol. 5262, pp. 298–314. Springer, Heidelberg (2008)
15. Karakasidis, A., Verykios, V.S.: Privacy preserving record linkage using phonetic codes. In: Proceedings of the 4th Balkan Conference of Informatics, pp. 101–106 (2009)
16. Karakasidis, A., Verykios, V.S.: Advances in privacy preserving record linkage. In: E-Activity and Intelligent Web Construction: Effects of Social Design, pp. 22–29. IGI Global (2011)
17. Karakasidis, A., Verykios, V.S.: Secure blocking + secure matching = secure record linkage. J. of Comp. Science and Engineering 5(3), 101–106 (2011)
18. Levenshtein, V.I.: Binary Codes Capable of Correcting Deletions, Insertions and Reversals. Soviet Physics Doklady 10, 707 (1966)
19. Morgenstern, M.: Security and inference in multilevel database and knowledge-base systems. In: Proceedings of the 1987 ACM SIGMOD International Conference on Management of Data, SIGMOD 1987, pp. 357–373. ACM, New York (1987)
20. BBC news (2010), http://news.bbc.co.uk/2/hi/business/8562381.stm
21. Odell, M., Russell, R.C.: The Soundex coding system. US Patents, 1261167 (1918)
22. Philips, L.: Hanging on the metaphone. Computer Language 7(12) (December 1990)
23. Rivest, R.L.: The MD5 message-digest algorithm (rfc 1321), http://www.ietf.org/rfc/rfc1321.txt?number=1321
24. Scannapieco, M., Figotin, I., Bertino, E., Elmagarmid, A.K.: Privacy preserving schema and data matching. In: SIGMOD Conference, pp. 653–664 (2007)
25. Schnell, R., Bachteler, T., Reiher, J.: Privacy-preserving record linkage using bloom filters. BMC Medical Informatics and Decision Making 9(1), 41+ (2009)
26. Shannon, C.E.: A mathematical theory of communication. The Bell System Technical Journal 27, 379–423 (1948)
27. Sweeney, L.: K-anonymity: A model for protecting privacy. International Journal of Uncertainty Fuzziness and Knowledge Based Systems 10(5), 557–570 (2002)
28. Taft, R.L.: Name search techniques. Technical report, New York State Identification and Intelligence System, Albany, N.Y. (February 1970)
29. Trepetin, S.: Privacy-preserving string comparisons in record linkage systems: A review. Information Security Journal: A Global Perspective 17(5&6), 253–266 (2008)
30. Verykios, V.S., Karakasidis, A., Mitrogiannis, V.K.: Privacy preserving record linkage approaches. Int. J. Data Mining, Modelling and Management 1(2), 206–221 (2009)

A Design Phase for Data Sharing Agreements*

Ilaria Matteucci[1], Marinella Petrocchi[1], Marco Luca Sbodio[2], and Luca Wiegand[1]

[1] IIT-CNR, Pisa, Italy
name.surname@iit.cnr.it
[2] HP Innovation Center, Italy
marco.sbodio@hp.com

Abstract. The number of factories, service providers, retailers, and final users that create networks and establish collaborations for increasing their productivity and competitiveness is constantly growing, especially by effect of the globalization and outsourcing of industrial activities. This trend introduces new complexities in the value supply chain, not last the need for secure and private data sharing among the collaborating parties. A Data Sharing Agreement (DSA) represents a flexible means to assure privacy and security of electronic data exchange. DSA is a formal document regulating data exchange in a controlled manner, by defining a set of policies specifying what parties are allowed, or required, or denied to do with respect to data covered by the agreement. A key factor in the adoption of DSAs is their usability. Here, we propose an approach for a consistent and automated design phase of the agreements. In particular, we present an authoring tool for a user-friendly and cooperative editing of DSA and an analysis tool to identify possible conflicts or incompatibilities among the DSA policies.

Keywords: Data Protection, Policy Specification, Policy Authoring, Policy Analysis.

1 Introduction

In the last twenty years, European and American manufacturing have experienced a deep restructuring, which has been increasingly characterized by globalization and outsourcing of industrial activities. These transformations contribute to maintaining and even improving the profitability of the manufacturing enterprises. However, they also introduce new complexities in the value supply chain:

- Some core manufacturing activities no longer happen within the central premises of manufacturing firms, but are more and more decentralized to partners and remote plants. Consequently, the relationships with partners and suppliers, as well as coordination and governance of the activities among them, become critical factors;
- Greater dependence on logistics and transport services for raw materials, components, and finished products;

---

* The research leading to these results has received funding from the European Union Seventh Framework Programme (FP7/2007-2013) under grant no 257930 (Aniketos) and under grant no 256980 (NESSoS), and from the IIT-funded project Mobi-Care.

J. Garcia-Alfaro et al. (Eds.): DPM 2011 and SETOP 2011, LNCS 7122, pp. 25–41, 2012.

- Need to execute operational processes at industrial plants located in areas where the availability of highly skilled workers and spare parts for reparation of sophisticated industrial devices (*e.g.*, robots, programmable logic controllers, measurement devices) is quite limited.

In summary, the organization of many manufacturing enterprises has dramatically changed and it is now based on decentralization and hybridization of productive models. This influences the management and sharing of sensitive data across the boundaries of the originating manufacturing enterprise. In this scenario, it is of utmost importance to ensure that data exchange happens in accordance with well defined and automatically manageable policies.

Data Sharing Agreements (DSA), which are formal agreements regulating how parties share data, enable secure, controlled, and collaborative data exchange. Consequently, infrastructures based on DSA become an increasingly important research topic and promise to be a flexible mechanism to ensure protection of critical data.

The main components of a DSA are the following (see also [1,2] for details):

Title gives a title to the DSA.
Parties defines the parties making the agreement.
Period specifies the validity period.
Data lists the data covered by the DSA.
Authorizations defines authorizations covered by the DSA.
Obligations defines obligations covered by the DSA.
Prohibitions defines prohibitions covered by the DSA.
Date and Signatures contains the date and (digital) signatures of the *Parties*.

In this paper, we focus on the DSA design phase. In order to define a DSA, the involved parties negotiate the respective authorizations, obligations, and prohibitions on data covered by the agreement. The design phase is iterative: the authoring of the DSA is followed by analysis of its content in order to identify possible inconsistencies and conflicts among the clauses. This process is iterated until all incompatibilities are solved, and parties have reached agreement on the content of the DSA.

In [2], we develop CNL4DSA, an authoring language for data sharing policies. In this paper, we are going to build on this language. In particular, we present an authoring tool for editing DSA authorization, obligation, and prohibition policies in CNL4DSA, and we provide a DSA analysis tool for detecting anomalies of the policies with respect to the author's intent. Indeed, through the analysis tool, it is possible to form a set of queries related to the DSA under investigation, regarding the possibility, or the necessity, to perform some actions under a list of contextual conditions. The authoring tool consists of a web application with a user interface that allows to write policies by choosing controlled terms from a drop-down menu. Such terms are predefined in a vocabulary configurable by the author. The authoring tool automatically encodes significant sections of a DSA in the CNL4DSA language. The analysis tool consists of two parts: a formal analysis engine allowing automated reasoning on the DSA policies, and a graphical interface through which the user can select the DSA and the contextual conditions in which that DSA is going to be analysed, can formulate a set of queries and can visualise the answers. Moreover, we present an executable version of CNL4DSA in the Maude language, which serves as the Maude input.

Authoring and analysis examples are presented through a reference agreement related to a scenario in which a set of industrial manufacturers and service providers need to share data in a controlled way.

The paper is structured as follows. Section 2 shows the reference scenario. In Section 3, we present the design and the implementation of the authoring tool. Section 4 introduces the design and implementation of the analysis tool. In Section 5, we comment on a usability study related to the proposed tools. Section 6 discusses related work in the area. Finally, Section 7 concludes with final remarks and insights for future work.

2   Example Scenario

We consider a scenario where a car manufacturer stocks produced cars using an outsourced parking service. The data related to production, stocks, and sale of cars flow across organizational boundaries.

The *XYZ car manufacturer* produces *custom-built* cars, *runabout* cars, and *station-wagons*. XYZ outsources stocking of produced cars to various parking services: XYZ custom-built cars are stored at *VeryExclusiveParking*, runabout cars are stored at *OrdinaryParking*, and station-wagons are stored at *HappyFamilyParking*. The kind of data we consider are: a) production data, *i.e.*, how many cars are produced by the car manufacturer within a certain period of time; b) sale data (how many cars are sold by the manufacturer); and c) employee's salary data (sensitive information related to the salary of XYZ manufacturer's employees).

The management of sensitive data across organisational boundaries and their different scope (production, sale, salaries) require some sort of agreement between the manufacturer and the parking providers. The set of data policies which can apply to each kind of data can be influenced by contextual factors like, *e.g.*, the role on an actor, her geographical location, the kind of data, and time.

In this scenario, we may consider the following information sharing policies.

- Authorizations
    A1 *OrdinaryParking* has access to the *production* data of XYZ runabout cars related to the next 6 months;
    A2 *HappyFamilyParking* has access to the past year *sale* data of XYZ station-wagons. Also, *HappyFamilyParking* can share the *sale* data of XYZ station-wagons cars after 1 year of receiving it;
    A3 Access to both XYZ *production* and *sale* data is only allowed to car manufacturers that are partners of XYZ;
    A4 Access to XYZ *sale* data on custom-built cars is allowed to car parks.
- Obligations
    O1 XYZ manufacturer will delete XYZ *employee's salary* data after 2 years of storing them.
    O2 After a car park accesses XYZ custom-built cars *sale* data, then XYZ must be notified.

– Prohibitions

  P1 Access to XYZ *sale* data on custom-built cars is not allowed to car parks outside the European Community.

3 DSA Authoring

In this section, we recall the language that we use for specifying Data Sharing Agreements and we describe the design and implementation of the authoring tool.

3.1 Authoring Language

In [2], a Controlled Natural Language for Data Sharing Agreements, namely CNL4DSA, has been proposed. The language allows to formally specify security policies without loosing simplicity of use for end-users. Aiming at making this paper as self-contained as possible, we briefly recall CNL4DSA.

  The core of CNL4DSA is the notion of *fragment*, a tuple $f = \langle s, a, o \rangle$ where s is the subject, a is the action, o is the object. The fragment expresses that "the subject s performs the action a on the object o", *e.g.*, "Bob reads Document1". It is possible to express authorizations, obligations, and prohibitions by adding the CAN / MUST / CANNOT constructs to the basic fragment. Fragments are evaluated within a specific *context*. In CNL4DSA, a *context* is a predicate c that usually characterizes environmental factors, such as time and location. Some examples of simple contexts are "more than 1 year ago" or "inside the European Community". Contexts are predicates that evaluate either to *true* or *false*. In order to describe complex policies, contexts need to be composable. Hence, we use the boolean connectors *and*, *or*, and *not* for describing a *composite context* C which is defined inductively as follows.

$$C := c \mid C \ and \ C \mid C \ or \ C \mid not \ c$$

The syntax of the *composite authorization fragment* F_A, used for expressing authorization policies, is inductively defined as follows.

$$F_A := nil \mid can \ f \mid F_A; F_A \mid if \ C \ then \ F_A \mid after \ f \ then \ F_A \mid (F_A)$$

The intuition is the following:

– *nil* can do nothing.
– *can f* is the atomic authorization fragment that expresses that f is allowed. Its informal meaning is *the subject s can perform the action a on the object o*.
– F_A; F_A is a list of composite authorization fragments (*i.e.*, a list of authorizations).
– *if C then* F_A expresses the logical implication between a context C and a composite authorization fragment: if C holds, then F_A is permitted.
– *after f then* F_A is the temporal sequence of fragments. Informally, after f has happened, then the composite authorization fragment F_A is permitted.

Similarly, the syntax of a composite obligation fragment, used for expressing obligation policies, is inductively defined as follows.

$$F_O := nil \mid must\ f \mid F_O; F_O \mid if\ C\ then\ F_O \mid after\ f\ then\ F_O \mid (F_O)$$

The intuition is the same as for F_A, except for *must f* that represents the atomic obligation: *the subject s must perform the action a on the object o. must f* expresses that *f* is required.

Finally, the syntax of a composite prohibition fragment, used for expressing prohibition policies, is inductively defined as follows.

$$F_P := nil \mid cannot\ f \mid F_P; F_P \mid if\ C\ then\ F_P \mid after\ f\ then\ F_P \mid (F_P)$$

The atomic prohibition is represented by *cannot f*: *the subject s cannot perform the action a on the object o. cannot f* expresses that *f* is not permitted.

CNL4DSA has an operational semantics based on a modal transition system, able to express *admissible* and *necessary* requirements to the behaviour of the CNL4DSA specifications [2,3].

3.2 Examples

Here, we show some simple examples of policy specification in CNL4DSA. Such examples refer to the scenario depicted in Section 2.

Authorization A1: OrdinaryParking has access to the production data of XYZ runabout cars related to the next 6 months.

We can rephrase it as

if a car parking service has role *OrdinaryParking*, and some data has category *Production*, and that data refer to *Runabout*, and that data refer to *the next six months*, and that data refer to *XYZ CarManufacturer* then that car parking service can access that data.

We can now use CNL4DSA syntax to express the authorization:

IF (c1 AND c2 AND c3 AND c4 AND c5) THEN CAN f1

- c1 = {Car Park has role OrdinaryParking} is a context;
- c2 = {Datum has data category Production} is a context;
- c3 = {Datum refers to Runabout} is a context;
- c4 = {Datum refers to Next6Months} is a context;
- c5 = {Datum refers to XYZ CarManufacturer} is a context;
- c1 AND c2 AND c3 AND c4 AND c5 is a composite context;
- f1 = {Car Park has access to Datum} is an atomic fragment with subject "Car Park", action "access", and object "Datum".

Obligation O2: After a car park accesses XYZ custom-built cars sale data, then XYZ must be notified.

After rephrasing the sentence, we can express it using CNL4DSA as:

IF (c1 AND c2 AND c3) THEN (AFTER f1 THEN MUST f2)

- c1 = {Datum refers to Custom-Built} is a context;
- c2 = {Datum has data category Sale} is a context;
- c3 = {Datum refers to XYZ} is a context;
- f1 = {Car Park has access to Datum} is an atomic fragment with subject "Car Park", action "access", and object "Datum".
- f2 = {System notifies XYZ} is an atomic fragment with subject "System", action "notify", and object "XYZ".

Prohibition P1: Access to XYZ sale data on custom-built cars is not allowed to car parks outside the European Community.

In CNL4DSA:

IF (c1 AND c2 AND NOT c3 AND c4) THEN CANNOT f1)

- c1 = {Datum refers to Custom-Built} is a context;
- c2 = {Datum has data category Sale} is a context;
- c3 = {Car Park has location EuropeanCommunity} is a context;
- c4 = {Datum refers to XYZ} is a context;
- f1 = {Car Park has access to Datum} is an atomic fragment with subject "Car Park", action "access", and object "Datum".

3.3 Authoring Tool

The DSA Authoring tool supports users in the creation of DSAs. Its main functionality consists of the simplified and controlled editing of a DSA, and the automatic encoding of its key sections in the CNL4DSA language. The resulting DSA document is in a XML file. CNL4DSA expressions are embedded into the XML representation of the DSA document, and they encode the sections Authorizations, Obligations and Prohibitions. The output of the DSA Authoring tool (*i.e.*, the XML file with the embedded CNL4DSA expressions) is the machine-processable document that enables the automation of the DSA lifecycle [1].

The DSA Authoring tool is a Web application that displays the DSA sections by using editable widgets, thus allowing the author to edit sections Authorizations, Obligations, and Prohibitions in a controlled way. The Web application guides the user in building semi-natural statements by using predefined terms taken from a controlled vocabulary. Such statements are automatically encoded in CNL4DSA and stored in the

---

[1] The DSA Authoring tool is the subject of the international patent application PCT/EP2011/058303 filed by Hewlett-Packard Development Company LP.

XML representation of the DSA. Additionally, the DSA Authoring tool automatically builds the Data section of XML DSA, which, for the sake of simplicity, is not displayed to the end user. Thus the DSA Authoring tool displays a human-readable version of the DSA, and allows the user to interactively edit its section in an assisted way.

Figures 1, 2, and 3 are snapshots of the DSA Authoring tool during the editing phase of our fictitious XYZ car manufacturer DSA. Fig. 1 shows the Authorizations and Obligations section of the DSA, where CNL4DSA is rendered in semi-natural language. Additionally, Fig. 1 shows the "highlight references" functionality of the DSA Authoring tool, which helps the end user in better understanding the statements structure. References are used when the subject or object of a CNL4DSA fragment are actually a reference to a previously used variable (either in the same, or in other statements). For example, Fig. 1 shows that the three expressions "those data" appearing in the first statement (highlighted in light blue), actually refer to previously used term "a datum" (highlighted in dark blue). When a DSA is complex and contains many authorizations and/or obligations and/or prohibitions, the "highlight references" functionality is very useful for end users authoring and/or reading the DSA.

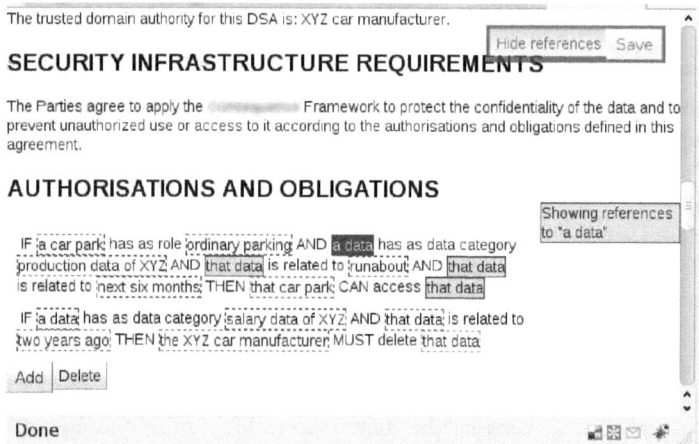

Fig. 1. Showing references

Fig. 2 shows how the DSA Authoring tool guides the user in writing a new CNL4DSA statement. The user is currently adding one of the example statements for the XYZ car manufacturer DSA. The vocabulary window on the bottom-right side of the screenshot shows a list of available terms. Terms are taken from a predefined controlled vocabulary, and their availability changes depending on the evolving structure of the statement currently being edited. In the example screenshot the user has previously selected the term "a datum", and therefore the tool is now suggesting to use one of the available predicates, in order to build a valid CNL4DSA statement.

Finally, Fig. 3 shows how the DSA Authoring tool helps the DSA author in using references. Following the previously described example statements, the DSA author should now enter the context ... AND { that datum is related to

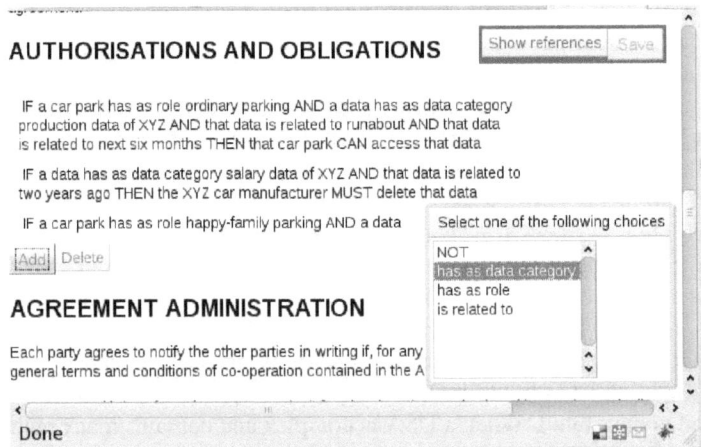

Fig. 2. Adding a predicate

station wagon }, where the term "that datum" refers to a previously defined "da-tum". To achieve this, the DSA author select "REFERENCE" from the vocabulary win-dow, and the DSA Authoring tool automatically shows with a light green background all the previously used terms that the user can refer to. When the user moves the mouse over these terms, the DSA Authoring tool highlights them in dark green. Finally, when the user clicks on the currently highlighted one ("a datum"), the DSA Authoring tool builds a reference to it (that will be displayed as "that datum").

Fig. 4 shows a fragment of the XML serialization of our example DSA for XYZ car manufacturer. The green box highlights an authorization statement. Each authorization (or obligation, or prohibition) has an automatically generated identifier, which is unique within the scope of the DSA; the DSA Authoring tool generates these identifiers. An authorization consists of several equivalent expressions based on different languages. Besides the UserText version, the figure shows the corresponding CNL4DSA ex-pression, and also the CNL4DSA-E expression. The latter is a simplified version of CNL4DSA, which is generated on the fly by the DSA Authoring tool while the user is building the authorizations/obligations/prohibitions statements. The DSA Authoring tool takes care of generating the formal CNL4DSA expressions when the DSA is saved and serialized in XML.

From the implementation perspective, the DSA Authoring tool is a lightweight Web application, in which the computation tasks (mostly related to CNL4DSA generation and processing) are carefully partitioned between the client-side and the server-side. Implementation-wise, there are two interesting aspects of the DSA Authoring tool: the agile web-based application, and the syntax driven editor.

Implementation of the Web application. The Web application is based on AJAX techniques, which allows the creation of rich client-side user interaction.

The client-side Web application (running inside a Web browser) asynchronously communicates with the server to retrieve data (for example the vocabulary), and to

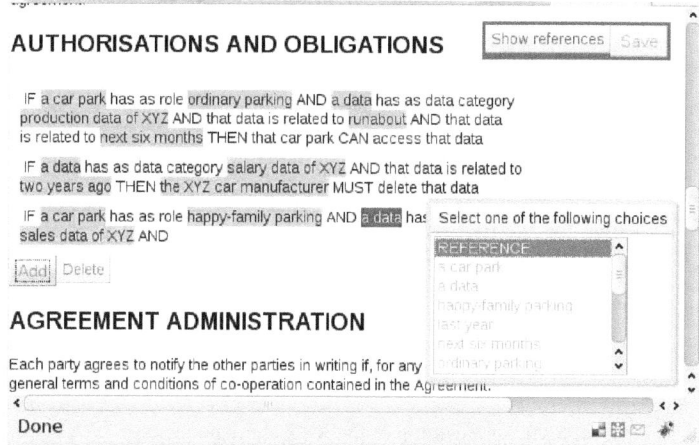

Fig. 3. Adding a reference

delegate computation-intensive tasks (for example the serialization of the DSA into XML with embedded CNL4DSA).

The server-side part, that runs in a Java application server, manages a DSA repository, that contains the XML serializations of the DSA documents. Additionally, the server-side part manages the vocabularies of terms that the DSA author can use when editing authorizations, obligations, and prohibitions. Such vocabularies are currently defined by XML files, that give the definitions of actions, subjects, objects and predicates. The architecture is flexible, and it allows for adding and configuring new vocabularies, which become instantly available for the DSA authors.

Implementation of the syntax driven editor. The most sophisticated part of the DSA Authoring tool is the editor guiding the user in building new statements. This editor is based on the formal definition of the CNL4DSA grammar. Based on an ANTLR [2] grammar definition we derived a Finite State Machine (FSM) that implements the CNL4DSA grammar, and we implemented the FSM on the client-side of the DSA Authoring tool. The type of the term selected by the user (action, subject, object, predicate) determines the state transitions of the FSM. The syntax driven editor essentially ensures that the user builds syntactically correct policies.

4   DSA Analysis

Here, we present the DSA analysis process, which allows to answer questions related to the allowance, or the necessity, to perform some particular actions, like the following.

– *Action list*: what are all the authorised actions in the investigated set of policies, under a set of contextual conditions?

---

[2] http://www.antlr.org/

```
-<datum id="DATUM_X79">
  -<expression language="CNL4DSA">
     ?X79 is-a <http://www ▓▓▓▓▓▓▓▓▓▓▓▓▓▓▓▓ #Data>
  </expression>
 </datum>
</data>
-<authorizations>
 -<authorization id="AUT_1271750718935">
  -<expression language="CNL4DSA-E">
     IF ?X77:CarPark has_role ?X78:OrdinaryParking AND ?X79:Data has_data_category ?X80:XYZProduction AND ?X79
     is_related_to ?X81:Runabout AND ?X79 is_related_to ?X82:NextSixMonths THEN ?X77 CAN access ?X79
  </expression>
  -<expression language="UserText">
     IF a car park has as role ordinary parking AND a data has as data category production data of XYZ AND that data is
     related to runabout AND that data is related to next six months THEN that car park CAN access that data
  </expression>
  -<expression language="CNL4DSA">
     IF has_role(?X77,?X78) AND has_data_category(?X79,?X80) AND is_related_to(?X79,?X81) AND
     is_related_to(?X79,?X82) THEN CAN [?X77, access, ?X79]
  </expression>
 </authorization>
```

Fig. 4. XML serialization of the XYZ car manufacturer DSA

- *Answer to specific authorization-related queries*: is it true that subject x is authorised to perform action z on object y, under a set of contextual conditions?
- *Answer to specific obligation-related queries*: is it true that subject x is obliged to perform action z on object y, under a set of contextual conditions, after that a subject w performs an action a on object o?
- *Check conflicts*: is it true that subject x can perform action z on object y and that, under the same context, subject x cannot perform action z on object y?

The main goal is to check if the authorization, obligation, and prohibition policies have been specified accordingly to the author intent. The analyser checks the execution trace of such policies, to understand if a particular action happens or not. This means checking if a certain safety property holds or not. It is possible to define a set of *security relevant actions*, *i.e.*, a set of actions that, when executed, may affect the security of the system. The safety properties we analyse are those stating that a certain security relevant action appears in an execution trace of the set of policies under investigation.

4.1   The Analysis Tool

The analysis tool consists of two parts:

- a formal engine that actually performs the analysis of the policies;
- a graphical user interface that allows the user to dynamically load contextual conditions and queries, launch the analysis process, and visualize the results.

The Engine. CNL4DSA has been designed with a precise formal semantics, based on a modal labelled transition system [3]. Thus, the language is governed by rules regulating states and transitions between these states. This allows for a precise translation of CNL4DSA in Maude. Maude is a programming language that models distributed systems and the actions within those systems [4]. Systems are specified by defining algebraic data types axiomatizing systems states, and rewrite rules declaring the relationships between the states and the transitions between them. Maude is executable and comes with a toolkit that allows formal reasoning of the specifications produced. In particular, the Maude facilities can be exploited to search for allowed traces, *i.e.*, sequence of actions, of a policy specified in CNL4DSA. These traces represent the sequences of actions that are authorised, or required, or denied by the policy.

CNL4DSA has been made executable by translating its syntax and formal semantics in Maude. An excerpt of the translation is shown in Fig. 9. The Maude template used for the analysis of DSA authorizations, obligations, and prohibitions is available online at: www.iit.cnr.it/staff/marinella.petrocchi/template.maude. This template contains static parts defining the translation from CNL4DSA to Maude and logic operators. Also, some modules are dynamically loaded depending on the kind of policies, contextual conditions, and queries that the user is going to deal with.

The Graphical User Interface. The GUI is deployed as a Web Application and it allows the user to query the analysis engine and visualize its results. The analysis engine exposes its functionalities as Web Service methods. The GUI is in charge of retrieving the set of policies that a user wants to analyse and the related vocabulary from a repository. Each vocabulary is implemented as an ontology and the inner logic of the GUI exploits it in order to create and show a set of menus whose information is consistent with the vocabulary.

The interface helps the user to create dynamic contexts, which represent the environment under which the analysis will be performed. The inner logic of the GUI updates the information according to the selected context. Furthermore, it is possible to compose different types of queries, related to authorizations, obligations, and prohibitions. Once the user has selected both context and queries, the GUI sends all the inputs, *i.e.*, the vocabulary, the CNL4DSA/Maude specification of the policies, the context defining the conditions on which the policies have to be evaluated, and the set of queries to the engine that performs the analysis. When the analysis has been performed, the results are shown through the GUI.

4.2 Analysis Example

Here, we show some example analyses over the policies of reference[3]. Fig. 5 and Fig. 6 show some snapshots of different phases of the analysis process.

The user can select the contextual conditions under which the analysis is carried out from a drop-down menu (see Fig. 5). The menu is dynamically created according to the vocabulary of the loaded policies. All the selected contexts are automatically set to *true*. We assume that everything that it is not explicitly specified does not hold. Hence, the user shall select each context that is supposed to be true.

---

[3] The GUI is available online at http://dev4.iit.cnr.it:8080/DsaAnalyzerWebGUI-0.1/? dsaID=cars.xml. The interested reader should press the *Submit for the Analysis* button in order to load our reference policies and the related vocabulary. This note has been written on October 11, 2011. Over the next years, the page could be moved. In case, the authors would be glad to provide a new pointer to the propotype.

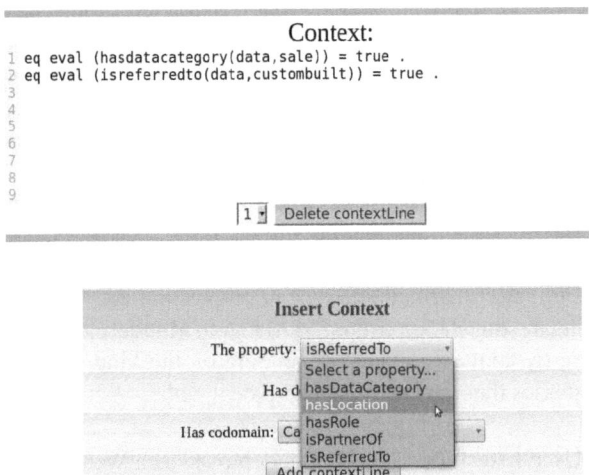

Fig. 5. Selection of context for the XYZ car manufacturer DSA analysis

Select Query

MUST

The action: Notify

Being performed by the subject: System

On the object: Carmanufacturer -> XYZ

After: Access

Being performed by the subject: Carparking

On the object: Data

?

Expected: True

Add query

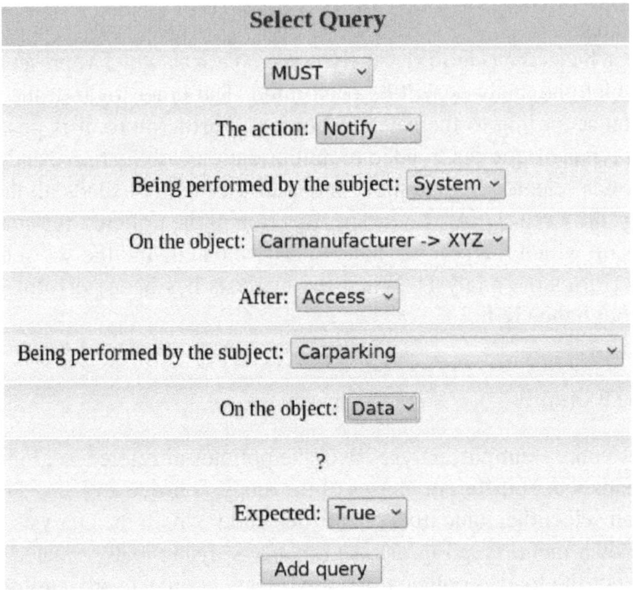

Fig. 6. Selection of queries for the XYZ car manufacturer DSA analysis

Then, the user can define the set of queries. In Fig. 6, we show an example of query composition. The user can select queries representing either authorizations, or obligations, or prohibitions. All the selected queries are shown to the user in the English natural language (see Fig. 7). Once that the user has selected both context and queries, she can start the analysis process by pressing the Submit button. This launches the inner analysis engine. At the end of the process, the GUI shows the analysis result to the user.

Finding the traces allowed by a set of policies is particularly useful to detect conflicts before the actual enforcement of those policies. As an example, we show how an authorization and a prohibition of our reference scenario leads to a conflict. They are authorization A4 and prohibition P1 listed in Section 2. Indeed, at the same time, they give and deny to car parkings the possibility of accessing sale data of custom-built cars manufactured by XYZ. This happens when the following contextual conditions are set:

- datum has data category *sale*
- datum refers to *custom-built*
- datum refers to *XYZ*

Indeed, according to authorization A4, a car park is allowed to access sale data of XYZ car manufacturer. On the other hand, prohibition P1 is activated since it is not explicitly stated that *the car parking has location European Community*. Recall that everything that is not explicitly said it is not true, thus the car park is located outside the European Community. A conflict occurs and an alert message is shown to the user. Thus, she can decide to go back to the authoring phase to modify the clauses that give the conflict, before their enforcement. The conflict detection is shown in Fig. 7. Currently, the system needs an explicit creation of queries that might capture conflicts. In the final remarks, we give some hints for a possible improvement of the conflict detection process.

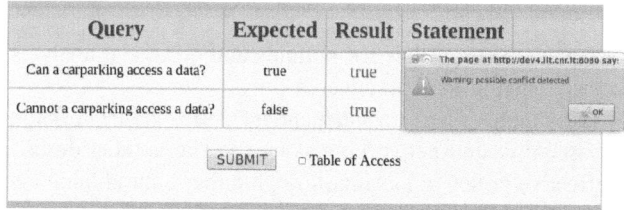

Fig. 7. Conflict detection

Finally, through the user interface it is possible to save the current configuration (*i.e.*, a set of contextual conditions and a set of queries) for successive elaborations (see Figure 8. This functionality allows to load a saved session without redefining contexts and queries. This is useful when the user, that possibly detects a conflict among the policies, modifies those policies. When checking the correctness of the modified clauses, there is no need to reformulate the contextual conditions and the queries.

5   Discussion

This paper presents two tools that can be exploited as the front-end for a data sharing agreements management system. To assess the degree of the user-friendliness of such tools, a first usability study has been carried out by external evaluators, both

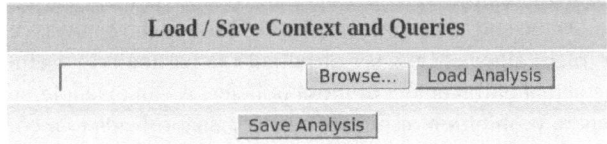

Fig. 8. Load and save a configuration

technicians and industrial managers, within the FP7 European Project Consequence (www.consequence-project.eu)[4]. Consequence designed and developed an integrated framework for DSA authoring, analysis, and enforcement. In particular, the authors of this paper worked on the DSA authoring and analysis phase. The Consequence results have been evaluated on two testbeds, and the results of those evaluations are available as public reports [5,6]. These two final deliverables accurately detail advantages and drawbacks of all the Consequence architecture components, including authoring and analysis. It was our intention to inherit the suggestions of the evaluators in order to improve the usability of the tools. For the time being, some updates have been done, like, *e.g.*, the insertion of a *help on line* facility that may help non expert users, like industrial managers. This facility is integrated in the online analysis GUI. However, we aim at fixing some further issues and to carry out a second usability survey.

6   Related Work

In the literature, there are proposals for policies authoring and analysis. We compare our framework with existing work in the area.

Work in [7] investigates platform-independent policy frameworks to specify, analyze, and deploy security and networking policies. The authors describe a prototype for usable and effective policy authoring through either natural language or structured lists that manage policies from the specification to the possible enforcement. Proposals in [8,9] specifically focus on DSA, by modeling the agreement as a set of obligation constraints. Obligations are expressed as distributed temporal logic predicates (DTL), a generalization of linear temporal logic including both past-time and future-time temporal operators. The authors of [10] proposes SPARCLE as an authoring language and the SPARCLE Policy Workbench as an application for editing privacy policies. Even if the proposed language is not based on a formal syntax and semantics, this work identifies some grammars for parsing natural language into SPARCLE. In [11], the authors propose a Datalog-like authoring language as the input for a policy editor. Focus is given on social and environmental aspects that can influence the interpretation and specification of the policies, like, *e.g.*, trust and privacy aspects. In [12], the authors offer a user-friendly, visual interface for the specification of the underlying concepts of privacy-preserving authorizations, such as roles, data types, actions, rules and contextual information, providing the appropriate level of abstraction. With respect to these

---

[4] The project ended in January, 2011. The website and all its content will be available online until Dec 31, 2013.

```
                COMPOSITE CONTEXT
                C  := c  |  C and C  |  C or C  |  not c

                COMPOSITE FRAGMENT
                F_A  := nil  |  can f  |  F_A; F_A  |
                       if  C  then  F_A  |  after f  then  F_A|  (F_A)
                F_O  :=   nil  |  must f  |  F_O; F_O  |
                       if  C  then  F_O  |  after  f  then  F_O|  (F_O)
                F_P  :=   nil  |  cannot f  |  F_P; F_P  |
                       if  C  then  F_P  |  after  f  then  F_P|  (F_P)
```

```
fmod FRAGMENT-CONTEXT is
--- this module declares fragments and contexts
...
sorts Term Action Basicfragment .
sorts Contesto CompCont . subsort Contesto < CompCont .
vars CC CC' : CompCont . var C : Contesto .
op eval : CompCont -> Bool .
--- logic operators for composing contexts:
op _ and _ : CompCont CompCont -> CompCont [ass comm prec 57 ] .
op _ or _ : CompCont CompCont -> CompCont [ass comm prec 59 ] .
op not_ : Contesto -> CompCont [prec 53] .
ceq eval(CC and CC') = true if eval(CC) ∧ eval(CC') .
ceq eval(not C) = true if eval(C) == false .
...
--- Basicfragment declaration:
op <_,_,_> : Term Action Term -> Basicfragment .
--- Context declaration:
op _(_,_) : Assertion Term Term -> Contesto . endfm

fmod CNL4DSA-SYNTAX is
inc FRAGMENT-CONTEXT .
sort Fragment .
--- syntax:
--- can/cannot/after
op _._ : Basicfragment Fragment -> Fragment [frozen prec 25] .
--- list
op _;_ : Fragment Fragment -> Fragment [frozen assoc comm prec 30] .
--- if
op _@_ : CompCont Fragment -> Fragment [frozen prec 25] .
--- obl
op * _ * _ : Basicfragment Fragment -> Fragment [frozen prec 25] .
endfm
```

Fig. 9. The syntax of CNL4DSA (top) and its translation in MAUDE (bottom)

work, we also deal with the problem of (automated) DSA verification: the formal foundation of CNL4DSA let us leverage existing analysis frameworks like Maude.

Other alternative approaches are possible for analysing DSA. Binder [13] is an open logic-based security language that encodes security authorizations among components of communicating distributed systems. It has a notion for context and provides flexible low-level programming tools to express delegation, even if Binder does not directly implement higher-level security concepts like delegation itself. Also, the Rodin platform provides animation and model-checking toolset, for developing specifications based on the Event-B language (www.event-b.org). In [14], it was shown that the Event-B language can be used to model obliged events. This could be useful in the case of analysing obligations in DSA. In [15], the authors present a formalization of DSA clauses in Event-B and the ProB animator and model checker are exploited in order to verify that a system behaves according to its associated DSA. The main difference with our approach is that CNL4DSA captures the events (or actions) that a system can perform, the order in which they can be executed and it can be easily extended for dealing with other aspects of this execution, such as time and probabilities. On the other hand, Event-B is a "state-oriented" language that models a state of a system rather than its transition.

Even if not specifically DSA-related, [16] presents a policy analysis framework which considers authorizations and obligations, giving useful diagnostic information. Also, a relevant work in [17] proposes a comprehensive framework for expressing highly complex privacy-related policies, featuring purposes and obligations. Also, a formal definition of conflicting permission assignments is given, together with efficient conflict-checking algorithms. Finally, the Policy Design Tool [18] offers a sophisticated way for modeling and analysing high-level security requirements in a business context and create security policy templates in a standard format.

To conclude, there exists generic formal approaches that could *a priori* be exploited for the analysis of some aspects of DSA. As an example, the Klaim family of process calculi [19] provide a high-level model for distributed systems, and, in particular, exploits a capability-based type system for programming and controlling access and usage of resources. Also, [20] consider policies that restrict the use and replication of information, *e.g.*, imposing that a certain information may only be used or copied a certain number of times. The analysis tool is a static analyser for a variant of Klaim.

7   Conclusions and Future Work

We focused on the authoring and analysis phase of DSAs. We developed a user-friendly authoring tool that can exploit capabilities of a background analysis tool. The combination of such tools allows to dynamically define DSAs ensuring privacy and security properties, and to detect conflicts before the actual enforcement of the resulting policies.

We leave some work for the future. Currently, the vocabularies collecting the terms used in a DSA do not carry semantic information, but we plan to evolve them towards more formal ontological definition of terms. Also, there are some open issues related to the detection of conflicts. First, in the current implementation, the conflict detection between an authorization and a prohibition is based on a user query. The analysis tool could be easily extended by automatically looking for all the possible actions that are at the same time allowed and prohibited under a certain context. Secondly, when a conflict is detected, the user manually re-edits the DSA and modifies the policies responsible for that conflict. We are currently working on supporting the user in automatically solving conflicts, once detected. Finally, as it is common for tools based on state exploration, the underlying analysis engine suffers from the problem of the state explosion. Thus, it may be convenient to further investigate the feasibility of using this engine for more complex DSA specifications.

References

1. The Consequence Team: D2.1: Methodologies and Tools for Data Sharing Agreements Infrastructure (2008),
   http://www.consequence-project.eu/Deliverables_Y1/D2.1.pdf
2. Matteucci, I., Petrocchi, M., Sbodio, M.L.: CNL4DSA: a Controlled Natural Language for Data Sharing Agreements. In: SAC: Privacy on the Web Track. ACM (2010)
3. Larsen, K.G., Thomsen, B.: A modal process logic. In: LICS, pp. 203–210 (1988)
4. Clavel, M., Durán, F., Eker, S., Lincoln, P., Martí-Oliet, N., Bevilacqua, V., Talcott, C. (eds.): All About Maude - A High-Performance Logical Framework. LNCS, vol. 4350, pp. 737–749. Springer, Heidelberg (2007)
5. The Consequence Team: D6.4: Final Evaluation of the Sensitive Data Test Bed (2011),
   http://www.consequence-project.eu/Deliverables_Y3/D6.4.pdf
6. The Consequence Team: D5.4: Final Evaluation of the Policy-Based Security for Crisis Management Test Bed (2011),
   http://www.consequence-project.eu/Deliverables_Y3/D5.4.pdf
7. Brodie, C., et al.: The Coalition Policy Management Portal for Policy Authoring, Verification, and Deployment. In: POLICY, pp. 247–249 (2008)
8. Swarup, V., Seligman, L., Rosenthal, A.: A Data Sharing Agreement Framework. In: Bagchi, A., Atluri, V. (eds.) ICISS 2006. LNCS, vol. 4332, pp. 22–36. Springer, Heidelberg (2006)
9. Swarup, V., et al.: Specifying Data Sharing Agreements. In: POLICY, pp. 157–162 (2006)
10. Brodie, C., et al.: An Empirical Study of Natural Language Parsing of Privacy Policy Rules using the SPARCLE Policy Workbench. In: SOUPS, pp. 8–19. ACM (2006)
11. Fisler, K., Krishnamurthi, S.: A Model of Triangulating Environments for Policy Authoring. In: SACMAT, pp. 3–12. ACM (2010)
12. Mousas, A.S., et al.: Visualising Access Control: The PRISM Approach. In: Panhellenic Conference on Informatics (2010)
13. Abadi, M.: Logic in Access Control. In: LICS, p. 228. IEEE (2003)
14. Bicarregui, J., Arenas, A., Aziz, B., Massonet, P., Ponsard, C.: Towards Modelling Obligations in Event-B. In: Börger, E., Butler, M., Bowen, J.P., Boca, P. (eds.) ABZ 2008. LNCS, vol. 5238, pp. 181–194. Springer, Heidelberg (2008)
15. Arenas, A., Aziz, B., Bicarregui, J., Wilson, M.D.: An Event-B Approach to Data Sharing Agreements. In: Méry, D., Merz, S. (eds.) IFM 2010. LNCS, vol. 6396, pp. 28–42. Springer, Heidelberg (2010)
16. Craven, R., et al.: Expressive Policy Analysis with Enhanced System Dynamicity. In: ASI-ACCS (2009)
17. Ni, Q., et al.: Privacy-aware Role-based Access Control. ACM Transactions on Information and System Security 13 (2010)
18. Policy Design Tool (2009),
   http://www.alphaworks.ibm.com/tech/policydesigntool
19. De Nicola, R., Ferrari, G.L., Pugliese, R.: Programming Access Control: The KLAIM Experience. In: Palamidessi, C. (ed.) CONCUR 2000. LNCS, vol. 1877, pp. 48–65. Springer, Heidelberg (2000)
20. Hansen, R.R., Nielson, F., Nielson, H.R., Probst, C.W.: Static Validation of Licence Conformance Policies. In: ARES, pp. 1104–1111 (2008)

A Privacy-Protecting Architecture for Collaborative Filtering via Forgery and Suppression of Ratings*

Javier Parra-Arnau, David Rebollo-Monedero, and Jordi Forné

Department of Telematics Engineering, Universitat Politècnica de Catalunya (UPC),
E-08034 Barcelona, Spain
{javier.parra,david.rebollo,jforne}@entel.upc.edu

Abstract. Recommendation systems are information-filtering systems that help users deal with information overload. Unfortunately, current recommendation systems prompt serious privacy concerns. In this work, we propose an architecture that protects user privacy in such collaborative-filtering systems, in which users are profiled on the basis of their ratings. Our approach capitalizes on the combination of two perturbative techniques, namely the forgery and the suppression of ratings. In our scenario, users rate those items they have an opinion on. However, in order to avoid privacy risks, they may want to refrain from rating some of those items, and/or rate some items that do not reflect their actual preferences. On the other hand, forgery and suppression may degrade the quality of the recommendation system. Motivated by this, we describe the implementation details of the proposed architecture and present a formulation of the optimal trade-off among privacy, forgery rate and suppression rate. Finally, we provide a numerical example that illustrates our formulation.

1 Introduction

From the advent of the Internet and the World Wide Web (WWW), the amount of information available to users has grown exponentially. Today, due to this information overload, users feel they have to separate the wheat from the chaff. Recommendation systems are a type of information-filtering systems that assist users in this task by suggesting information items they may be interested in. Among the existing recommendation systems, some of the most successful ones are based on collaborative filtering (CF) algorithms [1, 2]. Examples of CF-based systems include recommending books, music, and other products at Amazon.com [3], movies by MovieLens [4] and Netflix [5], and news at Digg [6].

* This work was supported in part by the Spanish Government through Projects CONSOLIDER INGENIO 2010 CSD2007-00004 "ARES" and TEC2010-20572-C02-02 "CONSEQUENCE", and by the Catalan Government under Grant 2009 SGR 1362. D.Rebollo-Monedero is the recipient of a Juan de la Cierva postdoctoral fellowship, JCI-2009-05259, from the Spanish Ministry of Science and Innovation.

J. Garcia-Alfaro et al. (Eds.): DPM 2011 and SETOP 2011, LNCS 7122, pp. 42–57, 2012.

One of the most popular forms of interaction in recommendation systems is that users communicate their preferences by rating items. This is the case of Movielens, where users assign *ratings* to movies they have already watched. Other strategies to capture users' interests include asking them to sort a number of items by order of predilection, or suggesting that they mark the items they like. On the other hand, recommendation systems may collect data from users without requiring them to explicitly convey their interests [7]. Such practices include observing the items clicked by users in an online store, analyzing the time it takes users to examine an item, or simply keeping a record of the purchased items.

The prolonged collection of these data allows the system to extract an accurate snapshot of user interests or *user profiles*. Once this information has been captured, the recommendation system applies an algorithm that returns a prediction of users' interests for those items they have not yet considered. For example, Movielens and Digg apply CF algorithms to predict the rating that a user would give to a movie and to create a personalized list of recommended news, respectively. Fig. 1 illustrates the case of Movielens and provides an example of user profile.

Despite the many advantages recommendation systems are bringing to users, the information collected, processed and stored by these systems prompts serious privacy concerns. One of the main privacy risks perceived by users is that of a computer "figuring things out" about them [8]. Namely, many users are worried about the idea that their profiles may reveal sensitive information such as health-related issues, political affiliation, salary or religion. On the other hand, other users are concerned that the system's predictions may be totally erroneous and be later used to defame them. The latter situation is illustrated in [9], where the accuracy of the predictions provided by TiVo digital video recorder and Amazon is questioned. Specifically, the author describes several real cases in which the recommender makes dubious, and in some cases aberrant, inferences about users' sexual preferences. Lastly, other privacy risks embrace unsolicited marketing, information leaked to other users of the same computer, court subpoenas, and government surveillance [8].

Therefore, it is not surprising that some users are reticent to disclose their interests. In fact, [10] reports that the 24% of Internet users surveyed provided false information in order to avoid giving private information to a Web site. In this line, another study [11] finds that 95% of the respondents refused, at some point, to provide personal information when requested by a Web site. In a nutshell, these studies seem to indicate that submitting false information and refusing to give private information are strategies accepted by users concerned with their privacy.

1.1   Contribution and Plan of This Paper

In this work, we tackle the problem of protecting user profiles in recommendation systems based on CF algorithms. Specifically, we propose an architecture aimed at preserving user privacy in those systems in which users are profiled on the basis of their ratings. Our approach relies upon the combination of two conceptually simple mechanisms: forgery and suppression of ratings. More accurately, in our

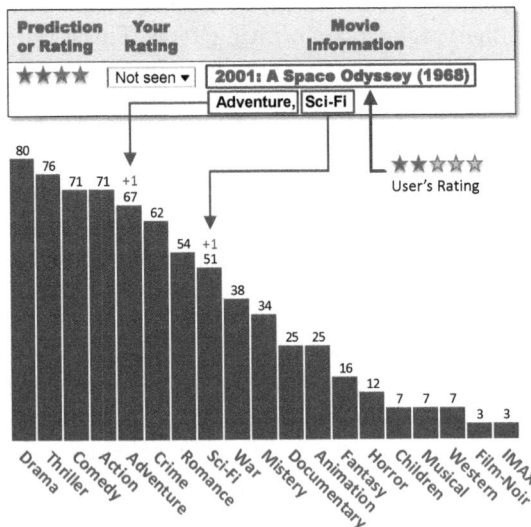

Fig. 1. The profile of a user is modeled in Movielens as a histogram of absolute frequencies of ratings within a set of movie genres (bottom). Based on this profile, the recommender predicts the rating that the user would probably give to a movie (top). After having watched the movie, the user rates it and their profile is updated.

scenario, users rate those items they have an opinion on. However, in order to prevent privacy risks, they may wish to refrain from rating some of those items, and/or rate items that are unknown to them and do not reflect their actual preferences. In order to hinder privacy attackers in their efforts to profile users' interests, the proposed architecture helps users decide which items should be rated and which should not. Consequently, this approach guarantees user privacy to a certain extent, without having to trust the recommendation system or the network operator, but at the cost a loss in utility, namely a degradation in the accuracy of the prediction. Our approach contemplates the impact that the forgery and suppression of ratings have on the quality of the recommendation, but tackles this in a more simplified manner, by using of a tractable measure of utility, in the absence of a future, more elaborated study.

In addition, we present an information-theoretic, mathematical formulation of the trade-off among privacy, forgery rate and suppression rate. More specifically, in this formulation we measure privacy as the entropy of the user's apparent profile, which is the profile observed by the system, after the forgery and suppression of ratings. Our formulation results in a convex optimization problem for which there exist efficient numerical methods to solve it. Finally, we would like to add that our approach could benefit from the combination with other alternatives in the literature.

Sec. 2 reviews some relevant approaches aimed at preserving user privacy in CF-based recommendation systems. Sec. 3 describes a privacy-protecting architecture based on the forgery and suppression of ratings. In addition, this section presents the model of user profile assumed, the adversarial model and our privacy measure. Sec. 4 introduces a formulation of the trade-off among privacy, forgery rate and suppression rate. Sec. 5 shows a simple but insightful example that illustrates this formulation. Conclusions are drawn in Sec. 6.

2 State of the Art

Numerous approaches have been proposed to protect user privacy in the context of recommendation systems using CF techniques. These approaches basically suggest three main strategies: perturbing the information provided by users, using cryptographic techniques, and distributing the information stored by recommenders.

In the case of perturbative methods for recommendation systems, [12] proposes that users add random values to their ratings and then submit these perturbed ratings to the recommender. After receiving these ratings, the system executes an algorithm and sends the users some information that allows them to compute the prediction. When the number of participating users is sufficiently large, the authors find that user privacy is protected to a certain extent and the system reaches a decent level of accuracy. However, even though a user disguises all their ratings, it is evident that the items themselves may uncover sensitive information. In other words, the simple fact of showing interest in a certain item may be more revealing than the ratings assigned to that item. For instance, a user rating a book called "How to Overcome Depression" indicates a clear interest in depression, regardless of the score assigned to this book. Apart from this critique, other works [13, 14] stress that the use of *randomized* data distortion techniques might not able to preserve privacy.

In line with this work, [15] applies the same perturbative technique to CF algorithms based on singular-value decomposition (SVD). More specifically, the authors focus on the impact that their technique has on privacy. For this purpose, they use the privacy metric proposed by [16], which is essentially equivalent to *differential entropy*, and conduct some experiments with data sets from Movielens and Jester [17]. The results show the trade-off curve between accuracy in recommendations and privacy. In particular, they measure accuracy as the mean absolute error between the predicted values from the original ratings and the predictions obtained from the perturbed ratings.

At this point, we would like to remark that the use of perturbative techniques is by no means new in other application scenarios such as private information retrieval (PIR). In this scenario, users send general-purpose queries to an information service provider. An example would be a user sending the query: "What was George Orwell's real name?". A perturbative approach to protect user profiles in this context consists in combining genuine with false queries. In this sense, [18] proposes a *non-randomized* method for query forgery and investigates the trade-off between privacy and the additional traffic overhead. Naturally, the perturbation of user profiles for privacy protection may be carried out not only by means of insertion of bogus activity, but also by suppression. This is exactly the alternative proposed in [19], aimed at protecting user privacy in the scenario of the semantic Web. More accurately, this approach recommends that users refrain from tagging some resources when their privacy is being compromised.

Regarding the use of cryptographic techniques, [20, 21] propose a method that enables a community of users to calculate a public aggregate of their profiles without revealing them on an individual basis. In particular, the authors use a homomorphic encryption scheme and a peer-to-peer (P2P) communication protocol for the recommender to perform this calculation. Once the aggregated profile is computed, the system sends it to users, who finally use local computation to obtain personalized recommendations. This proposal prevents the system or any external attacker from ascertaining the individual user profiles. However, its main handicap is assuming that an acceptable number of users is online and willing to participate in the protocol. In line with this, [22] uses a variant of Pailliers' homomorphic cryptosystem which improves the efficiency in the communication protocol. Another solution [23] presents an algorithm aimed at providing more efficiency by using the scalar product protocol.

In order to mitigate the potential privacy risks derived from the fact that users' private information is kept in a single repository, some approaches suggest that this information be stored in a distributed way. This is the case of [24], which presents a CF algorithm called PocketLens, specifically designed to be deployed to a P2P scenario. The algorithm in question enables users to decide which private information should exchange with other users of the P2P community. In addition, the authors provide several architectures for the problem of locating neighbors. Another alternative assumes a pure decentralized P2P scenario and proposes the use of several perturbative strategies [25]. In essence, this scheme could be regarded as a combination of the approaches in [24] and [12]. Namely, the mentioned scheme recommends replacing the actual ratings by fixed, predefined values, by uniformly distributed random values, and by a bell-curve distribution imitating the distribution of the population's ratings.

3   An Architecture for Privacy Protection in CF-Based Recommendation Systems

In this section, we present the main contribution of this work: an architecture for the protection of user profiles in recommendation systems relying on CF algorithms. Specifically, we consider the case in which users' preferences are exclusively derived from the ratings they assign to items. Bearing this in mind, we shall hereafter refer to the user's *known items* as those items they have an opinion on. In the case of Movielens, for example, the known items of a particular user would be those movies the user has already watched. Analogously, we shall refer to the user's *unknown items* as those items the user is not in the position to rate. For instance, this could be the case of a movie the user is not aware of or a movie the user has heard about, but has not watched yet.

Our approach is based on the combined use of two perturbative techniques, namely the submission of ratings of unknown items and the suppression of ratings of known items. For the sake of brevity, we shall occasionally refer to these techniques simply as the forgery and suppression of ratings, respectively. According to these mechanisms, in our scenario users rate known items. However, in order to avoid privacy risks, they may want to refrain from rating some of those known items, and/or rate some unknown items. Having said this, we would like to mention that the fact that forgery only applies to unknown items is basically because users may be reluctant to assign false ratings to known items. Despite the above, our approach could also give the user the option to forge ratings of known items. However, for brevity, we only describe the case where forgery applies just to unknown items. Lastly, we would like to say that our approach could be integrated with other systems, like for example, with some of the approaches mentioned in Sec. 2, and those using pseudonyms [26, 27].

In the rest of this section, we provide further insight into our proposal. Concretely, we propose a mathematical model of user profiles in Sec. 3.1. Afterwards, Sec. 3.2 examines the assumed adversarial model. Next, our privacy criterion is presented and justified in Sec. 3.3. Lastly, we delve into our architecture and analyze each of its internal components in Sec. 3.4.

3.1   User Profile

We pointed out in Sec. 1 that Movielens uses histograms of absolute frequencies to show user profiles. Other systems such Jinni and Last.fm represent this information by means of a tag cloud, which may be regarded as another kind of histogram. In this spirit, recent privacy-protecting approaches in the scenario of recommendation systems propose using histograms of absolute frequencies [28, 29].

According to all these examples, and as used in [30, 19, 18], we propose a tractable model of user profile as a probability mass function (PMF), that is, a histogram of relative frequencies of ratings within a predefined set of categories of interest. We would like to remark that, under this model, user profiles do not capture the particular scores given to items, but what we consider to be more sensitive: the categories these items belong to. This corresponds to the case of Movielens, which we illustrate in Fig. 1. In this example, a user assigns two stars to a movie, meaning that they consider it to be "fairly bad". However, the recommender updates their profile based only on the categories this movie belongs to.

Having assumed the above model, now we focus on how to estimate the profile of a user from their ratings. The reason is that our approach requires this information to help users decide which items should be rated and which should not. Clearly, the easiest way to obtain a user profile is by asking the recommender. Movielens users, for instance, can do that. Unfortunately, in most recommendation systems users do not have access to this information. In order to cope with this, we suggest an alternative for extracting users' preferences from their rating activity.

We consider two possible cases for the information that a system shows about its items. The trivial case is when the recommender provides users with a categorization of all of its items. In this situation, it is straightforward to keep a histogram based on these categories. This is the case of Netflix or Movielens, where the genres of all movies are available to users. On the contrary, it may happen that this categorization is not at the disposal of users. This applies to Digg, where the only information that the recommender provides about news is the headline, the first lines of the news and the source of information. In systems like this, the categorization of items may be accomplished by exploring web pages with information about those items. Specifically, this process could be carried out by using the vector space model [31], as normally done in information retrieval, to represent these web pages as tuples containing their most representative terms. Namely, the term frequency-inverse document frequency (TF-IDF) could be applied to calculate the weights of each term appearing in a web page. Next, the most weighted terms of each web page could be combined in order to create a category and assign it to the item. After obtaining the categories associated with all the items rated by a user, their profile would be computed as a histogram across these categories.

3.2   Adversarial Model

In our scenario, we suppose users interact with recommendation systems that infer their preferences based only on their ratings. This supposition is reinforced by the tractability of the model considered and also by the fact that implicit mechanisms are often less accurate than explicit ratings [32].

Under this assumption, we consider an adversarial model in which users submitting their ratings are observed by a passive attacker who is able to ascertain which ratings are associated with which items. Concretely, this could be the case of the recommendation system itself or, in general, any privacy attacker able to crawl through this information.

Bearing in mind the model of user profile assumed in Sec. 3.1, after the rating of a sufficiently large number of items, the attacker can compute a histogram with the actual interests of a particular user. However, when this user adheres to the forgery and suppression of ratings, the attacker observes a perturbed version of this histogram, which makes it more difficult for the attacker to discover the user's actual preferences. We shall refer to this perturbed profile as the user's *apparent* profile.

3.3   Privacy Metric

Any optimized mechanism aimed at protecting the privacy of users necessarily requires to evaluate the extent to which it is effective. In this work, just as in [19,18], we use an information-theoretic quantity to emphasize that an attacker will have gained some information about a user whenever their preferences are biased towards certain categories of interest.

Specifically, we measure privacy as the Shannon entropy [33] of the user's apparent distribution. Recall that the entropy is formulated in the following terms. Consider a random variable (r.v.) distributed according to a PMF t and taking on values in the alphabet $\{1, \ldots, n\}$. The entropy of this probability distribution is defined as $H(t) = \sum_{i=1}^{n} t_i \log_2 t_i$, which may be interpreted as a measure of the uncertainty of the outcome of that random variable, and also regarded as a special case of Kullback-Leibler (KL) divergence [34]. An interesting property of the entropy is that it is maximized, among all distributions on that alphabet, by the uniform distribution $u_i = 1/n$ for all i. This allows us to capture the intuitive observation that an attacker will have compromised user privacy as long as the user's apparent profile diverges from the uniform profile.

Having defined our measure of privacy, later in Sec. 4 we formulate the optimization problem given by the maximization of the entropy of the user's apparent distribution for a given forgery rate and a suppression rate. Precisely, our privacy criterion is justified by the rationale behind entropy maximization methods [35, 36]. Namely, some of the arguments in favor of these methods are related to the highest number of permutations with repeated elements associated with an empirical distribution [35], or more generally, the method of types and large deviation theory [34, §11].

In addition, we would like to stress that, although our privacy criterion is based on a fundamental quantity in information theory, the convergence of these two fields is by no means new. In fact, Shannon's work in the fifties introduced the concept of *equivocation* as the conditional entropy of a private message given an observed cryptogram [37], later used in the formulation of the problem of the wiretap channel [38, 39] as a measure of confidentiality. In addition, recent studies [40, 41] reassert the suitability and applicability of the concept of entropy as a measure of privacy.

3.4   Architecture

In this section, we describe an architecture that helps users decide which unknown items should be rated and which known items should not in order to hinder privacy attackers in their efforts to profile users' interests. Our architecture is conceived to be implemented by a software application running on the user's local machine. Fig. 2 shows the proposed architecture, which consists of a number of modules, each of them performing a specific task. Next, we provide a functional description of all of its modules and examine the details of a practical implementation.

Communication Manager. This module is in charge of interacting with the recommendation system. Specifically, it downloads information about the items the user finds when browsing the recommender's web site. This information may include a description about the items, the ratings that other users assigned to them, and the categories of interest these items belong to. In Amazon, for instance, all this information is available to users. However, as commented on in Sec. 3.1, this is not always the case. For this reason, our approach incorporates modules intended to retrieve the population's ratings and categorize all the items that the user explores.

On the other hand, this module receives the ratings of unknown items suggested by the *forgery alarm generator* and the ratings of known items sent by

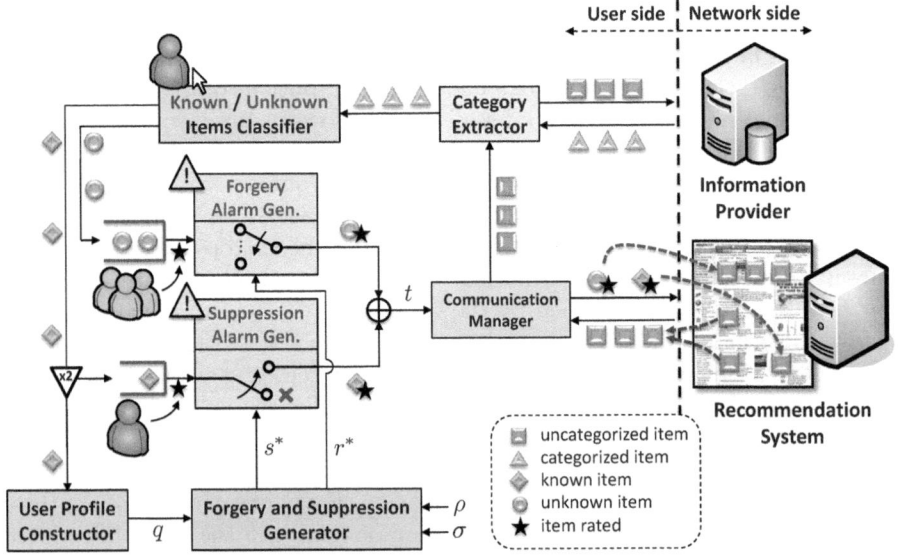

Fig. 2. Block diagram of the proposed architecture

the *suppression alarm generator*. Afterwards, the module submits these ratings to the recommendation system.

Category Extractor. This component is responsible for obtaining the categories the items belong to. To this end, the module uses the information provided by the communication manager. Should this information not be enough, the module will have to get additional data by searching the Web or by querying an information provider. Afterwards, the categorization of these items is carried out by using the vector space model and the TF-IDF weights as commented on in Sec. 3.1. In a last stage, this module sends the items and their corresponding categories to the *known/unknown items classifier*.

Known/Unknown Items Classifier. This module requires the active involvement of the user. Namely, it shows the user the items categorized by the category extractor module, and then asks the user to classify them as known or unknown. Evidently, this module will have previously checked whether these items have already been rated by the user. Should this be the case, the rated items would not be shown to the user, since these items would be classified as known items. For this purpose, the module keeps a record of all the items that the user rates. Once these items have been classified as known or unknown, they are sent to the *forgery alarm generator* and the *suppression alarm generator*, respectively. In addition, the known items are submitted to the *user profile constructor*.

User Profile Constructor. This module is responsible for the estimation of the user profile. To this end, the module is provided with the user's known items, i.e., those items capturing their preferences. Based on these items, it generates the user profile as described in Sec. 3.1. Obviously, during this process, the module discards those rated items that were already considered in the histogram computation.

Forgery and Suppression Generator. This block is the centerpiece of the architecture as it is directly responsible for the user privacy. First, the block is provided with the user profile. In addition, the user specifies a forgery rate ρ and a suppression rate σ. The former is the fraction of ratings of unknown items that the user is willing to submit. The latter is the relative frequency of ratings of known items that the user is disposed to eliminate. Having specified these two rates, the module computes the optimum tuples of forgery r^* and suppression s^*, which contain information about the ratings that should be forged and suppressed, respectively. More accurately, the component r_i is the percentage of ratings of unknown items that our architecture suggests submitting in the category i. The component s_i is defined analogously for suppression. An example of these tuples is represented in Fig. 3, where we suppose that the user agrees to forge and eliminate $\rho = 10\%$ and $\sigma = 15\%$ of their ratings, respectively. Based on these rates, the block calculates the optimal tuples r^* and s^*. In this example, the tuple s^* indicates that the user should refrain from rating 10% of the items belonging to the category 1 and 5% in the category 2. This is consistent with the fact the actual user profile is biased towards these categories.

In the end, these two tuples are sent to the forgery alarm generator and the suppression alarm generator, respectively. Later in Sec. 4, we provide a more detailed specification of this module by using a formulation of the trade-off among privacy, forgery rate and suppression rate, which will enable us to compute the tuples r^* and s^*.

Suppression Alarm Generator. This module is responsible for warning the user when their privacy is being compromised. Concretely, this module receives the tuple s^* and stores the known items provided by the known/unknown items classifier. These items are stored in an array. When the user decides to assign a rating to one of these items, the selected item is removed from the array. The user then rates this item, and the module proceeds as follows: if s^* has a positive component in at least one of the categories the item belongs to, a privacy alarm is generated to alert the user, and it is then for the user to decide whether to eliminate the rating or not. However, if s^* is zero for all components, our architecture does not become aware of any privacy risk and the rating is sent to the communication manager module. This process is repeated provided that the array is not empty.

In order to illustrate how this block works, suppose that it receives the tuples of forgery and suppression shown in Fig. 3. According to these tuples, the block would trigger an alarm if the user decided to rate an item classified into the categories 1 or 2. On the contrary, if the user wanted to rate an item belonging to any of the other categories, the system would forward this rating to the recommender.

Forgery Alarm Generator. Our approach also relies on the forgery of ratings. Precisely, this module selects, on the one hand, which unknown items should

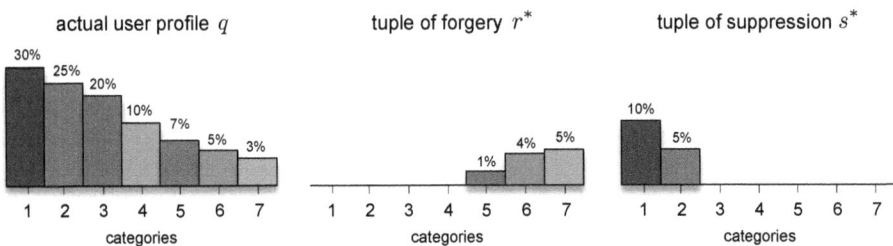

Fig. 3. Here we illustrate an example in which a user with profile q is disposed to forge and eliminate $\rho = 10\%$ and $\sigma = 15\%$ of their total number of ratings, respectively. Based on the user profile and the rates of forgery and suppression, our architecture computes the optimal tuples r^* and s^*. On the one hand, the tuple r^* gives us the percentage of unknown items that the user should rate in each category. And on the other hand, s^* provides the user with the proportion of known items that they should eliminate in each category.

be rated, and on the other hand, which particular ratings should be assigned to these unknown items. With regard to the ratings to be given to the items, we follow a method similar to the one pointed out in [20]. Namely, our approach assigns each unknown item a random rating, drawn according to the distribution of the other users' ratings to that item. Alternatively, we could also contemplate the distribution of ratings of a user with similar preferences, and the distribution of all ratings. In order to obtain this information, the module will have to query information providers or explore other recommenders. In the case of Amazon, for example, this is not necessary since users are provided with the population's ratings.

In parallel, the module receives unknown items and stores them in an array. After getting the tuple r^*, the module proceeds as follows: if r^* has positive components in one or several categories, a privacy alarm is triggered. Our architecture encourages then the user to submit a random rating to one of the unknown items in the array which belong to these categories. This is case shown in Fig. 3, where our approach recommends that the user rate items belonging to the categories 5, 6 and 7, which are those categories the user is not especially interested in. However, it is the user who finally decides whether to send this rating or not. If the user accepts the recommendation, then the rating is sent to the communication manager module, and the unknown item is removed from the array. This whole process is repeated provided that r^* has at least one positive component.

After having explored each of the modules of the architecture, next we shall describe how our approach would work. Initially, the user would browse the recommendation system's web site and would find some items. In order for the user to obtain future recommendations from the system, they would have to rate some of those items. Before proceeding, though, our approach would retrieve information about the items and extract the categories they belong to. Afterwards, the user would be asked to classify the items as known or unknown. The known items would allow the proposed architecture to build the user profile. After computing the tuples r^* and s^*, our approach could suggest submitting a random rating to one or more of the unknown items. Should this be the case, the user would have to decide whether to send the rating or not. Next, the user would start rating the known items. At a certain point, the user could receive a privacy alarm when trying to rate one of these items. Should this be the case, it would be up to the user to decide whether to eliminate the rating or not.

4   Formulation of the Trade-Off among Privacy, Forgery Rate and Suppression Rate

In this section, we present a formulation of the optimal trade-off among privacy, forgery rate and suppression rate. In the absence of a thorough study, our formulation considers these two rates as a measure of the degradation in the accuracy of the recommendations. This simplification allows us to formulate the problem of choosing a forgery tuple and a suppression tuple as a multiobjective optimization problem that takes into account privacy, forgery rate and suppression rate. As we shall show later, this formulation will enable us to go into the details of one of the functional blocks of the proposed architecture.

Next, we formalize some of the concepts that we introduced in previous sections. Specifically, we model the *items* in a recommendation system as r.v.'s taking on values in a common finite alphabet of categories, namely the set $\{1, \ldots, n\}$ for some $n \in \mathbb{Z}^+$. Accordingly, we define q as the probability distribution of the known items of a particular *user*, that is, the distribution capturing the actual preferences of the user. In line with Sec. 3.4, we introduce a *rating forgery* rate $\rho \in [0, 1)$, which is the ratio of forged items. Analogously, we define a *rating suppression* rate $\sigma \in [0, 1)$, modeling the proportion of items that the user consents to eliminate. Bearing this in mind, we define the user's *apparent* item distribution t as $\frac{q+r-s}{1+\rho-\sigma}$ for some forgery strategy $r = (r_1, \ldots, r_n)$ and some suppression strategy $s = (s_1, \ldots, s_n)$, satisfying, on the one hand, $r_i \geqslant 0$ and $\sum r_i = \rho$ for $i = 1, \ldots, n$, and on the other hand, $q_i \geqslant s_i \geqslant 0$ and $\sum s_i = \sigma$ for $i = 1, \ldots, n$. In light of this definition, the user's apparent item distribution may be interpreted as the result of the suppression of some genuine ratings from the actual user profile and the posterior addition of some forged ratings. Afterwards, this is normalized by $\frac{1}{1+\rho-\sigma}$ so that $\sum_i t_i = 1$.

According to the justification provided in Sec. 3.3, we use Shannon's entropy to quantify user privacy. More precisely, we measure privacy as the entropy of the user's apparent item distribution. Consistently with this measure, we define the *privacy-forgery-suppression* function

$$\mathcal{P}(\rho, \sigma) = \max_{\substack{r,s \\ r_i \geqslant 0, \sum r_i = \rho \\ q_i \geqslant s_i \geqslant 0, \sum s_i = \sigma}} \mathrm{H}\left(\frac{q+r-s}{1+\rho-\sigma}\right), \tag{1}$$

which characterizes the optimal trade-off among privacy, forgery rate and suppression rate, and enables us to specify the module *forgery and suppression generator* in Sec. 3.4. More accurately, this functional block will be in charge of solving the optimization problem in (1). Last but not least, we would like to remark that this optimization problem is convex [42], which in practice means that there are powerful and efficient numerical methods to solve it.

5   Numerical Example

This section provides a simple yet insightful numerical example that illustrates the formulation in Sec. 4 and sheds some light into the benefits from combining the forgery and suppression of ratings.

In this example, we assume two user's profiles $q_1 = (0.05, 0.35, 0.60)$ and $q_2 = (0.15, 0.15, 0.70)$, across three categories of interest. We define the user's *critical privacy* region as the set $\{(\rho, \sigma) : \mathcal{P}(\rho, \sigma) = H(u)\}$, and the *critical forgery* rate ρ_{crit} as $\min\{\rho : \mathcal{P}(\rho, 0) = H(u)\}$. Analogously, we define the *critical suppression* rate σ_{crit}. Fig. 4 shows the critical privacy region and the critical rates for these two users. In addition, we depicted several contour lines of function (1).

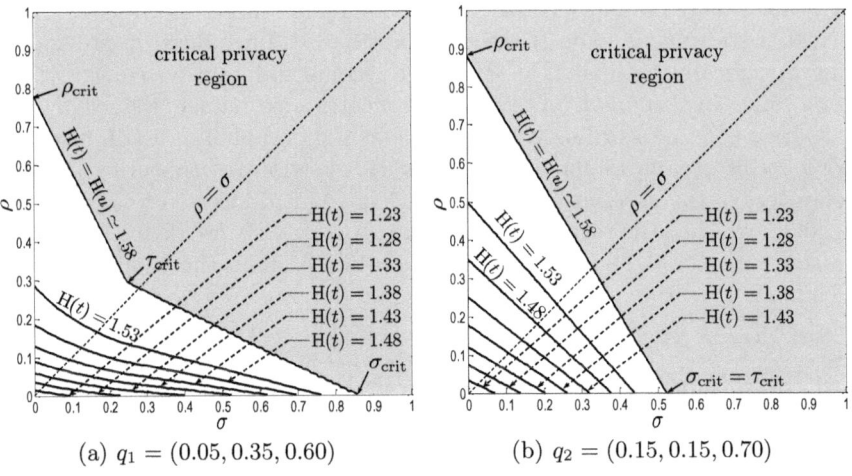

(a) $q_1 = (0.05, 0.35, 0.60)$ (b) $q_2 = (0.15, 0.15, 0.70)$

Fig. 4. We represent the critical privacy region and several contour lines of the privacy-forgery-suppression function, for two users with actual profiles q_1 and q_2

One important observation that emerges from these figures is that the combined use of forgery and suppression may be more effective than the sole application of one of these techniques. To illustrate this, consider the *cost* $\tau = \rho + \sigma$, where the impact of forgery and suppression is balanced. According to this, we define the *critical cost* τ_{crit} as $\min\{\tau : \mathcal{P}(\rho, \sigma) = H(u), \tau = \rho + \sigma\}$. Now we contemplate two possible strategies for the user: the *mixed* strategy, where forgery and suppression are used in conjunction, and the *pure* strategy, consisting in the application of one of these two mechanisms. In Fig. 4(a), we can appreciate a significant difference between these two strategies. Namely, when the user is not willing to eliminate any of their ratings, $\tau_{\mathrm{crit}}|_{\sigma=0} = \rho_{\mathrm{crit}} \simeq 0.78$. Similarly, when forgery is not applied, $\tau_{\mathrm{crit}}|_{\rho=0} = \sigma_{\mathrm{crit}} \simeq 0.85$. However, when the user adopts the mixed strategy, it turns out that $\tau_{\mathrm{crit}} \simeq 0.55$. Unfortunately, this is not always the case. For example, in Fig. 4(b) we find that $\tau_{\mathrm{crit}} = \sigma_{\mathrm{crit}}$, i.e., the pure strategy leads to the minimum cost. In a nutshell, the combination of forgery and suppression may result in a synergy that can help users protect their privacy more efficiently.

6   Concluding Remarks

There exist numerous proposals for the protection of user privacy in CF-based recommendation systems. Within these approaches, the forgery and suppression of ratings arise as two simple mechanisms in terms of infrastructure requirements, as users need not trust the recommender. However, the application of these mechanisms comes at the cost of some processing overhead and, more importantly, at the expense of a degradation in the accuracy of the recommendations.

Our main contribution is an architecture that implements the forgery and suppression of ratings in those recommendation systems that profile users exclusively from their ratings. We describe the functionality of the internal modules of this architecture. The centerpiece of our approach is a module responsible for computing a pair of tuples containing information about which ratings should be forged and which ones should be eliminated. Our architecture uses then this information to warn the user when their privacy is being compromised. The user is who finally decides whether to follow the recommendations made by our approach or not.

We present a mathematical formulation of the optimal trade-off among privacy, forgery rate and suppression rate, which arises from the definition of our privacy criterion. This formulation allows us to specify the module responsible for user privacy. Lastly, we illustrate the formulation with a simple albeit insightful numerical example.

References

1. Goldberg, D., Nichols, D., Oki, B.M., Terry, D.: Using collaborative filtering to weave an information tapestry. Commun. ACM 35(12), 61–70 (1992)
2. Su, X., Khoshgoftaar, T.M.: A survey of collaborative filtering techniques. Adv. Artif. Intell. (January 2009)
3. Amazon.com, http://www.amazon.com
4. Movielens, http://movielens.umn.edu
5. Netflix, http://www.netflix.com
6. Digg, http://digg.com
7. Oard, D., Kim, J.: Implicit feedback for recommender systems. In: Proc. AAAI Workshop Recommender Syst., pp. 81–83 (1998)

8. Cranor, L.F.: I didn't buy it for myself. Privacy and e-commerce personalization. In: Proc. ACM Workshop on Privacy in the Electron. Society, Washington, DC, pp. 111–117 (2003)

9. Zaslow, J.: If TiVo thinks you are gay, here's how to set it straight (November 2002), http://online.wsj.com/article_email/SB1038261936872356908.html

10. Fox, S.: Trust and privacy online: Why americans want to rewrite the rules. Pew Internet and Amer. Life Project, Res. Rep. (August 2000)

11. Hoffman, D.L., Novak, T.P., Peralta, M.: Building consumer trust online. Commun. ACM 42(4), 80–85 (1999)

12. Polat, H., Du, W.: Privacy-preserving collaborative filtering using randomized perturbation techniques. In: Proc. SIAM Int. Conf. Data Min. (SDM). IEEE Comput. Soc. (2003)

13. Kargupta, H., Datta, S., Wang, Q., Sivakumar, K.: On the privacy preserving properties of random data perturbation techniques. In: Proc. IEEE Int. Conf. Data Min. (ICDM), pp. 99–106. IEEE Comput. Soc., Washington, DC (2003)

14. Huang, Z., Du, W., Chen, B.: Deriving private information from randomized data. In: Proc. ACM SIGMOD Int. Conf. Manage. Data, pp. 37–48. ACM (2005)

15. Polat, H., Du, W.: SVD-based collaborative filtering with privacy. In: Proc. ACM Int. Symp. Appl. Comput. (SASC), pp. 791–795. ACM (2005)

16. Agrawal, D., Aggarwal, C.C.: On the design and quantification of privacy preserving data mining algorithms. In: Proc. ACM SIGMOD Int. Conf. Manage. Data, Santa Barbara, CA, pp. 247–255 (2001)

17. Jester: The online joke recommender, http://eigentaste.berkeley.edu/

18. Rebollo-Monedero, D., Forné, J.: Optimal query forgery for private information retrieval. IEEE Trans. Inform. Theory 56(9), 4631–4642 (2010)

19. Parra-Arnau, J., Rebollo-Monedero, D., Forné, J.: A privacy-preserving architecture for the semantic web based on tag suppression. In: Proc. Int. Conf. Trust, Privacy, Security, Digit. Bus. (TRUSTBUS), Bilbao, Spain (August 2010)

20. Canny, J.: Collaborative filtering with privacy via factor analysis. In: Proc. ACM SIGIR Conf. Res., Develop. Inform. Retrieval, pp. 238–245. ACM, Tampere (2002)

21. Canny, J.F.: Collaborative filtering with privacy. In: Proc. IEEE Symp. Security, Privacy (SP), pp. 45–57 (2002)

22. Ahmad, W., Khokhar, A.: An architecture for privacy preserving collaborative filtering on web portals. In: Proc. IEEE Int. Symp. Inform. Assurance, Security (IAS), pp. 273–278. IEEE Comput. Soc., Washington, DC (2007)

23. Zhan, J., Hsieh, C.L., Wang, I.C., Hsu, T.S., Liau, C.J., Wang, D.W.: Privacy-preserving collaborative recommender systems. IEEE Trans. Syst. Man, Cybern. 40(4), 472–476 (2010)

24. Miller, B., Bradley, N., Riedl, J.A.K.J.: Pocketlens: Toward a personal recommender system. ACM Trans. Inform. Syst. 22(3), 437–476 (2004)

25. Berkovsky, S., Eytani, Y., Kuflik, T., Ricci, F.: Enhancing privacy and preserving accuracy of a distributed collaborative filtering. In: Proc. ACM Conf. Recommender Syst. (RecSys), pp. 9–16. ACM (2007)

26. Bianchi, G., Bonola, M., Falletta, V., Proto, F.S., Teofili, S.: The SPARTA pseudonym and authorization system. Sci. Comput. Program 74(1-2), 23–33 (2008)

27. Benjumea, V., López, J., Linero, J.M.T.: Specification of a framework for the anonymous use of privileges. Telemat., Informat. 23(3), 179–195 (2006)

28. Toubiana, V., Narayanan, A., Boneh, D., Nissenbaum, H., Barocas, S.: Adnostic: Privacy preserving targeted advertising. In: Proc. IEEE Symp. Netw. Distrib. Syst. Security, SNDSS (2010)

29. Fredrikson, M., Livshits, B.: RePriv: Re-envisioning in-browser privacy. In: Proc. IEEE Symp. Security, Privacy (SP) (May 2011)
30. Domingo-Ferrer, J.: Coprivacy: Towards a Theory of Sustainable Privacy. In: Domingo-Ferrer, J., Magkos, E. (eds.) PSD 2010. LNCS, vol. 6344, pp. 258–268. Springer, Heidelberg (2010)
31. Salton, G., Wong, A., Yang, C.S.: A vector space model for automatic indexing. Commun. ACM 18(11), 613–620 (1975)
32. Adomavicius, G., Tuzhilin, A.: Toward the next generation of recommender systems: A survey of the state-of-the-art and possible extensions. IEEE Trans. Knowl. Data Eng. 17(6), 734–749 (2005)
33. Shannon, C.E.: A mathematical theory of communication. Bell Syst., Tech. J. 27 (1948)
34. Cover, T.M., Thomas, J.A.: Elements of Information Theory, 2nd edn. Wiley, New York (2006)
35. Jaynes, E.T.: On the rationale of maximum-entropy methods. Proc. IEEE 70(9), 939–952 (1982)
36. Jaynes, E.T.: Information theory and statistical mechanics II. Phys. Review Ser. II 108(2), 171–190 (1957)
37. Shannon, C.E.: Communication theory of secrecy systems. Bell Syst., Tech. J. (1949)
38. Wyner, A.: The wiretap channel. Bell Syst., Tech. J. 54 (1975)
39. Csiszár, I., Körner, J.: Broadcast channels with confidential messages. IEEE Trans. Inform. Theory 24, 339–348 (1978)
40. Díaz, C., Seys, S., Claessens, J., Preneel, B.: Towards Measuring Anonymity. In: Dingledine, R., Syverson, P.F. (eds.) PET 2002. LNCS, vol. 2482, pp. 54–68. Springer, Heidelberg (2003)
41. Díaz, C.: Anonymity and privacy in electronic services. Ph.D. dissertation, Katholieke Univ. Leuven (December 2005)
42. Boyd, S., Vandenberghe, L.: Convex Optimization. Cambridge University Press, Cambridge (2004)

On the Complexity of Aggregating Information for Authentication and Profiling

Christian A. Duncan and Vir V. Phoha

Center for Secure Cyberspace, Computer Science,
Louisiana Tech University, Ruston, LA 71270, USA
{duncan,phoha}@latech.edu

Abstract. Motivated by applications in online privacy, user authentication and profiling, we discuss the complexity of various problems generalized from the classic 0-1 knapsack problem. In our scenarios, we assume
the existence of a scoring function that evaluates the confidence in the
personal online profile or authenticity of an individual based on a subset
of acquired credentials and facts about an individual and show how the
specific properties of that function affect the computational complexity
of the problem, providing both NP-completeness proofs under certain
conditions as well as pseudo-polynomial-time solutions under others.

Keywords: user profiling, computational complexity.

1   Introduction

Privacy has long been a concern for those managing databases, particularly
databases that contain personal information. For example, a medical study might
result in the creation of a patient database containing personal private information such as ethnic background, gender, age, health habits, and incidences of
cancer over a certain time period. Access to the database might be granted so
that other researchers can then analyze the data to determine correlations such
as finding a statistical link between rates of lung cancer and smoking habits.
Privacy issues arise because the manager of the database needs to grant query
access to the database, for it to be useful, while ensuring that no actual personal
information is acquired, that private information remains private. Determining
how to and what it means to maintain privacy is the subject of much ongoing
research. See, for example, the review by Dwork [9] on differential privacy.

Due to the rise of social networks in recent years, many people have information about themselves scattered across the web on various online sites. In
terms of databases, this acquired information can lead to issues such as linkage
attacks whereby a user's information in an anonymized database is compromised by cross-referencing unique information in the anonymized database with
matching acquired information, such as birth date and gender. However, this acquired information is not always readily obtained. There is an inherent trade-off
between the cost of acquiring some information and the amount of new useful

J. Garcia-Alfaro et al. (Eds.): DPM 2011 and SETOP 2011, LNCS 7122, pp. 58–71, 2012.

information garnered. The complexity of analyzing this trade-off in obtaining and aggregating personal information is the focus of this paper.

Section 2 gives a brief general overview of our proposed theoretical model. In Section 3, we discuss the formal definitions of our model and problem as well as prove theoretical computation bounds, which depend on certain scoring functions used to measure success or failure and on their properties, the most surprising of which is that monotonicity is insufficient to guarantee tractability, but that a variant of monotonicity does allow a pseudo-polynomial time solution. In Section 4, we describe some empirical evidence showing the importance of reducing the number of facts used in obtaining more accurate profiling results. Finally, we present some concluding remarks in Section 5.

1.1   Motivation

Recently, the levels of sharing information have become more complex; no longer is information on the web simply accessible to everyone or to no-one. For example, the social-networking site Facebook now has the option to share information only with specific groups of individuals. Thus, information considered private could remain generally private. Or can it?

There is of course no complete guarantee of privacy. Companies managing the information could change policies at any moment, sell the information to a 3rd party, or become acquired by a large company desiring access to the information. To further complicate the matter, an individual might leave some personal information unpublished wisely due to concerns over privacy, yet the information might still become publicly available. Take the following simplified scenario: Bob has a personal email account with a strong password and a recovery mechanism involving a set of security questions. One question in particular involves knowing his exact birth date. Feeling that this information is personal for many reasons, Bob correctly avoids any mention of his age or birth date on any of his accounts including at the private level. Only his relatives and closest acquaintances know and only through verbal communication over many years. However, one day, Alice, Bob's sister, posts the following on her social account, "Getting ready to visit Bob for his 40th birthday this Saturday..." That one simple phrase has jeopardized Bob's careful planning, maybe due to Bob not having relayed the importance of this particular piece of personal information to those in the know, or to an accidental oversight by Alice. Regardless of the cause, a threshold has been crossed, and for Bob, his privacy and his security have been compromised possibly even without his knowledge.

Unlike traditional databases, where the managers of the databases can take most of the responsibility for ensuring and maintaining privacy and accessibility, the data on the web becomes more the responsibility of the user and even that, as described above, is not always sufficient. This begs the question, "What is privacy on the web?"

Besides the individual wishing to preserve privacy, there is another player in this game, the entity, which we refer to as the *aggregator*, wishing to collect that information and create an aggregate profile of an individual, or group of individuals, based on that information. The intent, of course, could be malicious. A recent paper by Altschuler *et al.* [2] discusses a new potential malware threat dubbed Stealing Reality attacks, where malicious software gathers personal and behavioral information about an individual. As opposed to previous profiling information containing vital information such as passwords and email addresses, this new type of attack steals far more static information such as family relationships and friendships, information that is far more difficult to change. Inherently, these programs require collecting information, at some cost, and collating that information to create profiles of individuals.

The intent, however, can also be benevolent. For example, Bettini *et al.* [1,4] discuss methods for helping mobile service providers sufficiently aggregate profile information to provide the user with a better personalized experience. In [14], Pareschi *et al.* consider methods of providing such context-aware personalized services while maintaining some level of privacy. In their example, they describe a gym service that monitors user's workout experience through sensor-equipped PDAs that track such information as body temperature, location, and mood. They go by the assumption that the user wishes to utilize the service but does not trust it sufficiently to provide it with complete information about themselves.

An example of an indifferent aggregator deals with the authentication of a user's identity, which is critical in maintaining strong system security. Although traditional user authentication typically requires a user to simply enter a secret password, more modern security systems require a myriad of credentials such as fingerprint authentication, voice recognition, facial recognition, keystroke pattern matching, and security tokens. Each credential necessarily reveals information about a user. The information might be innocuous or it might be extremely personal and private. For instance, a user may not wish to authenticate via a fingerprint scan because it requires that the system has access to and maintains their fingerprints. Thus, although each additional credential might enhance authentication strength providing various benefits, it comes at some cost both to the user, due to some inherent loss of privacy, and to the aggregator, due to costs associated with acquiring that information. For example, the use of facial recognition necessitates the installation of sophisticated cameras, and the use of security tokens requires that the user acquire and keep a FOB key or other cryptographic device. A versatile system might require any of several possible credentials for authentication and accept a user once sufficient evidence has been presented.

1.2   Related Work

Though there are some levels of privacy control available in all social networks, access control is not as fine grained as many users would want or need. Recent work by Carminati *et al.* [6,5] addresses this issue by providing a model allowing users to have strong control over access to their private information. Of course, users might wish to have some feedback as to when their shared information exceeds their privacy threshold. In [13], Liu and Terzi describe a method of estimating a user's privacy score, similar to a credit score but based on information they provide online rather than information about their financial activities. In [7], Domingo-Ferrer discusses trade-offs between maintaining privacy and functionality in a social network. In particular, he discusses game-theoretic ways that users can cooperate so that they can share information and acquire information while preventing "free-rides", acquiring without sharing. In doing so, he extends the privacy score of [13] to a privacy-functionality score. Further, in [8], Domingo-Ferrer introduces the notion of coprivacy where an individual's privacy is enhanced by the privacy of their peers.

As noted, social networks are not the only platform where private information can be released and aggregated. For example, Google Latitude[1] allows users to report their current physical location so they can meet up with friends nearby, rather innocuous but exploitable. In [10], Gambs *et al.* describe how such geolocated applications can inadvertently reveal information about an individual by sharing too much positional and mobility information and present both a model for representing a user's behavior from acquired geopositional data and, for administrators and researchers, a toolkit for testing the effectiveness of sanitized data.

2   Privacy and Profile Aggregation Model Overview

Though we model this notion more formally in the next section, to examine again the privacy issue from a web user's point of view, each user has a collection of known personal facts, each of which is shared by at least one entity, thus having the potential to become public without the user's control. The user has some level of importance of privacy, a set of privacy weights, attached to each fact, such as home address, phone number, birth date, and personal identification number. From a practical point of view, such information could be acquired for example via user attitude surveys, or one could adopt a privacy score as described in [13].

We also assume that an (adversarial) aggregator has an algorithm to generate a profile from a given subset of facts about an individual. Along with the profile, the algorithm provides a score weighing the confidence in the generated profile, based on the acquired information.

We model both the user and aggregator's point of view as functions. That is, we assume there are scoring functions associated with any given subset of credentials, one associated with the user and the other with the aggregator. A profile is thus successfully created, e.g., a user is authenticated, if the aggregation scoring function, based on the specifics of the aggregation algorithm, is above some acceptable confidence threshold, established by the aggregator. Similarly, a user's privacy is maintained if a similar scoring function, based on the specifics of the privacy weights associated with the personal information, is below some acceptable threshold.

Since the personal information is not immediately retrievable, not completely public, there is some known or more likely estimated acquisition cost associated with each fact. For example, home addresses and phone numbers could be

---

[1] http://www.google.com/mobile/latitude

acquired by purchasing access to phone directories, birth dates might require access to public registries, and personal identification numbers might require costly individually-tailored social engineering schemes. Thus, there is an inherent cost to the aggregator associated with acquiring any subset of personal information.

A privacy attack would thus be successful if an adversary manages to generate an acceptable profile, an aggregate score above a given threshold, within a given acquisition cost *and* the user's privacy function value, based on the privacy weights of the information acquired, is above some user-defined threshold. Clearly, an adversary with an unlimited budget and time can in theory collect all pieces of personal information. And, a user with no tolerance for any personal information being acquired will have little to no guarantee of privacy, at least for any facts that are shared by one other individual. Additionally, a (benevolent) aggregator might successfully create a profile, say for user authentication, within budget while simultaneously not violating a user's privacy threshold.

Motivated by such applications in social networks and user authentication, in this initial work on privacy attacks as outlined above, we are interested in analyzing the complexity of determining what information of a user or group is most valuable for an aggregator to collect given acquisition costs in order to create an acceptable profile of that individual or group. Normally, the more information that is available the better the profile that can be created, but that is not always the case. As mentioned, gathering information, might be difficult or costly. More importantly, some information might be incorrect or contradictory. Additionally, some facts might be highly valuable but only when coupled with other items. As the common expression goes, "the whole is greater than the sum of the parts." However, in other cases, too many features might even be detrimental. Therefore, it is often necessary to use only a small but very select subset of available facts.

To separate our complexity problem from that of actually generating profiles from aggregate information, in this paper, we assume that we know little about the aggregation scoring function itself, although some functions yield obvious results, and show how specific features of the function, such as monotonicity, affect the complexity of the problem.

3   Theory

As it shows the connection between privacy and aggregation particularly well, we describe our model using the example case where we wish to authenticate a single user while trying to minimize privacy concerns. Suppose a user has a set $S = \{f_1, f_2, \ldots, f_n\}$ of n **facts**, which could be any piece of information that can (but might not yet) be acquired about the user, for example, a voice pattern, fingerprint scan, keyboard entry pattern, or email address, and an inherent attitude about the external use of these facts. Suppose further that an aggregator has an algorithm that determines authenticity from some subset of these facts along with a confidence score. Since we are interested in the confidence score and are assuming the score is only based on the absence or presence of particular facts and not on the specific facts themselves, we can represent any subset of S as an n-dimensional **bit vector** $v = (v_1, \ldots, v_n)$ with $v_i \in \{0, 1\}$ and the authentication algorithm as a function $F^p : \{0, 1\}^n \to \Re$, called a **profiling** function, that takes a bit vector and returns a (confidence) score for the authentication profile generated. Similarly, we can model the user's privacy attitude as a function $F^u : \{0, 1\}^n \to \Re$, called a **privacy** function, with higher values indicating less satisfaction with privacy.

For example, the scores might be based on the fact that the correct password and keystroke pattern were collected but that a fingerprint scan was absent and not on the specifics of the password or pattern. In our current model, there is also no reliability score attached to any specific fact, so a fact is either used/accepted or not. However, such modifications could readily be made. In addition, we assume that both functions can be evaluated in polynomial time. It is easy to see how one might obtain a profiling function once a specific authentication algorithm is selected. However, the creation of a user's privacy function seems initially more problematic. Though it depends on individual tastes, a (benevolent) authentication site could determine general user attitudes towards privacy by conducting extensive user surveys, but this is reserved for future work.

The overall goal is to determine the highest confidence score under various conditions. As we shall see, the problem is quite similar to classic NP-complete problems such as the 0-1 Knapsack problem and Integer programming [11]. But, there are unique variations arising from the context of a profiling function that lead to different interesting results.

Suppose we wish to determine the smallest subset of S that produces a valid profile assuming all information is valid but possibly costly to acquire. Let $w = (w_1, w_2, \ldots, w_n)$ be an n-dimensional cost vector associated with the collection of the n facts. The **cost** of a particular subset of S is simply $v \cdot w$. First, assume the aggregator system is *indifferent* to the user's privacy concerns. In this case, we are given a single (profiling) function $F^p = F$ and some threshold T. We say a bit vector is **valid** if $F(v) \geq T$. Under these terms the goal is to find the minimum-cost valid vector. We refer to this problem as the Profile Aggregator problem.

Theorem 1. *Given an n-dimensional cost vector w, a cost goal W, a confidence threshold T and a profiling function F, it is NP-complete to determine if there exists a valid bit vector v such that $v \cdot w \leq W$.*

Proof. Observe that the problem is in NP since a valid certificate would be the bit vector and determining if the vector is valid using the function F and is below the weight threshold are both polynomial-time operations.

To show that the Profile Aggregator problem is NP-hard, we transform the 0-1 Knapsack problem [11] to the Profile Aggregator problem. Let an arbitrary instance of the 0-1 Knapsack problem be given by a maximum weight W, a goal T, and a set S of n items having benefits $b_1, \ldots, b_n$ and weights $w_1, \ldots, w_n$. We wish to determine if there exists a subset of S whose weights sum to no more than W and benefits sum to at least T.

To transform this instance into an instance of the Profile Aggregator problem, we represent any subset of S as a specific bit vector v where each bit is 1 if the item is in the subset and 0 otherwise. For example, $v = (1, 1, 0, 0, \ldots, 0)$ represents the subset $\{f_1, f_2\}$. We define our profiling function as $F(v) = v \cdot b$ where $b = (b_1, \ldots, b_n)$ is the vector associated with the benefits of each item. Similarly, the cost vector is $w = (w_1, \ldots, w_n)$. We now ask if there is a bit vector v such that $v \cdot w \leq W$ and $F(v) \geq T$.

Assume such a vector v exists. Let S' be the subset of S corresponding to the specific bit vector. Then the sum of the weights of items in S' is no more than W as it corresponds exactly to $v \cdot w$, and the sum of the benefits of items in S' is at least T as it corresponds exactly to $F(v) = v \cdot b$.

Assume now that a solution to the 0-1 Knapsack problem exists. Let S' be the subset of S corresponding to such a solution. Let v be the bit vector associated with S'. Then, $v \cdot w \leq W$ since it is the sum of the weights of items in S'. Similarly, $F(v) = v \cdot b \geq T$.

Therefore, a solution to the 0-1 Knapsack problem exists if and only if there is a corresponding solution to the Profile Aggregator problem. And, since 0-1 Knapsack is NP-hard, so is Profile Aggregator.   □

This result implies that it is difficult (if not impossible) to create a polynomial-time algorithm that would find a subset of facts of smallest cost that produces a valid profile or a subset whose cost is below a given threshold that produces the best profile. For a *benevolent* aggregator, the problem remains NP-complete as even a user with no privacy concerns leaves the problem in the same form as the original indifferent case.

This proof, though fairly straightforward, is included both as a formality and also to demonstrate that the NP-completeness of this problem relies on the fact that the profiling function is provided as input. For specific functions, the problem might not be NP-complete.

Clearly, there are simplistic functions for which the answer is trivial such as $F(v) = 0$. So, instead, let us consider the case where the profiling function is not given but has some mathematical property. For example, the function might be monotonic. Define the **OR** operation between two bit vectors u and v as $u|v = (u_1|v_1, u_2|v_2, \ldots, u_n|v_n)$, the bit-wise ORs between each component.

We call a function on a set of values **monotonic** if, for any two bit vectors u and v, $F(u) \leq F(u|v)$. That is, adding information to a profiling function does not produce a worse score. However, even in this more restrictive case of F, the problem remains NP-complete. This is because the function created in our proof reduction, which is simply the summation of the benefits, maintains this monotonic property.

We can go a little further in our restriction. Namely, we call a function on a set of values **consistently monotonic** if for any three bit vectors u, v, w, $F(u) \leq F(v) \rightarrow F(u|w) \leq F(v|w)$. That is, if a profile using elements from the set for u is worse than using elements from v then adding more elements to both will still leave the former with a worse score. Again, the problem remains NP-complete because the summation function we used still has this stricter monotonic property.

By considering the weights to be uniform or assuming that W is polynomial in n and assuming either an *indifferent* or *malevolent* aggregator, we can show a pseudo-polynomial-time solution to our problem for *consistently monotonic functions*, similar to the pseudo-polynomial-time solution for 0-1 Knapsack that uses dynamic programming (see e.g., [12, Chap. 5]). Namely, we have the following theorem:

Theorem 2. *Assume we are given an n-dimensional cost vector w with non-negative values, a cost goal W and a consistently monotonic profiling function F. One can find in $O(nW) * T(n)$ time a bit vector v such that $F(v)$ is maximized among all bit vectors with $v \cdot w \leq W$, where $T(n)$ is the worst-case time needed to evaluate function F on n elements.*

Proof. Define $A(i, j)$ to be the best score possible using only the first i entries with a cost of no more than j. In addition, $B(i, j)$ represents (one of) the specific bit vectors used to create the score for $A(i, j)$. Essentially, $A(i, j) = F(B(i, j)) \geq F(v)$ for all possible values of $v = (v_1, \ldots, v_i, 0, \ldots, 0)$ with $v \cdot w \leq j$. We wish to know $B(n, W)$.

Let $v^{(i)} = (0, \ldots, 0, 1, 0, \ldots, 0)$ represent the bit vector containing a 1 in the i-th location only. For entry $A(i, j)$ we have two choices: set the i-th bit (use fact f_i) or not. If we choose not to use the bit, the best solution for the first $i - 1$ bits suffices. If we choose to use the bit and the cost $w_i \leq j$, the best solution uses the first $i - 1$ bits at a cost of $j - w_i$. As we explain shortly, the latter case holds because our function is *consistently monotonic*. First, let us define $A(i, j)$ and $B(i, j)$ recursively.

$$A(i, j) = \max \begin{cases} F((0, \ldots, 0)) & \text{if } i = 0 \text{ or } j = 0 \\ A(i - 1, j) & \text{if } i > 0 \\ F(B(i - 1, j - w_i)|v^{(i)}) & \text{if } i > 0 \text{ and } w_i \leq j \end{cases}$$

and $B(i, j)$ is either $(0, \ldots, 0)$, $B(i - 1, j)$, or $B(i - 1, j - 1)|v^{(i)}$.

To prove correctness, we simply need to prove that $F(B(i, j))$ is in fact larger than all other candidates for entry $A(i, j)$. Clearly it works for the base cases, when i or j are 0. So, assume it is true for all previous entries, particularly $(i-1, j)$ and $(i-1, j-w_i)$. Let $v = (v_1, v_2, \ldots, v_i, 0, \ldots, 0)$ be the optimal solution for entry (i, j). If $v_i = 0$, then by our inductive assumption $F(v) = F(B(i - 1, j))$. Consequently, by definition $F(B(i, j)) = A(i, j) \geq F(B(i - 1, j)) = F(v)$ and our inductive assumption holds for entry $A(i, j)$. If $v_i = 1$, then let $v' = (v_1, v_2, \ldots, v_{i-1}, 0, \ldots, 0)$ be the bit vector v with the i-th bit set to 0. Note that $F(v) = F(v'|v^{(i)})$ and that $v' \cdot w = v \cdot w - w_i \leq j - w_i$. Our inductive assumption implies that $F(v') \leq A(i - 1, j - w_i) = F(B(i - 1, j - w_i))$. Since our function is *consistently monotonic*, we can see that $F(v'|v^{(i)}) \leq F(B(i-1, j-w_i)|v^{(i)})$. From definitions of $A(i, j)$ and $B(i, j)$, we know then that $F(v) \leq F(B(i, j)) = A(i, j)$ and our inductive assumption holds again for entry (i, j).

Observe that each entry needs one evaluation of the function F taking time at most $T(n)$. Since there are at most nW entries needed, we have our stated running time. As described, the entries in B require storing an n-bit vector. However, by reasonably assuming that the function F requires processing all the bit values to evaluate a score, we know that $T(n) \in \Omega(n)$ and hence the cost of creating the n-bit vector is subsumed by the cost of evaluating the function. The space used by this algorithm is also $\Theta(nW)$. Since row i only depends on row $i-1$, we only need to compute and store two rows at a time. Thus, the size for A is $\Theta(W)$. However, the entries in B require the n-bit vectors. $\square$

Again, the proof, though similar to other pseudo-polynomial-time solutions to NP-complete problems and shown more as a formality, highlights one key requirement, and that is that the profiling function is consistently monotonic. This is reasonable for many possible functions, such as the summation $\Sigma_{i=1}^{n} w_i$, and product (of non-negatives) $\Pi_{i=1}^{n} |w_i|$. But, there are other monotonic functions where this might not hold. To illustrate a practical example for a profiling function, take a system that authenticates users based on user name, password, keystroke press times, and keystroke release times taken while the user enters input text. This is similar to applications such as in [15]. Although the authentication is ideal when all information is present, the presence of both keystroke press time and keystroke release time is far stronger than the presence of either individually. The same would be reflected in the associated profile scores.

   Another example can be taken yet again from the 0-1 Knapsack problem. Suppose the choice is among a flashlight, a match, and a battery. The match by itself is useful for providing light. The flashlight by itself is fairly useless as is the battery; however, when combined the flashlight *and* the battery together provide a better benefit (possibly) than the match.

   Though monotonic in nature, these scoring functions are not consistently monotonic. This key difference though subtle leads to our final observation, which is that monotonicity itself is insufficient to provide a pseudo-polynomial-time solution. That is, the problem referred to as the Monotonic Profile Aggregator remains NP-complete even with a polynomial-sized weight W. Again, we assume the aggregator is malevolent or indifferent but as before the hardness bound applies to the benevolent aggregator as well.

Theorem 3. *Given an n-dimensional cost vector w with non-negative values, a cost goal W, a confidence threshold T and a monotonic profiling function F, it is NP-complete to determine if there exists a valid bit vector v such that $v \cdot w \leq W$, even if $W \in \Theta(n^k)$ for some constant $k \geq 1$.*

Proof. As with the proof for Theorem 1, the problem is in NP as the bit vector can serve as a certificate whose validity can be verified in polynomial time. To show that the Monotonic Profile Aggregator Problem is NP-hard, we show a reduction from the Vertex Cover (VC) problem [11]. Let an arbitrary instance of the VC (decision) problem be given by a graph $G = (V, E)$ and size K. The problem is to determine if there exists a subset $V' \subseteq V$ such that $|V'| \leq K$ and such that every edge is *covered* by a vertex; that is, for every edge $(a, b) \in E$, either a or b is in V'.

   To perform our reduction, again represent any subset V' of $V = (a_1, \ldots, a_n)$ as a specific bit vector $v = (v_1, \ldots, v_n)$ where $v_i = 1$ if and only if $a_i \in V'$. We define our profiling function as the total number of edges covered. That is, $F(v) = \Sigma_{(a_i,a_j) \in E} v_i | v_j$. Observe that $F(v)$ is monotonic since adding more vertices does not decrease the total number of edges covered. (But it is not consistently monotonic, since adding a vertex to one subset might increase the total number of edges covered by far more than adding the same vertex to another subset, depending on previously covered edges.) We define the cost vector as $w = (1, 1, \ldots, 1)$. We now ask if there is a bit vector v such that $v \cdot w \leq K$ and $F(v) \geq |E|$.

If such a vector v exists, let V' be the subset of V corresponding to this specific bit vector. Since $v \cdot w$ corresponds exactly to $|V'|$ and since $F(v)$ corresponds to the number of edges covered by V', the existence of v implies that V' is indeed a valid solution to the VC problem.

If a valid solution to the VC exists, let V' be such a vertex cover. Let v be the corresponding bit vector. Then, observe that $v \cdot w = |V'| \leq K$ and since every edge is covered we know that $F(v) = |E|$. Therefore, vector v is a valid solution to the Monotonic Profile Aggregator problem. Consequently, since VC is NP-hard, so is the Monotonic Profile Aggregator problem. Observe that our choice of W to be $K \leq n$ implies that the problem is NP-hard even if W is $\Theta(n)$. □

4 Experimental Results

To present justification as to why one might need to reduce the number of facts collected, we present empirical evidence using real data collected from volunteer users in order to perform fixed text keystroke authentication; see [15] for technical details on the data set and its applications. The data is a record of key press and key release times for each key that a user entered for a particular phrase, such as a password, performed multiple times. When a user wishes to authenticate, they not only must match the password but also the keystroke pattern, via a standard pattern recognition method. The key press and key release times are combined in various ways to create a high-dimensional feature vector used to represent one instance of a phrase. Recent work by Balagani et al. [3] discuss issues arising in the type of vectors one may choose. Our goal here is not to re-create their work but to enhance it by looking at a related issue.

We wish to determine what bounded-size subset of features maximizes the authentication capabilities of the system. A larger number of features, i.e. more keystrokes for a message, should provide better authentication capability, but this might come at a cost. For example, longer messages can be a burden to the user and might lead to more errors in recognition. They could also increase the likelihood of noise unless more training data per user is provided. Many pattern recognition algorithms suffer in some part to the curse of dimensionality so the more features available, the higher the dimension, and the longer it takes to authenticate. As discussed earlier, other scenarios could have even more obvious costs associated with more features, such as the inherent cost of acquiring the information itself, as an extreme but illustrative case consider the use of blood-drawn DNA samples for authentication. For each set of key press and key release times, we use the following three extracted features:

1. *Key hold latencies*: the time taken from pressing a key to releasing a key, defined for each key entered in the phrase;

2. *Key interval latencies*: the time from the release of one key to the pressing of the next key, defined for each pair of subsequent keys in the phrase; and

3. *Key press latencies*: the time from the pressing of one key to the pressing of the next key, defined for each pair of subsequent keys.

The 37-character phrase used is "master of science in computer science" yielding $37 * 3 - 2 = 109$ features per phrase entered. For each user, 9 samples of the phrase were taken during the training stage. Although [15,3] use only 33 users, we incorporate all 43 users from the dataset. In their study, 10 of the users did not return for subsequent testing phases involving other phrases and passwords, but we are not analyzing results using those particular values. Therefore, our data space consists of $43*9 = 387$ points from 43 classes in a 109-dimensional space. As our purpose is *not* about establishing the best method for fixed text keystroke authentication, we use a simple but well established supervised classification method: weighted k-nearest neighbors. However, we could have also used other classifiers such as naive Bayes, maximum entropy, or neural networks. In our tests, we used $k = 10$ and measured distance using the standard Euclidean metric. Thus, a test data point was classified by determining the k-nearest points from the training data, as measured by the Euclidean distance, and summing up, for each class found, the inverse distances to identify the class, user, with the highest value.

In our scenario, we needed to compute a profiling function, rather than do pure authentication. For this, we let the bit vector represent the inclusion or exclusion of one of the 109 features, causing the dimensionality of the problem to be determined by the number of bits set in the vector. We compute the function by doing a leave-one-out cross validation scheme (LOOCV). For a given subset of features, for each entry point, we remove the entry from the data set, determine the class using the weighted k-nearest neighbors classifier and compare the result to the actual class for that entry, with the function value being the percentage of correct classifications done. That is, $F(v)$ is the accuracy of the classifier using exactly the subset of features identified by v. The objective then is to determine the subset of features that maximizes the percentage of correct classifications. We further restricted the subsets to be within a specified total weight W.

Trying all possible subsets is almost certainly intractable, so we used the dynamic programming (DP) variant described in Theorem 2, which assumes among other things that the function is consistently monotonic. Figure 1(a) shows the performance of the classification as a function of W, with a comparison to a naive scheme that simply picks the first W features. In this example, each feature had unit cost so that the extracted ideal features were scattered throughout the set. Note that in our example after a value of $W \geq 54$, the same bit vectors were always selected. A more realistic scenario, to model user exhaustion with longer sequences, might be to give higher cost to later features. Figure 1(b) shows the performance when using a weight whose cost for feature i with $0 \leq i < 109$ is

$w_i = 1 + \lceil i/3 \rceil$, allowing for the fact that, other than the first key entered, all three latencies used have the same cost.

From the plot of the naive scheme in Figure 1, it should be clear that the function is far from consistently monotonic, or even monotonic; otherwise, the value of F, the y-axis, should never decrease as each new feature is added, the x-axis. However, as the problem is most likely intractable, we made the assumption so we could use the dynamic programming algorithm even if it does not produce an optimal answer, as it still illustrates that a subset of the features might prove more useful. For example, the largest accuracy obtained for the naive scheme was 61% whereas the one using the sub-optimal dynamic programming scheme reached an accuracy of 84%. It is meant to show the importance of wisely choosing features and, since the general problem is most likely intractable, the importance of understanding the properties of the profiling function when determining valid subsets and taking alternative approaches such as finding pseudo-polynomial or approximation solutions.

Leaving other heuristics to determine better subsets as future work, we point out an inherent difficulty. Techniques such as branch-and-cut will most likely perform poorly as one cannot place any bound on the profiling function and hence gain any useful cuts if monotonicity is not present or the function's range cannot be bounded based on other evaluations.

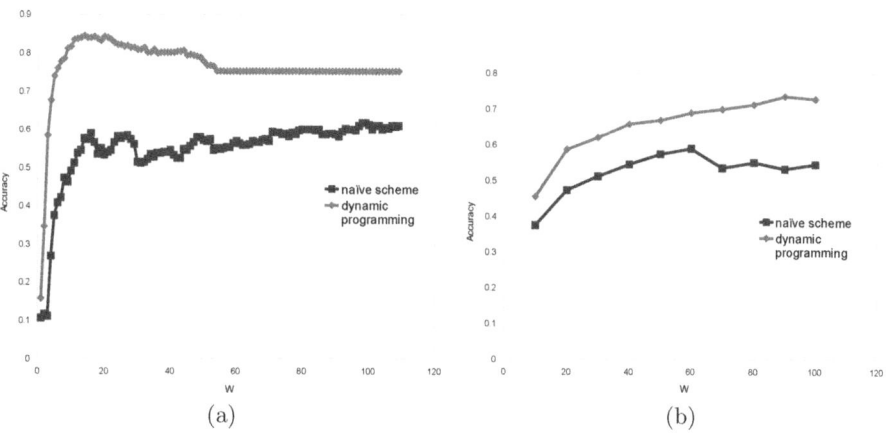

(a)   (b)

Fig. 1. A comparison of a naïve scheme to a dynamic programming scheme for selecting no more than W features while maximizing the profiling function for features with (a) equal weights and (b) increasing weights.

5   Discussion and Conclusions

In introducing the Profile Aggregator problems, we describe the complexity of determining how best to aggregate a collection of facts where for each fact one must weigh the benefits of using a fact as it affects a profile score to the detriments, including acquisition costs and users' privacy concerns. Unlike the similar

0-1 Knapsack problem, we incorporate a profiling function that is not simply a linear summation of the independent benefits of each fact but is instead a complex function based on the particular subset of facts used. We observe that specific properties of the profiling function affect the complexity of the problem. In particular, if the function is consistently monotonic as with summations and products, the problem has a pseudo-polynomial time solution. However, what is more surprising and interesting is this does not hold if the function is simply monotonic as one might initially suspect. If the property is that more facts lead to better scores, the problem remains NP-complete even for fixed costs. From a practical standpoint, this shows that optimizing for such an aggregation is most likely intractable without additional assumptions such as with the properties of the profiling function or concessions such as allowing for non-optimal solutions.

We also discussed a specific implementation of the technique using real-word data and, though our method is suboptimal due to a necessarily complex profiling function, we empirically show why selecting specific features can help improve overall performance. Of course, we do not claim that this technique is the best approach for solving the problem. Besides being application specific, techniques such as branch-and-cut can also not guarantee finding an optimal solution without some assumptions on the profiling function as well, so it will be interesting to see how they compare in terms of performance.

Besides exploring such experimentation, there are several directions that need further investigation. Polynomial-time approximation solutions to these particular problems are of particular interest. Additionally, a further exploration of other function properties besides monotonicity that lead to differing results would be worthwhile. As Theorem 2 does not directly apply to the benevolent case, it would be interesting to analyze what properties of the privacy function continue to allow similar bounds.

Acknowledgments. We thank the anonymous referees for their useful feedback. This work was supported in part by Louisiana Board of Regents through PKSFI Grant LEQSF (2007-12)-ENH-PKSFI-PRS-03 and by LA DEPSCoR grants N00014-08-1-0856 and FA9550-09-1-0715.

References

1. Agostini, A., Bettini, C., Riboni, D.: Loosely coupling ontological reasoning with an efficient middleware for context-awareness. In: 2nd Ann. Intl. Conf. on Mobile and Ubiquitous Systems: Networking and Services (MobiQuitous 2005), pp. 175–182 (July 2005), http://dx.doi.org/10.1109/MOBIQUITOUS.2005.34
2. Altshuler, Y., Aharony, N., Elovici, Y., Pentland, A., Cebrian, M.: Stealing reality. Tech. rep., arXiv (October 2010), http://arxiv.org/abs/1010.1028v1
3. Balagani, K.S., Phoha, V.V., Ray, A., Phoha, S.: On the discriminability of keystroke feature vectors used in fixed text keystroke authentication. Pattern Recogn. Lett. 32(7), 1070–1080 (2011), http://dx.doi.org/10.1016/j.patrec.2011.02.014

4. Bettini, C., Pareschi, L., Riboni, D.: Efficient profile aggregation and policy evaluation in a middleware for adaptive mobile applications. Pervasive and Mobile Computing 4(5), 697–718 (2008)
5. Carminati, B., Ferrari, E., Heatherly, R., Kantarcioglu, M., Thuraisingham, B.: Semantic web-based social network access control. Computers & Security 30(2-3), 108–115 (2011), http://dx.doi.org/10.1016/j.cose.2010.08.003
6. Carminati, B., Ferrari, E., Perego, A.: Enforcing access control in web-based social networks. ACM Trans. Inf. Syst. Secur. 13, 6:1–6:38 (2009),
   http://doi.acm.org/10.1145/1609956.1609962
7. Domingo-Ferrer, J.: Rational Privacy Disclosure in Social Networks. In: Torra, V., Narukawa, Y., Daumas, M. (eds.) MDAI 2010. LNCS, vol. 6408, pp. 255–265. Springer, Heidelberg (2010),
   http://dx.doi.org/10.1007/978-3-642-16292-3_25
8. Domingo-Ferrer, J.: Coprivacy: Towards a Theory of Sustainable Privacy. In: Domingo-Ferrer, J., Magkos, E. (eds.) PSD 2010. LNCS, vol. 6344, pp. 258–268. Springer, Heidelberg (2010),
   http://dx.doi.org/10.1007/978-3-642-15838-4_23
9. Dwork, C.: A firm foundation for private data analysis. Commun. ACM 54, 86–95 (2011), http://doi.acm.org/10.1145/1866739.1866758
10. Gambs, S., Killijian, M.O., del Prado Cortez, M.N.: Show me how you move and I will tell you who you are. Transactions on Data Privacy 4(2), 103–126 (2011)
11. Garey, M.R., Johnson, D.S.: Computers and Intractability: A Guide to the Theory of NP-Completeness. Series of Books in the Mathematical Sciences. W. H. Freeman & Co. Ltd. (January 1979), http://www.worldcat.org/isbn/0716710455
12. Goodrich, M.T., Tamassia, R.: Algorithm Design: Foundations, Analysis, and Internet Examples. Wiley (September 2001),
    http://www.worldcat.org/isbn/0471383651
13. Liu, K., Terzi, E.: A framework for computing the privacy scores of users in online social networks. ACM Trans. Knowl. Discov. Data 5, 6:1–6:30 (2010),
    http://doi.acm.org/10.1145/1870096.1870102
14. Pareschi, L., Riboni, D., Agostini, A., Bettini, C.: Composition and generalization of context data for privacy preservation. In: Sixth Annual IEEE International Conference on Pervasive Computing and Communications (PerCom 2008), pp. 429–433 (March 2008), http://dx.doi.org/10.1109/PERCOM.2008.47
15. Sheng, Y., Phoha, V.V., Rovnyak, S.M.: A parallel decision tree-based method for user authentication based on keystroke patterns. IEEE Transactions on Systems, Man, and Cybernetics, Part B 35(4), 826–833 (2005),
    http://dx.doi.org/10.1109/TSMCB.2005.846648

Secure and Privacy-Aware Searching in Peer-to-Peer Networks

Jaydip Sen

Innovation Labs, Tata Consultancy Services Ltd.
Bengal Intelligent Park, Salt Lake Electronic Complex, Kolkata 700091, India
jaydip.sen@acm.org

Abstract. The existing peer-to-peer networks have several problems such as fake content distribution, free riding, white-washing, poor search scalability, lack of a robust trust model and absence of user privacy protection mechanism. Although, several trust management and semantic community-based mechanisms for combating free riding and distribution of malicious contents have been proposed by some researchers, most of these schemes lack scalability due to their high computational, communication and storage overhead. This paper presents a robust trust management scheme for P2P networks that utilizes topology adaptation by constructing an overlay of trusted peers where the neighbors are selected based on their trust ratings and content similarities. While increasing the search efficiency by intelligently exploiting the formation of semantic community structures by topology adaptation among the trustworthy peers, the scheme provides the users a very high level of privacy protection of their usage and consumption patterns of network resources. Simulation results demonstrate that the proposed scheme provides efficient searching to good peers while penalizing the malicious peers by increasing their search times as the network topology stabilizes.

Keywords: P2P network, topology adaptation, trust, reputation, semantic community, malicious peer, user privacy.

1 Introduction

The term *peer-to-peer* (P2P) system encompasses a broad set of distributed applications which allow sharing of computer resources by direct exchange between systems. The goal of a P2P system is to aggregate resources available at the edge of Internet and to share it cooperatively among users. Specially, the file sharing P2P systems have become popular as a new paradigm for information exchange among large number of users in the Internet. They are more robust, scalable, fault tolerant and offer better availability of resources than the traditional client-server model. Depending on the presence of a central server, P2P systems can be classified as centralized or decentralized [11]. In decentralized architecture, both resource discovery and resource download are distributed. Decentralized P2P architectures may further be classified as structured or unstructured networks. In structured networks, there are certain restrictions on the placement of

J. Garcia-Alfaro et al. (Eds.): DPM 2011 and SETOP 2011, LNCS 7122, pp. 72–89, 2012.
© Springer-Verlag Berlin Heidelberg 2012

contents and the network topologies. In unstructured P2P networks, however, placement of contents is unrelated to the topologies of the network. Unstructured P2P networks perform better than their structured counterparts in dynamic environments. However, they need efficient search mechanisms and they also suffer from numerous problems such as: fake content distribution, free riding (peers who do not share, but consume resources), whitewashing (peers who leave and rejoin the system in order to avoid penalties) and lack of scalability in searching. Open and anonymous nature of P2P applications lead to complete lack of accountability of the contents that a peer may put in the network. The malicious peers often use these networks to do content poisoning and to distribute harmful programs such as Trojan Horses and viruses [12]. *Distributed reputation based trust management systems* have been proposed by researchers to provide protection against malicious content distribution [1]. The main drawbacks of these schemes are their high message exchange overheads and their susceptibility to misrepresentation. Guo et al. have proposed *trust-aware adaptive P2P topology* to control free-riders and malicious peers [7]. In [3] and [16], topology adaptation is used to reduce inauthentic file downloads. However, these schemes do not work well in unstructured networks. Poor search scalability is another problem. Traditional mechanisms such as controlled flooding, random walker and topology evolution all lack scalability. Zhuge et al. have proposed trust-based probabilistic search algorithm called *P-walk* to improve search efficiency and to reduce unnecessary traffic in P2P networks [18]. In P-walk, neighboring peers assign trust scores to each other. During routing, peers preferentially forward queries to the highly ranked neighbors. However, its performance in large-scale unstructured network is questionable. To combat free riders, various trust-based incentive mechanisms are presented in [17]. Most of these mechanisms involve high computational overhead.

To combat the problem of inauthentic downloads as well as to improve search scalability while protecting the privacy of the users, this paper proposes an adaptive trust-aware algorithm that is robust and scalable. This work is an extension of our already published scheme which is based on construction of an overlay of trusted peers where neighbors are selected based on their trust ratings and content similarities [14]. It increases search efficiency by taking advantage of implicit semantic community structures formed as a result of topology adaptation since most of the queries are resolved within the community [14]. However, the novel contribution of the current work is that it combines the functionalities of a robust trust management model and the semantic community formation to provide a secure and efficient searching scheme while protecting the privacy of the users. The trust management scheme segregates the good peers from malicious peers, based on both first-hand and second-hand information, and the semantic community formation allows topology adaptation to form cluster of peers sharing similar contents in the network. The semantic communities also form a neighborhood of trust which is utilized to protect user privacy in the network.

The rest of the paper is organized as follows. Section 2 discusses some related work. Section 3 presents the proposed algorithm. As mentioned earlier, the scheme presented in this paper has a robust trust management model and privacy preserving module which were not present in the scheme described in [14]. Section 4 introduces various metrics for performance measurement, and then presents the simulation results. A brief discussion is also made on the comparative analysis of the performance of the proposed scheme with some of the existing similar schemes in the literature. Section 5 concludes the paper while highlighting some future scope of work.

2   Related Work

In [5], a searching mechanism is proposed that is based on discovery of trust paths among the peers in a peer-to-peer network. A global trust model based on distance-weighted recommendations has been proposed in [10] to quantify and evaluate the peers in a peer-to-peer network. In [3], a protocol named *adaptive peer-to-peer technologies* (APT) for the formation of adaptive topologies has been proposed to reduce spurious file download and free riding, where a peer connects to those peers from whom it is most likely to download satisfactory content. It adds or removes neighbors based on *local trust* and *connection trust* which are decided by its transaction history. The scheme follows a defensive strategy for punishment where a peer equally punishes both malicious peers as well as neighbors through which it receives response from malicious peers. This strategy is relaxed in the *reciprocal capacity-based adaptive topology protocol* (RC-ATP), where a peer connects to others which have higher reciprocal capacity [16]. Reciprocal capacity is defined based on peers's capacity of providing good files and of recommending source of download. While RC-ATP provides better network connectivity than APT, and reduces the cost of inauthentic downloads, it has a large overhead of topology adaptation.

There are some significant differences between the proposed algorithm and APT and RC-ATP. First, in the proposed scheme, the links in the original overlays are never deleted to avoid network partitioning. Second, the robustness of the proposed protocol in presence of malicious peers is higher than that of APT and RC-ATP protocols as found in the experiments. Third, as APT and RC-ATP both use flooding to locate resource, they have poor search scalability. The proposed scheme takes the advantages of semantic communities to improve QoS of search. Fourth, APT and RC-ATP do not employ any robust trust model for security in searching and for user identity and data privacy protection. The central part of the proposed searching mechanism in this paper is a robust trust management model. Finally, unlike APT and RC-ATP, the proposed algorithm scheme punishes malicious peers by blocking their queries. This ensures that malicious peers are not allowed to consume the resources and services available in the network.

3   The Secure and Privacy-Aware Searching Algorithm

This section is divided into three sub-sections. In the first sub-section, the various parameters and network environment of P2P networks are discussed. In the second, the proposed search algorithm is presented, and in the third sub-section, the privacy aspects of users and data in the searching process are discussed.

3.1   The Network Environment

To derive meaningful conclusion from the proposed algorithm, the proposed scheme have been modeled in P2P networks in a realistic fashion. The factors that are taken into consideration for design of the scheme are as follows.

(1) Network topology: The topology of a P2P network plays an important role for the analysis of trust management among its peers and for designing a searching scheme. Following the work in [3] and [16], the network has been modeled as a *power law graph*. In a power law network, degree distribution of nodes follows power law distribution, i.e. fraction of nodes having degree L is L^{-k} where k is a network dependent constant. Prior to each simulation cycle, a fixed fraction of peers chosen randomly is marked as malicious. As the algorithm executes, the peers adjust topology locally to connect to those peers which have better chance to provide good files in future, and drop malicious peers from their neighborhood. The network links are categorized into two types: *connectivity link* and *community link*. The connectivity links are the edges of the original power law network which provide seamless connectivity among the peers. To prevent the network from being partitioned, these links are never deleted. On the other hand, community links are added probabilistically between the peers who know each other, and have already interacted with each other before. A community link may be deleted when the perceived trustworthiness of a peer falls in the perception of its neighbors. A limit is put on the additional number of edges that a node can acquire to control bandwidth usage and query processing overhead in the network. This increase in network load is measured relative to the initial network degree (corresponding to connectivity edges). Let *final_degree(x)* and *initial_degree(x)* be the initial and final degree of a node x. The *relative increase in connectivity* (RIC) as computed in (1) is constrained by a parameter called *edge_limit*.

$$RIC(x) = \frac{final\_degree(x)}{initial\_degree(x)} \leq edge\_limit \qquad (1)$$

(2) Content distribution: The dynamics of a P2P network are highly dependent on the volume and variety of files each peer chooses to share. Hence a model reflecting real-world P2P networks is required. It has been observed that peers are in general interested in a subset of the contents in the P2P network [4]. Also, the peers are often interested only in the files from a few content categories. Among these categories some are more popular than others. It has been shown that Gnutella content distribution follows *zipf distribution* [13]. Keeping this in mind, both content categories and file popularity within each category is modeled with *zipf distribution* with $\alpha = 0.8$.

Content distribution model: The content distribution model in [13] is followed for the purpose of simulation. In this model, each distinct file $f_{c,r}$ is abstractly represented by the tuple (c, r), where c represents the content category to which the file belongs, and r represents its popularity rank within a content category c. Let content categories be $C = \{C_1, C_2, ..., C_{32}\}$. Each content category is characterized by its popularity rank. For example, if $C_1 = 1$, $C_2 = 2$ and $C_3 = 3$, then C_1 is more popular than C_2 and hence it is more replicated than C_2 and so on. Also there are more files in category C_1 than C_2.

Table 1. Simulation Parameters

Peers	Content Categories
P_1	C_1, C_2, C_3
P_2	C_3, C_4, C_6, C_7
P_3	C_2, C_4, C_7, C_8
P_4	C_1, C_2
P_5	C_1, C_5, C_6

Each peer randomly chooses between three to six content categories to share files and shares more files belonging to more popular categories. Table 1 shows an illustrative content distribution among 5 peers. The category C_1 is more replicated as it is the most popular category. Peer 1 (P_1) shares files in three categories: C_1, C_2, C_3, where it shares maximum number of files in category C_1, followed by category C_2 and so on. On the other hand, Peer 3 (P_3) shares maximum number of files in category C_2 as it is the most popular among the categories chosen by it.

(3) Query initiation model: The authors in [13] suggest that peers usually query for files which are available in the network, and are in the content category of their interest. In each cycle of simulation, active peers issue queries. However number of queries a peer issues may vary from peer to peer. Using the *Poisson* distribution this is modeled as follows. If M is the total number of queries to be issued in each cycle of simulation, and N is the number of peers present in the network, query rate $\lambda = M / N$ is the mean of the Poisson process. The expression: $p(\# \, of \, queries = K) = \frac{e^{-K} \lambda^K}{K!}$ gives the probability that a peer issues K queries in a cycle. The probability that a peer issues query for the file $f_{c,r}$ depends on the peer's interest level in category c and rank r of the file within that category.

(4) Trust management engine: A trust management engine is designed which helps a peer to compute trust ratings of other peers from past transactions as well as recommendation from its neighbor. For computation of trust values for the peers, a method similar to the one proposed in [6] is followed. The framework employs a *beta distribution* for reputation representation, updates and integration.

The first-hand information and second-hand (recommendation from neighbors) are combined to compute the reputation value of a peer. The weight assigned by a peer i to a second-hand information received from a node k is a function of reputation of node k as maintained in node i. For each peer j, a reputation R_{ij} is computed by a neighbor peer i. The reputation is embodied in the *Beta model* which has two parameters: α_{ij} and β_{ij}. α_{ij} represents the number of successful transactions (i.e. authentic file downloads) that peer i had with peer j, and β_{ij} represents the number of unsuccessful transactions (i.e., unauthentic file downloads). The reputation of peer j as maintained by peer i is computed using (2).

$$R_{ij} = Beta(\alpha_{ij} + 1, \beta_{ij} + 1) \tag{2}$$

The trust metric of a peer is the expected value of its reputation and is given by (3).

$$T_{ij} = E(R_{ij}) = E(Beta(\alpha_{ij} + 1, \beta_{ij} + 1)) = \frac{\alpha_{ij} + 1}{\alpha_{ij} + \beta_{ij} + 2} \tag{3}$$

The second-hand information is presented to peer i by its neighbor peer k. The peer i receives the reputation R_{kj} of peer j from peer k in the form of the two parameters α_{kj} and β_{kj}. After receiving this new information, the peer i combines it with its current assessment R_{ij} to obtain a new reputation R_{ij}^{new} as shown in (4).

$$R_{ij}^{new} = Beta(\alpha_{ij}^{new}, \beta_{ij}^{new}) \tag{4}$$

In (4), the values of α_{ij}^{new} and β_{ij}^{new} are given by (5) and (6) as follows.

$$\alpha_{ij}^{new} = \alpha_{ij} + \frac{2\alpha_{ik}\alpha_{kj}}{(\beta_{ik} + 2)(\alpha_{kj} + \beta_{kj} + 2)(2\alpha_{ik})} \tag{5}$$

$$\beta_{ij}^{new} = \beta_{ij} + \frac{2\alpha_{ik}\beta_{kj}}{(\beta_{ik} + 2)(\alpha_{kj} + \beta_{kj} + 2)(2\alpha_{ik})} \tag{6}$$

The proposed trust model gives more weight to recent observations, which is used for updating the reputation value using direct observation. For updating the reputation value using the second-hand information, *Dempster-Shafer theory* [15] and the *belief discouting model* [8] are used. The reputation of a recommending peer is automatically taken into account while computing the reputation of the reported peer. This eliminates the need of a separate deviation test. As mentioned earlier in this section, the trust value of a peer is computed as the statistical expected value of its reputation. The trust value of a peer lies in the interval $[0, 1]$. Peer i considers peer j as trustworthy if $S_{ij} \geq 0.5$, and malicious if $S_{ij} < 0.5$.

(5) Identity of the peers: Each peer generates a 1024 bit public/private RSA key pair. The public key serves as the identity of the peer. The identities are persistent and they enable two peers that have exchanged keys to locate and connect to one another whenever the peers are online. In addition, a *distributed hash table* (DHT) is maintained that lists the transient IP addresses and port numbers for all peers for all applications running of the peers. DHT entries for the peer i are signed by i and encrypted using its public key. Each entry is indexed by a 20 byte randomly generated shared secret, which is agreed upon during the first successful connection between the two peers. Each peer's location in the DHT is independent of its identity and is determined by hashing the client's current IP address and DHT port. This inhibits systematic monitoring of targeted regions of the DHT key space since the region for which each peer is responsible is determined by that peer's network address and port.

(6) Node churning model: In P2P networks, a large number of peers may join and leave at any time. This activity is termed as *node churning*. To simulate node churning, prior to each *generation* (a set of consecutive searches), a fixed percentage of nodes are chosen randomly as inactive. These peers neither initiate nor respond to a query in that generation and join the system latter with their LRU structure cleared. Since in a real world network, even in presence of churning, the approximate distribu-tion of content categories and files remain constant, content of nodes undergoing churn is exchanged which in effect assigns each of them new content as well as keeps content distribution model of the network unchanged.

(7) Threat model: Malicious peers adopt various strategies (threat models) to conceal their behavior and disrupt activities in the network. Two threat models are considered in the proposed scheme. The peers who share good quality files enjoy better topological due to topology adaptation. In threat model A, malicious peers attempt to circumvent this by providing good file occasionally with probability, known as *degree of deception* to lure other peers to form communities with them. In threat model B, a group of malicious peer joins the system and provides good files until their connectivity reaches a maximum value, i.e., the *edge limit*. The peers then start acting maliciously by spreading fake contents in the network.

3.2   The Proposed Search Algorithm

The network learns trust information through the search and updates trust information and adapts topology based on the outcome of the search. The following criteria are kept in mind while designing the algorithm: (a) It should improve search efficiency as well as search quality (i.e., authentic file downloads). (b) It should have minimal overhead in terms of computation, storage and message passing. (c) It should provide incentives to the peers which share large number of authentic files. (d) It should be self-policing in the sense that a peer should be able adjust its search strategy based on the local estimate of network connectivity. (e) It should be able to protect the privacy of the users. The major steps of execution of the algorithm are: (i) search, (ii) trust computing and verification, and (iii) topology adaptation. Each of these steps is discussed in the following.

Search: A *time to live* (TTL) bound search is used. At each peer, the query is forwarded to a subset of neighbors; the number of neighbors is decided based on the local estimate connectivity. The *connectivity index* for peer x is denoted as $Prob_{com}(x)$ and is given by (7).

$$Prob_{comm}(x) = \frac{degree(x) - initial\_degree(x)}{initial\_degree(x)(edge\_limit - 1)} \quad (7)$$

When $Prob_{com}$ for a node is low, the peer has the capacity to accept new community edges and expand community structures. Higher the value of $Prob_{com}$, it is less likely that the neighbors will disseminate the queries. As the algorithm executes, the connectivity of good nodes increases and reaches a maximum value. At this time, the peers focus on directing the queries to appropriate communities which may host the specific file rather than expanding communities. For example, if peer i can contact at most 10 neighbors and $Prob_{com}$ of j is 0.6, it forwards query to: 10 x (1 - 0.6) = 4 neighbors only. The search strategy is changed from initial TTL limited BFS to directed DFS with the restructuring of the network. The search process has two steps: *query initiation* and *query forward*. These steps are described in the following.

(i) **Query initiation:** The initiating peer forms a query packet containing the name of the file (c, r) and forwards it to some of its neighbors along with $Prob_{com}$ and TTL values. The query is disseminated using the following *neighbor selection rule*. The neighbors are ranked based on both their trustworthiness and the similarity of interests. Preference is given to the trusted neighbors sharing similar contents. Among the trusted neighbors, community members having their contents matched to the query are preferred. If the number of community links is not adequate enough, the query is forwarded through connectivity links also. The various cases of neighbor selection are illustrated in [14].

When a query reaches to peer i from peer j, peer i forwards the query further in the network as discussed below.

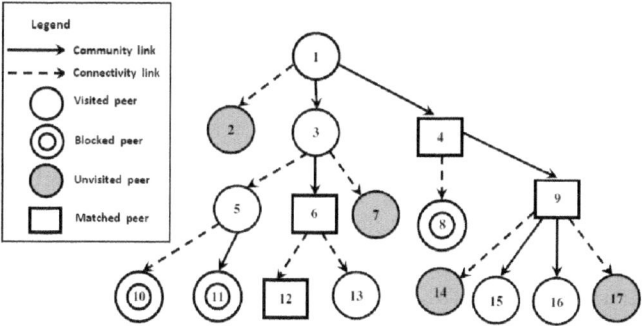

Fig. 1. The breadth first search (BFS) tree for the search initiated by peer 1

(ii) **Query forwarding:** (i) *Check the trust level of peer j*: Peer i checks trust rating of peer j through check trust rating algorithm (explained later in this section). Selection of peers for further forwarding the query is made accordingly.

(ii) *Check the availability of file*: If the requested file is found, response is sent to peer j. If TTL value has not expired, the following steps are executed. (iii) *Calculate the number of messages to be sent*: It is calculated based on the value of $Prob_{com}$. (iv) *Choose neighbors*: Neighbors are chosen in using neighbor selection rule. The search process is shown in Fig. 1. It is assumed that the query is forwarded at each hop to two neighbors. The matching community links are preferred over connectivity links to dispatch query. Peer 1 initiates the query and forwards it to two community neighbors 3 and 4. The query reaches peer 8 via peer 4. However, peer 8 knows from its previous transactions with peer 4 that peer 4 is malicious. Hence it blocks the query. The query forwarded by peer 5 is also blocked by peer 10 and 11 as both of them know that peer 5 is malicious. The query is matched at four peers: 4, 6, 9 and 12. The search process is shown in Fig. 1.

Topology Adaptation: The responses are sorted by the initiating peer i based on the reputations of the resource providers and the peer having the highest reputation is selected as the source for downloading. The requesting peer checks the authenticity of the downloaded file. If the file is found to be fake, peer i attempts to download the file from other sources until it is able to find the authentic resource or no more sources exist for searching. The peer then updates the trust ratings and possibly adapts the network topology after failed or successful download, to bring trusted peers to its neighborhood and to drop malicious peers from its community. The restructuring of network is controlled by a parameter known as *degree of rewiring* which provides the probability with which a link is formed between a pair of peers. This parameter allows trust information to propagate through the network. The topology adaptation consists of the following operations: (i) *link deletion*: Peer i deletes the existing community link with peer j if it finds peer j as malicious. (ii) *link addition*: Peer i probabilistically forms a community link with peer j if the resource provided by the peer j is found to be authentic. If $RIC \leq edge_{limit}$, for both peers i and j, only then an edge can be added subject to the approval of resource provider j. If peer j finds that peer i is malicious (i.e., its trust value is below the threshold), it doesn't approve the link.

Fig. 2 illustrates topology adaptation on the network topology shown in Fig. 1. In the example shown in Fig. 2, peer 1 downloads the file from peer 4 and finds that the file is spurious. It reduces the trust score of peer 4 and deletes the community link 1-4. It then downloads the file from peer 6 and gets an authentic file. Peer 1 now sends a request to peer 6, and the latter grants the request after checking its trust value and the community edge 1-6 is added. The malicious peer 4 loses one community link and peer 6 gains one community edge. However, the network still remains connected by connectivity edges, shown in dotted lines.

Checking of Trust Rating: Trust rating is used at various stages of execution of the algorithm to make decision about the possible source for download, to stop a query forwarded from a malicious node and to adapt the topology. A *least recently used* (LRU) data structure is used at each peer to keep track of 32 most

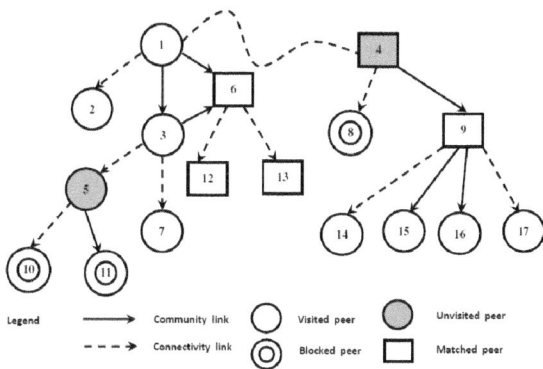

Fig. 2. Topology adaptation based on outcome of the search in Fig. 2. Malicious nodes are shaded in gray color.

recent peers it has interacted with. When no transaction history is available, a peer seeks recommendation from its neighbors using *trust query*. When peer i doesn't have trust score of peer j in its LRU history, it first seeks recommendation about j from all of its community neighbors. If none of its community neighbors possesses any information about j, peer i initiates a *directed DFS search*. The trust computation model has been presented in Section 3.1.

3.3 Privacy-Preservation in Searching

The trust-based searching scheme described above does not guarantee any privacy requirement of the requester (i.e. the initiator of the query). For protecting the privacy of the user, several enhancement of the algorithm are proposed. Following cases are identified for privacy preservation.

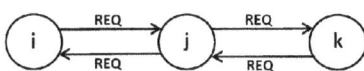

Fig. 3. Identity protection of the requesting peer i from the supplier peer k by use of trusted peer j. *REQ* and *RES* are the request and response message respectively.

(a) **Protection of the identity of the requesting peer:** In this case, as shown in Fig. 3, instead of sending the request straightway to the supplier peer, the requesting peer asks one of its trusted peers (which may or may not be its neighbor) to look up the data on its behalf. Once the query propagation module successfully identifies the possible supplier of the resource, the trusted peer serves as a proxy to deliver the data to the requester node. Other peers including the supplier of the resource will not be able to know the real requester. Hence, the requester's privacy is protected. Since the requestor's identity is only known to its trusted peer, the strength of privacy is dependent on the effort required to compromise the trusted peer. As mentioned in Section 3.1, the message communicated the peers are encrypted by 1024 bit RSA key, which is a provably secure algorithm. Hence, the privacy of the requester is highly protected.

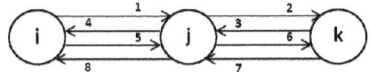

Fig. 4. Protecting data handle using trusted node. Peer i and k are the requester and the supplier peer respectively. Peer j is the trusted peer of the requester peer i.

(b) **Protecting the data handle:** To improve the achieved privacy level, the data handle may not be put in the request at the beginning. When a requester initiates the request, it computes the hash value of the handle and reveals only a part of the hash result in the request sent to its trusted peer. The steps 1 and 2 in Fig. 4 represent these activities. Each peer receiving the request compares the revealed partial hash to hash codes of the data handles that it holds. Depending on the length of the revealed part, the receiving peer may find multiple matches. This does not, however, imply that the peer has the requested data. Thus this peer will provide a candidate set, along with a certificate of its public key, to the requester. If the matched set is not empty, the peer will construct a *Bloom filter* [2] based on the left parts of the matched hash codes, and send it back to the trusted peer. The trusted peer forwards it back to the requester. These are represented by the steps 3 and 4 in Fig. 4. Examining the filters, the requester can eliminate from the candidate data supplier list all peers that do not have the required data. It then encrypts the complete request with the supplier's public key and gets the requested data with the help from its trusted node. The steps 5, 6, 7 and 8 in Fig. 4 represent these activities. By adjusting the length of the revealed hash code, the requestor can control the number of eliminated peers. The level of privacy is improved manifold since the malicious peers need to both compromise the trusted node and break the Bloom filter and hash function.

(c) **Hiding the data content:** Although the privacy-preservation level has been improved during the look-up phase using the previous two schemes, the privacy of the requester will be compromised if the trusted node can see the data content when it relays the packets for the requester. To improve the privacy level and prevent eavesdropping, we can encrypt the data handle and the data content. If the identity of the supplier is known to the requester, it can encrypt the request using the supplier's public key. The public key of the requester cannot be used because the certificate will reveal its identity. The problem is solved in the following manner. The requester generates a symmetric key and encrypts it using a supplier's public key. Only the supplier can recover the key and use it to encrypt data. To prevent the trusted node of the requester from conducting a man-in-the-middle attack, the trusted node is required to sign the packet. This provides a non-repudiation evidence, and shows that the packet is not generated by the trusted node itself. The privacy level has been improved since now the malicious nodes need to break the encryption keys as well.

4   Performance Evaluation

To analyze the performance of the proposed algorithm, several metrics are first defined. Due to constraints of space, the performance of the algorithm for some of the metrics are presented in this paper. More experimental results may be found in [14].

(a) **Attempt ratio (AR):** A peer keeps on downloading files from various sources based on their trust rating till it gets the authentic file. AR is the probability that the authentic file is downloaded in the first attempt. A high value of AR is desirable for a seraching scehme to be efficient and scalable.

(b) **Effective attempt ratio (EAR):** It measures the cost of downloading an authentic file by a good peer in comparison to the cost incurred by a malicious peer. If $P(i)$ be the total number of attempts made by the peer i to download an authentic file, EAR is given by (8).

$$EAR = (\frac{1}{M} \sum_{i=1}^{M} \frac{1}{P(i)} - \frac{1}{N} \sum_{j=1}^{N} \frac{1}{P(j)}) \tag{8}$$

In (8), M and N are the number of malicious and good peers issuing queries in a particular generation. For example, EAR $= 50$ implies that if a good peer needs one attempt to download an authentic file, a malicious peer will need two attempts.

(c) **Query miss ratio (QMR):** Since the formation of semantic communities takes some time, there will be a high rate of query misses in the first few generations of search. However, as the algorithm execuates, the rate of query miss is expected to fall for the good peers. QMR is defined as the ratio of the number of search failures to the total number of searches in a generation.

(d) **Relative increase in connectivity (RIC):** After a successful download, a requesting peer attempts to establish a community edge with the resource provider, if approved by the latter. This ensures that peers which provide good community services are rewarded by having increasing number of community neighbors. The metric RIC measures the number of community neighbors a peer gains with respect to its connectivity neighbors in the initial network topology. If $D_{init}(i)$ and $D_{final}(i)$ are the initial and final degrees of the peer i, and N is the number of peers, then RIC for peer i is computed using (9).

$$RIC(i) = \frac{1}{N} \sum_{i} \frac{D_{final}(i)}{D_{init}(i)} \tag{9}$$

(e) **Closeness centrality (CCen):** Since the topology adaptation effectively brings the good peers closer to each other, the length of the shortest path between a pair of good peers decreases. This intrinsic incentive for sharing authentic files is measured by the metric CCen. The peers with higher CCen values are topologically better positioned. If P_{ij} is the length of the shortest path between peer i and peer j through the community edges and if V denotes the set of peers, then CCen for peer i is given by (10).

$$CCen(i) = \frac{1}{\sum_{j \varepsilon V} P_{ij}} \qquad (10)$$

(f) **Clustering coefficient (CC):** It gives an indication about how well the network forms cliques. It has an important role in choosing the TTL value in the search algorithm. With higher values of CC, lower TTL values can be used. If K_i be the number of community neighbors of peer i, then clustering coefficient (CC) of peer i is computed using (11).

$$CC(i) = \frac{2E_i}{K_i(K_i - 1)} \qquad (11)$$

In (11), E_i is the actual number of community edges between the K_i neighbors. CC of the network is taken as the average value of all CC(i)s.

(g) **Largest connected component (LCC):** The community edges connect nodes which have similar content interests and sufficiently high mutual trust between each other. If we consider the peers which share a particular category of contents, then the community edges form a trust-aware community overlay. However, it will be highly probable that the trust-aware overly graph will be a disconnected graph. LCC is the largest connected component of this disconnected overlay graph. LCC of the network can be taken as a measure of the goodness of the community structure since it signifies how strongly the peers with similar contents and interests are connected with each other.

(h) **Trust query propagation overhead (TQPO):** The peers build trust and reputation information both by collection of first-hand and second-hand information. Trust query message is propagated when trust information about a peer is not available locally in a peer. A trust query message involves one DFS round without backtracking. The overhead incurred due to trust query propagation is measured by the metric called *trust query propagation overhead* (TQPO). TQPO is defined as the total number of distinct DFS search attempts per generation. It may be noted that a trust query may be initiated multiple times for a single file search operation: to select a trusted neighbor or to approve a community link.

A discrete time simulator written in C is used for simulation. In simulation, 6000 peer nodes, 18000 *connectivity edges*, 32 *content categories* are chosen. The *degree of deception* and the *degree of rewiring* are taken as 0.1 and 0.3 respectively. The value of the *edge_limit* is taken as 0.3. The TTL values for BFS and DFS are taken as 5 s and 10 s respectively. The discrete time simulator simulates the algorithm repeatedly on the power law network and outputs all the metrics averaged over generations. *Barabasi-Albert* generator is used to generate initial power law graph with 6000 nodes and approximately 18000 edges. The number of search per generation is taken as 5000 while the number of generations per cycle of simulation is 100.

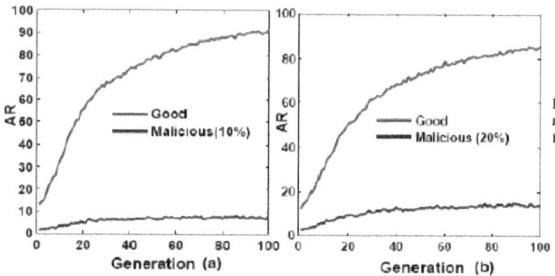

Fig. 5. AR vs. percentage of malicious peers. In (a) 10%, in (b) 20% nodes are malicious.

To check the robustness of the algorithm against attacks from malicious peers, the percentage of malicious peers is gradually increased. Fig. 5 illustrates the cost incurred (in terms of AR value) by each type of peers to download authentic files. As the percentage of malicious peers is increased, cost incurred by malicious peers to download authentic files decreases while that of good peers increases.

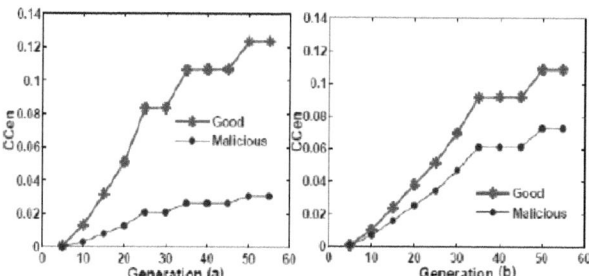

Fig. 6. Closeness centrality for various percentages of malicious nodes. In (a) 20% and (b) 40% nodes are malicious.

Fig. 6 presents how the *closeness centrality* (CCen) of good and malicious peers varies in the community topology. In computation of CCen, only the community edges have been considered. It may be observed that the steady state value of CCen for good peers is around 0.12. However, for the malicious peers, the CCen value is found to lie between 0.03 to 0.07. This demonstrates that the malicious peers are driven to the fringe of the network, while the good peers are allowed to form communities.

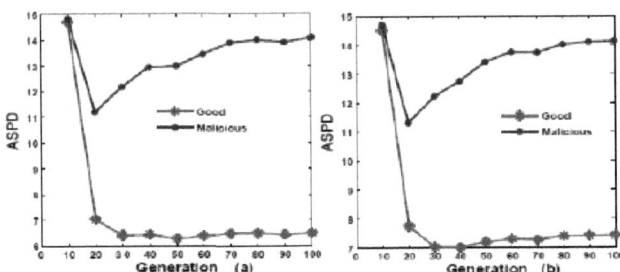

Fig. 7. Avg. shortest path distance vs. generations of search at the step of ten for various percentages of malicious peers. In (a) 30% and in (b) 40% nodes are malicious.

Higher values of CCen also indicate that good peers have smaller average shortest path length between them. In the simulation, the diameter of the initial network is taken as 5. At the end of one simulation run, if there is no path between a pair of peers using community edges, then the length of the shortest path between that pair is assumed to be arbitrarily long, say 15 (used in Fig. 7). As shown in Fig. 7, the *average shortest path distance* (ASPD) decreases form the initial value of 15 for both honest and malicious nodes. However, the rate and the extent of decrease for the good peers are much higher due to the formation of semantic communities around them. For malicious peers, after an initial fall, the value of ASPD increases consistently and finally almost reaches the maximum value of 15. On the other hand, the average value of ASPD for good peers is observed to be around 6. Since the good peers are connected with shorter paths, the query propagations and their responses will also be faster among these peers.

Fig. 8 shows *clustering coefficient* (CC) for each type of peers. Since community edges are added based on the download history and peers having good reputation gain more community edges, clustering coefficient (CC) is high for good peers. This leads to triangle formation in the communities. To counter this phenomenon, the search strategy adapts itself from BFS to DFS to minimize redundant message flows in the network. Since edges are added based on the download history and similarity of interest, community of peers are formed which are connected to other community by hub of peers having interest in multiple content categories. This leads to lower ASPD for good peers.

Fig. 9 depicts the size of the *largest connected component* (LCC) for each of the 32 content categories. It may be observed that the average size of LCC for all content categories remains constant even if the percentage of malicious peers in the network increases. This clearly shows that the community formation among the good peers is not adversely affected by the presence of malicious peers.

Fig. 10 shows that as the topology matures, the steady state value of *trust query propagation overhead* (TQPO) attains a low value. TQPO is less than 10 when 10% of the peers are malicious. Even when the network has 40% of its peers malicious, TQPO gradually decreases and reaches a value of 20 in 100 generations. Hence, the trust propagation module has little impact on the system overhead.

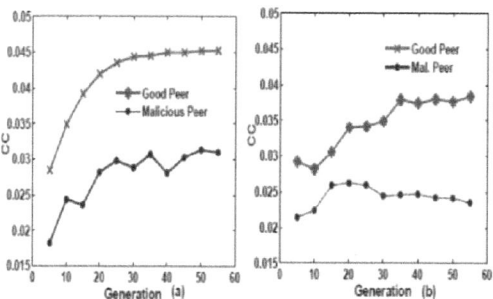

Fig. 8. Clustering coefficient for different percentages of malicious peers. In (a) 20% and in (b) 40% of the peers are malicious.

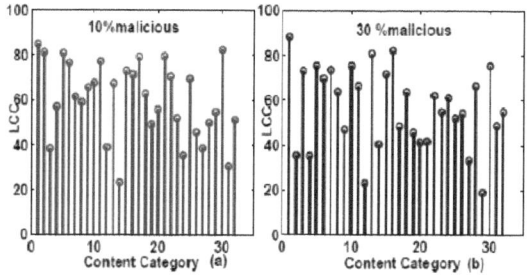

Fig. 9. Largest connected components (LCC) for different content categories

Comparisons with Existing Schemes: In the following, we provide a brief comparative analysis of the proposed protocol with two similar protocols existing in the literature. In [9], a method to minimize the impact of malicious peers on the performance of a peer-to-peer system has been proposed, where the global trust value for each peer is computed by calculating the left principal eigen vector of a matrix of normalized local trust value. Since the trust and reputation computations are robust, the mechanism is able to sustain a high value of AR (i.e. the fraction of authentic download) for good peers even when the percentage of malicious peers is as high as 80. In contrast, the proposed protocol in this paper can support high value of AR for good nodes as long as the percentage of malicious peers in the network does not exceed 60. However, the scehme based on eigen trust is computationally very intensive and it is susceptable to produce unreliable results in case of Byzantaine faliure of some peers. On the other hand, the proposed trust management algorithm in this paper is light-weight, and it can efficiently identify free riding and Byzantine failuer of peers while improving on the QoS of searching.

In the APT protocol[3], as the topology stabilizes, all the paths from the good peers to the malicious peers are blocked, and the characteristic path lenghts of these two types (good and malicious) of peers are distinctly different. However,

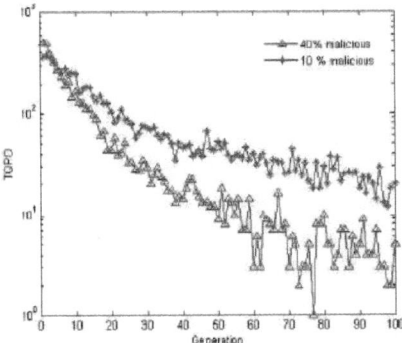

Fig. 10. Overhead of trust query propagation for 10% and 20% malicious peers in the network

in the proposed protocol in this paper, paths still exist between good peers and the malicious peers through the connectivity edges. Thee connectivity edges are not deleted. This prevents any possibility of network partitioning thereby making the protocol more robust. Moreover, the scalability is higher than that of the APT protocol, since it uses a light-weight trust management module. Finally, the APT protocol unlike the proposed scheme, does not have any mechanism to protect user and data privacy. This makes the protocol impractical for real-world deployment.

5   Conclusion

In this paper, a search mechanism is proposed that solves multiple problems in peer-to-peer networks e.g., inauthentic download, poor search scalability, combating free riders and protecting user privacy. The scheme exploits topology adaptation and robust trust management to isolate malicious peers. At the same time, the good peers are provided with topologically advantageous positions so that they get faster and authentic responses to their queries. Simulation results have demonstrated the efficiency and robustness of the scheme. As a future plan of work, we intend to carry out an analysis of the message overhead of the privacy module and a detailed comparative study of the performance of the proposed protocol with existing similar schemes.

References

1. Abdul-Rahman, A., Hailes, S.: A Distributed Trust Model. In: Proc. of the Workshop on New Security Paradigms, pp. 48–60 (1997)
2. Bloom, B.: Space-Time Trade-Offs in Hash Coding with Allowable Errors. Communications of the ACM 13(7), 422–426 (1970)

3. Condie, T., Kamvar, S.D., Garcia-Molina, H.: Adaptive Peer-to-Peer Topologies. In: Proc. of the 4th Int. Conf. on Peer-to-Peer Computing (P2P 2004), pp. 53–62 (2004)
4. Crespo, A., Garcia-Molina, H.: Semantic Overlay Networks for P2P Systems. Technical Report, Stanford University (2002)
5. De Mello, E.R., Moorsel, A.V., Fraga, J.D.S.: Evaluation of P2P Search Algorithms for Discovering Trust Paths. In: Proc. of 4th European Performance Engineering Conf. on Formal Models and Stochastic Models for Performance Evaluation, pp. 112–124 (2007)
6. Ganeriwal, S., Srivastava, M.: Reputation-Based Framework for High Integrity Sensor Networks. In: Proc. of the 2nd ACM Workshop on Security of Ad Hoc and Sensor Networks (SAN 2004), pp. 66–77 (2004)
7. Guo, L., Yang, S., Guo, L., Shen, K., Lu, W.: Trust-Aware Adaptive P2P Overlay Topology Based on Super-Peer-Partition. In: Proc. of the 6th Int. Conf. on Grid and Cooperative Computing, pp. 117–124 (2007)
8. Jsang, A.: A Logic for Uncertain Probabilities. Int. Journal of Uncertainty, Fuzziness and Knowledge-Based Systems 9(3), 279–311 (2001)
9. Kamvar, S.D., Schlosser, M.T., Garcia-Molina, H.: The Eigen Trust Algorithm for reputation Management in p2P Networks. In: Proc. of the 12th Int. Conf. on World Wide Web, WWW 2003 (2002)
10. Li, X., Wang, J.: A Global Trust Model of P2P Network Based on Distance-Weighted Recommendation. In: Proc. of IEEE Int. Conf. of Networking, Architecture, and Storage, pp. 281–284 (2009)
11. Risson, J., Moors, T.: Survey of Research Towards Robust Peer-to-Peer Networks. Computer Networks 50(7), 3485–3521 (2006)
12. Schafer, J., Malinks, K., Hanacek, P.: Peer-to-Peer Networks Security. In: Proc. of the 3rd Int. Conf. on Internet Monitoring and Protection (ICIMP), pp. 74–79 (2008)
13. Schlosser, M.T., Condie, T.E., Kamvar, S.D., Kamvar, A.D.: Simulating a P2P File-Sharing Network. In: Proc. of the 1st Workshop on Semantics in P2P and Grid Computing (2002)
14. Sen, J.: A Trust-Based Robust and Efficient Searching Scheme for Peer-to-Peer Networks. In: Soriano, M., Qing, S., López, J. (eds.) ICICS 2010. LNCS, vol. 6476, pp. 77–91. Springer, Heidelberg (2010)
15. Shafer, G.: A Mathematical Theory of Evidence. Princeton University (1976)
16. Tain, H., Zou, S., Wang, W., Cheng, S.: Constructing Efficient Peer-to-Peer Overlay Topologies by Adaptive Connection Establishment. Computer Communication 29(17), 3567–3579 (2006)
17. Tang, Y., Wang, H., Dou, W.: Trust Based Incentive in P2P Network. In: Proc. of the IEEE Int. Conf. on E-Commerce Technology for Dynamic E-Business, pp. 302–305 (2004)
18. Zhuge, H., Chen, X., Sun, X.: Preferential Walk: Towards Efficient and Scalable Search in Unstructured Peer-to-Peer Networks. In: Proc. of the 14th Int. Conf. on World Wide Web (WWW 2005), pp. 882–883 (2005)

On the Security of Mutual Authentication Protocols for RFID Systems: The Case of Wei *et al.*'s Protocol

Masoumeh Safkhani[1], Nasour Bagheri[2], Somitra Kumar Sanadhya[3], Majid Naderi[1], and Hamid Behnam[1]

[1] Electrical Engineering Department, Iran University of Science and Technology, Tehran, Iran
{M_Safkhani,M_Naderi,Behnam}@iust.ac.ir
[2] Electrical Engineering Department, Shahid Rajaee Teacher Training University, Tehran, Iran
N_Bagheri@iust.ac.ir
[3] Indraprastha Institute of Information Technology, Delhi (IIIT-Delhi), New Delhi, India
Somitra@iiitd.ac.in

Abstract. Authentication is one of the most basic and important cryptographic tasks. Mutual authentication protocols play a crucial role on the security of RFID systems. In this paper, we consider the security of a recently proposed mutual authentication protocol by Wei *et al.* which is a hash based protocol. We present efficient tag impersonation attack, two desynchronization attacks, reader impersonation attack and traceability attack against this protocol. The success probabilities of the attacks are "1" or $1 - 2^{-(n-1)}$, where n is the length of the secret value shared between the tag and the reader. The complexity of each one of the presented attacks is only two runs of protocol. Vulnerabilities presented in the present work rule out the practical usage of this protocol. To the best of our knowledge, this is the first security analysis of Wei *et al.*'s protocol. Finally, we exhibit an improved version of this protocol, which is immune against the attacks presented in this work.

Keywords: RFID, Authentication, Tag Impersonation Attack, Desynchronization Attack.

1 Introduction

Radio frequency identification (RFID) is a wireless technology which is employed for identifying and tracking objects in various applications of our daily life. Some common usage of this technology are in supply chain management in retail or wholesale stores, library access control, toll payments, theft prevention, human implants, e-Passports and so on. The basic components of a RFID system include the tag, the reader and the back-end database. The tag is attached to the target object and carries the identifier of its holder. The reader can read and/or modify

J. Garcia-Alfaro et al. (Eds.): DPM 2011 and SETOP 2011, LNCS 7122, pp. 90–103, 2012.
© Springer-Verlag Berlin Heidelberg 2012

the tag's information. Back-end database aids the reader, with extra storage space and computational capability to identify the objects.

RFID technology is slowly replacing Bar-coding method in grocery and retail stores, which are major users of this technology. Some of the reasons for wide deployment of RFID technology are:

1. The RFID technology can provide identification and authentication of tagged objects and allows data storage and data processing on the tags.
2. Data which can be stored on RFID tags is larger than what other competing methods such as Bar-coding can provide. In fact, bar-coding only provides the information about the "class" of the object, not the unique and personalized information about the object which is possible in RFID tags.
3. The distance of the RFID reader from the tags can vary from few centimeters to more than 20 meters.
4. Further, the RFID reader need not be in the line of sight of the tag. This is very useful for fast scanning and disposal of inventory and allows bulk object handling in short period of time.

Apart from the benefits mentioned above, widespread industrial adoption of RFID technology has partly also been due to the low cost of this technology. In particular, the tags are available for as little as few cents per piece. The power usage and the computational power of these low cost tags is quite restricted and this has motivated the researchers to study low cost methods and protocols for RFID systems.

1.1 Mutual Authentication Protocols in RFID Systems

Authentication is a process in which one party is assured of the identity of another party by obtaining corroborative evidence. In our case these parities are the Tag (T) and Reader/back-end database (R). In mutual authentication both the tag and the reader are authenticated to each other. However, if in a protocol, one of the parties is implicitly authenticated then it is enough that the other side (either the reader or the tag) authenticates itself. In general, such protocols include a game playing argument between the reader and the tag. One of the principals in the protocol poses some challenge(s) to the other principal and then verifies the received response(s). Protocols which provide this functionality are referred to as the authentication protocols. Commonly, RFID authentication protocols need to authenticate both the entities to each another.

If each of the parties involved in a transaction needs to verify the identity of the other then mutual authentication is necessary and critical. In that case, without mutual authentication, it may be possible for an adversary to impersonate the identity of either of the sides. The necessity of mutual authentication for RFID applications has been discussed in many earlier works such as [27, 7, 2, 18, 22]. The work [27], provides an example of an automated retail store check-out as an application of RFID mutual authentication between the customer (T) and the check-out mechanism (R). The lack of mutual authentication between the check-out mechanism and the customer would enable an active adversary to impersonate the customer to the store or vice versa. If the adversary impersonates the customer to the store then it could render the transaction useless for the store. The store would not only lose the goods but also the sale proceeds on those goods. On the other hand, if the adversary impersonates the store to the customer then it could violate the customer's privacy/security and steal his identity. Further, the customer may also incur financial losses due to fraudulent sales on his behalf.

Most RFID applications require both the communicating parties to need to prove their identity to the other party. This underscores the need for an efficient and secure mutual authentication protocol for RFID systems.

The aims of an adversary against such an authentication protocol may be manifold. First and foremost, an adversary would attempt to impersonate as either the tag or as the reader to the other principal in the communication. As already explained in the example of a retail store, it can have potential financial and/or privacy consequences for either principal. Secondly, an adversary may attempt to desynchronize the reader from the tag, thus causing a denial of service (DoS) attack on the system. Finally, the adversary may trace the tagged items to individual customers and may cause lose of privacy (Imagine a customer ordering a Viagra like drug and an adversary being able to trace the sale).

1.2   Standards for RFID Protocols

Many organizations have designed standards for RFID protocols. Some of these organizations are International Organization for Standards (ISO), International Electrotechnical Commission (IEC) and EPCGlobal. There is no unique global agency which has set standards for RFID protocols or frequencies. Based on their frequency, the RFID methods can be divided into three categories.

1. Low Frequency (LF): Typical range of LF is less than 150 KHz.
2. High Frequency (HF): Typical frequency is around 13.56 MHz.
3. Ultra High Frequency (UHF): Typical frequency is around 900 MHz.

Most industry uses of RFID are in the LF or HF category since they can be used without license. The UHF tags require prior local government approval before deployment and due to this reason are rather uncommon.

In 2004 [9,11], the Electronic Product Code Class-1 Generation-2 specification (EPC-C1 G2 in short) was announced by EPC Global which was approved as ISO18000-6C [14] in July 2006. It is widely believed that EPC-C1 G2 tags will be the mainstream to develop RFID applications because their effective reading range is larger. However, the security analysis that has been carried out in [1,24] has demonstrated important security flaws in the EPC-C1 G2 standard. For example, in this standard, the tag's identity (TID) is transmitted without any guard and it can be accessed by malicious readers.

Due to the flaws in the standard protocol as mentioned above, researchers have proposed several mutual authentication protocols in the literature [4, 41,

8, 16, 41, 15, 37, 38, 13, 5, 31, 6, 40, 32, 42, 39, 34, 33, 35]. However, there are many reports on their vulnerabilities [23, 43, 25, 30, 21, 26, 29]. The current work falls in the same line where we study the protocol proposed by Wei *et al.* [36] and show vulnerabilities in the proposal.

1.3 Overview of the Current Work

In Wei *et al.*'s protocol [36] each of the tag and the reader generate a random value, in every session, and the exclusive-or of these random values is used in the authentication process of the tag to the reader. We show that this property can be used as a drawback to present an efficient tag impersonation attack and desynchronization attack against this protocol. On the other hand, the reader authentication on the tag side is neither dependent on the random value generated by the tag nor the secret value which is updated in each session. We use this flaw in the design of the protocol to apply another desynchronization attack. Next we extend this second desynchronization attack to a reader impersonation attack and a traceability attack. The success probabilities of each of the attacks presented are at least $(1 - 2^{-(n-1)})$, where n is the length of the secret value S which has been shared between the tag and the reader which gets updated in each session. The complexity of each of our attacks is only two runs of the protocol.

Paper Organization: Notations used in the paper are presented in Section 2. The Wei *et al.*'s protocol is described in Section 3. In Section 4, we present our tag impersonation attack. In Section 5, we present two desynchronization attacks against the protocol. Further, we show how the adversary can impersonate the reader and trace a tag in this Section. In Section 6 we present our improvement to the the Wei *et al.*'s protocol to withstand the given attacks. Finally, we conclude the paper in Section 7.

2   Preliminaries

Throughout the paper, we use the following notations:
- R: RFID reader.
- T_i: RFID tag i.
- B: Back-end database.
- $\mathcal{A}$:   Adversary.
- ID :   Unique identifier of tag.
- RID : Unique identifier of Reader.
- S :   A secret value that the database B and the tag T share.
- S_{old} : Old value of S.
- S_{new} : New value of S.

- $R_{r_{(old)}}$: Old reader's random number.
- R_t :   Tag's random number.
- R_{db} :   Back-end database's random number.
- $h(.)$:   One way hash function.
- n: The output length of $h(.)$. This is also equal to the length of secret parameters, e.g. S.
- $\oplus$:   Exclusive-or operation.
- $A\|B$:   Concatenation of string A to string B.
- $B \leftarrow A$: Assigning the value of A to B.

3 Wei *et al.*'s Protocol Description

The Wei *et al.*'s [36] protocol, which is depicted in Fig. 1, is a hash based mutual authentication protocol. The protocol randomizes each authentication session by employing two random values R_r and R_t, generated by the reader and the tag respectively. The protocol works as follows:

1. The reader chooses a random number R_r and sends *Request* and R_r to the tag.

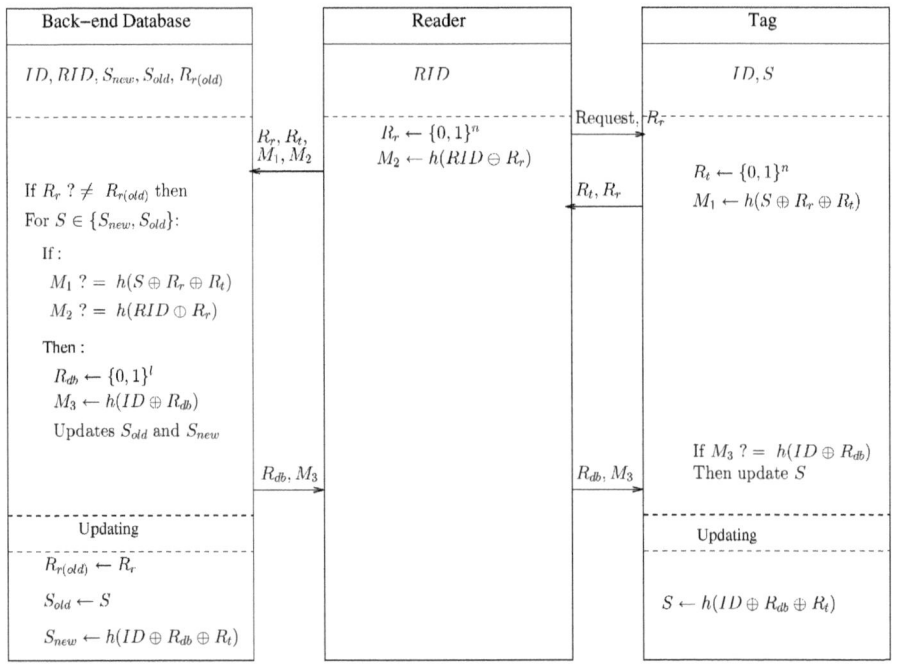

Fig. 1. The mutual authentication protocol proposed by Wei *et al.*

2. Upon receipt of the message, the tag proceeds as follows:
   (a) Generates another random number R_t,
   (b) Computes $M_1 = h(S \oplus R_r \oplus R_t)$,
   (c) Sends M_1 and R_t to the reader.
3. Upon receipt of the message, the tag proceeds as follows:
   (a) Computes $M_2 = h(RID \oplus R_r)$,
   (b) Sends M_1, M_2, R_r and R_t to the back-end database.
4. Upon receipt of the message, the back-end database proceeds as follows:
   (a) Verifies whether $R_r \overset{?}{\neq} R_{r_{(old)}}$ and $M_1 \overset{?}{=} h(S \oplus R_r \oplus R_t)$ and $M_2 \overset{?}{=}$ $h(RID \oplus R_r)$, either for S_{new} or S_{old}. If the verification fails then the session is aborted and the tag is not authenticated. If the verification succeeds, then the database proceeds as follows:
       − Authenticates the tag,
       − Generates another random number R_{db},
       − Computes $M_3 = h(ID \oplus R_{db})$,
       − Updates $R_{r_{(old)}} = R_r$
       − Updates S_{old} to the value of S for which the tag has been authenticated,
       − Updates $S_{new} = h(ID \oplus R_{db} \oplus R_t)$,
       − Sends M_3 and R_{db} to the reader.
5. Upon receipt of M_3 and R_{db}, the reader forwards them to the tag.
6. Upon receipt of M_3 and R_{db}, the tag proceeds as follows:
   (a) Verifies whether $M_3 \overset{?}{=} h(ID \oplus R_{db})$, if yes,
       − Authenticates the reader,
       − Updates $S = h(ID \oplus R_{db} \oplus R_t)$

It must be noted that although most of the other low cost RFID authentication protocols [37,38,20,5,31,6,40,32,34] consider the channel between the reader and back-end database secure, in Wei et al.'s protocol [36], the authors consider this channel to be insecure. However, this assumption does not affect our attacks. All the attacks described in the current paper work properly even when we consider the channel between the reader and back-end database secure.

4   Tag Impersonation Attack

Tag impersonation attack is a forgery attack in which the reader accepts a spoofed tag as a legitimate tag. Wei *et al.* [36] claim that only the legitimate tag can generate M_1 such that it gets accepted by the back-end database. More precisely, the authors of [36] state that to generate a valid M_1 and impersonate the tag, the adversary requires access to the secret value S which is protected by the hash function. However, we present a rather simple attack which can impersonate a legitimate tag without any knowledge of the secret values S. To impersonate the tag T_i, the adversary $\mathcal{A}$ follows the steps below:

Phase 1(Learning): $\mathcal{A}$ eavesdrops one run of protocol between the reader R and T_i and stores the transferred values between R and T_i. These values include R_r, $M_1 = h(S \oplus R_r \oplus R_t)$ and R_t. At the end of this step, the back-end database assigns the S value which has been used in the calculation of M_1 to S_{old}.

Phase 2 (Impersonation): To impersonate the legitimate tag, $\mathcal{A}$ waits until the reader initiates a new session of protocol, where:

1. R sends *Request* and R'_r.
2. Once $\mathcal{A}$ receipts the message, it will respond with the tuple R'_t and M'_1, where $R'_t = R_t \oplus R_r \oplus R'_r$ and $M'_1 = M_1 = h(S_{old} \oplus R_r \oplus R_t)$.
3. The reader receives R'_t and M'_1 and upon receipt of these values, it proceeds as follows:
   (a) Computes $M'_2 = h(RID \oplus R'_r)$,
   (b) Sends M'_1, M'_2, R'_r and R'_t to the back-end database.
4. The back-end database receives M'_1, M'_2, R'_r and R'_t. After receiving these values, it proceeds as follows:
   (a) Verifies whether $R'_r \neq R_{r_{(old)}}$ and $M'_1 \overset{?}{=} h(S_{old} \oplus R'_r \oplus R'_t)$ and $M'_2 \overset{?}{=} h(RID \oplus R'_r)$, where definitely $R'_r \neq R_{r_{(old)}}$ and $M'_2 = h(RID \oplus R'_r)$. On the other hand, $h(S_{old} \oplus R'_r \oplus R'_t) = h(S_{old} \oplus R'_r \oplus R'_r \oplus R_r \oplus R_t) = h(S_{old} \oplus R_r \oplus R_t) = M'_1 = M_1$.
   (b) Authenticates $\mathcal{A}$ as a legitimate tag.

Hence, following the above attack, the reader authenticates the adversary as a legitimate tag. The success probability of attack is "1" and the complexity of the attack is two runs of the protocol. The above adversary is a man in the middle adversary which controls the communications between the reader and the tags and interacts passively (Phase 1) or actively (Phase 2) with them. In the Impersonation phase of attack the affect of the tag's response is ignored because this step occurs in the absence of tag.

Remark 1. To fix the given attack, one may suggest that the protocol is modified in such a way that S_{old} can NOT be used for the verification. That is, the value S that must be used by the database in this verification must always be the last one, S_{new}, that he shares with the tag. However, in that case any adversary which blocks the last step of the protocol (M_3 and R_{db} forwarded from the reader to the tag) will desynchronize the tag and and the back-end database. Actually, the original protocol keeps the record of S_{new} and S_{old} to avoid such a trivial desynchronization attack.

5   Desynchronization Attack

In this Section we present two desynchronization attacks against the Wei *et al.*'s [36] protocol. In desynchronization attack, the adversary forces the tag and the reader to update their common values to different values. If the adversary can succeed in forcing the tag and the reader to do so, they will not authenticate each other in further transactions. Wei *et al.* [36] claim that their protocol is secure against desynchronization attack. More precisely, the authors state that to prevent the desynchronization attack they keep a record of old secret value (It helps to remain in sync when the adversary blocks the last message sent from the back-end database to the tag). However, we present two attacks where the adversary forces the tag to update its secret value such that it does not match the value that back-end database keeps in its records.

5.1 The First Desynchronization Attack

Our first desynchronization attack is similar to the tag impersonation attack described in Section 4. The steps of this attack are as follows:

Phase 1(Learning) : $\mathcal{A}$ eavesdrops one run of the protocol between R and T_i and stores the transferred values between R and T_i. These values include R_r, $M_1 = h(S \oplus R_r \oplus R_t)$ and R_t. At the end of this step, the back-end database has two record of S, the S value which has been used in the calculation of M_1 denoted by S_{old} and $S_{new} = h(ID \oplus R_{db} \oplus R_t)$. Further, the tag has updated its secret value to $S = h(ID \oplus R_{db} \oplus R_t)$.

Phase 2 (Desynchronization) : To desynchronize the tag and the reader, $\mathcal{A}$ waits until the reader initiates a new session of protocol, where:

1. R sends *Request* and R'_r.
2. Once $\mathcal{A}$ receipts the message, it will respond with the tuple R'_t and M'_1, where $R'_t = R_t \oplus R_r \oplus R'_r$ and $M'_1 = M_1 = h(S_{old} \oplus R_r \oplus R_t)$.
3. Following the argument of step 4 in Section 4, the back-end database authenticates $\mathcal{A}$ as the legitimate tag T_i, generates a new random value R'_{db} and updates its secret value. However, since S_{old} has been used throughout the authentication process, the reader R assigns it to S_{old} and updates $S'_{new} = h(ID \oplus R'_{db} \oplus R'_t) = h(ID \oplus R'_{db} \oplus R'_r \oplus R_r \oplus R_t)$.
4. Since the secret key S in tag remains $h(ID \oplus R_{db} \oplus R_t)$, if $S \neq S_{old}$ and $S \neq S'_{new}$, then R and T_i have different secret values in their database and they will not authenticate each other any more.

Hence, following the above attack the adversary can desynchronize the tag and the reader if $S \neq S_{old}$ and $S \neq S'_{new}$. From Step 3 of the attack we know that the probability of $S = S_{old}$ is 2^{-n}. Similarly, the probability for $S = S'_{new}$ is also 2^{-n}. Therefore, The success probability of the given attack is $1 - 2^{-(n-1)}$ where n is the length of the secret value S. The interesting point in this attack is that although T_i has been desynchronized, the adversary can impersonate it at any time following the given attack in Section 4.

Similar to the given impersonation attack, the above adversary is a man in the middle adversary which controls the communications between the reader and the tags and interacts passively (Phase 1) or actively (Phase 2) with them. In the Desynchronization phase of attack the affect of the tag's response is ignored because this step occurs in the absence of tag or the adversary blocks the tag's responses.

5.2   The Second Desynchronization Attack

The second desynchronization attack is based on the observation that on the last step of the protocol, where the back-end database sends $M_3 = h(R_{db} \oplus ID)$ and R_{db} to the tag, the adversary can replace this message by any eavesdropped $M_3' = h(R_{db}' \oplus ID)$ and R_{db}' from the previous sessions and also get authenticated by the tag. Similar to the previously given attacks, the adversary is a man in the middle adversary which controls the communications between the reader and the tags and interacts passively (Phase 1) or actively (Phase 2) with them. The steps of our second desynchronization attack are as follows:

Phase 1(Learning) : $\mathcal{A}$ eavesdrops one run of protocol between the reader R and T_i and stores the transferred values between R and T_i at the last step of protocol, $M_3 = h(R_{db} \oplus ID)$ and R_{db}. At the end of this step, the back-end database has two records of S, S_{old} and $S_{new} = h(ID \oplus R_{db} \oplus R_t)$ and the tag updates its secret value to $S = h(ID \oplus R_{db} \oplus R_t)$.

Phase 2 (Desynchronization) : To desynchronize the tag and the reader, $\mathcal{A}$ waits until the reader initiates a new session of protocol, where:

1. R sends *Request* and R_r'.
2. Once $\mathcal{A}$ receipts the message, it will forward *Request* and R_r' to the tag.
3. Once $\mathcal{A}$ receipts the tag's response R_t' and M_1' to R, where $M_1' = h(S_{new} \oplus R_r' \oplus R_t')$, it will forward them to R.
4. The back-end database authenticates T_i, generates a new random number R_{db}', assigns the current secret $S_{new} = h(ID \oplus R_{db} \oplus R_t)$ to S_{old}, updates $S_{new}' = h(ID \oplus R_{db}' \oplus R_t')$ and sends $M_3' = h(R_{db}' \oplus ID)$ and R_{db}' to R to forward them to T_i.
5. $\mathcal{A}$ blocks $M_3' = h(R_{db}' \oplus ID)$ and R_{db}' and instead sends $M_3 = h(R_{db} \oplus ID)$ and R_{db} to T_i.
6. As the tag receives M_3 and R_{db} it does as follows:
   (a) Verifies whether $M_3 \stackrel{?}{=} h(ID \oplus R_{db})$, which it is,
      – Authenticates the reader,
      – Updates $S_{new}' = h(ID \oplus R_{db} \oplus R_t')$
7. Now, the records of secret value S that back-end database has are $S_{old} = h(ID \oplus R_{db} \oplus R_t)$ and $S_{new}' = h(ID \oplus R_{db}' \oplus R_t')$, while the secret value stored in T_i is $S = h(ID \oplus R_{db} \oplus R_t')$. Since with the probability of $(1 - 2^{-n})$ we have $h(ID \oplus R_{db} \oplus R_t') \neq h(ID \oplus R_{db}' \oplus R_t')$ and similarly for $h(ID \oplus R_{db} \oplus R_t') = h(ID \oplus R_{db} \oplus R_t)$, the tag and the reader would be desynchronized with a good probability.

Hence, following the above attack the adversary can desynchronize the tag and the reader if $S \neq S_{old}$ and $S \neq S_{new}'$, where from Step 7 of the attack we know that the probability of $S = S_{old}$ is 2^{-n} and similarly for $S \neq S_{new}$. Therefore, the success probability of the given attack is $(1 - 2^{-(n-1)})$ where n is the length of the secret value S. Although T_i has been desynchronized, if the adversary eavesdropped the transferred R_r', $M_1' = h(S \oplus R_r' \oplus R_t')$ and R_t' at the last run of protocol in the above attack, it can impersonate T_i at any time following the attack described in Section 4.

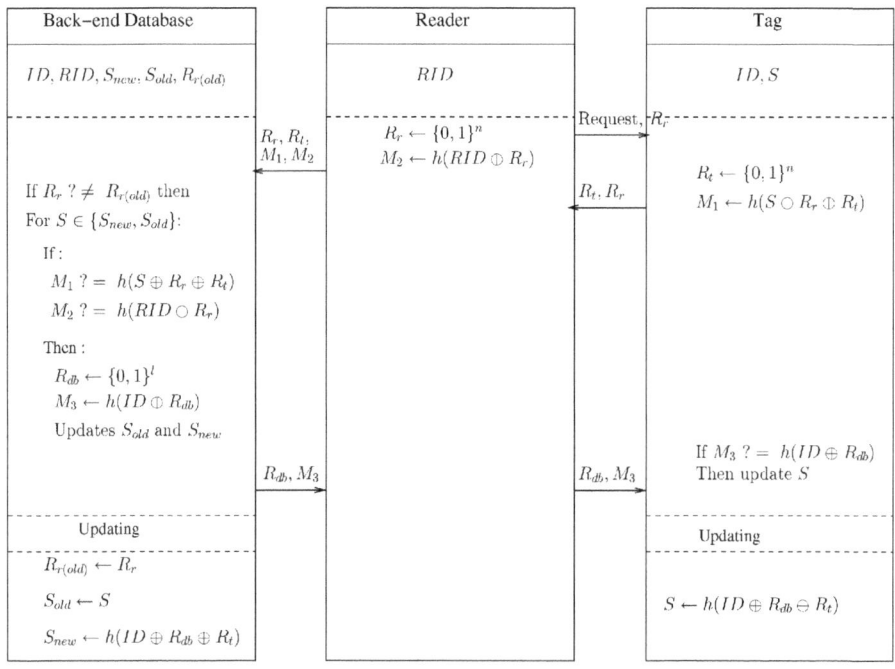

Fig. 2. The strengthened version of Wei *et al.*'s mutual authentication protocol proposed in the current work

Remark 2. The above attack can be used as a reader impersonation attack. In this attack, the adversary has eavesdropped tuple M_3 and R_{db} in one session of protocol. Now, to impersonate the reader, $\mathcal{A}$ supplants a new session and at the last step of the protocol, the adversary replies with the eavesdropped M_3 and R_{db}. Definitely, the tag authenticates $\mathcal{A}$ as a legitimate reader. The success probability of the attack is "1" while the complexity is two runs of protocol.

Remark 3. The above attack can also be used as a traceability attack. In this attack, to trace T_i, the adversary eavesdrops values of M_3 and R_{db} in one session of the protocol that T_i has been involved in. Now given a tag T_j, the adversary will try to impersonate the reader based on the eavesdropped M_3 and R_{db}. If T_j authenticated $\mathcal{A}$ then adversary concludes that the given tag is T_i, otherwise it is not. The success probability of the attack is $(1 - 2^{-(n)})$ while the complexity is two runs of protocol.

6   Strengthening Wei *et al.*'s Protocol

In this Section, we attempt to strengthen Wei *et al.*'s protocol against the attacks described in this paper. We show that the protocol can be modified slightly to withstand our attacks. Fig. 2 shows the revised protocol which works as follows:

1. The reader chooses a random number R_r and sends *Request* and R_r to the tag.
2. Upon receipt of the messages, the tag proceeds as follows:
   (a) Generates another random number R_t,
   (b) Computes $M_1 = h((S \oplus R_r)\|R_t)$,
   (c) Sends M_1 and R_t to the reader.
3. Upon receipt of the messages, the reader proceeds as follows:
   (a) Computes $M_2 = h(RID \oplus R_r)$,
   (b) Sends M_1, M_2, R_r and R_t to the back-end database.
4. Upon receipt of the messages, the back-end database proceeds as follows:
   (a) Verifies whether $R_r \overset{?}{\neq} R_{r(old)}$ and $M_1 \overset{?}{=} h((S \oplus R_r)\|R_t)$ and $M_2 \overset{?}{=} h(RID \oplus R_r)$, either for S_{new} or S_{old}. If the verification fails then the session is aborted and the tag is not authenticated. If verification succeeds, then the database does as follows:
   - Authenticates the tag,
   - Generates another random number R_{db},
   - Computes $M_3 = h((ID \oplus R_{db})\|(R_t \oplus R_r))$,
   - Updates $R_{r(old)} = R_r$
   - Updates S_{old} to the value of S for which the tag has been authenticated,
   - Updates $S_{new} = h(((ID \oplus R_t)\|(R_r \oplus R_{db})) \oplus S)$,
   - Sends M_3 and R_{db} to the reader.
5. Upon receipt of M_3 and R_{db}, the reader forwards them to the tag.
6. Upon receipt of M_3 and R_{db}, the tag proceeds as follows:
   (a) Verifies whether $M_3 \overset{?}{=} h((ID \oplus R_{db})\|(R_t \oplus R_r))$, if yes,
   - Authenticates the reader,
   - Updates $S = h(((ID \oplus R_t)\|(R_r \oplus R_{db})) \oplus S)$

After the simple modifications proposed, the above protocol can resist the attacks described in this paper. This is because the adversary has no control over all of R_t or R_r and R_{db}. Hence, it is not possible for the adversary to run the protocol again and control the hash function output. Therefore, on any run of protocol, the output of the hash function will be different and unexpected, and thus it can prevent the proposed attacks. In order to attack the modified proposal, one will need to construct a non-trivial attack.

Remark 4. Replacement of the XOR operation in the protocol by the concatenation extends the length of the message that must be hashed. However, the most common way to hash messages is to call a compression function of fixed length iteratively. For example, the Merkle-Damgård (MD) [17, 10] is a well known hash construction, which is used in almost all popular hash functions such as MD5 [28], SHA-1 [19] and SHA-2 [12]. Given a message $M = M_1\|...\|M_l$ and $g : \{0,1\}^n \times \{0,1\}^m \to \{0,1\}^n$ as the compression function, MD hash function computes the hash value of M as follows:

$$h^g(M) = g(g(...g(IV, M_1), ...), M_l)$$

where IV is the initial value. Hence, the modified protocol will need few extra calls to the underlying compression function which will increase the computational complexity of the protocol. However, this increase in the complexity is providing more security.

7 Conclusion

In this paper we considered the Wei *et al.* 's RFID mutual authentication protocol and presented several efficient attacks against the protocol. Our attacks succeed in tag impersonation, reader impersonation, desynchronization of the tag and the reader (in two different ways) and tracing a tag. The success probability of the attacks are "1" or $(1 - 2^{-(n-1)})$ and the complexity is two runs of the protocol. This study shows that Wei *et al.*'s protocol is not a secure protocol at all. In addition, we proposed a slight modification of this protocol to withstand the attacks presented in this paper. However, this modification may cost the protocol extra calls to the hash function.

Acknowledgments. The authors would like to acknowledge helpful comments by anonymous reviewers of DPM 2011. These comments helped improve the technical content as well as the readability of the paper.

References

1. Bailey, D.V., Juels, A.: Shoehorning Security into the EPC Tag Standard. In: De Prisco, R., Yung, M. (eds.) SCN 2006. LNCS, vol. 4116, pp. 303–320. Springer, Heidelberg (2006)
2. Blundo, C., Cimato, S. (eds.): SCN 2004. LNCS, vol. 3352, pp. 149–164. Springer, Heidelberg (2005)
3. Brassard, G. (ed.): CRYPTO 1989. LNCS, vol. 435, pp. 416–427. Springer, Heidelberg (1990)
4. Chen, C.-L., Deng, Y.-Y.: Conformation of EPC class 1 generation 2 standards RFID system with mutual authentication and privacy protection. Eng. Appl. of AI 22(8), 1284–1291 (2009)
5. Chen, Y.-Y., Tsai, M.-L., Jan, J.-K.: The design of RFID access control protocol using the strategy of indefinite-index and challenge -response. Computer Communication 34(3), 250–256 (2011)
6. Chien, H.-Y.: Secure Access Control Schemes for RFID Systems with Anonymity. In: MDM, page 96. IEEE Computer Society (2006)
7. Chien, H.-Y., Chen, C.-H.: Mutual authentication protocol for RFID conforming to EPC Class 1 Generation 2 standards. Computer Standards & Interfaces 29(2), 254–259 (2007)
8. Choi, E.Y., Lee, D.H., Lim, J.I.: Anti-cloning protocol suitable to EPCglobal class-1 generation-2 RFID systems. Computer Standards & Interfaces 31(6), 1124–1130 (2009)
9. Class-1 generation 2 UHF air interface protocol standard version 1.2.0, Gen2. In: Gen-2 Standard. EPCGlobal (2008), http://www.epcglobalinc.org/standards/

10. Damgård, I.: A Design Principle for Hash Functions. In: Brassard [3], pp. 416–427
11. EPC Tag data standar dversion (January 4, 2008); Yearly report on algorithms and keysizes, Technical Report D.SPA.13Rev.1.0,ICT-2007-216676. In: Gen2 Standard. ECRYPT (2010), http://www.epcglobalinc.org/standards/
12. FIPS. Secure Hash Standard. National Institute for Standards and Technology (NIST) (August 2002)
13. Hung-Yu, C.: SASI: A New Ultralightweight RFID Authentication Protocol Providing Strong Authentication and Strong Integrity. IEEE Transactions on Dependable and Secure Computing 4(4), 337–340 (2007)
14. Information technology - Radio frequency identification for item management. Part 6: Parameters for air interface communications at 860 MHz to 960MHz (2005), http://www.iso.org
15. Jin, G., Jeong, E.Y., Jung, H.-Y., Lee, K.D.: RFID authentication protocol conforming to EPC class-1 generation-2 standard. In: Arabnia, H.R., Daimi, K. (eds.) Security and Management, pp. 227–231. CSREA Press (2009)
16. Lo, N.W., Yeh, K.-H.: An Efficient Mutual Authentication Scheme for EPCglobal Class-1 Generation-2 RFID System. In: Denko, M.K., Shih, C.-s., Li, K.-C., Tsao, S.-L., Zeng, Q.-A., Park, S.H., Ko, Y.-B., Hung, S.-H., Park, J.-H. (eds.) EUC-WS 2007. LNCS, vol. 4809, pp. 43–56. Springer, Heidelberg (2007)
17. Markle, R.: One way Hash Functions and DES. In: Brassard [3], pp. 428–446
18. Molnar, D., Wagner, D.: Privacy and security in library RFID: issues, practices, and architectures. In: Atluri, V., Pfitzmann, B., McDaniel, P.D. (eds.) ACM Conference on Computer and Communications Security, pp. 210–219. ACM (2004)
19. National Institute of Standards and Technology. Secure Hash Standard (SHS). FIPS Publication 180 (May 1993)
20. Ohkubo, M., Suzuki, K., Kinoshita, S.: Hash-chain based forward-secure privacy protection scheme for low-cost RFID. In: Proc. of the 2004 Symposium on Cryptography and Information Security (SCI 2004), pp. 719–724 (2004)
21. Rizomiliotis, S.G.P., Rekleitis, E.: Security analysis of the Song Mitchell authentication protocol for low-cost RFID tags. IEEE Communications Letters 13(4), 274–276 (2009)
22. Peris-Lopez, P., Hernandez-Castro, J.C., Estevez-Tapiador, J.M., Ribagorda, A.: M^2AP: A Minimalist Mutual-Authentication Protocol for Low-Cost RFID Tags. In: Ma, J., Jin, H., Yang, L.T., Tsai, J.J.-P. (eds.) UIC 2006. LNCS, vol. 4159, pp. 912–923. Springer, Heidelberg (2006)
23. Peris-Lopez, P., Castro, J.C.H., Estévez-Tapiador, J.M., Ribagorda, A.: Cryptanalysis of a novel authentication protocol conforming to EPC-C1G2 standard. Computer Standards & Interfaces 31(2), 372–380 (2009)
24. Peris-Lopez, P., Hernandez-Castro, J.C., Estevez-Tapiador, J.M., Ribagorda, A.: RFID specification revisited. In: The Internet of Things: From RFID to The Next-Generation Pervasive Networked Systems, pp. 311–346. Taylor & Francis Group (2008)
25. Peris-Lopez, P., Hernandez-Castro, J.C., Tapiador, J.E., van der Lubbe, J.C.A.: Cryptanalysis of an EPC class-1 generation-2 standard compliant authentication protocol. Eng. Appl. of AI 24(6), 1061–1069 (2011)
26. Phan, R.C.-W.: Cryptanalysis of a New Ultralightweight RFID Authentication Protocol - SASI. IEEE Transactions on Dependable and Secure Computing 6(4), 316–320 (2009)
27. Piramuthu, S.: RFID mutual authentication protocols. Decision Support Systems 50(2), 387–393 (2011)

28. Rivest, R.L.: RFC 1321: The MD5 Message-Digest Algorithm. Internet Activities Board (April 1992)
29. Safkhani, M., Bagheri, N., Naderi, M., Luo, Y., Chai, Q.: Tag Impersonation Attack on Two RFID Mutual Authentication Protocols. In: FARES (2011)
30. Safkhani, M., Naderi, M.: Cryptanalysis and Improvement of a Lightweight Mutual Authentication Protocol for RFID system. In: 7th International ISC Conference on Information Security and Cryptology (ISCISC 2010), pp. 57–59 (2010)
31. Shen, J., Choi, D., Moh, S., Chung, I.: A Novel Anonymous RFID Authentication Protocol Providing Strong Privacy and Security. In: 2010 International Conference on Multimedia Information Networking and Security (2010)
32. Song, B., Mitchell, C.J.: RFID Authentication Protocol for Low-cost Tags. In: WiSec 2008, pp. 140–147 (2008)
33. Song, B., Mitchell, C.J.: Scalable RFID security protocols supporting tag ownership transfer. Computer Communications 34(4), 556–566 (2011)
34. Sun, H.-M., Ting, W.-C.: A Gen2-Based RFID Authentication Protocol for Security and Privacy. IEEE Transactions on Mobile Computing 8(8), 1052–1062 (2009)
35. Tan, C.C., Sheng, B., Li, Q.: Secure and Serverless RFID Authentication and Search Protocols. IEEE Transactions on Wireless Communications 7(4), 1400–1407 (2008)
36. Wei, C.-H., Hwang, M.-S., Chin, A.Y.: A Mutual Authentication Protocol for RFID. IT Professional 13(2), 20–24 (2011)
37. Weis, S.: Security and Privacy in Radio Frequency Identification Devices. Masters Thesis, Massachusetts Institute of Technology, MIT (2003)
38. Weis, S.A., Sarma, S.E., Rivest, R.L., Engels, D.W.: Security and Privacy Aspects of Low-Cost Radio Frequency Identification Systems. In: Hutter, D., Müller, G., Stephan, W., Ullmann, M. (eds.) Security in Pervasive Computing 2003. LNCS, vol. 2802, pp. 201–212. Springer, Heidelberg (2004)
39. Xueping, R., Xianghua, X.: A Mutual Authentication Protocol For Low-cost RFID System. In: 2010 IEEE Asia-Pacific Services Computing Conference, pp. 632–636 (2010)
40. Wu, W., Gu, Y.: A light-weight mutual authentication protocol for ISO 18000-6B standard RFID system. In: Proceedings of ICCTA 2009, pp. 21–25 (2009)
41. Yeh, K.-H., Lo, N.-W.: Improvement of an EPC gen2 compliant RFID authentication protocol. In: Fifth International Conference on Information Assurance and Security, IAS 2009, pp. 532–535. IEEE Computer Society (2009)
42. Yiyuan Luo, G.G., Chai, Q., Lai, X.: A lightweight Stream Cipher WG-7 for RFID Encryption and Authentication. In: IEEE Globecom 2010 Proceedings (2010)
43. Yoon, E.-J.: Improvement of the securing RFID systems conforming to EPC class 1 generation 2 standard. Expert Systems with Applications (in press, corrected proof, 2011)

Inference-Proof View Update Transactions with Minimal Refusals*

Joachim Biskup and Cornelia Tadros

Technische Universität Dortmund, Germany
{joachim.biskup,cornelia.tadros}@cs.tu-dortmund.de

Abstract. Publishing information to clients of an information system may leak confidential information. Even more, update transaction protocols must ensure both integrity and confidentiality of information which results in a conflicting situation rather involved. To avoid confidentiality breaches, previous work allow views with misinformation provided to clients. In order to maintain correctness and reliability of information, we propose query and update protocols that refuse client requests for the sake of confidentiality. Further, this article focuses on availability of information in two ways: confidentiality policy specification can impose less strict confidentiality in favor of availability; the proposed transaction protocol is shown to be as cooperative and to provide as much information as possible among a discussed class of transaction protocols. Regarding the confidentiality policy, in our approach the security administrator can choose between protecting only sensitive information in the current instance or even outdated information of previous instances.

1 Introduction

Sharing of information via an information system is commonly restricted by access control to publish sensitive information only selectively to authorized clients. Yet, as known under the *inference problem* [1], plain access control is not sufficient to prevent the leakage of sensitive information. A user can exploit, for example, schema knowledge and previously received data to acquire information that is not represented in the accessed individual data items. Moreover, the user may exploit the notification of the database management system (DBMS) in response to a view update transaction initiated by this user. Such inferences cause a well-known conflict between integrity and confidentiality (cf. [2,3]). Integrity constraints (e.g., key constraints) included in the database schema permit only reasonable database instances in the application context. Consequently, a database instance is not allowed to be updated by a view update transaction if these constraints are violated afterwards. Further, users may only contribute or modify data given sufficient authorization which is commonly known under

---

* Part of this work has been supported by Deutsche Forschungsgemeinschaft (DFG) within the Collaborative Research Center SFB 876 "Providing Information by Resource-Constrained Analysis", project A5.

integrity as unmodified content in computer security and not covered in this article. Enforcement of the integrity constraints may conflict confidentiality due to the user's schema knowledge. For example, assume the constraint that "each employee is manager of at most one project". The user requests to insert "Smith is manager of project A". From a successful insertion the user can conclude that Smith is manager of no other project than A whereas from a failed insertion (due to the integrity constraint) he can conclude that Smith is already manager of some other project. The user may combine the latter fact with the prior knowledge "there are only two projects A and B" and infer the confidential fact "Smith is manager of project B". In this situation, insertion is to fail due to integrity but the user must not be informed about this failure due to confidentiality so that an *immediate conflict* between the two requirements emerges. In order to resolve this conflict, other work (cf. Sec. 2) insert misinformation to the user's view, i.e., by *lying* or *polyinstantiation*. Following the example, an appropriate lie would be a successful insertion although conforming to the constraint no insertion has been performed.

In contrast, we present inference-proof protocols that may only refuse a user's request so that correctness and reliability of information in the user's view is not affected. We consider a single client, e.g., a human user, who may query a complete propositional database instance and modify the instance by view update transactions, leaving extensions to the relational or incomplete data models and multiple clients for future research. Outdated sensitive information may either be released (*temporary confidentiality*) or still be protected (*continuous confidentiality*) on the discretion of the security administrator, as suggested in [4]. The presented protocols assess at run-time, i.e., dynamically, whether ordinary processing of a request would enable the client to infer confidential information. Herein, the protocols respect the client's immediate information needs by an availability policy of *last-minute intervention* [5]: the protocol should only intervene the usual processing of requests if it detects a harmful inference (cf. Sec. 7 for an illustrative example). To judge the performance of the protocols under this availability policy, we list other desirable properties of view update transaction protocols (beside inference-proofness). Then, we show that the presented view update transaction protocol achieves all these properties while no other protocol can increase availability under the last-minute intervention policy without lacking one of these properties. In summary, our main achievements are:

- inference-proof protocols for queries and view update transactions employing *refusal* instead of misinformation as contrasted with *polyinstantiation* in multilevel secure databases or *lying* in controlled query evaluation;
- the choice to declare the sensitivity of information depending on its actuality;
- a proof that availability cannot be improved for any reasonable refusal protocol for view update transactions based on *last-minute intervention*.

Section 2 explains each contribution in the context of the related work. Section 3 introduces the client-server scenario with query–update requests on the client's part and basic definitions; Section 4 gives two inference-proofness properties for confidentiality preservation; Section 5 discusses a necessary condition for the client's view to prevent harmful inferences; Section 6 presents the protocols; Section 7 evaluates the protocol design under the availability aspect and, lastly, Section 8 concludes this article with a discussion of our achievements.

2 Related Work

Controlled (Query) Evaluation (C(Q)E), originally designed as an inference-proof query processing protocol (cf. [5] as a survey), has been extended to view update transactions, provider updates and view refreshments (cf. [3] for the overall framework; cf. [6] for a detailed study of view update transactions including refreshments). This extension uses the complete propositional data model and the lying approach only. To track released information, the protocol maintains a materialized view (called logfile) for each client with possibly distorted data. The client can request to update this view which the protocol translates to the database instance in an inference-proof integrity-preserving way. Essentially, a view update transaction involves several implicit queries to ensure acceptability [7] and integrity. If the client cannot be notified about an integrity violation, the view update transaction pretendedly succeeds, yet actually, without updating the database instance (cf. Sec. 1). This solution is close to polyinstantiation used in the area of multilevel secure (MLS) databases. By allowing spontaneous updates added by the server, which might affect the correctness of the data, the authors of [6] achieve continuous confidentiality. In our case, such spontaneous updates would thwart the advantages of the refusal over the lying approach. Temporary confidentiality, however, has not been studied in [3,6].

In an MLS database instance, data items and schema objects are assigned a security level as a classification. Likewise subjects receive a security level as a clearance. The set of security levels must be partially ordered. Information flow is only permitted from a lower level to a higher level in the partial order. The conflict illustrated in Section 1 may be caused by the fact "Smith is manager of project B" classified high. To resolve it, the fact "Smith is manager of project A" is inserted but classified to the user's clearance low. As a consequence, the instance is *polyinstantiated*, i.e., Smith is a manager of two projects where each project is associated with a different security level [2,8]. The inserted fact is implicitly considered as a *cover story* (i.e., a lie) [8].

As a different approach, the protocol presented in this article identifies situations in which the enforcement of integrity may lead to a confidentiality violation, i.e., there is a potential conflict. In such situations, the protocol aborts the transaction to escape a possible immediate conflict in the future. This approach comes at the cost of availability because the protocol aborts in situations with no immediate, but a potential conflict between integrity and confidentiality.

Other solutions to the inference problem care for sharing information to the farthest degree possible by optimizing some availability measure, e.g., minimizing the number of distorted database entries [9] or selecting a lowest classification of data in MLS databases [10]. These solutions precompute a view to be published or a classification, respectively, whereas in this article inferences are checked dynamically. As the dynamic approach depends on the client's behavior, the above measures are not applicable in our case (cf. Sec. 7). In Section 8, we briefly discuss the advantages and drawbacks of the dynamic approach compared to precomputed views. There is also a variety of research on preprocessing data that is released for statistical queries or data mining so that after the release the loss of privacy is minimized whereas subordinately data utility is maximized (cf. [11] for a survey).

There are several aspects beyond the scope of this article, e.g., update transactions requested by high level users [2], in particular the data provider [3], and the refreshment of aged views [3,6,1]. Further, there are other types of unwanted information flow during the execution of an update transaction protocol. This has been extensively studied in the MLS area, such as covert channels in concurrency control protocols etc [12].

3   Server and Protocol for Inference-Proof Interactions

3.1   Components

We consider a simplified scenario of one client C communicating with one server, the data provider. In a multiple client scenario an inference-proof refreshment protocol would be necessary (cf. [3]). As the refusal approach aims at correct and reliable views, the refreshment of an outdated view may be considered obligatory (as opposed to the lying approach in [3]), yet, conflicting with confidentiality. An immediate and conservative solution would be to assume total collaboration among the clients and maintain a single view representing the information available to all the clients. However, this assumption may be too conservative while a single inference-proof view cannot serve the information needs of all the individual clients at the same time. We leave this issue for future work.

To start with, we describe the components of the server, our database model, ordinary query evaluation and ordinary view update transaction. The components of the server are as follows:

- *definition language*: the set $\mathcal{L}_{pl}$ of propositional formulas over an alphabet $\mathcal{A}$ of propositional variables
- *schema*: comprised of the alphabet $\mathcal{A}$ and the integrity constraints $con \subseteq \mathcal{L}_{pl}$
- *instance*: a finite set $db \subseteq \mathcal{A}$ with $db \models con$ ($\models$ denotes the propositional model-of operator with $a \in \mathcal{A}$ being interpreted as *true* iff $a \in db$)
- *view*: a consistent set $view \subset \mathcal{L}_{pl}$
- *interaction language*: requests θ of the following forms: queries $que(\phi)$ with $\phi \in \mathcal{L}_{pl}$ and view update transactions $vtr(\langle \mathcal{X}_1, \ldots, \mathcal{X}_l \rangle)$ with literals $\mathcal{X}_j$ over pairwise distinct variables[1]
- *performed updates*: a sequence $S\Delta$ of subsets of $\mathcal{A}$ (see Sec. 5)
- *confidentiality policy*: a collection $psec$ of two sets of formulas (see Sec. 4)

---

[1] This avoids that a data item (referred to by a variable, e.g., a) is requested to be both deleted (by the literal $\neg a$) and inserted (by the literal a) at the same time, as well as duplicated requests.

Example 1. As a running example, consider the following: a database instance $db_0 = \{s_1, s_2, a\}$ over alphabet $\mathcal{A} := \{s_1, s_2, a, b\}$ with constraints $con = \{a \Rightarrow s_2, s_1 \vee s_2, a \Rightarrow \neg b\}$. The view is initialized by $view_0 := con$. The client issues the following requests $que(a)$, $vtr(\langle \neg a, b \rangle)$ and $vtr(\langle \neg b, \neg s_2 \rangle)$ in succession.

The view contains information from db (here: valid formulas) that is visible to the client C. Commonly, this information is frequently needed by the client and, thus, maintaining a view avoids more costly access to the instance itself (cf. [13] for the concept of database views and view update transactions). In our case, we assume the integrity constraints con as visible to C and, thus, we have to include them in the view throughout the article.

3.2   Uncontrolled Interaction

Next, we introduce the ordinary processing of requests before we move to the controlled processing. The ordinary query evaluation function eval over the instance db is defined as follows: Let $\phi \in \mathcal{L}_{pl}$ be a query, then $\mathsf{eval}(\phi)(db) := (db \models \phi)$. By means of a view update a client can contribute or modify some information in his view, but as this information should be made valid also in the underlying instance db, these modifications must be translated to db (which is involved for relational databases, cf. [13,7]). A view update transaction must adhere to the ACID principles (here, we neglect (C)oncurrency and (D)urability, cf. Sec. 1), in particular, either a transaction is committed as a whole or the previous database state is restored ((A)tomicity) and further, after committing, the integrity constraints are preserved ((I)ntegrity). Overall, the server processes an ordinary view update transaction $vtr(\langle \mathcal{X}_1, \ldots, \mathcal{X}_l \rangle)$ as follows:

1. filter out void update requests from the list $L = \{\mathcal{X}_1, \ldots, \mathcal{X}_l\}$ and keep the outstanding updates in $Inc\Delta := \{\mathcal{X} \in L \mid \mathsf{eval}(\mathcal{X})(db) = false\}$;
2. check whether for the outstanding updates the necessary modifications of the instance would preserve the integrity constraints, that is whether the modified instance would be a model of all formulas in con;
3. if the constraints are violated, notify the client about the violation;
4. else modify the instance by deleting all variables x with $\neg x \in Inc\Delta$ and inserting all variables $x \in Inc\Delta$, and
5. update the view to $\mathsf{neg}(view, Inc\Delta) \cup L \cup con$.

A successful view update modifies all formulas in the view by the operation of *variable negation* neg (Definition 1, below) so that all of them are valid in the modified instance and no information is lost (Lemma 1, below). Moreover, because the transaction ensures that all literals in L are valid as well as the integrity constraints, they are added to the view.

Before we give the details of the computation in step (5), we illustrate the ordinary processing by continuing our running example:

Example 2. The client receives the answer *true* on his query $que(a)$. The server adds this new information to the client's view: $view_1 = con \cup \{a\}$ (here, $db_1 = db_0$).

During the view update transaction $vtr(\langle \neg a, b \rangle)$, a is removed from db_1 and b is added: $db_2 := \{s_1, s_2, b\}$ which complies with the integrity constraints con. The information a in the view $view_1$ is obviously outdated and must be replaced by $\neg a$. Moreover, the information con in $view_1$ (validity of integrity constraints in db_1) must not be lost: The constraint $a \Rightarrow s_2$ was valid before modifying a and b whereas s_2 was not touched by these modifications. Therefore $\neg a \Rightarrow s_2$ must be valid afterwards (similarly, consider the constraint $a \Rightarrow \neg b$). Altogether, the view is updated to $view_2 = \{\neg a, \neg a \Rightarrow s_2, \neg a \Rightarrow b, b\} \cup con = \mathsf{neg}(view_1, \{\neg a, b\}) \cup \{\neg a, b\} \cup con$. The operator neg is defined as follows:

Definition 1 (Variable Negation neg, cf. [6]). *Let $M \subseteq \mathcal{L}_{pl}$ be a set of formulas and L a set of literals over pairwise distinct variables. Variable negation on M by L is defined as $\mathsf{neg}(M, L) := \{\mathsf{neg}(\phi, L) \mid \phi \in M\}$ where $\mathsf{neg}(\phi, L)$ is the result of replacing each occurrence of a variable $x \in \mathsf{Var}(L)$ in ϕ by $\neg x$ (here $\mathsf{Var}(L)$ is the set of variables occurring in L).*

We required literals in L instead of variables for later convenience. By definition, $\mathsf{neg}(\phi, L) = \mathsf{neg}(\phi, \mathsf{Var}(L))$.

The relation between modifications of the database instance and variable negation is subject of the following lemma.

Lemma 1 (Negation Equivalence, cf.[6]). *Let db be a database instance, $M \subseteq \mathcal{L}_{pl}$ a set of formulas, $\phi \in \mathcal{L}_{pl}$ a formula and L a set of literals over pairwise distinct variables. Further, $Inc\Delta$ denotes the outstanding updates in L as introduced above and $db^{Inc\Delta}$ the modified instance. It holds that*

1. $\mathsf{eval}(\phi)(db) = \mathsf{eval}(\mathsf{neg}(\phi, Inc\Delta))(db^{Inc\Delta})$, *and*
2. $\mathsf{eval}(\mathsf{neg}(\phi, Inc\Delta))(db) = \mathsf{eval}(\phi)(db^{Inc\Delta})$.

In our example, $true = \mathsf{eval}(a \Rightarrow s_2)(db_1) = \mathsf{eval}(\neg a \Rightarrow s_2)(db_2)$.

3.3   Employing Inference-Proof Protocols

To ensure confidentiality, instead of the ordinary processing the server invokes dedicated inference-proof protocols as sketched in the architecture in Figure 1. These protocols process the client's requests, accessing all components and returning a notification $REACT$ to the server. The notification may contain a query-answer or a notification of success or failure of a transaction and is forwarded to the client by the server. For inference detection, both protocols essentially need the components $view$ and $S\Delta$ where the former keeps track of the information in the current instance visible to the client and the latter records the performed updates during the history of the instance. The details of the protocols are introduced in Section 6.

Definition 2 (Protocols for Controlled Client-Server Interactions). *Let θ_i be the ith request. A protocol P for controlled client-server interactions offers the following interface to the server:*

$$P(con, db_{i-1}, psec, view_{i-1}, S\Delta_{i-1}, \theta_i) = (REACT_i; db_i, view_i, S\Delta_i).$$

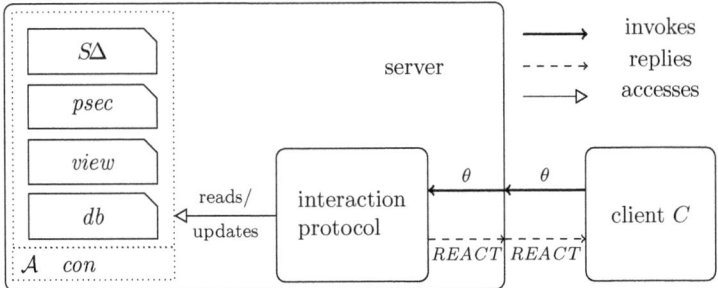

Fig. 1. Architecture

Here, REACT$_i$ is a string output to the server while db$_i$, view$_i$ and SΔ$_i$ denote the components after the execution of the protocol. Thereof REACT$_i$, view$_i$ and SΔ$_i$ are visible to the client: this fact is denoted by $\nu^C(P(\ldots)) := (REACT_i, view_i, SΔ_i)$. All parts of the input are visible to the client except for db$_{i-1}$. The instances db$_{i-1}$ and db$_i$ must be hidden from the client. This interface is extended to sequences of requests in the usual way.

In particular, we assume an open design, i.e., the client knows the implementation of the protocols and of the server and the schema definition, i.e., $\mathcal{A}$ and *con*, as well as the confidentiality policy. Further, the client is assumed to have unlimited computing power so that we neglect the computational efforts spent by the client to actually infer a confidential piece of information.

4   Two Kinds of Confidentiality Preservation

On the one hand, some information may be sensitive and confidential when up-to-date but may be disclosed when outdated, such as a person's bank account number, a password or phone number. In this case, only a current sensitive value must be protected. On the other hand, some information is sensitive even when outdated, such as severe diseases or crimes. In this case, a sensitive value must not be released regardless of its actuality. We formalize the former confidentiality need by *temporary confidentiality preservation* (TCP) and the latter by *continuous confidentiality preservation* (CCP). Continuous confidentiality preservation is stricter than temporary, so we expect an enforcement protocol to be more restrictive and to release less information. Conversely, by choosing temporary confidentiality preservation you offer more availability of information. The security administrator declares the sensitive information as two disjoint sets *psec*(*TCP*) and *psec*(*CCP*) of propositional formulas collected in the confidentiality policy *psec* for the client C, i.e., $psec = psec(TCP) \uplus psec(CCP)$. The declaration aims at guaranteeing confidentiality as an indistinguishability property: For each $\psi \in psec$, the client cannot distinguish a 'safe' situation assuring a current database instance without the sensitive content ψ (*TCP*) or a sequence of such instances (*CCP*) from the actual situation.

Definition 3 (Confidentiality Preservation). *A protocol P of Definition 2 for controlled client-server interactions preserves confidentiality with respect to a client C iff*

> *for all sets of integrity constraints con,*
> *for all initial instances db_0 satisfying con,*
> *for every confidentiality policy psec,*
> *for all initial views $view_0$ of client C, such that $con \subseteq view_0$ and $db_0 \models view_0$ and $view_0 \nvdash \psi$ for each $\psi \in psec(TCP) \uplus psec(CCP)$ (with propositional entailment $\vdash$),*
> *for all finite sequences Q of requests,*
> *for all $\psi \in psec(TCP) \uplus psec(CCP)$:*
> *there exists an alternative instance db_0^S satisfying con and $db_0^S \models view_0$ such that the following two properties hold:*

1. *[indistinguishability: same visible outputs]*
   $\nu^C(P(con, db_0, psec, view_0, Q)) = \nu^C(P(con, db_0^S, psec, view_0, Q))$
2. (a) *[temporary preservation: safe current instance]*
   If $\psi \in psec(TCP)$ then $\mathsf{eval}(\psi)(db_{|Q|}^S) = false$
   (b) *[continuous preservation: safe sequence of instances]*
   If $\psi \in psec(CCP)$ then $\mathsf{eval}(\psi)(db_i^S) = false$ for all $i = 0, \ldots, |Q|$

Immediately, from this definition it follows that continuous confidentiality preservation implies temporary confidentiality preservation. A confidential piece of information $\psi \in psec$ is called a *potential secret*: The situation that ψ does not hold in a database instance is not confidential.

5 Enforcing CCP

At first, we illustrate by the running example how the client might infer a potential secret in some preceding instance (a breach of continuous confidentiality preservation) and how this inference can be detected:

Example 3. The two sets $psec(TCP) = \emptyset$ and $psec(CCP) = \{s_1 \wedge s_2\}$ define the confidentiality policy. After the remaining view update request $vtr(\langle \neg b, \neg s_2 \rangle)$ from Example 2 is processed with the ordinary procedure (see Sec. 3), the view is $view_3 = \{\neg a, \neg b, \neg s_2, \ldots\} \cup con$ and the current instance is $db_3 := \{s_1\}$. The client can infer s_1 from $\neg s_2$ in his view and the integrity constraint $s_1 \vee s_2$ by propositional entailment, so that he knows that $s_1 \wedge \neg s_2$ is valid in db_3. Now, the client can reason by Lemma 1 that $\mathsf{eval}(s_1 \wedge s_2)(db_2) = \mathsf{eval}(\mathsf{neg}(s_1 \wedge s_2, \{\neg b, \neg s_2\}))(db_3) = \mathsf{eval}(s_1 \wedge \neg s_2)(db_3) = true$ (in fact, the client can determine db_3 and all preceding instances). Thus the sensitive information $s_1 \wedge s_2$ in db_2 is revealed to him. The confidentiality breach is caused by the client's reasoning from the fact that $s_1 \wedge \neg s_2 \equiv {}^2\mathsf{neg}(s_1 \wedge s_2, \{\neg b, \neg s_2\})$ is valid in db_3. Regarding db_1, the client can trace back all updates from db_1 to db_3 (by the history of his requests), sort out all duplicated or revoked updates (b and $\neg b$) and ends up with

---

^{2} The symbol $\equiv$ denotes logical equivalence.

the effective updates from db_1 to db_3 (which are $\{\neg a, \neg s_2\}$). Then, by Lemma 1 he can reason $\mathsf{eval}(s_1 \wedge s_2)(db_1) = \mathsf{eval}(\mathsf{neg}(s_1 \wedge s_2, \{\neg a, \neg s_2\}))(db_3) = \textit{true}$.

In general, let Δ_j denote the effective updates from instance db_j to the current instance db_k with $j < k$ and $\psi \in psec(CCP)$. For all preceding instances db_j, we must prevent the client to infer that $\mathsf{neg}(\psi, \Delta_j)$ is valid in db_k. Therefore he must consider possible that

$$\mathsf{eval}(\neg \mathsf{neg}(\psi, \Delta_0) \wedge \ldots \wedge \neg \mathsf{neg}(\psi, \Delta_{k-1}) \wedge \neg \psi)(db_k) = \textit{true}. \qquad (1)$$

So, if the client reasons about db_k (by means of propositional entailment $\vdash$ applied to his view), he must not rule out that db_k has property (1), i.e., that $view_k$ still has models with property (1):

$$view_k \not\vdash \neg(\neg \mathsf{neg}(\psi, \Delta_0) \wedge \ldots \wedge \neg \mathsf{neg}(\psi, \Delta_{k-1}) \wedge \neg \psi)$$
$$\equiv \mathsf{neg}(\psi, \Delta_0) \vee \ldots \vee \mathsf{neg}(\psi, \Delta_{k-1}) \vee \psi.$$

Definition 4 (CCP). *For a finite sequence $S\Delta$ of k sets of literals and a potential secret ψ we define the formula*

$$\mathsf{ccp}(\psi, S\Delta) := \mathsf{neg}(\psi, S\Delta[0]) \vee \ldots \vee \mathsf{neg}(\psi, S\Delta[k-1]) \vee \psi.$$

If $S\Delta = \langle \rangle$ then we set $\mathsf{ccp}(\psi, S\Delta) = \psi$.

You may read the formula as "ψ previously held at some point of time or currently holds with respect to the sequence $S\Delta$". Its negation $\neg \mathsf{ccp}(\psi, S\Delta)$ can be read as "ψ never held, neither previously nor currently".

Example 4. In the situation of Example 3, the client's inference of the outdated sensitive information $s_1 \wedge s_2$ is detected by $view_3 \vdash s_1$ and $\mathsf{ccp}(s_1 \wedge s_2, S\Delta) \equiv \mathsf{neg}(s_1 \wedge s_2, \{\neg a, \neg s_2\}) \vee \mathsf{neg}(s_1 \wedge s_2, \{\neg b, \neg s_2\}) \vee (s_1 \wedge s_2) \equiv (s_1 \wedge \neg s_2) \vee (s_1 \wedge s_2) \equiv s_1$ with $S\Delta = \langle \{\neg a, \neg s_2\}, \{\neg b, \neg s_2\} \rangle$.

As a conclusion, we see that continuous confidentiality relies on the enforcement of the invariant $view \not\vdash \mathsf{ccp}(\psi, S\Delta)$ whereas the invariant $view \not\vdash \psi$ will prove sufficient for temporary confidentiality in the following sections.

6   Protocols

This section presents protocols for view update transactions and for query processing which together enforce temporary and continuous confidentiality preservation. We illustrate the execution of each protocol with our running example. At initialization time, we set $view_0 = con$ and $S\Delta = \langle \rangle$.

An inference-proof protocol with refusals must handle *meta-inferences* (in contrast to the lying method, cf. [14]) which are inferences drawn by the client when he reasons about the execution of the protocol. For example, for a query ϕ an incautious protocol may refuse the answer *ans* to ϕ (which is either *true* or *false*) if and only if adding *ans* to *view* reveals confidential information according to *psec*. Because *view* is visible to the client, who is additionally assumed to know *psec*, he can figure out the refused set of answers by himself. In the worst case, this set is a singleton and, thus, the original but refused answer is revealed to the client.

6.1   Inference-Proof Query Processing

The protocol for query processing implements Definition 2 and is essentially the refusal censor from [14] extended with continuous confidentiality preservation. Let client C pose the query request $que(\phi)$ at step i of the interaction. Then, the following three major cases are checked by the protocol:

1. The answer ans to ϕ returned by ordinary query evaluation is already included in the current view $view_{i-1}$.
2. In some situations, being informed about the evaluation of ϕ lets the client infer the validity of a potential secret in the current instance (TCP) or during the interaction (CCP). This check is independent of the ordinary query evaluation result (instance independent) to preclude meta-inferences.
3. The answer ans is to be forwarded to the client.

Protocol 1 (Query Processing[3]) $\theta_i = que(\phi)$

case1. ***Answer Known to Client***
  if $view_{i-1} \vdash \phi$ then $REACT_i := \phi$
  else if $view_{i-1} \vdash \neg\phi_i$ then $REACT_i := \neg\phi$
case2. ***Answer Reveals a Potential Secret***
  else if $[view_{i-1} \cup \{\phi\} \vdash \mathsf{ccp}(\psi, S\Delta_{i-1})$ or
        $view_{i-1} \cup \{\neg\phi\} \vdash \mathsf{ccp}(\psi, S\Delta_{i-1})]$ *for a* $\psi \in psec(CCP)$
        or
        $[view_{i-1} \cup \{\phi\} \vdash \psi$ *or* $view_{i-1} \cup \{\neg\phi\} \vdash \psi]$
        for a $\psi \in psec(TCP)$
  then $REACT_i := refuse$
case3. ***Query Evaluation***
  else if $\mathsf{eval}(\phi)(db_{i-1}) = true$ then $REACT_i := \phi$; $view_i := view_{i-1} \cup \{\phi\}$
  else $REACT_i := \neg\phi$; $view_i := view_{i-1} \cup \{\neg\phi\}$

Example 5. The query $que(a)$ is processed with $view_0 = con = \{a \Rightarrow s_2, s_1 \vee s_2, a \Rightarrow \neg b\}$: The protocol passes *case1* and *case2*, because $\{a, s_2\}$ is a model of $view_0 \cup \{a\}$ and $\{s_2\}$ of $view_0 \cup \{\neg a\}$ which falsify the potential secret $s_1 \wedge s_2$. Afterwards, the answer a is returned and $view_1 = con \cup \{a\}$ as well as $db_1 = db_0$.

6.2   Inference-Proof View Update Transactions

The view update transaction protocol follows the ordinary procedure of a view update transaction (especially, achieves atomicity and integrity, Sec. 3) while it ensures that the client's view does not disclose a potential secret in the current instance or during its history. For the latter, it tracks the effective updates in the sequence $S\Delta$ (Sec. 5). After the client issues $vtr(\langle \mathcal{X}_1, \ldots, \mathcal{X}_l \rangle)$ at step i, the following four major cases are checked:

1. For at least one input literal $\mathcal{X}_j$ the client cannot be informed whether it is a void or outstanding update request due to a conflict with the confidentiality policy. In this case, the transaction aborts.

---

[3] If not explicitly stated, a component of the server is not modified.

2. A successful transaction necessarily ends up in a confidentiality violation (because the updated view implies a current or outdated potential secret). In this case, the transaction aborts.
3. Either a potential conflict between integrity and confidentiality arises or integrity cannot be preserved. In this case, the transaction aborts.
4. The instance is to be updated.

Protocol 2 (View Update Transaction) $\theta_i = vtr(\langle \mathcal{X}_1, \ldots, \mathcal{X}_l \rangle)$
In the protocol we use the following notations:

$Inc\Delta := \{\mathcal{X}_j \in \theta \mid \mathsf{eval}(\mathcal{X}_j)(db) = false\}$ *outstanding updates,*
$db_{i-1}^{Inc\Delta} := \{a \in db_{i-1} \mid \neg a \notin Inc\Delta\} \cup (\mathcal{A} \cap Inc\Delta)$ *the modified instance,*
$con\_conj := \bigwedge\limits_{\phi \in con} \phi.$

case1 Outstanding Updates
Pose queries $\mathcal{X}_1, \ldots, \mathcal{X}_l$ *successively to Protocol 1*
(which adds the answer $\mathcal{X}_j$ *or* $\neg \mathcal{X}_j$ *to* $view_{i-1}$ *if not already contained*
implicitly).
If refuse is returned on some query,
    then $REACT_i :=$ transaction refused
        exit protocol.
case2 Performing Transaction Reveals a Potential Secret
    Compute the effective updates for all preceding instances
    after the modification with $Inc\Delta$ *in* $\overline{S\Delta}$.[4]
    if $\mathsf{neg}(view_{i-1}, Inc\Delta) \cup con \vdash \mathsf{ccp}(\psi, \overline{S\Delta})$ *for a* $\psi \in psec(CCP)$ (2)
    or $\mathsf{neg}(view_{i-1}, Inc\Delta) \cup con \vdash \psi$ *for a* $\psi \in psec(TCP)$ (3)
    then $REACT_i :=$ transaction violates confidentiality
        exit protocol
case3 Integrity Check
    Integrity violation possible
    if $\mathsf{neg}(view_{i-1}, Inc\Delta) \not\vdash con$ (4)
    then
        Integrity violation known to C
        if $view_{i-1} \vdash \mathsf{neg}(\neg con\_conj, Inc\Delta)$ (5)
        then $REACT_i :=$ transaction violates integrity
            exit protocol
        Notification of integrity violation harms confidentiality
        else if $view_{i-1} \cup \mathsf{neg}(\neg con\_conj, Inc\Delta) \vdash \mathsf{ccp}(\psi, S\Delta_{i-1})$
            for a $\psi \in psec(CCP)$ (6)
            or
            $view_{i-1} \cup \mathsf{neg}(\neg con\_conj, Inc\Delta) \vdash \psi$
            for a $\psi \in psec(TCP)$ (7)
        then $REACT_i :=$ integrity check conflicts confidentiality
            exit protocol

---

[4] All effective updates can be computed incrementally from the input $S\Delta_{i-1}$.

Integrity check fails
else if eval$(con)(db_{i-1}^{Inc\Delta}) = false$ (8)
  then $REACT_i$:= transaction violates integrity
     $view_i$:= $view_{i-1} \cup$ neg$(\neg con\_conj, Inc\Delta)$
  exit protocol
 else skip
else skip

case4 Performing Update Transaction
 $REACT_i$:= transaction successful
 db_i := $db_{i-1}^{Inc\Delta}$
 $view_i$:= neg$(view_{i-1}, Inc\Delta) \cup con$

In *case1*, to ensure confidentiality, a transaction is refused if at least one answer to a query $\mathcal{X}_j$ violates confidentiality. In this case, que$(\mathcal{X}_j)$ is refused by Protocol 1 and, accordingly, we let Protocol 2 immediately exit. In particular, the refusal of the query $\mathcal{X}_j$ by Protocol 1 means that the client must not be aware whether or not $\mathcal{X}_j$ is in $Inc\Delta$. Rather than deciding to let the protocol exit, we could try to find an alternative way to let the protocol hide (parts of) $Inc\Delta$ from the client. However, we would face the problem that the knowledge, whether or not $\mathcal{X}_j \in Inc\Delta$, may be disclosed to the client *implicitly* since $Inc\Delta$ is used by the protocol in the integrity check and view refreshment neg$(view_{i-1}, Inc\Delta)$. Preventing such disclosures presumably would lead to significantly more complicated inference checks in *case2* and *case3*.

In *case2*, there is no need to check for meta-inferences: Passing *case1*, $Inc\Delta$ can be made visible to the client, so that the client is able to execute *case2* by himself and, thus, the execution of *case2* by the protocol releases no additional information to the client. Therefore the client cannot exploit the execution of *case2* to draw meta-inferences.

In *case3*, the integrity check can be understood as the implicit query neg$(\neg con\_conj, Inc\Delta)$ (posed to db_{i-1}): "Does the updated instance violate the integrity constraints?" This query can be evaluated in db_{i-1} due to the relation eval$($neg$(\neg con\_conj, Inc\Delta))(db_{i-1}) =$ eval$(\neg con\_conj)(db_{i-1}^{Inc\Delta})$ in Lemma 1. The protocol first checks if the client knows the result of the integrity check by his current view $view_{i-1}$ in (4) and (5) (this is important to avoid refusal due to inconsistency in the premises of (6) and (7)). Further, the protocol checks whether a notification of integrity violation breaches confidentiality in (6) and (7). This check is instance-independent (i.e., evaluated independently of integrity violation or preservation with respect to the current database instance and update transaction) to prevent the meta-inference that a refusal in *case3* occurs if and only if integrity is violated. In contrast to Protocol 1, the protocol does not check whether $view_{i-1} \cup$ neg$(con, Inc\Delta) \vdash$ ccp$(\psi, S\Delta_{i-1})$ for $Pol = CCP$ or ψ for $Pol = TCP$. In the situation of an implication, the notification of *integrity preservation* after the update transaction reveals a potential secret in the current instance db_{i-1} (or some preceding instance for CCP). As for continuous confidentiality preservation, such a violation is already prevented by condition (2) (due to ccp$(\psi, S\Delta)$). As for temporary confidentiality preservation, this situation is no confidentiality threat because, when integrity is preserved, the insecure db_{i-1} is going to be updated to db_i which is secure for the following reason: from the client's point of view db_i might not contain a potential secret by condition (3).

Theorem 1 (Confidentiality Preservation). *Protocols 1 and 2 together preserve continuous and temporary confidentiality preservation.*

Sketch of Proof. In the proof, essentially, $view_i \not\vdash \psi$ and $view_i \not\vdash \mathsf{ccp}(\psi, S\!\Delta_i)$ are identified as invariants of the protocols. These invariants guarantee secure alternative sequences of database instances as demanded by Definition 3. The relationship between these sequences and the invariants is hinted at in Section 5.

Example 6. Continuing our running example, the client's view on $db_1 = \{s_1, s_2, a\}$ is $view_1 = con \cup \{a\} \equiv \{a \wedge \neg b \wedge s_2\}$. Therefore, the implicit queries $\neg a$ and b of $vtr(\langle \neg a, b \rangle)$ are already contained in the view, so that the protocol proceeds with *case2* and $Inc\Delta = \{\neg a, b\}$ as follows:

case	inference checks (condition)	computations
2	$\mathsf{neg}(view_1, Inc\Delta) \cup \{\neg a, b\} \cup con$ $\equiv \{\neg a \wedge b \wedge s_2\} \cup \{a \Rightarrow s_2, \ s_1 \vee s_2, \ a \Rightarrow \neg b\}$ $\equiv \{\neg a \wedge b \wedge s_2\} \not\vdash s_1 \wedge s_2 \equiv \mathsf{ccp}(s_1 \wedge s_2, \overline{S\!\Delta}) \ (2)$	$\overline{S\!\Delta} = \langle \{\neg a, b\} \rangle$
3	$\mathsf{neg}(view_1, Inc\Delta) \cup \{\neg a, b\}$ $\equiv \{\neg a \wedge b \wedge s_2\} \vdash con \hspace{3.2cm} (4)$	

Case3 reveals that the client would already know at protocol termination that integrity is preserved by knowing $Inc\Delta$, con and $view_1$. According to *case4*, db_1 is updated to $db_2 = \{s_1, s_2, b\}$ and the client's view is $view_2 \equiv \{\neg a \wedge b \wedge s_2\}$.

Now, the request $vtr(\langle \neg b, \neg s_2 \rangle)$ is processed: $view_2$ contains the answers to the queries $\neg b$ and $\neg s_2$ in *case1*. In *case2*, with $\overline{S\!\Delta} = \langle \{\neg a, \neg s_2\}, \{\neg b, \neg s_2\} \rangle$ and $Inc\Delta = \{\neg b, \neg s_2\}$ an inference is detected: $\mathsf{neg}(view_2, \{\neg b, \neg s_2\}) \cup \{\neg b, \neg s_2\} \cup con \equiv \{\neg a \wedge \neg b \wedge \neg s_2, s_1 \vee s_2\} \vdash s_1 \equiv \mathsf{ccp}(s_1 \wedge s_2, \overline{S\!\Delta})$ (see Example 4). Note that $s_1 \wedge s_2$ (the original potential secret) is not implied.

Example 7. Whereas the previous example demonstrated a successful transaction and a transaction that reveals some potential secret after its execution, another situation of interest is an immediate conflict between confidentiality and integrity. Let $\mathcal{A} = \{a, b, c\}$ and $con = \{\neg c \Rightarrow a\}$ be the schema and $db_1 = \{a, c\}$ the instance with view $view_1 = con \cup \{a \vee b, c\}$. Further, let $psec(TCP) = \{\neg a \wedge b\}$ and $psec(CCP) = \emptyset$ constitute the policy.

The client requests $vtr(\langle \neg c \rangle)$. Because $c \in view_1$ the client knows that $\neg c$ is an outstanding update in *case1*. Further, *case2* passes since it holds that

$$\mathsf{neg}(view_1, \{\neg c\}) \cup con = \{c \Rightarrow a, a \vee b, \neg c, \neg c \Rightarrow a\} \equiv \{\neg c, a\} \not\vdash \neg a \wedge b.$$

Afterwards, *case3* passes until the check of condition (7):

$$view_1 \cup \mathsf{neg}(\neg con\_conj, \{\neg c\}) = \{a \vee b, c, \neg c \Rightarrow a\} \cup \mathsf{neg}(\neg c \wedge \neg a, \{\neg c\})$$
$$\equiv \{c, \neg a, b\} \vdash \neg a \wedge b.$$

Therefore, the protocol exits independently from the actual instance db_1.

7   Availability Considerations

In this section, we review Protocol 2 in terms of availability of information and justify our design decisions under the availability aspect. The design of Protocols 1 and 2 follows the policy of last-minute intervention (Sec. 1). Inherently, this policy lets the client choose implicitly which information should be available. The next example illustrates the principle of last-minute intervention by Protocol 1:

Example 8. Let $view_0 = \{medB \rightarrow (cancer \vee flu)\}$, $db_0 = \{cancer, medB\}$, $S\!\varDelta_0 = \langle\rangle$ and $psec(TCP) = \emptyset$, $psec(CCP) = \{cancer\}$ ($\mathsf{ccp}(cancer, S\!\varDelta_0) \equiv cancer$). The query sequence $Q_1 = \langle flu, medB\rangle$ is answered with $\langle\neg flu, refuse\rangle$, whereas $Q_2 = \langle medB, flu\rangle$ is answered with $\langle medB, refuse\rangle$. Thus, by the order of his queries the client can choose implicitly whether $medB$ or $\neg flu$ is published.

Imagine another protocol P that answers Q_1 with $\langle refuse, medB\rangle$, then clearly this protocol followed another availability policy and does not let the client choose implicitly. In this situation, one cannot compare the availability of information offered by P and Protocol 1. For this reason in the availability analysis of Protocol 2, we consider only a single view update transaction instead of sequences, so that we can compare the availability of different view update transaction protocols under the principle of last-minute intervention.

  For simplicity in Definitions 5 and 6 we assume that the client has issued the query sequence $\langle \mathcal{X}_1, \dots, \mathcal{X}_l\rangle$ without a refusal before the view update transaction $\theta = vtr(\mathcal{X}_1, \dots, \mathcal{X}_l)$. Along with the confidentiality requirements in the design of the protocol we aim to achieve the following properties:

Definition 5 (Proper Truthful Deterministic Protocols). *Let P be a deterministic protocol for controlled view update transactions adhering to Definition 2 and the atomicity and integrity requirement (ACID). A proper truthful protocol has the following properties for each admissible input, i.e., $db_{i-1} \models view_{i-1} \supseteq con$, $view_{i-1} \not\vdash \psi$ for all $\psi \in psec(TCP)$ and $view_{i-1} \not\vdash \mathsf{ccp}(\psi, S\!\varDelta_{i-1})$ for all $\psi \in psec(CCP)$:*

1. **No Misinformation:** *$db_i \models view_i$.*
2. **No Loss of Information:** *If the transaction does not perform an update (i.e., $db_i = db_{i-1}$) then $view_i \vdash view_{i-1}$ else $view_i \vdash \mathsf{neg}(view_{i-1}, Inc\varDelta)$.*
3. **Cooperativeness:** *If the transaction does not perform an update then $view_{i-1} \cup \mathsf{neg}(\neg con\_conj, Inc\varDelta) \vdash view_i$ else $\mathsf{neg}(view_{i-1}, Inc\varDelta) \cup con \vdash view_i$. Further, the client is truthfully notified about the success of the update transaction in REACT forwarded to him by the server.*
4. **Soundness of Client View:** *If for db'_{i-1} admissible $\nu^C(P(con, db'_{i-1}, psec, view_{i-1}, S\!\varDelta_{i-1}, \theta)) \neq \nu^C(P(con, db_{i-1}, psec, view_{i-1}, S\!\varDelta_{i-1}, \theta))$ then*
   - *if the transaction does not perform an update then $db'_{i-1} \not\models view_i$*
   - *else $db'^{Inc\varDelta}_{i-1} \not\models view_i$.*
5. **Confidentiality:** *P adheres to the requirements of Definition 3.*

These properties meet the following objectives:

No Misinformation: The protocol does not attempt to mislead the client and thus the current instance is a possible instance with respect to the view $view_i$.

No Loss of Information: The protocol does not suppose the client to forget information already disclosed to him.

Cooperativeness: The update performed by the protocol is requested by the client's view update transaction. More precisely, without success the client may only be informed about a failed integrity check whereas $view_{i-1}$ is prior knowledge. With a successful update, the client may only be informed about the success of the operation. Given all this additional information, $\mathsf{neg}(view_{i-1}, Inc\Delta) \cup con$ can be determined by the client using his prior knowledge.

Soundness of Client View: If after the execution of P the client rules out an admissible instance db'_{i-1} (by simulating P with instance db'_{i-1} and comparing the visible results of both computations, cf. Definition 2 regarding the clients capabilities), then, depending on the success of the operation, db'_{i-1} (no success) or $db'^{Inc\Delta}_{i-1}$ (success) is ruled out as an instance by the computed view $view_i$. Note that the success of the operation is reported to the client (Cooperativeness).

Example 9. Reviewing Example 7, we illustrate the relation among these properties and their influence on availability. In Example 7, the admissible instances are all models of $view_1$, i.e., $db_1 = \{a, c\}$, $db'_1 = \{b, c\}$, $db''_1 = \{a, b, c\}$. The immediate conflict between integrity and confidentiality in that example can be explained further by the client's reasoning about the processsing of his request $vtr(\langle \neg c \rangle)$ on all admissible instances: Only for instance db'_1 deleting c violates the integrity constraint $\neg c \Rightarrow a$, but db'_1 also makes valid the potential secret $\neg a \wedge b$. Therefore a notification of integrity violation would reveal a use of db'_1 and must consequently be refused. Consider now an attempt to improve Protocol 2 in terms of availability: Different from Protocol 2 we allow the transaction $vtr(\langle \neg c \rangle)$ for db''_1 (but not for db_1 so that a refusal would not reveal a use of db'_1). Then after the transaction for db''_1, the client is able to distinguish db''_1 (not refused) from db_1 (refused) from the observed success. Now, consider first that the altered protocol updates the view by $view''_2 = \mathsf{neg}(view_1, \neg c) \cup con \equiv \{\neg c, a\}$. Then, soundness of client view is not ensured because $db_1^{\{\neg c\}} \models view''_2$. To avoid loosing this property, consider that the altered protocol updates the view by $view''_2 = \{a, b, \neg c\}$ (removing db_1 from the models of $\{\neg c, a\}$). Then, cooperativeness is not ensured:

$$\mathsf{neg}(view_1, \{\neg c\}) \cup \{\neg c\} \cup con \equiv \{a \vee b, \neg c\} \cup \{\neg c \Rightarrow a\} \not\vdash b \in view''_2.$$

Here, the altered protocol arbitrarily provides the client with the information b that is not related to his request $vtr(\langle \neg c \rangle)$ and may not be needed by him.

A protocol P offers more availability than another protocol $\tilde{P}$ if for any admissible input the view on the current database instance provided by P to the client offers more information than the one provided by $\tilde{P}$. Here, we assume that the update transaction does not necessarily end up in a confidentiality violation (conditions (2) or (3) in Protocol 2).

Definition 6 (Local Optimality). *A proper truthful protocol (Definition 5) is said to be locally optimal, if for each proper truthful protocol $\tilde{P}$ the following properties hold on each admissible input to which conditions (2),(3) not apply:*

- $\Delta_i^{\tilde{P}} \subset \Delta_i^P$: $\tilde{P}$ performs strictly less updates than P,[5] or
- $\Delta_i^{\tilde{P}} = \Delta_i^P$ and $view_i^P \vdash view_i^{\tilde{P}}$: $\tilde{P}$ performs the same updates as P, but offers at most the information provided by P.

Here Δ_i^P denotes the variables updated by protocol P.

Theorem 2 (Local Optimality of Protocol 2). *Protocol 2 is locally optimal.*

Sketch of Proof. In the proof, the situation of major interest is when an immediate conflict between integrity and confidentiality can arise. To not let the client be aware of a present conflict, a protocol has to refuse a transaction in at least one situation with no integrity violation (No Misinformation). Nevertheless, the proof reveals that, actually, no protocol adhering to Definition 5 can complete a transaction if such a conflict is possible for this transaction, i.e., there is a potential conflict. A successful transaction would disclose information to the client by meta-inferences (Deterministic), which have to be recorded in the view (Soundness of Client View). But this disclosure contradicts (Cooperativeness).

8 Summary and Discussion

As our first contribution, we presented (propositional) query and view update transaction protocols with refusal in a scenario of a server with one client, and we proved confidentiality preservation of these protocols. Further, these protocols offer the declaration of a weaker policy (temporary confidentiality preservation), which can increase the availability of information. Other research addressing the inference problem in transactions without data distortion is presented, e.g., in [15,16]. First, the authors of [15] test predefined transaction procedures at compile time for confidentiality breaches through inferences, whereas we allow updates of arbitrary information. Second, for MLS databases a special attribute value *Restricted* hides the actual value from unauthorized users while inherently revealing its existence [16]. Because the *Restricted* values are inserted into a MLS database at instantiation time, this approach differs from our work which prevents inference at runtime under a last-minute intervention policy.

As our second contribution, we studied local optimality of the view update protocol. The local optimality result shows that availability cannot be further improved in a view update transaction, if we decide to employ a deterministic refusal protocol with an availability policy of last-minute intervention. Although common in C(Q)E, the choice of a deterministic protocol is arguable. A potential conflict between confidentiality and integrity in a transaction must not force a protocol to refuse this transaction if the protocol can randomly choose to refuse

---

[5] Because of the atomicity requirement (ACID) on the transaction either $\Delta_i^P = Inc\Delta$ or $\Delta_i^P = \emptyset$, the same with $\tilde{P}$.

this transaction. Another open aspect is a comparison of local optimality of our protocols with protocols applying data distortion, i.e., lying such as [6] or cover stories such as [8]. At first sight, our approach seems to pay the rather high price of forcefully refusing a transaction with a potential conflict between integrity and confidentiality. Yet, lying or polyinstantiation provide misinformation, which obviously reduces the availability of correct or reliable information, so that a more thorough comparison is needed. For such a comparison, we would have to modify Definition 6 in order to account for pretended success of an update or misinformation in the view.

A drawback of the dynamic approach is the high computational cost of the employed propositional entailment operator combined with the increasing size of the view as well as the increasing length of the sequence of effective updates. Alternatively, the security administrator may create a precomputed inference-proof view for the client, but then is recommended to define an availability policy that estimates the client's information needs [9,17]. Similarly, but on the schema rather than on the data level, the authors of [18] split a relation into vertical views (fragments, i.e., several columns of the original relation) in order to break sensitive associations among the attributes, but inference based on integrity constraints is not considered.

The authors of [19] introduce a richer language for confidentiality policies by means of which the security administrator can declare a combination of attributes (of a relation) sensitive, e.g., the combination of "personnel number" and "employee name". For the time being, in this article we considered a simpler language (lacking this feature) but, in practice, the extension is desirable and should be straightforward.

References

1. Toland, T.S., Farkas, C., Eastman, C.M.: The inference problem: Maintaining maximal availability in the presence of database updates. Computers & Security 29(1), 88–103 (2010)
2. Jajodia, S., Meadows, C.: Inference problems in multilevel secure database management systems. In: Abrams, M.D., Jajodia, S., Podell, H.J. (eds.) Information Security: An Integrated Collection of Essays, pp. 570–584. IEEE (1995)
3. Biskup, J., Gogolin, C., Seiler, J., Weibert, T.: Requirements and Protocols for Inference-Proof Interactions in Information Systems. In: Backes, M., Ning, P. (eds.) ESORICS 2009. LNCS, vol. 5789, pp. 285–302. Springer, Heidelberg (2009)
4. Biskup, J., Tadros, C.: Policy-based secrecy in the Runs & Systems framework and controlled query evaluation. In: Echizen, I., Kunihiro, N., Sasaki, R. (eds.) Short Paper of IWSEC 2010. IPSJ, pp. 60–77 (2010)
5. Biskup, J.: Usability Confinement of Server Reactions: Maintaining Inference-Proof Client Views by Controlled Interaction Execution. In: Kikuchi, S., Sachdeva, S., Bhalla, S. (eds.) DNIS 2010. LNCS, vol. 5999, pp. 80–106. Springer, Heidelberg (2010)
6. Biskup, J., Gogolin, C., Seiler, J., Weibert, T.: Inference-proof view update transactions with forwarded refreshments. Journal of Computer Security 19(3), 487–529 (2011)

7. Bancilhon, F., Spyratos, N.: Update semantics of relational views. ACM Transactions on Database Systems (TODS) 6(4), 557–575 (1981)
8. Gabillon, A.: Multilevel databases. In: Rivero, L.C., Doorn, J.H., Ferraggine, V.E. (eds.) Encyclopedia of Database Technologies and Applications, pp. 386–389. Idea Group (2005)
9. Biskup, J., Wiese, L.: A sound and complete model-generation procedure for consistent and confidentiality-preserving databases. Theoretical Computer Science 412(31), 4044–4072 (2011)
10. Dawson, S., di Vimercati, S.D.C., Lincoln, P., Samarati, P.: Maximizing sharing of protected information. Journal of Computer and System Sciences 64(3), 496–541 (2002)
11. Aggarwal, C.C., Yu, P.S. (eds.): Privacy-Preserving Data Mining - Models and Algorithms. Advances in Database Systems, vol. 34. Springer, Heidelberg (2008)
12. Jajodia, S., Atluri, V., Keefe, T.F., McCollum, C.D., Mukkamala, R.: Multilevel security transaction processing. Journal of Computer Security 9(3), 165–195 (2001)
13. Abiteboul, S., Hull, R., Vianu, V.: Foundations of Databases. Addison-Wesley (1995)
14. Biskup, J., Bonatti, P.A.: Controlled query evaluation for enforcing confidentiality in complete information systems. International Journal of Information Security 3(1), 14–27 (2004)
15. Mazumdar, S., Stemple, D.W., Sheard, T.: Resolving the tension between integrity and security using a theorem prover. In: Boral, H., Larson, P.Å. (eds.) SIGMOD Conference 1988, pp. 233–242. ACM Press (1988)
16. Cuppens, F., Gabillon, A.: Logical foundations of multilevel databases. Data & Knowledge Engineering 29(3), 259–291 (1999)
17. Biskup, J., Wiese, L.: Preprocessing for controlled query evaluation with availability policy. Journal of Computer Security 16(4), 477–494 (2008)
18. Ciriani, V., De Capitani di Vimercati, S., Foresti, S., Livraga, G., Samarati, P.: Enforcing Confidentiality and Data Visibility Constraints: An OBDD Approach. In: Li, Y. (ed.) DBSec 2011. LNCS, vol. 6818, pp. 44–59. Springer, Heidelberg (2011)
19. Biskup, J., Lochner, J.-H., Sonntag, S.: Optimization of the Controlled Evaluation of Closed Relational Queries. In: Gritzalis, D., Lopez, J. (eds.) SEC 2009. IFIP AICT, vol. 297, pp. 214–225. Springer, Heidelberg (2009)

Representation-Independent Data Usage Control

Alexander Pretschner, Enrico Lovat, and Matthias Büchler

Karlsruhe Institute of Technology, Germany
{pretschner,lovat,buechler}@kit.edu

Abstract. Usage control is concerned with what happens to data after access has been granted. In the literature, usage control models have been defined on the grounds of *events* that, somehow, are related to data. In order to better cater to the dimension of data, we extend a usage control model by the explicit distinction between *data* and *representation* of data. A data flow model is used to track the flow of data in-between different representations. The usage control model is then extended so that usage control policies can address not just one single representation (e.g., delete file1.txt after thirty days) but rather all representations of the data (e.g., if file1.txt is a copy of file2.txt, also delete file2.txt). We present three proof-of-concept implementations of the model, at the operating system level, at the browser level, and at the X11 level, and also provide an ad-hoc implementation for multi-layer enforcement.

1 Introduction

If usage control requirements are to be enforced on data, one must take into account that this data exists in multiple representations. For instance, there can be multiple copies of a file, or multiple clones of an object. Similarly, an image can exist as network packet, Java object, window pixmap, data base record, or file. The representations potentially reside at different system layers, including operating system, runtime system, window manager, and DBMS. High-level usage control requirements such as "don't copy" have different meanings at different layers (copy a file, take a screenshot, duplicate a database record, copy&paste in a word processor). While in principle, it is possible to enforce these requirements at the level of CPU instructions, it turns out to be hard to identify, *in general*, precisely those instructions that pertain to copying a file, taking a screenshot, etc. Therefore, we consider it convenient to simultaneously enforce usage control requirements at all relevant system layers. This, however, requires following the flow of data from one representation to another within and across system layers.

We present a framework and its implementation for combining usage control enforcement with data flow tracking technology. One example of the resulting system is a social network in which users may view pictures in their browsers (first representation, first layer) but not copy cache files (second representation, second layer) or take screenshots (third representation, third layer) [1]. We describe the model and its prototypical implementation; detailed security and performance analyses are not in the scope. We organize our paper along six steps.

J. Garcia-Alfaro et al. (Eds.): DPM 2011 and SETOP 2011, LNCS 7122, pp. 122–140, 2012.
© Springer-Verlag Berlin Heidelberg 2012

Step 1: Specification-level usage control policies based on events We start with a policy language from the literature [2] that allows us to state requirements on future events ("at most three copies," "whenever data is accessed, notify me," "don't delete for five years," "do delete after thirty days"). In this model, usage control policies are interpreted as sets of allowed sequences of sets of events. We call these policies *specification-level policies*.

Step 2: Data and containers; data state In order to cater to the dimension of data, we distinguish between data and containers. Containers (files, pixmaps, memory regions, network packets) reflect different representations of data. This is captured by the *data state* $\sigma \in \Sigma$ of a system which essentially maps containers to sets of data items. Independent of any policies, the data state of a system changes with every step of the system. We capture this by a transition function ϱ that maps a data state and a set of events to another data state. This data flow model has been described and instantiated to various levels of the system before [3,4,5]. In this paper, we embody the data flow model in a usage control policy language and an integrated semantic model; together with the prototype implementation, this constitutes the core contribution of this paper.

Step 3: Specification-level usage control policies based on data In the language of step 1, we can only express container usages, i.e., usage events that pertain to *one specific representation*. Since we deem it natural to express *data usages* which pertain to all representations of the same data as well, we augment the language by (1) data usages and (2) special operators for data rather than containers— e.g., some *data* may not flow into a specific container such as a network socket.

Step 4: Implementation-level policies based on data Specification-level policies are enforced by mechanisms that are configured by *implementation-level* policies. Implementation-level policies are event-condition-action (ECA) rules that perform an action provided that a trigger event has happened and the respective condition has evaluated to true. The action can be to inhibit or to modify the trigger event (which requires the distinction between desired and actual events) or to execute some other event (which does not require this distinction). Since these mechanisms are actually implemented, it is convenient to express the condition part of the ECA rules in a language that expresses requirements on the past rather than on the future. This language then is the natural past dual of the language of step 1 [6]. In this paper, we also augment this implementation-level policy language by data usages and special state-based operators.

Step 5: Runtime monitors for events and data Using our specification-level (future) and implementation-level (past) languages, we can leverage results from runtime monitoring to synthesize efficient monitors both for specification-level and (the condition part of) implementation-level policies. In the first case, we can detect violations (detective enforcement) whereas in the second case, we can also prevent violations from happening by blocking or modifying attempted events, and by performing compensating, penalizing, or notifying actions. Efficient runtime monitoring technology is readily available [7].

It is straightforward to implement the evolution of the data state. At each moment in time, we intercept the current event and update the data state by consulting the transition function ϱ. This simple implementation yields a state machine that computes the data state at every given moment in time.

In terms of the combined model, if a *data usage* is specified in a policy (and thus in the synthesized monitor), we consult the state machine that implements the information state $\sigma \in \Sigma$ from within the usage control monitor to retrieve all the containers that contain the respective data item, and evaluate the policy w.r.t. *all these containers*. Function *states* is independent of any given policy; since our framework is intended to be deployed at different system layers, there hence is one data state tracker per system layer, and one runtime monitor per layer per policy. While pure usage control monitors [8] as well as data flow tracking systems [3,4,5] have been implemented before, we provide implementations of *combined* data flow tracking and usage control enforcement mechanisms here.

Step 6: Multi-Layer enforcement As the above example of the social network application shows, data representations may exist at several different layers of abstraction (cache file, pixmap, web page content), and we must track the flow of data and enforce usage control requirements not only at single layers of the system, but also across different layers. In full generality, this problem is still subject of investigation. However, tailored solutions are possible. For instance, in this paper, we propose as an example an ad-hoc solution for a multi-layer instantiation in a social network scenario: we show that it is possible to enforce usage control requirements with data flow tracking for a picture when this is represented as a browser object, as a cache file and as content of a window.

Research Problem. In sum, we tackle the problem of how to do usage control on data that exists in multiple representations at different system layers.

Solution. We present, firstly, a formal model that extends one usage control model by the notion of data representations and that hence allows us to track data flows within and in-between different representations at different layers of the system. Secondly, as a proof of concept, we show how to implement such a system. We do not present a security analysis, and we do not claim that our implementation cannot be circumvented [9].

Contribution. Data flow tracking at specific system layers has been done in a multitude of ways [3,4,10,11,12,13,14,15,16,17,18,19], also in the form of information flow analyses where implicit flows are also taken into account [20,21]. As far as we are aware, this work ends where sensitive (or tainted) data is moved to illegal sinks, e.g., when a file is written or an http post request is sent. If such an illegal sink is reached, something bad has happened, and an exception is thrown. In contrast, our work adds the dimension of usage control that allows to specify and enforce more fine-grained constraints on these sinks. Conversely, usage control models are usually defined on the grounds of technical events, including specific technologies such as complex event processing or runtime verification [22,7], but do not cater to the flow of data. We add the distinction between representation and data to these models. We see our contribution in the marriage of the research areas of usage control and dynamic data flow tracking.

Organization. §2 recapitulates (1) a semantic model and a language for usage control and (2) a semantic model for data flow. §3 presents our combined model. §4 describes three different instantiations as well as an ad-hoc multi-layer enforcement implementation. §5 puts our work in context, and §6 concludes. An extended version of this paper is available as a technical report [23].

2 Background

In this section, we recapitulate the specification-level policy specification language [2] and the data flow model [3,4,5] that we will combine in §3.

Step 1: Usage Control. We consider a usage control system model [2] based on classes of parameterized events where parameters represent attributes. Every event in set *Event* ⊆ *EventName* × *Params* consists of the event's name and parameters, represented as a partial (↠) function from names to values: *Params* ⊆ *ParamName* ↠ *ParamValue* for basic types *ParamName, ParamValue, EventName*. We denote event parameters by their graph, i.e., as (*name, value*) pairs. We assume a reserved parameter name, *obj*, to indicate on which data item the event is performed. An example is the event $(show, \{(obj, x)\})$, where *show* is the name of the event and the parameter *obj* has value x. We reserve a Boolean parameter *isTry* which indicates if the event is desired or actual (this is necessary if events should be blocked or modified in order to enforce policies) [6].

In policies, events are usually under-specified. For instance, if a policy specifies that event $(show, \{(obj, x)\})$ is prohibited, then the actual event $(show, \{(obj, x), (window, w)\})$ should also be prohibited. For this reason, events are partially ordered with respect to a refinement relation *refinesEv*. Event e_2 refines event e_1 iff e_2 has the same event name as e_1 and all parameters of e_1 have the same value in e_2. e_2 can also have additional parameters specified, which explains the subset relation in the definition. Let $x.i$ identify the i-th component of a tuple x. Formally, we then have *refinesEv* ⊆ *Event* × *Event* with $\forall\, e_1, e_2 \in Event \bullet e_2\ refinesEv\ e_1 \Leftrightarrow e_1.1 = e_2.1 \wedge e_1.2 \subseteq e_2.2$. In the semantic model, we will assume traces to be maximally refined (all parameters carry values; this seems natural in an actually running system): $maxRefinedEv = \{e \in Event : \forall\, e' \in Event \bullet e'\ refinesEv\ e \Rightarrow e' = e\}$. The semantics of the usage control policy language is defined over traces. Traces map abstract points in time —the natural numbers— to possibly empty sets of maximally refined actual and desired events: $Trace : \mathbb{N} \to \mathbb{P}(maxRefinedEv)$.

Specification-level usage control policies are then described in language Φ^+ (+ for future). It is a temporal logic with explicit operators for cardinality and permissions where the cardinality operators turn out to be mere macros [24], and where we omit the permission operator for brevity's sake. We distinguish between purely propositional (Ψ) and temporal and cardinality operators (Φ^+).

$$\Psi ::= \underline{true} \mid \underline{false} \mid E(\mathit{Event}) \mid T(\mathit{Event}) \mid \underline{not}(\Psi) \mid \underline{and}(\Psi, \Psi) \mid \underline{or}(\Psi, \Psi) \mid \underline{implies}(\Psi, \Psi)$$
$$\Phi^+ ::= \Psi \mid \underline{not}(\Phi^+) \mid \underline{and}(\Phi^+, \Phi^+) \mid \underline{or}(\Phi^+, \Phi^+) \mid \underline{implies}(\Phi^+, \Phi^+) \mid$$
$$\underline{until}(\Phi^+, \Phi^+) \mid \underline{after}(\mathbb{N}, \Phi^+) \mid \underline{within}(\mathbb{N}, \Phi^+) \mid \underline{during}(\mathbb{N}, \Phi^+) \mid$$
$$\underline{always}(\Phi^+) \mid \underline{repmax}(\mathbb{N}, \Psi) \mid \underline{replim}(\mathbb{N}, \mathbb{N}, \mathbb{N}, \Psi) \mid \underline{repuntil}(\mathbb{N}, \Psi, \Phi^+)$$

We also distinguish between *desired* or *attempted* (T) and *actual* (E) events. These syntactically reflect the (semantic-level) parameter *isTry* introduced above. The semantics of events is captured by relation $\models_\varepsilon \subseteq Event \times \Phi^+$ that relates events (rather than traces) to formulae of the form $E(\cdot)$ or $T(\cdot)$ as follows:

$$\forall e, e' \in Event \bullet e \models_\varepsilon E(e') \Leftrightarrow e \; refinesEv \; e' \wedge e.2(isTry) = false \text{ and}$$
$$\forall e, e' \in Event \bullet e \models_\varepsilon T(e') \Leftrightarrow e \; refinesEv \; e' \wedge e.2(isTry) = true.$$

not, *and*, *or*, *implies* have the usual semantics. The *until* operator is the weak-until operator from LTL. Using *after*(n), which refers to the time after n time steps, we can express concepts like *during* (something must constantly hold during a specified time interval) and *within* (something must hold at least once during a specified time interval). Cardinality operators restrict the number of occurrences or the duration of an action. The *replim* operator specifies lower and upper bounds of times within a fixed time interval in which a given formula holds. The *repuntil* operator does the same, but independent of any time interval. Instead, it limits the maximal number of times a formula holds until another formula holds (e.g., the occurrence of some event). With the help of *repuntil*, we can also define *repmax*, which defines the maximal number of times a formula may hold in the indefinite future. As an example of a cardinality operator, *replim*$(100, 0, 3, E((login, \{(user, Alice), (obj, \varnothing)\})))$ specifies that user Alice may login at most 3 times in the next 100 time units.

Step 2: Data Flow Tracking. We base our work on data flow tracking on approaches from the literature [3,4,5]. In this model, data flow is defined by a transition relation on states that essentially map data representations, so-called *containers*, to data. Transitions are triggered by principals that perform actions. Formally, we describe systems as tuples $(P, Data, Event, Container, \Sigma, \sigma_i, \varrho)$ where P is a set of principals, *Data* is a set of data elements, *Event* is the set of events (or actions), *Container* is a set of data containers, Σ is the set of states of the system with σ_i being the initial state, and ϱ is the state transition function. In the following, we assume that the principals executing actions (making an event happen) are provided as a parameter of the action.

States are defined by three mappings (for simplicity's sake, we concentrated on just one mapping in the introduction): a *storage function* of type *Container* $\rightarrow$ $\mathbb{P}(Data)$, to know which set of data is stored in which container; an *alias function* of type *Container* $\rightarrow \mathbb{P}(Container)$ that captures the fact that some containers may implicitly get updated whenever other containers do; and a *naming function* that provides names for containers and that is of type $F \rightarrow Container$. F is a set of identifiers. We need identifiers to correctly model renaming activities. We thus define $\Sigma = (Container \rightarrow \mathbb{P}(Data)) \times (Container \rightarrow \mathbb{P}(Container)) \times (F \rightarrow Container)$ and $\sigma_i = (\varnothing, \varnothing, \varnothing)$. We define transitions between two states by ϱ :

$\Sigma \times \mathbb{P}(\textit{Event}) \rightarrow \Sigma$. For simplicity's sake, in this paper, we assume independent actions only: if $(\sigma, E) \in \varrho$, then the target state of this transition is independent of the ordering in which actions in E are executed in an actual implementation. In real systems is usually possible to sort events within the same timestep (e.g. by timestamp), hence this assumption is, in general, not restrictive.

3   A Combined Model

In the usage control model of § 2, data is addressed by referring to its specific representations as event parameters. For instance, $\underline{after}(30, \underline{always}(\underline{not}(E(\ (play, \{(obj, song1.mp3)\})))))$ stipulates that a file (a specific representation and a specific container) called $song1.mp3$ must not be played after thirty days. We address the situation where a copy of that file, $song2.mp3$, should not be played either. To this end, we extend the semantic model by *data usages* that allow us to specify protection requirements for all representations rather than just one. Using the data flow tracking model, we compute, at each moment in time t, the current data state of the system: we simply take the usage control model's system trace until t, extract the respective events in each step, iteratively compute the successor data states for each data state and eventually get the data state at time t. In an implementation, we will not store the system history but rather use state machines to record the data state at each moment in time (step 5).

Data, Containers, and Events. We need to distinguish between *data* items and *containers* for data items. At the specification level, this leads to the distinction between two classes of events according to the "type" of the *obj* parameter: events of class *dataUsage* define actions on data objects. The intuition is that these pertain to *every representation*. In contrast, events of class *containerUsage* refer to one single container. In a real system, only events of class *containerUsage* can happen. This is because each monitored event in a trace is related to a specific representation of the data (a file, a memory region, etc). *dataUsage* events are used only in the definition of policies, where it is possible to define a rule abstracting from the specific representation of a data item. We define a function *getclass* that extracts if an event is a data or a container usage.

$EventClass = \{dataUsage, containerUsage\}$ $getclass : Event \rightarrow EventClass$

$Data \cup Container \subseteq ParamValue$ $\{(obj, d) \mid d \in Data\} \subseteq Params$

$Container \cap Data = \varnothing$ $\{(obj, c) \mid c \in Container\} \subseteq Params$

$\forall e : Event \bullet getclass(e) = dataUsage \Leftrightarrow \exists x : ParamValue \bullet ((obj, x) \in e.2) \wedge x \in Data$
$\qquad \wedge\ getclass(e) = containerUsage \Leftrightarrow \exists x : ParamValue \bullet ((obj, x) \in e.2) \wedge x \in Container$

Step 3: Adding Data State. In our semantic model, policies are defined on traces. We want to describe certain situations to be avoided or enforced. In practice there usually is an almost infinite number of different sequences of events that lead to the same situation, e.g., the creation of a copy or the deletion of a file. Instead of listing all these sequences, it appears more convenient in situations of this kind to define a policy based on the description of the (data flow state of the) system at that specific moment. To define such formulas we introduce a new set of *state-based operators*, $\Phi_i ::= \underline{isNotIn}(Data, \mathbb{P}\ Container)\ |$ $\underline{isCombinedWith}(Data, Data)\quad |\quad \underline{isOnlyIn}(Data, \mathbb{P}\ Container)$ and define $\Phi_i^+ ::= \Phi^+\ |\ \Phi_i$. Intuitively, $\underline{isNotIn}(d, C)$ is true if data d is not present in any of the containers in set C. This is useful to express constraints such as "song s must not be distributed over the network", which becomes $\underline{always}(\underline{isNotIn}(s, \{c_{net}\}))$ for a network container (any socket) c_{net}. The rule $\underline{isCombinedWith}(d_1, d_2)$ states whether data items d_1 and d_2 are combined in one container. This is useful to express Chinese Wall policies. $\underline{isOnlyIn}(d, C)$ is syntactic sugar for $\underline{isNotIn}(d, Container \setminus C)$ and expresses that data d can only be in containers of set C, e.g., $\underline{isOnlyIn}(d, \varnothing)$ for "data d has been deleted."

We have seen above that we implicitly quantify over unmentioned parameters when specifying events in policies by using relation *refinesEv*. We now extend this definition to *dataUsages*. An event of class *dataUsage* is refined by an event of class *containerUsage* if the latter is related to a specific representation of the data the former refers to. As in the original definition, in both cases the more refined event may have more parameters than the more abstract event. An event e_2 refines an event e_1 if (1) e_1 and e_2 both have the same class (*containerUsage* or *dataUsage*) and we have e_2 *refinesEv* e_1; or (2) if e_1 is a *dataUsage* and e_2 a *containerUsage* event. In this latter case, e_1 and e_2 must have the same event name, and there must exist a data item d stored in a container c such that $(obj, d) \in e_1.2$; $(obj, c) \in e_2.2$; all parameters (except for obj) of e_1 have the same value in e_2; and e_2 can possibly have additional parameters. Formally, these requirements are specified by relation *refinesEv$_i$* $\subseteq (Event \times \Sigma) \times Event$, which checks whether one event e_2 refines another event e_1 also w.r.t. data and containers (Σ is needed to access the current information state):

$$\forall e_1, e_2 \in Event;\ \sigma \in \Sigma \bullet (e_2, \sigma)\ refinesEv_i\ e_1 \Leftrightarrow$$
$$(getclass(e_1) = getclass(e_2) \wedge e_2\ refinesEv\ e_1)$$
$$\vee\ ((getclass(e_1) = dataUsage \wedge getclass(e_2) = containerUsage \wedge e_1.1 = e_2.1$$
$$\wedge\ \exists d \in Data, c \in Container \bullet d \in \sigma.1(c)$$
$$\wedge\ e_1.2(obj) = d \wedge e_2.2(obj) = c \wedge (e_1.2\backslash\{(obj, d)\} \subseteq e_2.2\backslash\{(obj, c)\})))$$

With the help of *refinesEv$_i$*, we now define the satisfaction relation for event expressions in the context of data and container usages. We simply add one argument to $\models_\varepsilon$ and obtain $\models_{\varepsilon,i} \subseteq (Event \times \Sigma) \times \Phi_i^+$ as follows:

$$\forall e, e' \in Event, \sigma \in \Sigma \bullet (e, \sigma) \models_{\varepsilon,i} E(e') \Leftrightarrow (e, \sigma)\ refinesEv_i\ e' \wedge e.2(isTry) = false$$
$$\wedge\ (e, \sigma) \models_{\varepsilon,i} T(e') \Leftrightarrow (e, \sigma)\ refinesEv_i\ e' \wedge e.2(isTry) = true$$

As a last ingredient, we need function $states : (Trace \times \mathbb{N}) \to \Sigma$ to compute the information state at a given moment in time via $states(t, 0) = \sigma_i$ and $n > 0 \Rightarrow states(t, n) = \varrho(states(t, n-1), t(n-1))$. On these grounds, we finally define the semantics of the specific data usage operators in Φ_i with semantics $\models_i \subseteq (Trace \times \mathbb{N}) \times \Phi_i$:

$\forall t \in Trace;\ n \in \mathbb{N};\ \varphi \in \Phi_i;\ \sigma \in \Sigma \bullet\ (t,n) \models_i \varphi \Leftrightarrow \sigma = states(t,n) \wedge$
$\exists d \in Data, C \in \mathbb{P}\ Container \bullet\ \varphi = \underline{isNotIn}(d,C) \wedge \forall c' \in Container \bullet\ d \in \sigma.1(c') \Rightarrow (c' \notin C)$
$\vee\ \exists d_1, d_2 \in Data \bullet\ \varphi = \underline{isCombinedWith}(d_1,d_2) \wedge \exists c' \in Container \bullet\ d_1 \in \sigma.1(c') \wedge d_2 \in \sigma.1(c')$

This leads to the definition of the semantics augmented by data flow, $\models_i^+ \subseteq$ $(Trace \times \mathbb{N}) \times \Phi_i^+$ depicted in Figure 1. The definitions for the cardinality operators are complex because of the refinement relation: it is possible that two simultaneously happening events e_1, e_2 that both refine the same event e both make $E(e) \in \Psi$ true. For a trace t, it is thus not sufficient to simply count those moments in time, n, that satisfy $(t,n) \models_i^+ E(e)$ [2,6].

Step 4: Mechanisms enforce specification-level policies. Specification-level policies expressed in Φ_i^+ describe which runs of a system are allowed and which ones are not. There are usually several ways of enforcing such policies, by modification, inhibition, or execution [19]. Since there is not the one right choice, a user must explicitly stipulate this by selecting an operational mechanism. These operational mechanisms embody *implementation-level policies* and are conveniently expressed as event-condition-action (ECA) rules [6]; whether or not satisfaction of an implementation-level usage control policy entails enforcement of a specification-level policy can be checked automatically [24]. In our case, the semantics is as follows: if a triggering event is detected, the condition is evaluated; if it evaluates to true, the action (modify, inhibit, execute) is performed. Since mechanisms are operational in nature, we decided to formulate the conditions in a past variant of our language, Φ^- with semantics $\models^-$ [6,24]. The fact that mechanisms can inhibit or modify motivates the conceptual distinction between desired and actual events ($E(\cdot)$ and $T(\cdot)$; we could well have restricted the usage of Ψ in specification-level policies to actual events ($E(e)$) which, however, slightly complicates the combined definitions).

Implementation-level policies—for the time being without data flow tracking semantics—hence come in the following forms. We assume a trigger event e and a condition $\varphi \in \Phi^-$. Modifiers are formulas $(T(e) \wedge (E(e) \Rightarrow \varphi)) \Rightarrow$ $T(e') \wedge \neg E(e)$ where e' is like e but with some parameters modified. The idea is that if e is attempted ($T(e)$) and the actual execution of e makes the trigger true ($E(e) \Rightarrow \varphi$), then e' should happen in lieu of e ($T(e') \wedge \neg E(e)$; the reason for having $T(e')$ rather than $E(e')$ is that there might be multiple concurrently executing mechanisms). Inhibitors are formulas $(T(e) \wedge (E(e) \Rightarrow \varphi)) \Rightarrow \neg E(e)$ that simply prohibit the desired event $T(e)$ by requiring $\neg E(e)$ in case $E(e)$ would make φ true. Finally, executors are expressed as $(T(e) \wedge (E(e) \Rightarrow \varphi)) \Rightarrow T(e') \wedge E(e)$ for some event e' to be executed; again, since there may be multiple mechanisms in place, e' can only be attempted at this stage. The formal semantics of a set of combined mechanisms as well as conflict detection has been described elsewhere [6,24].

The structure of Φ^- reflects that of Φ^+. Observe that the semantics of Φ_i, $\models_i$, "does not look into the future" and makes use of the *states* function *that already is defined solely in terms of the past*. As a consequence, we use

$$\forall t \in \textit{Trace}, n \in \mathbb{N}, \varphi \in \Phi_i^+ \bullet (t, n) \models_i^+ \varphi \Leftrightarrow$$

$$\exists e, e' \in \textit{Event} \bullet (\varphi = E(e) \vee \varphi = T(e)) \wedge e' \in t(n) \wedge (e', states(t, n)) \models_{\varepsilon, i} \varphi$$

$$\vee\ \varphi \in \Phi_i \wedge (t, n) \models_i \varphi$$

$$\vee\ \exists \psi \in \Phi_i^+ \bullet \varphi = \underline{not}(\psi) \wedge \neg ((t, n) \models_i^+ \psi)$$

$$\vee\ \exists \psi, \chi \in \Phi_i^+ \bullet \varphi = \underline{or}(\psi, \chi) \wedge ((t, n) \models_i^+ \psi \vee (t, n) \models_i^+ \chi)$$

$$\vee\ \exists \psi, \chi \in \Phi_i^+ \bullet \varphi = \underline{until}(\psi, \chi)$$
$$\wedge (\exists u \in \mathbb{N} \bullet (((t, n+u) \models_i^+ \chi \wedge (\forall v \in \mathbb{N} \bullet v < u \Rightarrow (t, n+v) \models_i^+ \psi))$$
$$\vee\ \forall v \in \mathbb{N} \bullet (t, n+v) \models_i^+ \psi))$$

$$\vee\ \exists i \in \mathbb{N};\ \psi \in \Phi_i^+ \bullet \varphi = \underline{after}(i, \psi) \wedge (t, n+i) \models_i^+ \psi$$

$$\vee\ \exists l, x, y \in \mathbb{N};\ \psi \in \Psi \bullet \varphi = \underline{replim}(l, x, y, \psi)$$
$$\wedge\ x \leq \sum_{j=1}^{l} |\{S \subseteq \textit{Event} \mid S \subseteq t(n+j) \wedge \exists t' \in \textit{Trace} \, \forall m \in \mathbb{N} \bullet$$
$$t'(n+j) = S \wedge (m < n+j \Rightarrow t'(m) = t(m)) \wedge (t', n+j) \models_i^+ \psi$$
$$\wedge \nexists S' \subseteq \textit{Event} \bullet S' \subset S \wedge \exists t' \in \textit{Trace} \, \forall m \in \mathbb{N} \bullet$$
$$t'(n+j) = S' \wedge (m < n+j \Rightarrow t'(m) = t(m)) \wedge (t', n+j) \models_i^+ \psi\}| \leq y$$

$$\vee\ \exists l, u \in \mathbb{N};\ \psi \in \Psi;\ \chi \in \Phi^+ \bullet \varphi = \underline{repuntil}(l, \psi, \chi)$$
$$\wedge\ ((t, n+u) \models_i^+ \chi \wedge \forall v \in \mathbb{N} \bullet v < u \Rightarrow \neg((t, n+v) \models_i^+ \chi)$$
$$\wedge \sum_{j=1}^{u} |\{S \subseteq \textit{Event} \mid S \subseteq t(n+j) \wedge \exists t' \in \textit{Trace} \, \forall m \in \mathbb{N} \bullet$$
$$t'(n+j) = S \wedge (m < n+j \Rightarrow t'(m) = t(m)) \wedge (t', n+j) \models_i^+ \psi$$
$$\wedge \nexists S' \subseteq \textit{Event} \bullet S' \subset S \wedge \exists t' \in \textit{Trace} \, \forall m \in \mathbb{N} \bullet$$
$$t'(n+j) = S' \wedge (m < n+j \Rightarrow t'(m) = t(m)) \wedge (t', n+j) \models_i^+ \psi\}| \leq l)$$
$$\vee \sum_{j=1}^{\infty} |\{S \subseteq \textit{Event} \mid S \subseteq t(n+j) \wedge \exists t' \in \textit{Trace} \, \forall m \in \mathbb{N} \bullet$$
$$t'(n+j) = S \wedge (m < n+j \Rightarrow t'(m) = t(m)) \wedge (t', n+j) \models_i^+ \psi$$
$$\wedge \nexists S' \subseteq \textit{Event} \bullet S' \subset S \wedge \exists t' \in \textit{Trace} \, \forall m \in \mathbb{N} \bullet$$
$$t'(n+j) = S' \wedge (m < n+j \Rightarrow t'(m) = t(m)) \wedge (t', n+j) \models_i^+ \psi\}| \leq l$$

$$\vee\ \exists \psi, \chi \in \Phi_i^+ \bullet \varphi = \underline{and}(\psi, \chi) \wedge (t, n) \models_i^+ \underline{not}(or(\underline{not}(\psi), \underline{not}(\chi)))$$

$$\vee\ \exists \psi, \chi \in \Phi_i^+ \bullet \varphi = \underline{implies}(\psi, \chi) \wedge (t, n) \models_i^+ \underline{or}(not(\psi), \chi)$$

$$\vee\ \exists \psi \in \Phi_i^+ \bullet \varphi = \underline{always}(\psi) \wedge (t, n) \models_i^+ \underline{until}(\psi, false)$$

$$\vee\ \exists i \in \mathbb{N};\ \psi \in \Phi_i^+ \bullet \varphi = \underline{within}(i, \psi) \wedge (t, n) \models_i^+ \bigvee_{x=1}^{i} \underline{after}(i, \varphi)$$

$$\vee\ \exists i \in \mathbb{N};\ \psi \in \Phi_i^+ \bullet \varphi = \underline{during}(i, \psi) \wedge (t, n) \models_i^+ \bigwedge_{x=1}^{i} \underline{after}(x, \varphi)$$

$$\vee\ \exists l \in \mathbb{N};\ \psi \in \Psi \bullet \varphi = \underline{repmax}(l, \psi) \wedge (t, n) \models_i^+ \underline{repuntil}(l, \psi, false)$$

Fig. 1. Semantics of Φ_i^+

$$\Phi^- ::= \Psi \mid \underline{not}^-(\Phi^-) \mid \underline{and}^-(\Phi^-, \Phi^-) \mid \underline{or}^-(\Phi^-, \Phi^-) \mid \underline{implies}^-(\Phi^-, \Phi^-) \mid \underline{since}^-(\Phi^-, \Phi^-) \mid$$
$$\underline{before}^-(\mathbb{N}, \Phi^-) \mid \underline{within}^-(\mathbb{N}, \Phi^-) \mid \underline{during}^-(\mathbb{N}, \Phi^-) \mid$$
$$\underline{always}^-(\Phi^-) \mid \underline{repmax}^-(\mathbb{N}, \Psi) \mid \underline{replim}^-(\mathbb{N}, \mathbb{N}, \mathbb{N}, \Psi) \mid \underline{repsince}^-(\mathbb{N}, \Psi, \Phi^-);$$

let $\Phi_i^- ::= \Phi_i \mid \Phi^-$, verbatim reuse the definition of $\models_i$, and get the combined semantics of Φ_i^-, $\models_i^-$, in Figure 2, where we omit the definition of the propositional operators. Because of space limitations, we do not provide the semantics of entire mechanisms (that is: entire ECA rules, not just conditions) here; this straightforwardly generalizes the case without data flow tracking [6].

Step 5: Architecture. Our generic architecture is the same for each concrete system layer at which the infrastructure is instantiated. We distinguish three main components: a *Policy Enforcement Point* (PEP), able to observe, intercept and possibly modify and generate events in the system; a *Policy Decision Point* (PDP), representing the core of the usage control monitoring logic; and a *Policy Information Point* (PIP), which provides the data state $\sigma \in \Sigma$ to the PDP.

$$\forall\, t \in \mathit{Trace}, n \in \mathbb{N}, \varphi \in \Phi_i^- \bullet (t, n) \models_i^- \varphi \Leftrightarrow$$
$$\exists\, e, e' \in \mathit{Event} \bullet (\varphi = E(e) \vee \varphi = T(e)) \wedge e' \in t(n) \wedge (e', \mathit{states}(t, n)) \models_{\varepsilon, i} \varphi$$
$$\vee\ \varphi \in \Phi_i \wedge (t, n) \models_i \varphi$$
$$\vee\ \exists\, \psi, \chi \in \Phi_i^- \bullet \varphi = \underline{\mathit{since}}^-(\chi, \psi)$$
$$\qquad \wedge\, (\exists\, u \in \mathbb{N} \bullet u \leq n \wedge (t, n - u) \models_i^- \chi \wedge (\forall\, v \in \mathbb{N} \bullet u < v \leq n \Rightarrow (t, n - v) \models_i^- \psi)$$
$$\qquad\quad \vee\, \forall\, v \in \mathbb{N} \bullet v \leq u \Rightarrow (t, n - v) \models_i^- \psi)$$
$$\vee\ \exists\, i \in \mathbb{N};\ \psi \in \Phi_i^- \bullet \varphi = \underline{\mathit{before}}^-(i, \psi) \wedge i \leq n \wedge (t, n - i) \models_i^- \psi$$
$$\vee\ \exists\, l, x, y \in \mathbb{N};\ \psi \in \Psi \bullet \varphi = \underline{\mathit{replim}}^-(l, x, y, \psi)$$
$$\qquad \wedge\, x \leq \sum_{j=0}^{min(l,n)} \big| \{ S \subseteq \mathit{Event} \mid S \subseteq t(n - j) \wedge \exists\, t' \in \mathit{Trace}\ \forall\, m \in \mathbb{N} \bullet$$
$$\qquad\qquad t'(n - j) = S \wedge (n \geq m > n - j \Rightarrow t'(m) = t(m)) \wedge (t', n - j) \models_i^- \psi$$
$$\qquad\qquad \wedge \not\exists\, S' \subseteq \mathit{Event} \bullet S' \subset S \wedge \exists\, t' \in \mathit{Trace}\ \forall\, m \in \mathbb{N} \bullet$$
$$\qquad\qquad t'(n - j) = S' \wedge (n \geq m > n - j \Rightarrow t'(m) = t(m)) \wedge (t', n - j) \models_i^- \psi \} \big| \leq y$$
$$\vee\ \exists\, l, u \in \mathbb{N};\ \psi \in \Psi;\ \chi \in \Phi^- \bullet \varphi = \underline{\mathit{repsince}}^-(l, \chi, \psi)$$
$$\qquad \wedge\, \big(u \leq n \wedge (t, n - u) \models_i^- \chi \wedge \forall\, v \in \mathbb{N} \bullet u < v \leq n \Rightarrow \neg((t, n - v) \models_i^- \chi)$$
$$\qquad\quad \wedge \sum_{j=0}^{u} \big| \{ S \subseteq \mathit{Event} \mid S \subseteq t(n - j) \wedge \exists\, t' \in \mathit{Trace}\ \forall\, m \in \mathbb{N} \bullet$$
$$\qquad\qquad t'(n - j) = S \wedge (n \geq m > n - j \Rightarrow t'(m) = t(m)) \wedge (t', n - j) \models_i^- \psi$$
$$\qquad\qquad \wedge \not\exists\, S' \subseteq \mathit{Event} \bullet S' \subset S \wedge \exists\, t' \in \mathit{Trace}\ \forall\, m \in \mathbb{N} \bullet$$
$$\qquad\qquad t'(n - j) = S' \wedge (n \geq m > n - j \Rightarrow t'(m) = t(m)) \wedge (t', n - j) \models_i^- \psi \} \big| \leq l\big)$$
$$\qquad \vee \sum_{j=0}^{n} \big| \{ S \subseteq \mathit{Event} \mid S \subseteq t(n - j) \wedge \exists\, t' \in \mathit{Trace}\ \forall\, m \in \mathbb{N} \bullet$$
$$\qquad\qquad t'(n - j) = S \wedge (n \geq m > n - j \Rightarrow t'(m) = t(m)) \wedge (t', n - j) \models_i^- \psi$$
$$\qquad\qquad \wedge \not\exists\, S' \subseteq \mathit{Event} \bullet S' \subset S \wedge \exists\, t' \in \mathit{Trace}\ \forall\, m \in \mathbb{N} \bullet$$
$$\qquad\qquad t'(n + j) = S' \wedge (n \geq m > n - j \Rightarrow t'(m) = t(m)) \wedge (t', n - j) \models_i^- \psi \} \big| \leq l$$
$$\vee\ \exists\, \psi \in \Phi_i^- \bullet \varphi = \underline{\mathit{always}}^-(\psi) \wedge (t, n) \models_i^- \underline{\mathit{since}}^-(\mathit{false}, \psi)$$
$$\vee\ \exists\, i \in \mathbb{N};\ \psi \in \Phi_i^- \bullet \varphi = \underline{\mathit{within}}^-(i, \psi) \wedge i < n \wedge (t, n) \models_i^- \bigvee_{x=1}^{i} \underline{\mathit{before}}^-(i, \varphi)$$
$$\vee\ \exists\, i \in \mathbb{N};\ \psi \in \Phi_i^- \bullet \varphi = \underline{\mathit{during}}^-(i, \psi) \wedge i < n \wedge (t, n) \models_i^- \bigwedge_{x=1}^{i} \underline{\mathit{before}}^-(x, \varphi)$$
$$\vee\ \exists\, l \in \mathbb{N};\ \psi \in \Psi \bullet \varphi = \underline{\mathit{repmax}}^-(l, \psi) \wedge (t, n) \models_i^- \underline{\mathit{repsince}}^-(l, \mathit{false}, \psi)$$

Fig. 2. Semantics of Φ_i^-

The role of the PEP is to implement the mechanisms of step 4. PEPs intercept desired and actual events, signal them to the PDP and, according to the response, allow, inhibit or modify them. Using the events signaled by the PEP, the PDP evaluates the policies, more specifically, the condition of the ECA rules. While we implemented one specific algorithm [25] for the PDP, any runtime verification algorithm can be used [7]. Due to its generic nature, the same implementation can be reused at different system layers: only the binding of events in the system to events specified in the policies has to be performed. In order to take a decision, the PDP may need additional information (e.g., in case of state-based formulae or data usages) concerning the distribution of data among the different representations. For this reason the PDP queries the PIP. The PIP represents a (layer-specific) implementation of the data-flow tracking model presented in step 3. In order to properly model the evolution of the data-flow state, the PEP notifies the PIP about every actual event that happens in the system, and the PIP then updates its data state $\sigma \in \Sigma$ according to ϱ.

The interplay of PEP, PDP, and PIP is shown in Figure 3. Whenever the PDP checks an actual (container) event e against a data usage event u in a policy, the PIP is consulted to check if the data item referred to by u is contained in the container referred to by e.

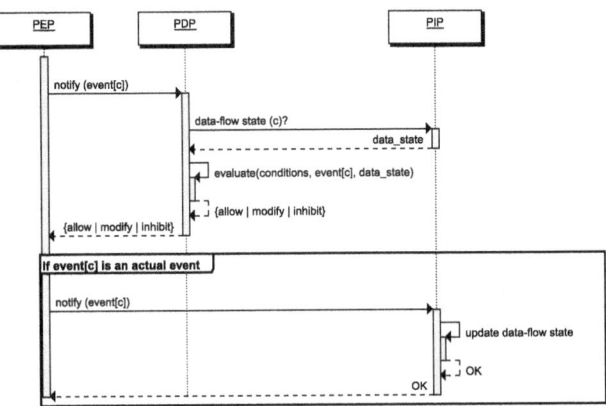

Fig. 3. Interplay of PEP, PDP, PIP

Step 6: Multi-layer data flow detection and usage control enforcement.
In the example of the social network application in Section 1 we have three
monitors: one at the level of the operating system, one at the level of the web
browser, and one at the level of the X11 system. Now, some events, together with
the data that they operate on, at one layer imply related events at a different
layer. For instance, saving a page in the web browser (event *save*) implies a
write() system call at the operating system layer. As a consequence, data flows
from one layer to another one.

We introduce a set of layers, L, that includes layers such as X11, the operating
system, a browser, etc. For each event, we assume that there is precisely one
layer at which this event happens (if there is more than one layer, then this is
captured by the following function π). This motivates the definition of a function
$\lambda : Event \to L$ that partitions the set of events. Note that neither our definition
of the transition relation ϱ nor the definition of the data state σ nor the definition
of languages Φ_i^+ and Φ_i^- require events, containers, and data to reside at one level
of abstraction. As a consequence, we may assume that our system is specified
globally, i.e. encompassing all levels of abstraction. We can then use function
λ to separate the different layers: $Event_\ell = \{e \in Event : \lambda(e) = \ell\}$ contains the
events relevant at layer ℓ, and, using graph notation, $\varrho_\ell = \{(\sigma, E, \sigma') : E \subseteq
Event_\ell \wedge \varrho(\sigma, E) = \sigma'\}$ projects the data flow transition relation to layer ℓ
(remember that in step 2 of Section 2, we required independence of events in the
definition of ϱ for simplicity's sake). With ϱ_ℓ and $Event_\ell$, we can implement the
data flow monitor for layer ℓ as described in step 5. The usage control monitor
part is synthesized from a policy; the only layer-specific part is $Event_\ell$. In the
implementation, the set of ϱ_ℓ and $Event_\ell$ hence defines the set of independent
enforcement mechanisms for all layers $\ell \in L$.

We now consider the flow of data in-between different layers. To this end, we introduce a relation $\pi : Event \rightarrow 2^{Event}$. With this relation, it is possible to specify, *at the model level*, that whenever an event happens at one layer ℓ_1, a set of simultaneous events at another layer ℓ_2 necessarily take place. Formally, we can capture this intuition by a constraint on the set of traces of a system: $\forall s \in Trace \, \forall t \in \mathbb{N} \, \forall e \in Event : e \in s(t) \Rightarrow \pi(e) \subseteq s(t)$. In other words, via π we require *in the semantic model* that, for instance, there must be a write() system call whenever there is a save action in the web browser, thus capturing the data flow from browser to operating system.

In this way, cross-layer data flow tracking and data-driven usage control enforcement can be *specified* in a conceptually very simple way. However, in terms of the *implementation*, this is far more challenging. While every layer-specific infrastructure instantiates the general model, our current cross-layer enforcement solution is an ad-hoc implementation that relates an event at one layer to an event at another layer in a hard-coded way (Section 4).

4   Instantiations

Operating System: OpenBSD. At the operating system level, system calls are the events that can change the state of the system. The complete description of the data-flow tracking model can be found in [3]. Here, we show how to extend this implementation with a usage control monitor, thus providing an instance of the combined model of this paper. Events are system calls, and they are invoked by processes on data containers. Containers include files, pipes, message queues and the network. A process itself is also considered as a data container because the process state, CPU registers and the memory image of the process are possible locations for data. Data containers are identified by a set of names, which includes file names, descriptors and sockets. Each state consists of the three mappings presented in Section 3: *storage, alias* and *naming*. As an example, aliases are created if memory is mapped to a file system (mmap() system call). The transition relation ϱ is described in [3].

The combined usage control and data flow tracking system is implemented using *Systrace*, a policy enforcement tool for monitoring, intercepting and modifying system calls in OpenBSD. In contrast to our earlier work [3], the combined implementation of this paper can enforce advanced usage control policies that address all the instances of the same data at the same time.

One example policy is from the DRM world: the content (dataUsage, lines 11 and 16) of a file, song.mp3, can be used, i.e. opened, (lines 10 and 15) at most 4 further times and within 30 seconds (1 timestep = 1 second) after the first use (lines 7-19); further attempts of opening the file will result in opening a predefined error message (lines 21-23). We provide it to demonstrate the use of complex conditions. Further examples are available [23].

```
1   <controlMechanism>
2    <id>OS_DRM_example</id>
3    <triggerEvent> <id>open</id>
4                   <param name="obj" value="song.mp3" type="dataUsage"/>
5                   <param name="isTry" value="true"/>
6    </triggerEvent>
7    <condition>
8    <or>
9      <not><before timeInterval="30"><always><not>
10         <event> <id>open</id>
11                 <param name="obj" value="song.mp3" type="dataUsage"/>
12         </event>
13       </not></always></before></not>
14       <not><repmax limit="5">
15         <event> <id>open</id>
16                 <param name="obj" value="song.mp3" type="dataUsage"/>
17         </event>
18       </repmax></not></or>
19    </condition>
20    <actions> <allow> <modify>
21       <param name="obj" value="/etc/UCmon/expired.msg" />
22    </modify> </allow> </actions>
23   </controlMechanism>
```

The effect of our implementation can be seen by executing the following sequence of commands:

```
> vlc song.mp3 && cp song.mp3 song2.mp3 && mv song2.mp3 song3.mp3 &&
  cat song3.mp3 > song4.mp3 &&
  ... (after more than 30 seconds) ... && vlc song4.mp3   --> ERROR!
```

When trying to play (command *vlc*) the file *song4.mp3* (a copy of the original *song.mp3*) more than 30 seconds after the first play, an error message is played instead of the song. The same error is generated when trying to open whatever instance of the song after the fifth time.

Windowing System: X11 X11 is a distributed system and a protocol for GUI environments on Unix-like systems. In X11, events that change the state of the system are network packets exchanged between clients and servers. The model for data-flow tracking and primitive usage control is described elsewhere [4]. Events are requests, replies, events and errors, invoked on specific X11 resources by principals that, because of the distributed setting, are identified by IP address and port. Resources form the containers that potentially carry sensitive information, like windows, pixmaps (memory areas that are valid destinations for drawing functions), atoms (unique names for accessing resources or for communication between different clients), attributes and properties (variables attached to windows), etc. States consists of the three mappings presented in Section 3: *storage, alias* and *naming*. Among others, aliases are created whenever windows overlap translucently. The transition relation ϱ is described in [4].

The combined usage control and data flow tracking system is implemented using *Xmon*, an X11 debugging tool for monitoring, intercepting and modifying network packets from/to an X server. As opposed to [4], thanks to the usage control runtime monitor, it is able to enforce advanced usage control policies, with temporal and cardinality operators, addressing all instances of the same data at the same time. One example policy is the following.

```
1   <controlMechanism>
2    <id>X11_Screenshot</id>
3    <triggerEvent> <id>GetImage</id>
4                   <param name="obj" value="0x1a00005" type="dataUsage"/>
5                   <param name="isTry" value"true"/>
6    </triggerEvent>
7    <condition> <true /> </condition>
8    <actions> <allow>
9      <modify> <param name="planeMask" value="0x0" /> </modify>
10   </allow> </actions>
11  </controlMechanism>
```

In this example, the enforcement mechanism prevents the X client from taking a screenshot (X11 action *GetImage*, line 3) of the content of window 0x1a00005 (line 4; in the multi-layer example, this data is filled in by the web browser PEP). If a client requests a screenshot of that window, the action is permitted (line 8), but the parameter *planeMask* is modified to the value 0x0 (line 9). *planeMask* represents which set of drawable objects should be included in the screenshot: a *planeMask* of 0xffff means that every plane is contained in the screenshot, whereas invoking *GetImage* with *planeMask* equal to 0x0 returns a black image because no plane is included. Further examples are available [23].

Web Browser: Firefox. A third instance of our model at the browser level extends an existing usage control extension for the Firefox web browser [26]. In this scenario, we want to protect sensitive web page content from malicious usage by the user of the browser. Here, we show how to instantiate the data-flow tracking model to objects of the browser domain, in order to extend the existing implementation to another instance of the combined model presented so far.

Events include the user actions "copy", "paste", "print", "save as", etc., and are performed by a user on web page content. Content is stored in two types of containers: read-only (the non-editable part of a web-page) and read-write (text fields where it is possible to type); in addition, there is the clipboard. The only principal in this scenario is the user of the browser. The browser-level instantiation does not require the alias function, because no alias relations are created among containers. Similarly, the naming function is constant. Therefore, a state of the system is given only by the state of the storage function $\Sigma = (Container \rightarrow 2^{Data})$. Due to space constraints, we do not present the definition of the transition relation ϱ here. The resulting system can enforce advanced policies that address all the representations of the same data. Our example is from the social network scenario: a user is allowed to print a profile picture (lines 3-6) only once (lines 8 and 14). More examples are available [23].

```
1   <controlMechanism>
2   <id>Browser_Print</id>
3     <triggerEvent> <id>print</id>
4                    <param name="obj" value="imgprofile" type="dataUsage"/>
5                    <param name="isTry" value"true"/>
6   </triggerEvent>
7   <condition>
8     <not> <repmax limit="1">
9       <event> <id>print</id>
10              <parameter name="obj" value="imgprofile" type="dataUsage"/>
11      </event>
12      </repmax> </not>
13  </condition>
14  <actions> <inhibit/> </actions>
15  </controlMechanism>
```

Multi-Layer Enforcement. We also implemented multi-layer usage control by combining the three implementations presented above [1]. To do so, we deployed the three monitors, each consisting of PEP, PDP, and PIP, on the same physical system and made them communicate with each other. A general protocol for such a communication among arbitrary parties is the subject of current work, so we hard-coded a solution tailored for this specific scenario: we made the Firefox monitor able to instruct the OS and X11 monitors about new policies and data flows from the browser layer to the operating system and the windowing system.

We consider a social network [26] where a user watches a picture on someone else's profile page. Since the picture is considered sensitive, its usage is restricted. In particular, no local usage is allowed after download, except for printing, and whenever the picture is printed, a notification must be sent to the owner. The respective specification policy is *"This picture cannot be copied to the clipboard (not even as a screenshot) nor saved to disk and its cached version can be used only by Firefox. No printing of the picture without notification of the owner."* We do not show the implementation-level policies here. Together with a description of the interplay of the components, they are provided elsewhere [23].

In our implementation, at each layer we distinguish between the business logic and the monitoring component which instantiates the model presented in this paper (PEP, PDP and PIP in step 5 of Section 3). If the user requests the page with picture Pic, the browser downloads the profile page together with a policy that contains a sub-policy related to the figure. Upon reception by the web browser, Pic takes new representations: it is rendered as a set of pixels inside the browser window, it is cached as a file, and it is internally represented by the browser in some memory region referenced by a node in the DOM tree. Each representation must be protected at its layer in the system.

To do so—and this is the ad hoc part of the implementation—the browser monitor instantiates the generic policy it got from the remote server to each layer by adding runtime information including the name of the cache file and the ID of the window. Because this data is created at runtime, it cannot be statically determined by the server a priori. After instantiating and deploying the policies to the OS and X11 layers, the browser monitor allows rendering the picture and creating the cache file. From this point onward, all three instantiations of the policy are enforced at different levels of abstraction.

5   Related Work

The subject of this paper is the combination of data flow detection with usage control, a policy language, and a prototype enforcement infrastructure.

Enforcement of usage control requirements has been done for the OS layer [27,28,3], for the X11 layer [4], for Java [10,11,29], the .NET CIL [12] and machine languages [13,14,30]; at the level of an enterprise service bus [15]; for dedicated applications such as the Internet Explorer [16] and in the context of digital rights management [17,18,19]. These solutions focus on either data flow tracking or event-driven usage control. Our model, in contrast, tackles both at the same time and since it is layer-independent, it can be instantiated to each of these layers. At the level of binary files, the Garm tool [30] combines data tracking with an enforcement mechanism for basic usage control. This model focuses on access control, trust and policy management aspects, while our goal is a generic model and a policy language to express and enforce advanced usage control requirements for arbitrary system layers. Data flow confinement is also intensely studied at the operating system level [27,28]; here, our work differs in that we aim at enforcing complex usage control policies.

A multitude of policy languages has been proposed in literature, but as far as we know, none of them addresses the data dimension like ours does; they allow for definitions of usage restrictions for specific rather than all representations of data, and their semantic models do not consider data flows.

In terms of data flow tracking, our approach restricts the standard notion of information flow which also caters to implicit flows and aims at non-interference assessments [31,32,20,21]: our system detects only flows from container to container. This explains why we prefer to speak of data flow rather than information flow. Moreover, even if we plan to leverage results of static analyses, like [33], we want to detect these flows at runtime. Implementations of such data-flow tracking system have been realized for OS [3], X11 [4], OpenOffice [5] and Java byte code and can be used as PIP component to instantiate our model. This cited work, however, only addresses data flow detection without full usage control.

In terms of general-purpose usage control models, there are similarities with the models underlying XACML [34], Ponder2 [35] and UCON [36]. The first two, however, do not provide formalized support for cardinality or temporal operators (free text fields exist, but the respective requirements are hard to enforce). UCON supports complex conditions [37], and has been used in applications at different system layers, such as the Java Virtual Machine [38] and the Enterprise Service Bus [39]. Data flow is not considered, however.

Complex event processing [22] and runtime monitoring [7] are suitable for monitoring conditions of usage control policies. As such, they address one aspect of the problem, namely the monitoring part, and do not cater to data flow.

6   Conclusions

The contribution of this paper is a combination of usage control with data flow detection technology. Rather than specifying and enforcing usage control policies on specific representations of a data item (usually encoded in usage-controlled events), our work makes it possible to specify and enforce usage control policies for all representations of a data item (files, windows contents, memory contents, etc.). We provide a model, a language, an architecture and a generic implementation for data-centric usage control enforcement that we instantiate to several system layers. Our implementation consists of combined usage control and data flow monitors for an operating system, a windowing system, and a web browser, together with a multi-layer enforcement infrastructure for them. As an example, this system makes it possible that a user can download a picture on a web page and watch it in the browser but not copy&paste or print the content without notification (enforced at the browser layer); nor take a screenshot (enforced at the X11 layer); nor access the cache files (enforced at the OS layer) [1].

Because of space restrictions, we have not provided security nor performance analyses. While we do not claim that our system cannot be circumvented, we believe that a reasonable level of security can be attained [26,9]. Performance-wise, we currently are faced with an overhead of one to two orders of magnitude [3,4]. This, however, heavily depends on the kind of events that happen in our system; moreover, our system is not optimized at all. Security and performance analyses and improvements are the subject of current work. This paper also does not solve the problem of policy deployment, livecycle management, delegation and media breaks (e.g., taking a photograph of the screen).

Our current data flow model is very simple. While it is appropriate for use cases of the kind we presented here, the involved overapproximations quickly lead to a label creep in practice. For instance, at the OS-level, if a process reads a file that contains one tainted bit, then every subsequent output of the process is tainted. We are currently investigating how to adopt McCamant and Ernst's quantitative information flow model [40] as well as dynamic declassification techniques to overcome this problem. The system layers we catered to in this paper do not exhibit indirect information flow caused by control flow; this is, however, the case for runtime systems. We plan to combine static and dynamic analyses at this level to get more precise data flow models for these layers.

In terms of further future work, we need a generic implementation for cross-layer enforcement, a formal model that caters to dependent events at one moment in time, and a way of protecting the enforcement infrastructure that not necessarily inherits the disadvantages of trusted computing technology [9].

Acknowledgments. This work was supported by the DFG under grant no. PR 1266/1-1 as part of the priority program SPP 1496, "Reliably Secure Software Systems." Florian Kelbert provided valuable comments.

References

1. Lovat, E., Pretschner, A.: Data-centric multi-layer usage control enforcement: A social network example. In: Proceedings of the 16th ACM Symposium on Access Control Models and Technologies, SACMAT 2011, pp. 151–152 (2011)

2. Hilty, M., Pretschner, A., Basin, D., Schaefer, C., Walter, T.: A Policy Language for Distributed Usage Control. In: Biskup, J., López, J. (eds.) ESORICS 2007. LNCS, vol. 4734, pp. 531–546. Springer, Heidelberg (2008)
3. Harvan, M., Pretschner, A.: State-based Usage Control Enforcement with Data Flow Tracking using System Call Interposition. In: Proc. 3rd Intl. Conf. on Network and System Security, pp. 373–380 (2009)
4. Pretschner, A., Buechler, M., Harvan, M., Schaefer, C., Walter, T.: Usage control enforcement with data flow tracking for x11. In: Proc. 5th Intl. Workshop on Security and Trust Management, pp. 124–137 (2009)
5. Schaefer, C., Walter, T., Pretschner, A., Harvan, M.: Usage control policy enforcement in OpenOffice.org and information flow. In: Proc. Annual ISSA (2009)
6. Pretschner, A., Hilty, M., Basin, D., Schaefer, C., Walter, T.: Mechanisms for Usage Control. In: Proc. ACM Symposium on Information, Computer & Communication Security, pp. 240–245 (2008)
7. Leucker, M., Schallhart, C.: A brief account of runtime verification. J. Log. Algebr. Program. 78(5), 293–303 (2009)
8. Hilty, M., Pretschner, A., Basin, D., Schaefer, C., Walter, T.: Monitors for usage control. In: Proc. Trust Management, vol. 238, pp. 411–414 (2007)
9. Neisse, R., Holling, D., Pretschner, A.: Implementing trust in cloud infrastructures. In: CCGrid (2011), http://zvi.ipd.kit.edu
10. Dam, M., Jacobs, B., Lundblad, A., Piessens, F.: Security Monitor Inlining for Multithreaded Java. In: Drossopoulou, S. (ed.) ECOOP 2009. LNCS, vol. 5653, pp. 546–569. Springer, Heidelberg (2009)
11. Ion, I., Dragovic, B., Crispo, B.: Extending the Java Virtual Machine to Enforce Fine-Grained Security Policies in Mobile Devices. In: Proc. Annual Computer Security Applications Conference, pp. 233–242. IEEE Computer Society (2007)
12. Desmet, L., Joosen, W., Massacci, F., Naliuka, K., Philippaerts, P., Piessens, F., Vanoverberghe, D.: The S3MS.NET Run Time Monitor: Tool Demonstration. ENTCS 253(5), 153–159 (2009)
13. Erlingsson, U., Schneider, F.: SASI enforcement of security policies: A retrospective. In: Proc. New Security Paradigms Workshop, pp. 87–95 (1999)
14. Yee, B., Sehr, D., Dardyk, G., Chen, J., Muth, R., Ormandy, T., Okasaka, S., Narula, N., Fullagar, N.: Native Client: A Sandbox for Portable, Untrusted x86 Native Code. In: Proc. IEEE Symposium on Security and Privacy, pp. 79–93 (2009)
15. Gheorghe, G., Neuhaus, S., Crispo, B.: xESB: An Enterprise Service Bus for Access and Usage Control Policy Enforcement. In: Nishigaki, M., Jøsang, A., Murayama, Y., Marsh, S. (eds.) IFIPTM 2010. IFIP AICT, vol. 321, pp. 63–78. Springer, Heidelberg (2010)
16. Egele, M., Kruegel, C., Kirda, E., Yin, H., Song, D.: Dynamic spyware analysis. In: Proceedings of USENIX Annual Technical Conference (June 2007)
17. Adobe livecycle rights management es (August 2010), http://www.adobe.com/products/livecycle/rightsmanagement/indepth.html
18. Microsoft. Windows Rights Management Services (2010), http://www.microsoft.com/windowsserver2008/en/us/ad-rms-overview.aspx
19. Pretschner, A., Hilty, M., Schutz, F., Schaefer, C., Walter, T.: Usage control enforcement: Present and future. IEEE Security & Privacy 6(4), 44–53 (2008)
20. Mantel, H.: Possibilistic definitions of security - an assembly kit. In: IEEE Computer Security Foundations Workshop, p. 185 (2000)
21. Hammer, C., Snelting, G.: Flow-sensitive, context-sensitive, and object-sensitive information flow control based on program dependence graphs. International Journal of Information Security 8, 399–422 (2009), 10.1007/s10207-009-0086-1

22. Luckham, D.C.: The Power of Events: An Introduction to Complex Event Processing in Distributed Enterprise Systems. In: Bassiliades, N., Governatori, G., Paschke, A. (eds.) RuleML 2008. LNCS, vol. 5321, p. 3. Springer, Heidelberg (2008)
23. Pretschner, A., Lovat, E., Büchler, M.: Representation-Independent Data Usage Control. Technical Report 2011,23, Karlsruhe Institute of Technology (August 2011), http://digbib.ubka.uni-karlsruhe.de/volltexte/1000024005
24. Pretschner, A., Rüesch, J., Schaefer, C., Walter, T.: Formal analyses of usage control policies. In: ARES, pp. 98–105 (2009)
25. Havelund, K., Rosu, G.: Efficient monitoring of safety properties. Int. J. Softw. Tools Technol. Transf. 6 (August 2004)
26. Kumari, P., Pretschner, A., Peschla, J., Kuhn, J.M.: Distributed data usage control for web applications: a social network implementation. In: Proc. of 1st ACM Conference on Data and Application Security and Privacy, CODASPY (2011)
27. Efstathopoulos, P., Krohn, M., VanDeBogart, S., Frey, C., Ziegler, D., Kohler, E., Mazières, D., Kaashoek, F., Morris, R.: Labels and event processes in the asbestos operating system. In: Proc. SOSP, pp. 17–30 (2005)
28. Zeldovich, N., Boyd-Wickizer, S., Mazières, D.: Securing distributed systems with information flow control. In: Proc. of NSDI, pp. 293–308 (2008)
29. Enck, W., Gilbert, P., Chun, B., Cox, L., Jung, J., McDaniel, P., Sheth, A.: Taintdroid: An information-flow tracking system for realtime privacy monitoring on smartphones. In: Proc. of USENIX OSDI (2010)
30. Demsky, B.: Garm: cross application data provenance and policy enforcement. In: Proceedings of the 4th USENIX Conference on Hot Topics in Security, HotSec 2009, pages 10. USENIX Association, Berkeley (2009)
31. Rushby, J.: Noninterference, transitivity and channel-control security policies (1992)
32. Goguen, J.A., Meseguer, J.: Security policies and security models. In: Proc. of IEEE Symposium on Security and Privacy, pp. 11–20 (1982)
33. Vachharajani, N., Bridges, M.J., Chang, J., Rangan, R., Ottoni, G., Blome, J.A., Reis, G.A., Vachharajani, M., August, D.I.: Rifle: An architectural framework for user-centric information-flow security. In: Proc. of 37th Annual IEEE/ACM International Symposium on Microarchitecture, MICRO 37, pp. 243–254 (2004)
34. Rissanen, E.: Extensible access control markup language v3.0 (2010), http://docs.oasis-open.org
35. Twidle, K., Lupu, E., Dulay, N., Sloman, M.: Ponder2 - a policy environment for autonomous pervasive systems. In: IEEE International Workshop on Policies for Distributed Systems and Networks (2008)
36. Park, J., Sandhu, R.: The UCON ABC usage control model. ACM Trans. Inf. Syst. Secur. 7(1), 128–174 (2004)
37. Zhang, X., Park, J., Parisi-Presicce, F., Sandhu, R.: A logical specification for usage control. In: SACMAT (2004)
38. Nair, S.K., Tanenbaum, A.S., Gheorghe, G., Crispo, B.: Enforcing drm policies across applications. In: Proceedings of the 8th ACM Workshop on Digital Rights Management, DRM 2008, pp. 87–94. ACM, New York (2008)
39. Gheorghe, G., Mori, P., Crispo, B., Martinelli, F.: Enforcing UCON Policies on the Enterprise Service Bus. In: Meersman, R., Dillon, T., Herrero, P. (eds.) OTM 2010, Part II. LNCS, vol. 6427, pp. 876–893. Springer, Heidelberg (2010)
40. McCamant, S., Ernst, M.D.: Quantitative information flow as network flow capacity. In: PLDI, pp. 193–205 (2008)

Using Personal Portfolios to Manage Customer Data

Aimilia Tasidou and Pavlos S. Efraimidis

Department of Electrical and Computer Engineering,
Democritus University of Thrace,
University Campus, 67100 Xanthi, Greece
{atasidou,pefraimi}@ee.duth.gr

Abstract. Transactions today are conducted in a way that leaves no real option to the customers to protect their privacy. Sensitive private information is left uncontrolled at the companies' disposal and is often (un)intentionally leaked to unauthorized parties. There is a growing demand for privacy-preserving management of private information that will make individuals feel safer during their transactions and assist companies with customer data management. In this work we propose that individuals store and manage their transaction data locally, in a personal portfolio, allowing them to retain control of their private information. Using contemporary cryptographic techniques, companies are given access to the accountable, certified data of portfolios in a privacy-preserving way.

Keywords: Personal Data Management, Privacy Enhancing Technologies, Economics of Privacy.

1 Introduction

During electronic and physical transactions today, users are required to provide their personal information, without being offered the option to carry on with their purchase anonymously. In most e-purchases customers are requested to register, creating a profile with the company, upon which they have no or little control. Even with physical transactions, it is often required that the customers register their information with the shop in order to complete a purchase. Some shops offer membership cards that entitle customers to member privileges and offers. These shopping profiles provide valuable information to interested parties, but can be a significant source of private information leakages. By giving away their personal information, customers often do not realize the dangers their actions entail and the possible impact on their lives (identity theft, discrimination, etc.). All sorts of data collected about an individual can be used against them. The obvious categories are sensitive information like financial or health records, but the collection of GPS data or shopping habits should not be considered risk-free either. Electronic trails can be combined to compose an individual's detailed profile. Companies thrive at exploiting customer transaction data nowadays to an extent never imagined before.

J. Garcia-Alfaro et al. (Eds.): DPM 2011 and SETOP 2011, LNCS 7122, pp. 141–154, 2012.

It is, therefore, important that individuals are protected from unauthorized usage of their information and compensated for the service and profit they offer to legitimate data processing companies, whenever their data is processed. At the same time, service providers require data accountability in order to provide their services.

To address the above requirements we propose an electronic portfolio system that offers utilization and simultaneous protection of individuals' transaction data. We argue that today the enabling technologies exist to create such accountable privacy preserving services, protecting parties from fraud and identity theft. Each individual in the system has a portfolio that is stored locally at their side and contains their transaction history. Interested parties acquire access to the portfolio data in a controlled way and always with the user's consent.

Giving control of the data back to the user raises accountability issues on the accuracy of the data the user reveals to the data collector. By combining contemporary advanced cryptographic techniques to create appropriate transaction protocols, the proposed system provides information accountability while preserving the owner's privacy. The portfolio functionality is supported by an agent-based system where software agents representing users exchange portfolio information according to the users' preferences.

Apart for keeping transaction profiles, the portfolio approach can be used in many other applications. Some characteristic examples are tax records, health records, biographic or even opinion records for statistics and polls. Although each application entails different challenges and requirements, the main requirements remain unchanged:

- Protecting the individual's private information.
- Providing an efficient and accountable method of accessing the portfolio data for legitimate users.
- Offering strong accountability, protecting data processing entities from ill behaving and malicious users.

In this paper we propose and design a shopping portfolio, containing information on individuals' shopping transactions (super market products, electronics, music, services, etc), electronic and physical ones.

Related Work
We first examined the idea of personal information residing at and being controlled by it's owner by designing and implementing the Polis personal data management prototype [11]. The Polis system studied identity management issues and did not handle any transaction history information. We further extended the idea of Polis by introducing the idea that individuals should be compensated when their personal information is used for commercial purposes, while retaining control of their data in FPIT (Fair Personal Information Trades) [18]. The FPIT work focuses primarily on the economic aspects of identity management and the way the information owner is compensated when their personal information is being utilized. In this work we examine the possibility for

privacy-preserving transaction management, utilizing the Polis and FPIT principle that users should remain in charge of their information to handle a different problem.

A major project on personal data management that also uses cryptography to protect personal data is Prime [4]. Prime also studies identity management and the proposed approach is that data is provided to data consumers for them to store under well-defined policies. Within Prime, advanced techniques for privacy policy negotiations and enforcement were designed and implemented. Prime's relation to our work is that it also utilizes cryptographic components as building blocks to construct a privacy-preserving architecture. The PrimeLife project [16] is the successor of Prime, examining lifelong privacy maintainance and privacy protection in emerging Internet applications. An innovative product on personal data management that caught the attention of major companies like IBM and Microsoft is U-Prove [19].

The economic aspects of personal privacy are discussed in [20,2,3]. The value of private information and the fact that individuals need to be in control of the dissemination of their information, as well as be compensated for disclosing it, is discussed in [12]. According to Odlyzko [15], privacy violation stems from the need for price differentiation according to the user's profile. This way service providers can determine how much clients are willing to pay for their services. Although price differentiation is usually perceived as a negative idea, it can be have positive economic and social results as it allows products and services to be sold in profitable prices (on average) for the service seller and advantageous prices for each buyer. Therefore, the availability of the customers' profile is important for service and price personalization, as long as privacy protection is ensured and the information processing is performed with the individuals' control and consent.

A privacy-preserving National Identity Card is proposed in [10], where a smart card is used to store individuals' personal information and allows them to prove binary statements about themselves. The smart card data is inserted from an authority (e.g. the city hall) and does not support adding new data on the card. However some of the enabling technologies used to support the privacy-preserving functions of the card are similar to those used in the portfolio. Cards or Portable devices that record individuals' actions regarding taxes, identification or health information are being introduced into everyday life in order to offer quick and reliable data recording and utilization. These profiles need to be protected while retaining their usability. Accountable privacy preserving services need to be used to facilitate this goal.

In this work we utilize contemporary advanced cryptographic techniques to propose an information portfolio that acts towards the benefit of the individual. The proposed idea can be implemented using existing hardware and technologies, leading to applications that can enhance user privacy protection in everyday practice.

Paper Outline

In Section 2 we introduce the basic concepts and architecture of the portfolio, explaining the main entities and components, as well as the requirements of the proposed functionality. In Section 3 we describe the protocols that enable portfolio operations and the building blocks used to achieve the desired protocol attributes. In Section 4 the conclusions of this work are presented and possible future work is discussed.

2   Portfolio Concepts and Architecture

In this Section we first present the motivation of this work, the main concepts and definitions of the portfolio approach. Subsequently, the proposed architecture is presented and the requirements of its functionality are discussed.

2.1   Problem Statement - Privacy Preserving Transactions

Personal privacy during physical and electronic transactions is not being protected today. Customer profiles containing individuals' sensitive information are created and stored outside the information owners' control. Even when given the choice, customers often have to choose between gaining customer privileges and giving up their privacy or protecting their privacy and losing customer privileges. Such examples are the profiles that track customer transactions in super markets in exchange for personalized offers and discounts.

We believe that accountable privacy-preserving services are needed to increase customer trust in everyday transactions and allow for privacy-supporting utilization of their data. Following the principle of least information [7], customers should be able to perform transactions in a way that only the necessary information about them is revealed to the service provider and preferably remain anonymous. Service providers on the other side, should be able to utilize the transaction information of their customers to draw useful conclusions about their products, without violating customer privacy. It would be even better if companies could acquire access to accountable transaction data besides their own to derive general market trends and patterns, compensating the data owners for their service.

In order to address this issue, we propose a distributed architecture, described in the following sections, where users keep their transaction information in a local portfolio, managed by software agents. Shops are only allowed to keep anonymized information about their client transactions; no customer profile information should be maintained.

2.2   Portfolio Definition and Architecture

The main idea of the portfolio approach is the following:

A user's portfolio contains the user's transaction history. The portfolio is stored at the owner's side and is managed by a software agent that allows access to the portfolio information under well-defined rules.

Using the portfolio functionality, the individual's transactions are recorded in their portfolio. Data consumers can acquire controlled access to specific information from the individual's portfolio with their consent. Although the focus of this work is primarily on privacy preserving transaction history management, some identity management issues also arise. While individuals use anonymous credentials during their transactions, we propose the storage of the individual's Personal Identifiable Information in the portfolio as well, in order to use demographic data to support the filtering of data based on such fields (e.g. shopping records for women of age 30 to 40). The possible conclusions that can be drawn about the individual's identity from the retrieved data is a separate, very interesting problem, also discussed in [13].

The entities that interact in the portfolio system are the following:

- The individual who owns a portfolio (I) and acts as a customer during transactions.
- Shops and service providers that the individuals perform transactions with (S), e.g., super markets and e-shops.
- Companies that act as data consumers, interested in acquiring data from a users' portfolios (C).
- An identity provider that issues credentials to the portfolio users (IDP).
- A notarization service that supports verification of the integrity of the portfolio data (N).
- A notice board that is used to post public information about portfolios and support retrieval operations by data consumers.

The identity provider and the notarization service are considered trusted third parties. Individuals, shops and companies are all considered portfolio users (U). Software agents, i.e., software that acts on behalf of the user, manage the users' portfolios. This means that they act as always-on local services which represent the users and allow for the communications and the data exchanges between the participants.

Understandably, in some cases a service provider can also be a data consumer interested in acquiring access to portfolio data. For example, such a case could be a super market wanting access to all coffee-related transactions of individuals between ages 25-35, in order to detect correlations between products. However, in general the service provider and data consumer entities are different. There can be shops that are not interested in transaction data management, but individuals would like to import their transactions with them into their portfolio. Additionally there can be data processing companies that do not perform any transactions with the individuals and are only interested in transaction data mining.

Portable devices are used to facilitate physical transactions. We assume that any portable computing device, such as a PDA, smartphone or tablet, able to perform basic computation and storage tasks is suitable for this role.

The main system components are the following:

- The portfolio $P_j=\{T_i, T_{i+1}, ...\}$ that belongs to an individual, where i is the transaction id number and j is the portfolio version id.
- The software agent (A_u) of user u, representing the user in the system and controlling access to the user's portfolio data.

The critical resource within the portfolio system is the transaction (T_i) between an individual and a shop, which is stored into the individual's portfolio, where i is the transaction id number in the portfolio database. The transaction (T_i) also constitutes the system's information unit. An individual's portfolio contains and manages a set of transactions and a transaction is the least amount of information that enters the portfolio.

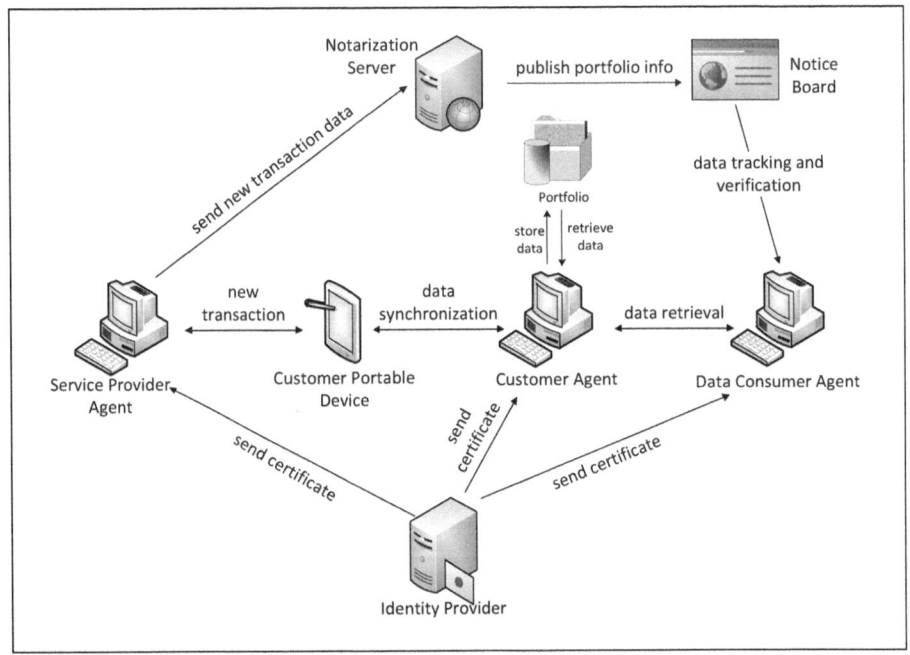

Fig. 1. The Portfolio Architecture

The portfolio system architecture is presented in Fig. 1, where the portfolio entities and their interactions are illustrated. The two main operations of the portfolio are data insertion during new transactions and data retrieval by data consumers. Transaction data is created during new transactions between a service provider and a customer, and is stored into the customer's porfolio, either directly form the customer's portfolio agent during electronic transactions, or using a portable device during physical transactions and then synchronizing the data with the portfolio agent. During new transactions the notarization server is informed of the new transaction and relevant information is published onto the notice board. Transaction data is retrieved by a data consumer agent from an individual's agent. Data verification is performed by querying the notice board. These operations and the protocols for them will be described and analyzed in Section 3.

2.3   Requirements

Before developing the actual protocols for the portfolio operations, we need to identify their main functional, privacy and accountability requirements. These requirements will be addressed later on by utilizing and combining appropriate cryptographic techniques (analyzed in Section 3.1).

The main functional requirements of the portfolio operations are:

- There exist a function that allows the insertion of new transaction data in the portfolio.
- There exist a function that allows the retrieval of transaction data from the portfolio.
- The above functions are practical and efficient.

The main privacy requirements of the portfolio operations are:

- Customer privacy is preserved while transaction information is retrieved.
- The notarization service cannot determine the contents of the portfolio or the identity of its owner (oblivious transactions, anonymity).
- Shops do not keep any other information about their customers, apart from anonymous transaction information. This requires for secure anonymity: untraceability of communication and unlinkability of sessions between the shop, the notarization service and the individual.

The main accountability requirements of the portfolio operations are:

- Individuals cannot tamper with the portfolio data. Data integrity needs to be ensured.
- The returned results of a data consumer query contain all the relevant transactions that exist in the latest version of the portfolio.

3   Privacy Preserving Protocols

To address the above requirements we examine the use of the following building blocks based on cryptographic primitives. We believe that their attributes, appropriately combined, adequately fulfill the portfolio architecture requirements and can be used to design the portfolio operation protocols.

3.1   Portfolio Building Blocks

In the following paragraphs, the building blocks used to construct the portfolio operations and protocols are briefly described focusing on their functionality and attributes.

Private Credentials
Anonymous credential systems allow users to acquire credentials and demonstrate them without revealing their identity. Using the privacy credential system described in [9], individuals can use different unlinkable pseudonyms with each service provider they interact with, based on the same credential issued for their portfolio by the identity provider. The private credential system can also provide certified attributes by the identity provider, for the individual to selectively reveal attributes (e.g. their age range, based on their date of birth). Anonymity revocation is also supported by the private credential system, allowing identities of ill-behaving users to be revealed under well-specified conditions. The private credential system apart from users who receive credentials and the certification authority that verifies user public-private key pairs, comprises of organizations which grant user credentials, verifiers who verify them and an anonymity revocation manager that allows revocable anonymity. We use private credentials as a "black box" component in the portfolio architecture, therefore we will not go into the details of its functionality. The ideal system offers unforgeability of credentials, anonymity of users, unlinkability of credential showings and consistency of credentials [8].

Public Key Encryption with Keyword Search (PEKS)
PEKS [6] allows for keyword searches within encrypted data. Using PEKS the transactions within the portfolio database can be encrypted with the owner's public key and retrieval of specific transactions can be achieved using the PEKS keywords of the transactions as search trapdoors. The PEKS keywords of transactions (which are encrypted and do not reveal any information on their own) can be posted on the notice board and be used during the retrieval process to track and verify transaction data.

Unlike private credentials, PEKS functions are incorporated into the portfolio protocols, therefore we will briefly describe and explain them in the portfolio context. Supposing that we want to store an encrypted transaction T_i with keywords $W_1, \ldots, W_k$, the following entry is created:

$$[E_{I_{pub}}(T_i), PEKS(I_{pub}, W_1), ..., PEKS(I_{pub}, W_k)] \tag{1}$$

where $E_{I_{pub}}(T_i)$ denotes the encryption function (E) of transaction i (T_i) with the individual's public key (I_{pub}), and $PEKS(I_{pub}, W_k)$ denotes the generation of the searchable encryption of keyword W_k with the individuals' public key (I_{pub}) using the PEKS algorithm. The PEKS values do not reveal any information about the transactions, but enable searching for specific keywords.

Apart from the public-private key pair generation algorithm and the PEKS searchable encryption generation algorithm, the public key encryption with keyword search scheme also consists of the following algorithms:

- Trapdoor(I_{priv},W): given the individual's private key and a word W produces a trapdoor Tr_W.
- Test(I_{pub}, S, Tr_W): given the individual's public key, a searchable encryption $S = PEKS(I_{pub}, W_k)$, and a trapdoor $Tr_W = Trapdoor(I_{priv}, W)$, produces a positive output if $W = W_k$ and a negative otherwise.

The basic PEKS work [6] does not deal with the issue of the trapdoor for a certain keyword being stored and reused by the searcher. This fact does not pose a significant threat to the portfolio application, as the trapdoors are used by data consumers for data verification purposes and not for data retrieval (see Section 3.2). However, subsequent works propose some solutions for this problem [1,5]. The proposed solutions contain the use of time-limited keywords and trapdoors, that expire after a certain period of time.

Audit Logs - Tamper Detection
Audit logs and tamper detection mechanisms [17], can be used within the portfolio in order to ensure data accountability. Individuals should not be able to alter, remove or hide transactions from their portfolio, thus presenting invalid profile attributes. The notarization service is introduced in the architecture to serve towards this end.

Apart from removing transactions from the portfolio, users are prohibited from tampering with the transaction contents themselves by using digital signatures. The transactions are signed by both the service provider and the individual at the time of the transaction, ensuring their integrity. Additionally, using a cryptographically strong one-way hash function, the hash value of the transaction is computed. This value is then sent to the notarization service where a notary ID is calculated and sent back to the portfolio agent. This process allows for tamper detection of the portfolio contents in case the portfolio data integrity is questioned. If the transaction contents are altered in any way, their hash value will not match the one used to produce the notary ID and the inconsistency will be revealed.

3.2   Portfolio Protocols

Two protocols were designed to complement agent interaction in the portfolio system. The first is the "transaction insertion protocol" (Fig.2), that defines the way new transaction records are added in the individual's portfolio when they conduct new transactions. The second is the "data retrieval protocol" (Fig.3), that describes the data retrieval process when a company tries to access specific information from a portfolio. Both protocols achieve the desired functionality, while offering privacy protection and information accountability. The protocols are discussed and analysed in the following paragraphs.

Adding a new transaction to the portfolio
A new transaction is inserted in an individual's portfolio according to the following protocol:

1. When an individual makes a new transaction (T_i) with a shop, the shop signs it, creating $Sg_s(T_i)$, where Sg_s denotes the signature of the shop, and sends it to the individual.
2. The individual verifies the contents of the transaction (T_i) and signs it creating $Sg_I[Sg_s(T_i)]$, stores it and sends it back to the service provider, along

with the relevant PEKS keywords of the transaction: PEKS(I_{pub}, W_1), ...,
PEKS(I_{pub}, W_n). The key used for the creation of the PEKS keywords is
not part of the credentials used for the interaction with the service provider,
but a specific set of keys used for the generation of the PEKS keywords and
trapdoors.

3. The shop calculates the transaction's hash value $H(Sg_I[Sg_S(T_i)])$, using a
cryptographically strong one-way hash function and sends it to the notarization service, along with the PEKS keywords of the transaction.

4. The notarization service calculates the notary ID on the received hash value,
stores the transaction hash value and its relevant keywords and sends the
notary ID to the individual's portfolio agent.

5. The notarization service publishes the transaction hash value and its keywords on the notice board, to be used later by data consumers for verification.

We accept that the PEKS keywords created by the individual during step 2
derive from the products the customer bought, for example beer, sugar, dvd, etc
and possibly the date of the transaction in standard format. It would be useful
to ensure consistency of used terms, in order to facilitate the retrieval process.
Therefore, the systems could be aided by a common, agreed upon vocabulary or
an appropriate ontology representing knowledge of the domain and organizing
information, like the WordNet lexical ontology [14].

There is an issue of the individual not creating valid PEKS keywords or all the
PEKS keywords for the transaction. For the transaction portfolio scenario this
is not a major problem, as the user does not really have an incentive to do so.
Declaration of false keywords will be revealed when the transaction data is sent
to the data consumer. Omission of keywords is not to the individual's benefit,
as the keywords are the means through which they acquire benefits by proving
some attributes regarding their buying habits. Even if some individuals decided

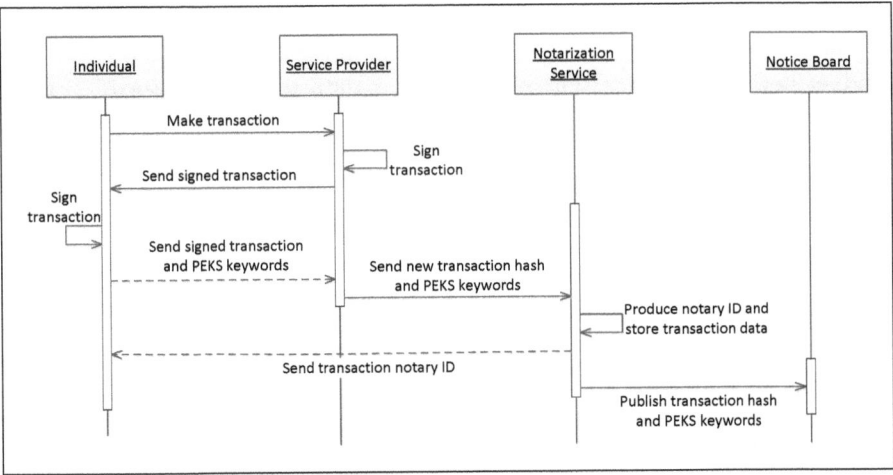

Fig. 2. Transaction Insertion Protocol

to omit some keywords from transactions, this would not be a major threat to the system functionality. However, in other applications of the portfolio, like in health records, it is critical that all the keywords are declared for the PEKS functionality. We plan to examine the possibility of the service provider/organization checking the validity of the keywords provided by the individual.

Data retrieval Protocol

Given an individual's portfolio containing transaction records, we design the following protocol in order for a company to retrieve data on specific transactions:

1. The company contacts the portfolio agent, stating the keywords they are interested in. The portfolio agent sends the Trapdoors of those keywords to the company.
2. The company queries the notice board on the PEKS keywords they are interested in, using the received Trapdoors. The returned results, produced using the PEKS Test algorithm, determine the relevant transactions by returning the hash values of the transactions that contain those keywords.
3. The company requests these transactions from the portfolio agent, sending the hash values of the transactions returned from the notice board query.
4. The portfolio agent sends the transaction data to the data consumer. This data is anonymous and the data consumer is not allowed to store it for further use. Appropriate policies and licenses can be used to define the terms of use for the received data.

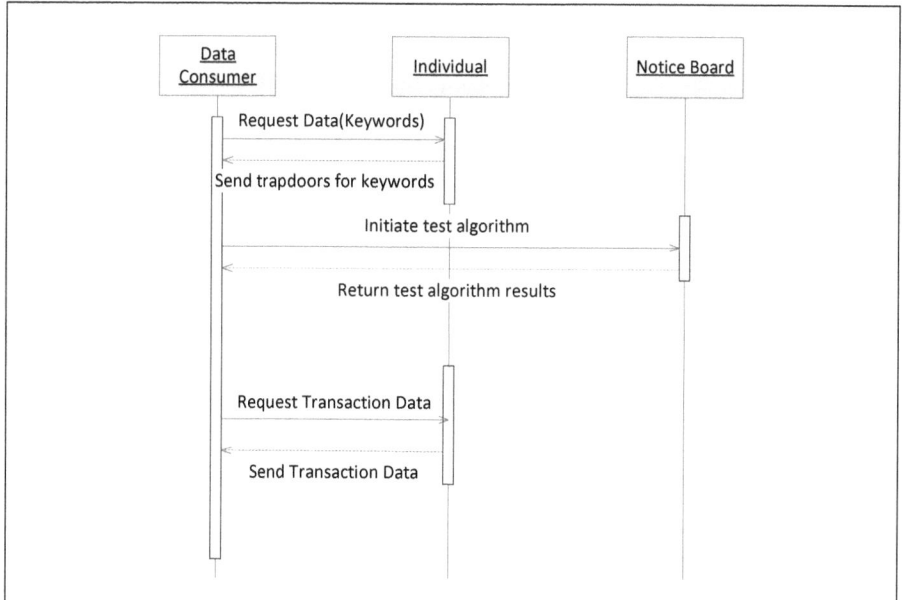

Fig. 3. Data Retrieval Protocol

An alternative data retrieval protocol could omit the notice board query described in step 2 and have the company directly request the transactions regarding specific keywords from the portfolio agent. After receiving the data from the portfolio agent the company can optionally verify the received information by submitting the query described in step 2 and matching the returned results to the provided received portfolio data.

The contact details of a portfolio agent can be retrieved either from the notice board or from individuals themselves. For example, a possible scenario is an individual wishing to show previous purchases of certain products to a super market, in order to prove eligibility for special offers and prices.

4   Discussion and Conclusions

Data mining of customer data is a popular method of extracting valuable information to serve commercial interests. Patterns of customer behavior and habits can provide valuable insights to companies on how to promote their products and handle their customer relationships. Loyalty cards are today a common way for companies to acquire customer transaction data in exchange for personalized prices and offers. These profiles often contain customer Personal Identifiable Information and can be used to extract sensitive information about a person's attributes, habits and beliefs.

In this work we propose an alternative approach to the way customer data is handled by moving the control of the transaction profile to the customer. We believe that the availability of contemporary cryptographic techniques allows for today's paradigm to change and offers increased data protection and simultaneously an opportunity for trustworthy utilization of transaction data, in a way that can be usable with the existing common infrastructure. The proposed system is constructed from existing and efficient building blocks, therefore we believe that it will be adequately efficient. However, it remains for future work to thoroughly examine the implementation possibilities and adjust the system's efficiency.

We expect that this new paradigm will appeal to individuals, whose personal information will be protected, as well as well-meaning companies interested in processing transaction data without the risk of violating the customer's privacy. Our approach allows for shops and service providers to retain anonymized information on transactions individuals conducted with them, relieving them from the responsibility of protecting their customers' data. Additionally, companies are given the opportunity to legitimately access entire transaction profiles of individuals, containing transactions with multiple shops and thus acquiring access to more information for processing. On the other hand, individuals retain control of their transaction information and are able to provide controlled access to it, whenever they choose. Motives for doing so contain special offers and privileges based on the individual's profile, or even integration with a compensation system like FPIT [18]. A real world adoption of the proposed approach does not depend only on its technical feasibility, but mainly on the attitude of the individuals and data protection authorities, who need to demand better privacy-preserving services and stricter privacy regulations.

The issue of enforcing prohibition of storage of the retrieved data by the data consumer also depends on the existence of strict privacy regulations. However, the proposed system is to some extent protected from misuse. The retrieved transaction data will no longer be useful to data consumers once they become out of date. The only way to get access to new, updated information is through the portfolio system. Additionally, data processing entities should be able to prove the legitimate acquisition of their data. The use of policies and licenses like the ones used in Polis [11] could be introduced in the system, in order to better regulate the conditions under which access to transaction data is granted.

4.1 Future Work

In this work we describe the main concepts and operations of the portfolio approach without going into detailed description of the implementation of the portfolio functionality. Future work entails determining the specifics of every aspect of the portfolio functionality, considering a threat model for the system and possibly implementing a prototype or simulation of the proposed approach. In this context, the portfolio protocols could be further enhanced and expanded. Possible extensions include the support of distributed computations directly by the portfolio agent to relieve the notice board of some of its work, as well as the examination of protocols for introducing the portfolio into the Cloud.

Another possible future task is the integration of the portfolio system with a compensation system for private information like FPIT [18], to enable controlled exchanges regarding portfolio data, that provide fair compensation to the data owner. Appropriate policies and licenses will be added to the system to improve misuse detection and prohibition.

The use of the portfolio approach in other contexts, like health records, tax records, etc, or the design of a general portfolio that can handle any or all of these types of information is another interesting extension of this work.

Acknowledgments. This work was performed in the framework of and partially funded by the GSRT/CO-OPERATION/SPHINX Project (09SYN-72-419) (http://sphinx.vtrip.net) and the GSRT research grant 09SYN-62-1129, 'myVisitPlanner'. The authors would also like to thank Vasilis Katos for his helpful ideas regarding the portfolio concept and applications and Remous-Aris Koutsiamanis for his support and help during the writing of this paper.

References

1. Abdalla, M., Bellare, M., Catalano, D., Kiltz, E., Kohno, T., Lange, T., Malone-Lee, J., Neven, G., Paillier, P., Shi, H.: Searchable Encryption Revisited: Consistency Properties, Relation to Anonymous IBE, and Extensions. In: Shoup, V. (ed.) CRYPTO 2005. LNCS, vol. 3621, pp. 205–222. Springer, Heidelberg (2005)

2. Acquisti, A.: Privacy and security of personal information: Technological solutions and economic incentives. In: Camp, J., Lewis, R. (eds.) The Economics of Information Security, pp. 165–178. Kluwer (2004)
3. Anderson, R., Moore, T.: The economics of information security. Science 314(5799), 610 (2006)
4. Ardagna, C.A., Camenisch, J., Kohlweiss, M., Leenes, R., Neven, G., Priem, B., Samarati, P., Sommer, D., Verdicchio, M.: Exploiting cryptography for privacy-enhanced access control: A result of the PRIME project. Journal of Computer Security 18(1), 123–160 (2010)
5. Baek, J., Safavi-Naini, R., Susilo, W.: Public Key Encryption with Keyword Search Revisited. In: Gervasi, O., Murgante, B., Laganà, A., Taniar, D., Mun, Y., Gavrilova, M.L. (eds.) ICCSA 2008, Part I. LNCS, vol. 5072, pp. 1249–1259. Springer, Heidelberg (2008)
6. Boneh, D., Di Crescenzo, G., Ostrovsky, R., Persiano, G.: Public Key Encryption with Keyword Search. In: Cachin, C., Camenisch, J.L. (eds.) EUROCRYPT 2004. LNCS, vol. 3027, pp. 506–522. Springer, Heidelberg (2004)
7. Camenisch, J., Groß, T., Heydt-Benjamin, T.: Accountable privacy supporting services. Identity in the Information Society 2(3), 241–267 (2009)
8. Camenisch, J.L., Lysyanskaya, A.: An Efficient System for Non-transferable Anonymous Credentials with Optional Anonymity Revocation. In: Pfitzmann, B. (ed.) EUROCRYPT 2001. LNCS, vol. 2045, pp. 93–118. Springer, Heidelberg (2001)
9. Camenisch, J., Pfitzmann, B.: Federated identity management. In: Petković, M., Jonker, W. (eds.) Security, Privacy, and Trust in Modern Data Management, pp. 213–238. Springer, Heidelberg (2007)
10. Deswarte, Y., Gambs, S.: A proposal for a privacy-preserving national identity card. Transactions on Data Privacy 3(3), 253–276 (2010)
11. Efraimidis, P.S., Drosatos, G., Nalbadis, F., Tasidou, A.: Towards privacy in personal data management. Information Management and Computer Security (IMCS) 17(4), 311–329 (2009)
12. Kleinberg, J., Papadimitriou, C.H., Raghavan, P.: On the value of private information. In: Proceedings of the 8th Conference on Theoretical Aspects of Rationality and Knowledge, pp. 249–257. Morgan Kaufmann Publishers Inc. (2001)
13. Lindell, Y., Pinkas, B.: Secure multiparty computation for privacy-preserving data mining. Journal of Privacy and Confidentiality 1(21), 59–98 (2009), http://repository.cmu.edu/jpc/vol1/iss1/5
14. Miller, G.A.: Wordnet: a lexical database for english. Commun. ACM 38, 39–41 (1995)
15. Odlyzko, A.: Privacy, economics, and price discrimination on the internet. In: Proceedings of the 5th International Conference on Electronic Commerce, pp. 355–366. ACM (2003)
16. PrimeLife. Bringing sustainable privacy and identity management to future networks and services, http://www.primelife.eu
17. Snodgrass, R.T., Yao, S.S., Collberg, C.: Tamper detection in audit logs. In: VLDB 2004, pp. 504–515 (2004)
18. Tasidou, A., Efraimidis, P.S., Katos, V.: Economics of personal data management: Fair personal information trades. In: Sideridis, A.B., Patrikakis, C.Z. (eds.) Next Generation Society. Technological and Legal Issues, vol. 26, ch. 14, pp. 151–160. Springer, Heidelberg (2010)
19. U-Prove, http://www.credentica.com/
20. Varian, H.: Economic aspects of personal privacy. U.S. Dept. of Commerce, Privacy and Self-Regulation in the Information Age (1996)

Using Requirements Engineering in an Automatic Security Policy Derivation Process

Mariem Graa[1,3], Nora Cuppens-Boulahia[1], Fabien Autrel[1], Hanieh Azkia[1], Frédéric Cuppens[1], Gouenou Coatrieux[2], Ana Cavalli[3], and Amel Mammar[3]

[1] Télécom-Bretagne, 2 Rue de la Châtaigneraie, 35576 Cesson Sévigne, France
[2] Télécom-Bretagne, 655 Avenue du technople, 29200 Brest, France
[3] Télécom SudParis, 9 Rue Charles Fourier 91011 Evry Cedex, France

Abstract. Traditionally, a security policy is defined from an informal set of requirements, generally written using natural language. It is then difficult to appreciate the compatibility degree of the manually generated security policy with the informal requirements definition. The idea of this paper is to automate the process of deriving the formal security policy, using a more structured specification of the security objectives issued by the administrator of the information system to be secured. We chose the goal-oriented methodology KAOS to express the functional objectives, then based on the results of a risk analysis, we integrate the security objectives to the obtained KAOS framework. Finally, through a process of transformation applied to this structured security objectives specification, we automatically generate the corresponding security policy. This policy is consistent with the access control model OrBAC (Organization Access Control).

Keywords: requirement engineering, security policy, KAOS, OrBAC.

1 Introduction

Millions of dollars of losses are the result of attacks on unsecured systems and software of poor quality, easily exploitable by hackers. The percentage of vulnerabilities has increased significantly. The CERT Coordination Center (Carnegie Mellon University) has listed more than six thousand of such vulnerabilities between January and September 2010. Therefore, software security is still a major problem in practice. It affects not only financial aspects but also human issues like in the case where the management of emergency ambulances, due to misunderstanding of requirements, has resulted in several deaths [10]. For these reasons, it is an important objective in the development of software to produce secure systems. In order to achieve this goal and avoid the high impact of software vulnerabilities, it is necessary to specify security requirements early in the initial phases of the development process. Several studies demonstrate that the correction of defects of requirements engineering costs from 10 to 200 times more than when they are detected during the development of the requirements. Since the efforts required to correct such errors are very important [13], it is necessary

J. Garcia-Alfaro et al. (Eds.): DPM 2011 and SETOP 2011, LNCS 7122, pp. 155–172, 2012.

to develop methods and tools to elucidate, validate and represent adequately and structurally the needs related to developed systems. It is the goal that was set by engineering needs. The requirements engineering (RE) is the activity that transforms a vague idea into a precise specification of needs, requirements expressed by a community of users so it defines the relationship between a system and its environment. There are two kinds of needs, i) a functional requirement is what the system should do and ii) a non-functional requirement (NFRs) specifies under what constraints the system must satisfy (safety, security, accuracy, performance, etc.). Security requirements are neglected by the traditional RE. Thus, the community of security and the community of RE invest more and more methods and techniques to integrate and/or adapt the requirements of security in the initial process of the RE but they cannot achieve optimal solutions. Security requirements are generally expressed by security rules which constitute a security policy. They generally conform to a security model (BLP [17], RBAC [3], OrBAC [14], ...). However, although the expression of this policy is based on a formal model the process which leads to the policy specification has always been informal. In this paper, we propose to formalize this process which generates the formal security policy from the security objectives.

This paper is organized as follows. Section 2 discusses related work. Section 3 overviews the derivation of formal security policy process. Section 4 introduces the OrBAC model into which security requirements are translated. Section 5 details the formal specification of requirements. Section 6 explains extraction of the specification of the security requirements. Section 7 describes the generation of security policies. Section 8 demonstrates the approach with a case study. Finally, Section 9 concludes with an outline of future work.

2   Security Requirements and Related Work

Appropriate management of security requirements plays an essential role in the success or the failure of systems. The chances of success for the software system are maximized when they are modeled from the initial phases of the development process. Many interests are dedicated to the development and analysis of security requirements. For example, *"The CC (common criteria) permits the comparability between the results of independent security evaluations. The CC does so by providing a common set of requirements for the security functionality of IT products and for assurance measures applied to these IT products during a security evaluation"* [2]. So, the integration of standard CC in the requirements engineering process occurs in three steps: (1) analyzing all possible threats to which the system is exposed, (2) identifying security objectives which can respond to these threats and (3) selecting the CC functional components to specify the security requirements that meet the system security objectives. Misuse cases [12,11] are other approaches, based on UML, to handle NFRs such as security requirements. They are a special kind of use cases that are used to analyze and specify security threats concentrate on interactions between the application and those who seek to violate its security. In [12], the authors develop a misuse based method to derive detailed NFRs. The authors argue that the analysis of NFRs in terms of assets, threats, misuses and countermeasures help to complement software and project requirements.

Since the success criteria for a misuse case is a successful attack against an application, misuse cases are effective ways of analyzing security threats but are inappropriate for the analysis and specification of security requirements [1,19]. After discussing the relationships between misuse cases, security use cases, and security mechanisms, [11] provide examples and guidelines for properly specifying essential (requirements-level) security use cases. The Anti-Models [21] is a method based on the goal-oriented framework KAOS for generating and resolving obstacles to goal satisfaction. The extended framework addresses malicious obstacles (called anti-goals) set up by attackers to threaten security goals. Threat trees are built systematically through anti-goal refinement until leaf nodes are derived that are either software vulnerabilities observable by the attacker or anti-requirements implementable by this attacker. New security requirements are then obtained as countermeasures by application of threat resolution operators to the specification of the anti requirements and vulnerabilities revealed by the analysis. It also introduces formal epistemic specification constructs and patterns that may be used to support a formal derivation and analysis process. Requirements are expressed in Sysml in textual form, and the semantic of the relations between requirements is not precise and can lead to ambiguities. The authors of [15] noted that these drawbacks can be alleviated by extending Sysml with the KAOS model. But KAOS does not allow representing explicit non-functional needs such as security requirements. Non-functional needs in KAOS are taken into account at the level of system architecture design. [15] proposes an extension to the KAOS method to represent the non-functional needs at the same level as functional needs.

Our work is compliant with the CC approach and is based on Anti-Models for the derivation of security requirements. The CC method allows generating complete results that are easy to analyze. The Anti-Models approach ensures that application-specific security requirements are made explicit, precise, adequate, non-conflicting with other requirements and complete.

In order to determine security requirements, a risk analysis of the information system or software is needed. It is used to identify threats, vulnerabilities, environmental assumptions, like attack scenarios, constraints, and results in the establishment of an aversion matrix grouping the whole set of security properties that are expected from the system and their degree of criticality. There are several choices of risk analysis method like OCTAVE[1], EBIOS[2], MEHARI[3] or CRAMM[4]. We adopt the EBIOS risk analysis method [8], which meets the

---

[1] http://www.cert.org/octave/

[2] http://www.ssi.gouv.fr/en/the-anssi/publications-109/methods-to-achieve-iss/ebios-2010-expression-of-needs-and-identification-of-security-objectives.html

[3] https://www.clusif.asso.fr/en/production/mehari/

[4] http://www.cramm.com/

criteria of simplicity, free distribution of the support tool, goals orientation and stays in the spirit of KAOS.

3   Derivation of Formal Security Policy Process

Our process is essentially based on four phases illustrated in figure 1:

- *EBIOS risk analysis of the information system or software which we intend to specify the security policy.* It identifies threats, vulnerabilities, environmental assumptions, potential attacks scenarios, constraints and results in the establishment of an aversion matrix that gathers all the expected security properties of the system and their degree of criticality.
- *KAOS specification of the considered system which takes into account the first phase to integrate and differentiate security objectives.* It will be refined to derive the requirements of the target system. A KAOS XML file related to functional and non functional requirements will be generated (Requirement Acquisition phase in figure 1).
- *Extraction of the security requirements specification from the target system specification defined in the previous phase.* The XML output file contains only the security requirements specification (Requirement Extraction phase in figure 1).
- *Formal security policy generation.* The KAOS security specification of the target system is transmitted to an OrBAC Translator wich generates an XML OrBAC file. Then, MotOrBAC (a tool designed to handle and manage OrBAC policies) uses this XML file to generate the formal security policy (KAOS to OrBAC Translation phase in figure 1).

The next section introduces the OrBAC model that has been chosen as a target model to translate KAOS security requirements into a formal security policy.

4   The OrBAC Model

OrBAC [14] aims at modelling a security policy centered on the organization which defines it or manages it. Intuitively, an organization is any entity responsible for managing a security policy. An OrBAC policy specification is done at the organizational level, also called the abstract level, and is implementation-independent. The enforced policy, called the concrete policy, is inferred from the abstract policy. This approach makes all the policies expressed in the OrBAC model reproducible and scalable. Actually once the concrete policy is inferred, no modification or tuning has to be done on the inferred policy since it would possibly introduce inconsistencies. Everything is done at the abstract policy specification level. The inferred concrete policy expresses security rules using subjects, actions and objects. The abstract policy, specified at the organizational level, is specified using *roles*, *activities* and *views* which respectively abstract the concrete subjects, actions and objects.

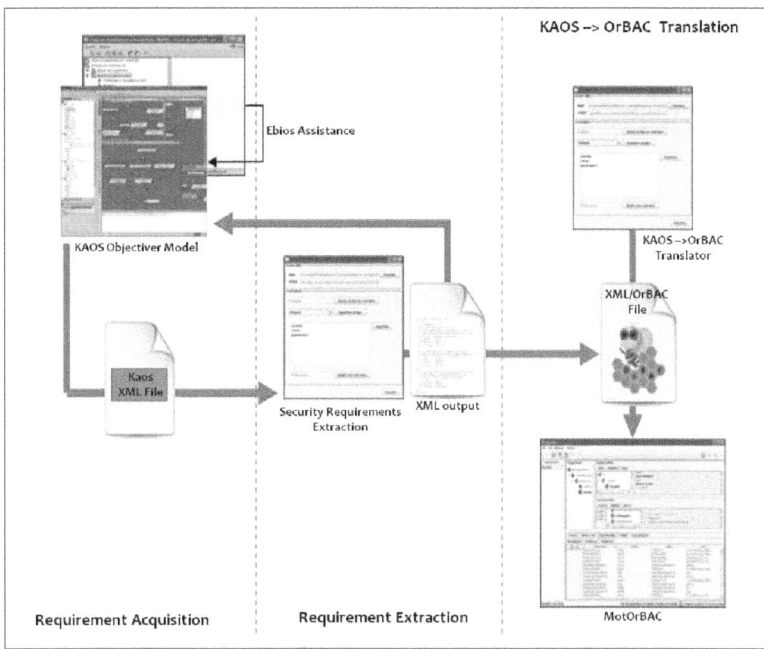

Fig. 1. The KAOS target elements for the extraction of formal security requirements

The OrBAC model uses a first order logic formalism with negation. However since first order logic is generally undecidable, the model is restricted in order to be compatible with a stratified Datalog program [20].

Using this formalism, each organization specifies its own security rules. Some *role* may have the permission, prohibition or obligation to do some *activity* on some *view* given an associated *context* is true. The *context* concept [6] has been introduced in OrBAC in order to express dynamic rules. These security rules are represented using 5-ary and 6-ary predicates:

- *permission*(*org, role, activity, view, context*) means that in organization *org*, *role* is authorized to perform *activity* on *view* if *context* is true.
- the *prohibition* predicate has the same arguments as the *permission* predicate but expresses a prohibition for a role to do an activity on a view in an organization when a context is true.
- *obligation*(*org, role, activity, view, context, violationCtx*): compared to the *permission* and *prohibition* predicates, an obligation has an extra context, the violation context, which expresses the condition, for example a deadline, in which the obligation is violated.

Security rules can be hierarchically structured so that they are inherited through the organization, role, activity and view hierarchies (see [5]).

Once the security policy has been specified at the organizational level, it is possible to test it by assigning concrete entities to abstract entities. To do so, three ternary predicates have been defined to assign a subject to a role, an action to an activity and an object to a view:

- *empower*(*Org*, *Subject*, *Role*): specifies that in organization *Org*, *Subject* is empowered in *Role*.
- *consider*(*Org*, *Action*, *Activity*): specifies that in organization *Org*, *Action* implements *Activity*.
- *use*(*Org*, *Object*, *View*): specifies that in organization *Org*, *Object* is used in *View*.

For example, the fact *empower*(*hospital*, *john*, *surgeon*) states that in the *hospital* organization *john* is empowered in role *surgeon*.

Contexts are defined through logical rules which express the condition that must be true in order for the context to be active. In the OrBAC model such rules have the predicate *hold* in their conclusion:

$$hold(Org, Subject, Action, Object, Context)$$

specifies that in organization *Org*, *Subject* executes *Action* on *Object* in *Context*.

A context definition is expressed into an organization, hence multiple definitions can be expressed for the same context but in different organizations.

The following derivation rule shows how concrete permissions, represented by the *is_permitted* predicate, are derived from abstract permissions:

$$is\_permitted(Subject, Action, Object) : -$$
$$permission(Org, Role, Activity, View, Context),$$
$$empower(Org, Subject, Role),$$
$$consider(Org, Action, Activity),$$
$$use(Org, Object, View),$$
$$hold(Org, Subject, Action, Object, Context).$$

The *is_permitted*(*s*, *a*, *o*) predicate says that subject *s* is authorized to do action *a* on object *o*. Similar rules exist for prohibitions and obligations.

5   Formal Specification of Requirements

The specification phase was conducted by adopting an approach based on the requirements engineering, a branch of software engineering dealing with the goals (or objectives) of the real world, the functions and the constraints of the software system. It manages also the relationships between these factors to determine the specifications of the system and software behaviors and their evolution in time. There exists a dozen of RE methods : GDC, ISAC, i*, NFR, GBRAM, ... and the most well known methodology, KAOS. In comparison to other methods (Kavalki and al in [4] give an assessment of some of them), KAOS is based on easy to use concepts. It is not difficult to introduce security aspects in the original concepts or extend some of them.

5.1   KAOS Goal-Oriented Methodology

KAOS (Knowledge Acquisition in autOmated Specification) [23,16] is a goal-based requirements engineering method which allows analysts to build

requirements models and to derive requirements documents. KAOS is composed
of several sub-models related through inter-model consistency rules:

- *The goal model* is the driving model of KAOS. It declares the goals of the
  composite system. A goal defines an objective which the composite system
  should meet, usually through the cooperation of multiple KAOS agents.
  Goals are different from domain properties which describe statements about
  the environment. They must be refined and specified precisely to support the
  development process. Some of these requirements will be used to generate
  the formal security policy.
- *The object model* declares the objects of interest in the application domain.
  An object is classified as entity, relationship, event or agent depending on
  whether the object is autonomous, subordinate, instantaneous or active. The
  objects and their relationships are elements that will be extracted from the
  model to derive the formal security policy.
- *The agent responsibility model* declares responsibility assignments of goals
  to agents. Agents include the existent software components to be developed
  and external devices and humans in the environment. Responsibility assignment provides a criterion for stopping the goal refinement process. A goal
  assigned to a single agent will not undergo further refinements. Agents and
  the responsibility relationship are used for the generation of the formal security policy.
- *The operation model* sums up all the behaviors that agents need to have
  to fulfill their requirements. Behaviors are expressed in term of operations
  performed by agents. These operations use objects described in the object
  model and are defined through domain pre- and post-conditions. Further
  requirements on operations are necessary to ensure the goals assigned to
  individual agents. Such requirements are specified through required trigger,
  pre- and post-conditions. They are related to the goal they ensure through
  operationalization links. Operations, agents, objects are the elements that
  will be extracted from the model and used to derive the formal security rules.
- *The behavior model* captures the required behaviors of system agents in
  terms of temporal sequences of state transitions for the variables they control.

KAOS includes the concept of goal refinements, which are of two kinds. The
AND refinement generates subgoals which conjunction is sufficient to achieve the
parent goal. The second type of refinement is the OR refinement, that generates
subgoals such that at least one of these subgoals needs to be satisfied for the
parent goal to be achieved. A priority (low, medium, or high) is assigned to each
goal or requirements in KAOS.

KAOS provides an optional formal assertion layer for the specification of goals,
constraints and objects in Real-Time Linear Temporal Logic (RT-LTL). This formalization step [22,7] verifies if the goal refinements are correct and complete
using a theorem prover and formal refinement patterns. Such checking is important in order to detect missing subgoals in incomplete requirements.

KAOS offers several category labels used to classify goals and requirements
(e.g. Accuracy, Adaptability, Capacity, Consistency, Efficiency, Information, etc.),

we focus and use essentially the "security" one in the refinement of goals process to tag the security requirement and ease the extraction procedure. Besides, in KAOS there are four goal patterns: the "achieve" goal pattern, which specifies that a property will be achieved "some time in the future", the "cease" goal pattern, which specifies that, "some time in the future", a property will be disallowed, the "maintain" goal pattern, which specifies that a property must hold "at all times in the future", and the "avoid" goal pattern, which specifies that, "at all times in the future", a property must not hold. The type of security rule is derivable from the links that are pre-established with pattern metadata in the case of security requirements (those assigned a "security" category).

5.2 KAOS Guided by an Analysis of Risk

In the KAOS specification methodology, there is not a real distinction between functional and security aspects. Generally, the requirements for protecting a system are subsidiary. In order to take security into account in KAOS, it is necessary to integrate gradually a risk analysis process. KAOS is neither a risk analysis nor a requirement analysis method. So, the best way to consider security aspect in KAOS is to use a method of risk analysis, which supplies and guides KAOS specification. The output of the risk analysis process helps to identify appropriate controls for reducing or eliminating risks. Risk analysis performs two main activities. The first one is "risk identification" and the second is "risk assessment". The first step includes a series of activities as below:

- Characterization of the system: it specifies authorized functions and provides information about resources (e.g., hardware, software) of the analyzed system.
- Threat identification: In this step, the process looks for probable threats that can affect the system. The common threat can be natural, human, or environmental.
- Vulnerability identification: The goal of this step is to develop a list of system vulnerabilities. It means flaws or weaknesses of system that could be exploited by the potential threat.
- Impact analysis: the consequences or damages that could be caused by an attack scenarios are evaluated in terms of high, medium or low impact on the three common security goals: integrity, availability and confidentiality.
- Control analysis: The goal of this step is to analyze the existing countermeasures which have been implemented by the organization to reduce or remove potential vulnerabilities.

The second step is "risk assessment" which takes as input a list of attack scenarios with their occurrence probability and their consequences on the assets and the organization's processes. The estimated risk is a combination of the likelihood of an attack scenario and its consequences. As output, it defines an aversion matrix containing security properties expected for the system and their risk level value.

In our study, we chose the EBIOS method [8] that meets the criteria of simplicity, maintenance and assured evolution, and goal orientation. According to the diagram showed in figure 2, EBIOS meets all the main steps of the aforementioned generic risk analysis method. It allows expression of requirements and identification of security goals for an existing system and determines security actions that should be undertaken, which, apart from the security aspect, is compliant with KAOS philosophy. In figure 2, we give some simple examples to explain the mapping between KAOS and EBIOS concepts used to integrate the risk analysis and assessment into the goal refinement process.

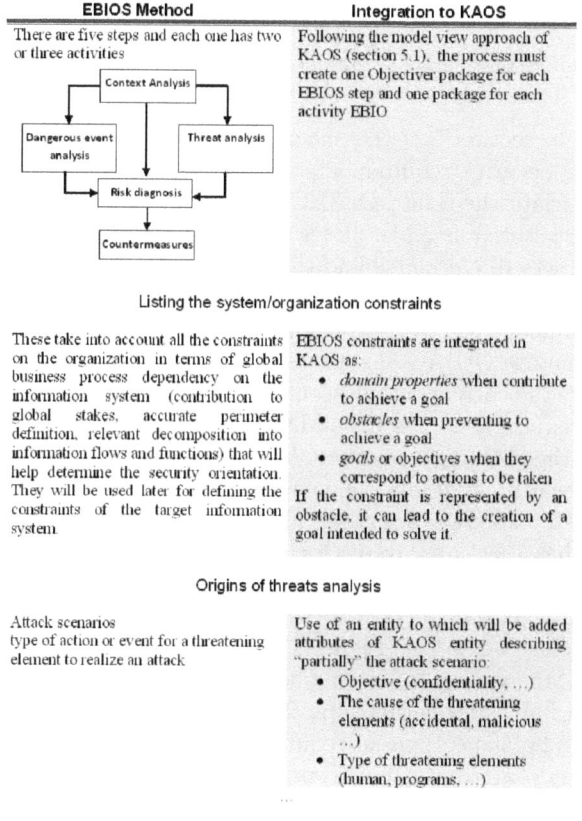

EBIOS Method	Integration to KAOS
There are five steps and each one has two or three activities	Following the model view approach of KAOS (section 5.1), the process must create one Objectiver package for each EBIOS step and one package for each activity EBIO

Listing the system/organization constraints

These take into account all the constraints on the organization in terms of global business process dependency on the information system (contribution to global stakes, accurate perimeter definition, relevant decomposition into information flows and functions) that will help determine the security orientation. They will be used later for defining the constraints of the target information system.	EBIOS constraints are integrated in KAOS as: • *domain properties* when contribute to achieve a goal • *obstacles* when preventing to achieve a goal • *goals* or objectives when they correspond to actions to be taken If the constraint is represented by an obstacle, it can lead to the creation of a goal intended to solve it.

Origins of threats analysis

Attack scenarios type of action or event for a threatening element to realize an attack	Use of an entity to which will be added attributes of KAOS entity describing "partially" the attack scenario: • Objective (confidentiality, ...) • The cause of the threatening elements (accidental, malicious ...) • Type of threatening elements (human, programs, ...)

Fig. 2. EBIOS/KAOS

6   Security Requirements Extraction

We have used the Objectiver [18] tool to apply the KAOS methodology. Objectiver is a requirement engineering tool implementing the KAOS methodology which can be used to identify project requirements, create models that take user agents and the system environment into account, represent user scenarios, model business processes and workflows and produce structured requirements documents. Objectiver can save requirements files in two formats, binary and XML. Since the two formats are not documented, we have chosen the XML format in order to understand how requirements are stored. Figure 3 shows a security requirement part of an Objectiver XML requirement file.

```
<C id="1286526578515:4422" n="Maintain network connection security"
                        p="MM.xml#Method:NewKaos2003:MetaModel:Requirement" t="E">
    <AV n="Name" v="Maintain network connection security"/>
    <AV n="Pattern" v="Maintain"/>
    <AV n="Category" v="Security"/>
</C>
```

Fig. 3. Example of security requirement recorded in an Objectiver XML file

As specified in section 5.1, the *security* category is used in the refinement of a goal to tag security requirements. Those requirements must be extracted in order to translate them into OrBAC abstract security policy rules. Security requirements are stored as XML nodes of type C having a child node AV with the n attribute sets to *Category* and the v attribute sets to *Security*. The first step in building the set of security requirements S is to identify those nodes. Once identified, these nodes will be used in the policy generation process presented in section 7 to generate OrBAC abstract security rules. The requirement name is used to generate the corresponding security rule name. Each node corresponding to a security requirement has an additional parameter called *pattern*, which corresponds to the KAOS goal pattern. This parameter is also extracted to know which type of security rule must be generated during the translation process.

The second step consists in finding all agents (the $\mathcal{A}$ set), operations (the $\mathcal{O}$ set), entities (the $\mathcal{E}$ set) and events (the $\mathcal{C}$ set) specified in the requirement file and related to the previously extracted security requirements. The KAOS binary relationships linking elements of those sets between them are also extracted while those sets are constructed (see Figure 4).

The XPath language is used to query the KAOS XML file to build the above sets and find the relationships. More precisely, the target nodes in the XML file have the same type as requirement nodes, i.e the C type, and are identified by the p attribute. For example agents have the p attribute sets to $Method : NewKaos2003 : MetaModel : Agent$, similar attributes are defined to identify operations, entities and events. Relationships (*Performance*, *Input*, *Cause*, *Responsability* and *Operationalization*) are represented in the XML file as nodes with the same type as the previously extracted data, i.e the C type, and are also identified by the p attribute. For example instances of the performance relationship have the p attribute sets to $Method : NewKaos2003 : MetaModel : Performance$.

Before being able to generate the security rules, we must extract the relationships linking agents, operations, entities and events to security requirements. The following predicates are used to represent these relationships and are used in the next section to define the translation process:

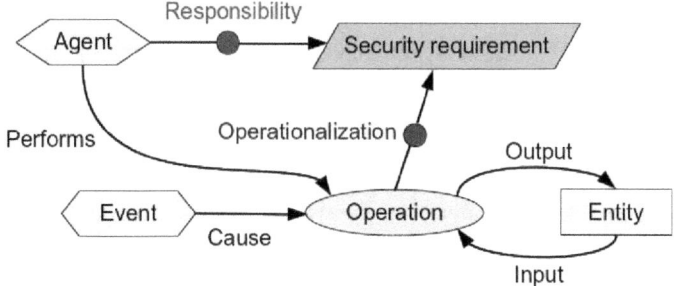

Fig. 4. Graph with KAOS concepts as nodes and KAOS relationships as edges

- $\forall a \in \mathcal{A}, \forall o \in \mathcal{O}, performs(a, o)$ is true iff a *Performs* relationship exists between agent a and operation o
- $\forall c \in \mathcal{C}, \forall o \in \mathcal{O}, cause(c, o)$ is true iff a *Cause* relationship exists between event c and operation o
- $\forall e \in \mathcal{E}, \forall o \in \mathcal{O}, input(e, o)$ is true iff an *Input* relationship exists between entity e and operation o
- $\forall a \in \mathcal{A}, \forall s \in \mathcal{S}, responsibility(a, s)$ is true iff a *Responsibility* relationship exists between agent a and security requirement s
- $\forall o \in \mathcal{O}, \forall s \in \mathcal{S}, operationalization(o, s)$ is true iff a *Operationalization* relationship exists between operation o and security requirement s
- $\forall s \in \mathcal{S}, achieve(s)$ is true iff s is a security requirement with the *Achieve* pattern, $avoid(s)$ is true iff s is a security requirement with the *Avoid* pattern and $maintain(s)$ is true iff s is a security requirement with the *Maintain* pattern.

In addition, obligations in the OrBAC model have two contexts, one specifying the activation condition and the other the violation condition. In order to distinguish between normal KAOS events mapped to OrBAC contexts and events mapped to violation contexts, we add a boolean attribute to the events defined in a KAOS model. This attribute is called *violation* and is set to true if the associated event must be used to generate a violation context. This attribute is represented by the following predicate:

$\forall c \in \mathcal{C}, violationEvent(c)$ is true iff the *violation* boolean attribute of event c is set to true

Once the $\mathcal{S}$, $\mathcal{A}$, $\mathcal{O}$, $\mathcal{E}$ and $\mathcal{C}$ sets have been built and the *Performance*, *Input*, *Cause*, *Responsability* and *Operationalization* relationships instances have been extracted, the translation process from KAOS security requirements to an OrBAC policy can take place.

7   Security Policy Generation

Generating an OrBAC security policy from the data extracted in the previous section from a KAOS requirement file consists of the following steps:

– Create the organization in which the rules and abstract entities will be created. The OrBAC organization concept having no counterpart in the KAOS model, the OrBAC policy is generated into one organization whose name is given at translation time by the administrator.
– For each element in $\mathcal{A}$, $\mathcal{O}$, $\mathcal{E}$ and $\mathcal{C}$, create the corresponding OrBAC abstract entities in the organization specified by the administrator, i.e for each agent create a role, for each operation create an activity, for each entity create an object and for each event create a context. Notice that the created contexts have no definition, it is left to the policy designer to specify them.
– For each security requirement in $\mathcal{S}$, if one or more graphs corresponding to figure 4 can be built from the *Performance, Input, Cause, Responsability* and *Operationalization* relationships instances and the $\mathcal{A}$, $\mathcal{O}$, $\mathcal{E}$ and $\mathcal{C}$ sets, an OrBAC security rule is generated. The rule type is determined by the *pattern* attribute associated with each security requirement. Security requirements with the *Achieve* pattern are translated into permissions, those with the *Avoid* pattern are translated into prohibitions and those with the *Maintain* pattern are translated into obligations.

Using the predicates defined in the previous section, three derivation rules specify how OrBAC abstract security rules are derived. The following rules show how abstract permissions and abstract prohibitions are derived:

$$permission(Agent, Operation, Entity, Event) : -$$
$$performs(Agent, Operation),$$
$$cause(Event, Operation),$$
$$input(Entity, Operation),$$
$$responsibility(Agent, Requirement),$$
$$operationalization(Operation, Requirement),$$
$$achieve(Requirement).$$
$$prohibition(Agent, Operation, Entity, Event) : -$$
$$performs(Agent, Operation),$$
$$cause(Event, Operation),$$
$$input(Entity, Operation),$$
$$responsibility(Agent, Requirement),$$
$$operationalization(Operation, Requirement),$$
$$avoid(Requirement).$$

Note that the *permission* and *prohibition* predicates have no parameter specifying the organization in which it is defined as the rule is implicitly derived in the organization specified by the administrator. The rule for obligations slightly differs since there is an extra context:

$obligation(Agent, Operation, Entity, Event, ViolationEvent) : -$
      $performs(Agent, Operation),$
      $cause(Event, Operation),$
      $cause(ViolationEvent, Operation),$
      $violationEvent(ViolationEvent),$
      $input(Entity, Operation),$
      $responsibility(Agent, Requirement),$
      $operationalization(Operation, Requirement),$
      $achieve(Requirement).$

The translation process has been implemented as a MotOrBAC plugin [9]. The plugin displays the $\mathcal{S}$, $\mathcal{A}$, $\mathcal{O}$, $\mathcal{E}$ and $\mathcal{C}$ sets extracted from an Objectiver KAOS project file saved in XML as well as the *Performance, Input, Cause, Responsability* and *Operationalization* extracted relationships. The user can choose which requirements must be translated.

The user can choose to run the plugin on an empty OrBAC policy or can use it with an existing policy to inject the translated security requirements into it. The plugin can also be used as a standalone application, in this case the policy is not generated inside MotOrBAC but in a file which can later be loaded in MotOrBAC or interpreted by the OrBAC API once concrete entities have been created.

8   Case Studies

In this section, we illustrate the proposed approach through the embedded secure system and echo Doppler case studies. We briefly describe the requirements then we show how to elaborate these requirements in KAOS and how to generate the corresponding formal security policies. It is an access and usage control policy in the first case study and reaction policy in the second one.

8.1   The Echo Doppler Case Study

In this use case, we are interested in generating the formal access policy from the functional goals. We illustrate here how functional specifications can be enriched with security objectives derived from risk analysis results. In ultrasound scanner service, there are several main activities that support a patient from the examination request to the examination results. An examination consists in exploring the patient using an ultrasound scanner. During the examination, the physician records meaningful and important images that will be transmitted to the archiving system. The physician then dictates the examination report to the secretary. Finally, the images are transmitted to the patient. The main activities in this scenario are: making an appointment for a patient, reception of the patient in the service, patient image acquisition, diagnostic of the image by the physician, saving images with their associated reports.

Now we apply the overall process described in the previous sections to generate access control rules. So, we specify goal model, object model, agent responsibility model and operation model using Objectiver. Here, we chose an example of goal model named "patient identification" which is one of the refinement branches of the "patient reception" requirement. "Patient reception" supports the patient from identification to image acquisition. First, the secretary must verify if the patient was already present at the hospital reception service before arriving in acquisition service or not. Then she must verify the patient identification such as name, date of birthday, file number, etc. Once the identification of patient is confirmed, she schedules the patient examination.

As aforementioned, in order to inject security aspects into the KAOS specification, we use EBIOS. Figure 5 shows the "Patient Reception" diagram which illustrates the main security objectives resulting from applying an EBIOS risk analysis. This diagram is then linked to the main functional diagram.

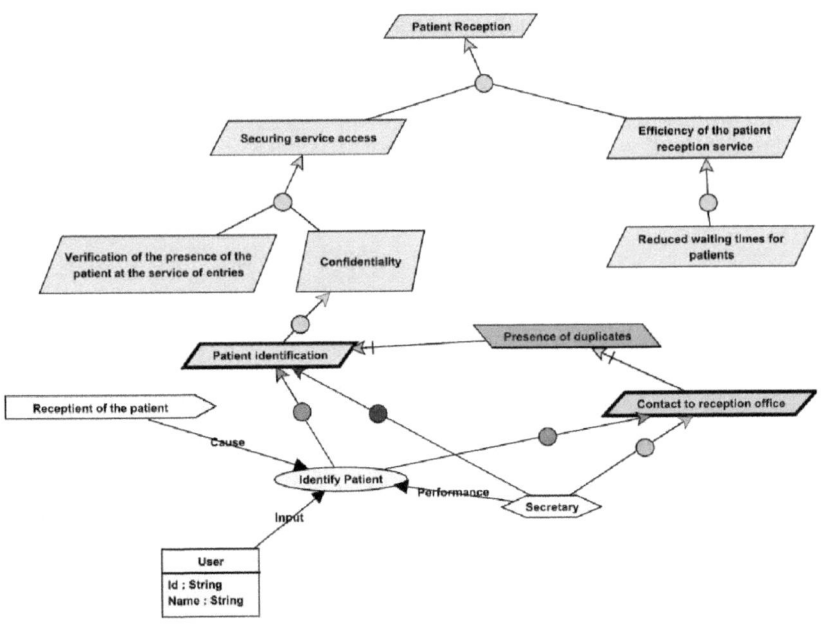

Fig. 5. PatientReception Diagram

As explained in section 5.2, the risk analysis consists in several steps. Here, we explain briefly some of them. First of all, security functions must be defined, in our example, "identify patient" is such a function. Then, the security requirements related to the resource used by this function must be determined. Specification of these security requirements is used to estimate the risks, according to some security properties. If these requirements are not satisfied, the organization will be impacted. This impact can take many forms, for example: loss of integrity, loss of confidentiality, unavailability or financial loss. After these steps, threatening elements and attack methods must be defined and analyzed.

Examples of threatening elements and attack methods for the "identify patient" function are: Lack of reliable means for identification, ability to alter communications, ignorance of the importance of qualification information, lack of awareness of the identity usurpation risk.

Once the list of threatening elements is specified, identification of security properties (integrity, confidentiality, etc.) and estimation of risk level (intolerable risk, tolerable risk, etc) for each target element is determined. The results of this analysis are used to tag the KAOS elements and assign them meta data like priority or pattern. Figure 6 illustrates this enrichment.

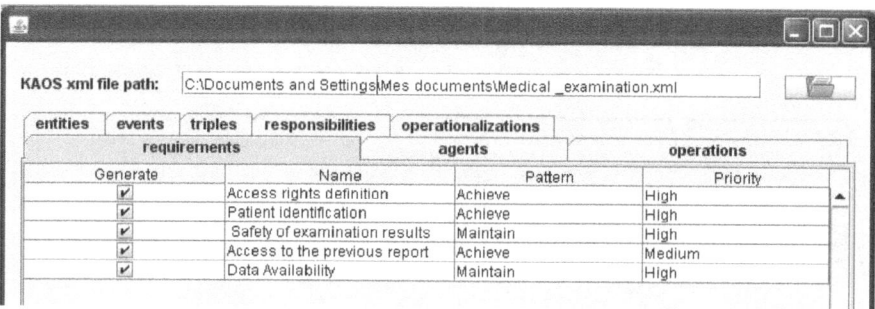

Fig. 6. KAOS to ORBAC Translator

In the next steps, as explained in section 6 and 7, we extract security requirements from the obtained KAOS specifications and generate formal security policy. An example of the result of these processes is illustrated in figure 7.

Rule name	Role	Activity	View	Context
Access_rights_definition1	Secretary	Definition_of_access_rights	Previous_report	Request_for_information_on_the_patient_during_the_examination
Access_to_the_previous_report_3	Praticien	Access_to_the_previous_report_of_the_service	Previous_report	Request_for_information_on_the_patient_during_the_examination
Patient_identification_2	Secretary	Identify_Patient	User	Receptient_of_the_patient

Fig. 7. Some Generated Abstract Rules

8.2 The Embedded Secure System Case Study

Several systems such as personal computers, PDAs, cell phones, network routers and smart cards access and manipulate sensitive information, therefore security is a serious concern in their design. In this context, our approach can be applied to generate the formal reaction to intrusion policy from the security goals of embedded systems (ES).

Risk analysis allowed the identification of threats and vulnerabilities that may be encountered in this kind of systems. We were interested in software

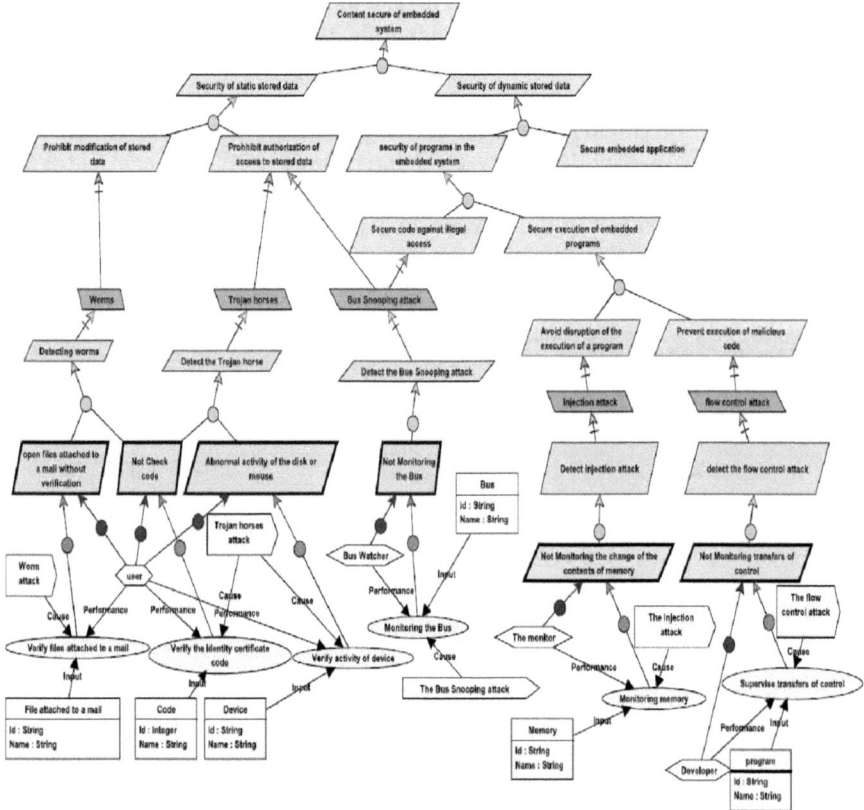

Fig. 8. KAOS specification of secure content of embedded system

	Rule name	Role	Activity	View	Context
add	Not_Monitoring_the_Bus3	Bus_Watcher	Monitoring_the_Bus	Bus	The_Bus_Snooping_att...
del	Not_Monitoring_transfers...	Developer	supervise_transfers_of_control_	program	The_flow_control_attack_
edit	Abnormal_activity_of_the...	user	verify_activity_of_device	Device	Trojan_horses_attack
	Not_Monitoring__the_cha	The_monitor_	Monitoring_memory	Memory	The_Injection_attack
	open_files_attached_to_...	user	Verify_files_attached_to_a_mail	File_attached_to_a_mail	Worm_attack
	Not_Check_code4	user	Verify_the_identity_certificate_code	Code	Trojan_horses_attack

Abstract entities | Contexts | Abstract rules | Conflicts | Entity definitions | Simulation

Permissions (0) | Prohibitions (6) | Obligations (0)

Fig. 9. Some detection/reaction rules related to secure content of embedded system

attacks such as worms, Trojan horses, bus snooping, injection attacks and flow controls attacks that can compromise the confidentiality and integrity of ES. In a second step, we specified the security objectives dedicated to these systems using KAOS (Figure 8 gives an idea of how it may appear). The security of an ES requires the protection of the content (static and dynamic data). We have refined these goals by ensuring integrity and confidentiality of static data, embedded programs and applications by protecting them against the attacks (represented by obstacles). We have obtained security requirements which define procedures to detect these attacks. Then we have operationalized these security requirements by specifying the corresponding actions and linking them to agents, entities and events as specified in figure 4. Using our extraction process of the KAOS-XML security specification part and applying our translator process, we generate a formal detection and reaction policy (see some examples of rules generated by MotOrBAC in Figure 9).

9   Conclusion

Usually, the document of specifications is written in natural language and security policies are often defined according to the interpretation one can do when reading them. So, the resulting policies are not always consistent with the expected requirements. We propose in this paper to enhance and automate the derivation of formal security policies. We define, develop and implement the corresponding process based on three building blocks: KAOS, a goal-oriented formal model to specify functional requirements, EBIOS, a risk analysis methodology to integrate security requirements and OrBAC, a formal security model to express the security policies. The next near future step, though the process we have defined is "correct by construction", is to conduct proofs of some security properties.

Acknowledgement. Meriam Graa's Phd is funded by the "Futur et Ruptures" programme of the Institut Telecom. Hanieh Azkia's PhD is funded by a grant from the Britany region. Frédéric Cuppens, Nora Cuppens-Boulahia and Gouenou Coatrieux would like to thank the ANR for its support within the SELKIS project.

References

1. Alexander, I.: Misuse cases help to elicit non-functional requirements. Computing and Control Engineering Journal 14(1), 40–45 (2003)
2. Card, I., Profile, P.: Common Criteria for Information Technology Security Evaluation (2001)
3. Coatrieux, G., Maitre, H., Sankur, B.: Strict integrity control of biomedical images. In: Proceedings of SPIE
4. Cuppens, F., Cuppens-Boulahia, N.: Modeling contextual security policies. International Journal of Information Security 7(4), 285–305 (2008)
5. Cuppens, F., Cuppens-Boulahia, N., Miège, A.: Inheritance hierarchies in the Or-BAC model and application in a network environment. In: Second Foundations of Computer Security Workshop (FCS 2004), Turku, Finland (2004)
6. Cuppens, F., Miège, A.: Modelling contexts in the Or-BAC model. In: 19th Annual Computer Security Applications Conference, Las Vegas (2003)
7. Darimont, R., Van Lamsweerde, A.: Formal refinement patterns for goal-driven requirements elaboration. ACM SIGSOFT Software Engineering Notes 21

8. DCSSI: Expression des Besoins et Identification des Objectifs de Securite (February 2004),
   `http://www.ssi.gouv.fr/IMG/pdf/ebiosv2-section1-introduction-2004-02-05.pdf` (Online; accessed April 20, 2011)
9. Autrel, F., Cuppens, F., Cuppens-Boulahia, N., Coma, C.: Motorbac 2: a security policy tool. In: Third Joint Conference on Security in Networks Architectures and Security of Information Systems (SARSSI), Loctudy, France (2008)
10. Finkelstein, A., Dowell, J.: A Comedy of Errors: the London Ambulance Service case study. In: Proceedings of 8th International Workshop on Software Specification and Design (IWSSD-8),
11. Firesmith, D.: Security use cases. Technology 2
12. Herrmann, A., Paech, B.: Quality Misuse. In: Proceedings of the Fourteenth International Workshop on Requirements Engineering: Foundation of Software Quality
13. Johnson, J.: Chaos: The dollar drain of IT project failures. Application Development Trends 2
14. Jonker, W., Linnartz, J.: Digital rights management in consumer electronics products. IEEE Signal Processing Magazine 21
15. Laleau, R., Semmak, F., Matoussi, A., Petit, D., Hammad, A., Tatibouet, B.: A first attempt to combine SysML requirements diagrams and B. Innovations in Systems and Software Engineering (2010)
16. Letier, E.: Reasoning about agents in goal-oriented requirements engineering (2001)
17. Miller, M., Cox, I., Linnartz, J., Kalker, T.: A review of watermarking principles and practices. Digital Signal Processing for Multimedia Systems, 461–485 (1999)
18. Sa, R.I.: Objectiver: un atelier de gnie logiciel pour l'ingnierie des exigences (2004), `http://www.objectiver.com`
19. Sindre, G., Opdahl, A.: Templates for misuse case description. In: Proc. of the 7th International Workshop on Requirements Engineering, Foundation for Software Quality (REFSQ 2001), Citeseer (2001)
20. Ullman, J.D.: Principles of database and knowledge-base systems. Computer Science Press (1989)
21. Van Lamsweerde, A.: Elaborating security requirements by construction of intentional anti-models
22. Van Lamsweerde, A.: Goal-oriented requirements engineering: From system objectives to UML models to precise software specifications. In: Proceedings of the 25th International Conference on Software Engineering
23. Van Lamsweerde, A.: Goal-oriented requirements engineering: A guided tour. In: Proceedings of the 5th IEEE International Symposium on Requirements Engineering, p. 0249 (2001)

Web Services Verification and Prudent Implementation*

Tigran Avanesov[1], Yannick Chevalier[2],
Mohammed Anis Mekki[1], and Michaël Rusinowitch[1]

[1] INRIA Nancy Grand Est,
615 allée du jardin botanique, 54000 Vandœuvre-lès-Nancy, France
{avanesot,mekkimoh,rusi}@loria.fr
[2] Université de Toulouse,
118 Route de Narbonne, F-31062 Toulouse, France
ychevali@irit.fr

Abstract. Alice&Bob notation is widely used to describe conversations between partners in security protocols. We present a tool that compiles an Alice&Bob description of a Web Services choreography into a set of servlets. For that we first compute for each partner an executable specification as prudent as possible of her role in the choreography. This specification is expressed in ASLan language, a formal language designed for modeling Web Services tied with security policies. Then we can check with automatic tools that this ASLan specification verifies some required security properties such as secrecy and authentication. If no flaw is found, we compile the specification into Java servlets that real partners can use to execute the choreography.

Keywords: Web Services, Security Policy, Automated deployment.

1 Introduction

Alice&Bob notation (A&B) primarily intended for specifying Security Protocols permits also to capture complex and secured standard conversations between Web Services (WS's). Figure 1 shows a choreography view of the *Needham-Schroeder Public Key* security protocol (NSPK). In the following we discuss how such conversations can be extracted from the specification files documenting the services and the processes involved in a choreography.

1.1 Web Services

According to the Web Services Description Language (WSDL) a WS is defined as a list of *operations* which can be called to use a computation or processing skill proposed by the WS. These operations are organized into *ports* and each port can be bound to one or different networks addresses (and possibly to

---

* This work is supported by FP7 AVANTSSAR [2] and FP7 NESSoS [1] projects.

J. Garcia-Alfaro et al. (Eds.): DPM 2011 and SETOP 2011, LNCS 7122, pp. 173–189, 2012.

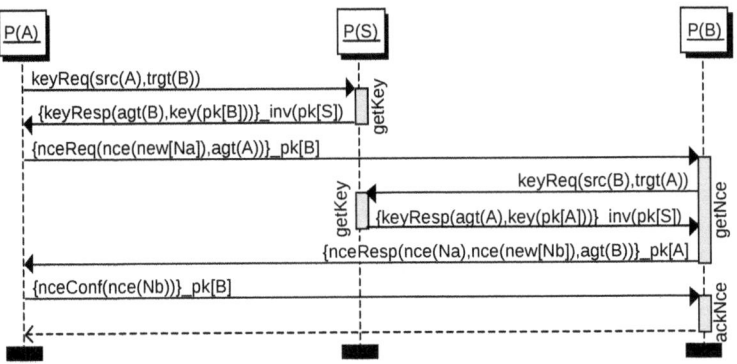

Fig. 1. The NSPK Choreography

specific transport protocols). Each operation is described by giving the precise XML structure of three messages: the request message the operation expects when it is called, the response message the operation returns as a result of a regular execution and the third is the error message returned after a faulty one. Moreover security policies are possibly defined to constrain the use of a service. They address different levels of protection targeting either the entire service, a specific port, a given operation or even a specific message associated to an operation. Within the WS-SecurityPolicy (WS-SP) standard, these policies can express either the need to use secure transport protocols to communicate with the service (*e.g.* SSL over HTTP) or the need for cryptographic protection for the operations' messages (using encryption or digital signature) but also for satisfying some access control rules by requiring some certificates to be present in the exchanged messages. Figure 2(a) shows a graphical representation of the *Key Server WS* (*S*). S exposes one operation called getKey which belong to a default port (not represented). We represent here the XML patterns bound to the input and output messages using first-order terms over a signature described in § 2.1. Moreover a security policy is associated to S and targets the outbound message of getKey which have to be digitally signed using a private key available to the service: #0. More generally such policies may specify which parts of one operation's message have to be digitally signed and/or ciphered. These parts are identified inside the corresponding XML schemata using XPATH [23] queries.

1.2   Business Processes

The *Business Process Execution Language* (*BPEL*) is an XML-based language describing *business processes* (BP's) as aggregation of WS's interactions achieving particular goals. While an *abstract* BPEL specification describes only the behavioral aspects of these interactions, *e.g.* following a specific order, an *executable* BPEL specification (also called WS *orchestration*) may describe in addition internal actions that are performed by the process, *e.g.* applying basic XML data transformation. An executable BPEL process can be executed by

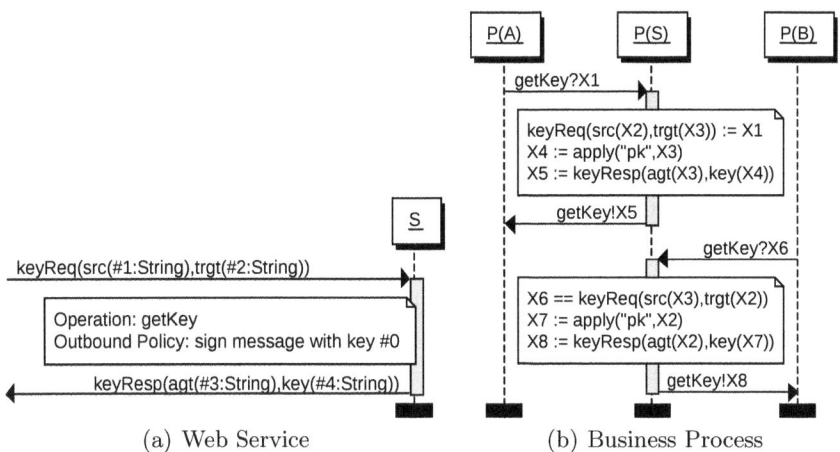

Fig. 2. The Key Server

an orchestration engine which performs the WS's invocations and the internal actions in the order specified in its BPEL specification. The process itself can then be offered as a new WS, in this sense BPEL implements the composability principle of SOA by encompassing an aggregation of WS operation calls into a single one.

Figure 2(b) shows a graphical representation of $P(S)$ a BP playing the NSPK Choreography with partners $P(A)$ and $P(B)$. Each arrow represents a communication activity involving $P(S)$. Annotations of the form getKey?Xi stands for receptions of requests Xi targeting the getKey operation of the service S while those of the form getKey!Xj stands for sending back the corresponding responses Xj returned by getKey to the caller. The Xi's are typed variables the orchestration engine manipulates during the process execution. These variables are either initially instantiated or assigned to values carried by received messages or to new values by applying simple XML transformations on already valuated variables. For example the line keyReq(src(X2),trgt(X3)) := X1 freshly assigns the variables X2 and X3 to the corresponding parts inside X1 which is implicitly supposed to be of the correct type. In the line X6 == keyReq(src(X3),trgt(X2)) all the variables are already valuated and thus it represents a condition to check. This check is important in order to play the NSPK Choreography correctly since $P(S)$ have to correlate the two requests *w.r.t.* the identities of the two partners $P(A)$ and $P(B)$. Correlation is explicitly supported by BPEL and naturally introduces the need of a multi-session handling which was not visible at WS level where operations are serving their answers in a synchronous way.

A BPEL orchestration engine is not in charge of enforcing the security policies associated to the invoked services or to the executed process. This is too restrictive from the general point of view of security protocols. Indeed it discards processes that receive messages they cannot totally decipher at the moment of reception but which could be more finely analyzed in a further step after receiving the right keys. The tool we propose in this paper overcomes this restriction and permits thus to correctly handle such protocols. For this we need to take into account the effect of the security policies on messages exchanged by the process and we sketch in the following how we can proceed. First we reconstruct from the BPEL process specification the terms t_i corresponding to the XML schematas of its exchanged messages m_i. Each t_i have its minimal subterms (or leaves) ranging over a set of fresh variables. Then we identify in the t_i variables that correspond to the same value by analyzing the effect of the correlation relations and the internal actions (the assignments) of the process on the m_i. Finally we apply to each t_i the effect of the security policy attached to the operation of m_i. This amounts to first identify the subterms of t_i corresponding to parts in m_i that have to be cryptographically protected and then to replace them in t_i by terms expressing this protection. For $P(S)$ these transformations lead to the following sequence of interactions:

```
1 ?msg(par(A),opt(getKey),pld(keyReq(src(Y1),trgt(Y2))))
2 !msg(par(A),opt(getKey),pld({keyResp(agt(Y2),key(pk[Y2]))}_Y0))
3 ?msg(par(B),opt(getKey),pld(keyReq(src(Y2),trgt(Y1))))
4 !msg(par(B),opt(getKey),pld({keyResp(agt(Y1),key(pk[Y1]))}_Y0))
```

where $node_3^{msg}$, $node_1^{par}$, $node_1^{opt}$ and $node_1^{pld}$ are wrapping function symbols permitting to hold the other partner's name in the communication activity, the called operation in addition to the exchanged message (the payload). Since our objective is to provide an executable implementation for a given role we need to keep track of these information for all its communication activities in order to compute the network address of the receiver in the case of an emission or the called operation in the case of a reception. $\{\#1\}\_\#2$ (resp. $\#1[\#2]$) is a shorthand for the asymmetric encryption of the message $\#1$ by the key $\#2$ (resp. a shorthand for apply("$\#1$",$\#2$)) and Y0 is the private key of $P(S)$.

1.3   Choreographies

The choreography is a collaborative effort focused on exchange of messages from a global point of view where all participating services are treated equally [7]. This definition contrasts with the one for orchestration where a BPEL process is distinguished as a central coordinator of the WS's interactions. The *Web Services Choreography Description Language* (WS-CDL) [24] is a standard language that permits to define multi-party contracts describing only the externally observable behaviors of WS's, *i.e.* the description of the messages they exchange. WS-CDL models are not meant to be directly executed but are often used in conjunction with executable BPEL models especially to implement choreographies. When this is the case, the WS-CDL specification may be used to distinguish the subset of the desired collaborations between a set of existing BPEL processes within the set of all the possible ones. Indeed WS-CDL permits to define execution in sequence, in parallel or in choice mode of structured and possibly (conditioned or repetitive) abstract interactions which can be matched with local communication activities of the involved BPEL processes.

For the NSPK Choreography the WS-CDL file simply interconnects in sequence the BPEL processes representing the involved partners: $P(A)$, $P(B)$ and $P(S)$. We claim that after collecting all the BPEL specifications involved in the NSPK Choreography (and enriched by the effect of security policies on the exchanged messages as explained in the end of § 1.2) and after analyzing the WS-CDL specification file we obtain the result in Figure 1 which is a graphical illustration of an A&B specification of the NSPK Choreography.

1.4   Contributions

We propose a tool that:

- Translates an A&B specification of a WS choreography played by a set of BP's into its formal specification permitting its verification against classical security properties (such as secrecy, authentication);
- Compiles the A&B specification into Java servlets that partners can use to execute the choreography as safely as possible.

We stress out here the fact that both results can be reused in the security protocol world, obtaining thus an automated procedure permitting to formalize protocols described using the A&B semi-formal notation but also to obtain their operational implementations. Moreover the obtained formal specification and Java servlets implement *as prudently as possible* the different business processes involved in the choreography permitting to establish strong security guarantees for the generated code (the *prudence* property is defined in § 3.1). We also note that our tool generates the Java servlets even if the formal specification of the choreography is flawed. Finally, we show how in some interesting cases the prudence property is sufficient to use the generated servlets in a multi-sessions-aware context.

The remainder of this paper is organized as follows: in § 2 we provide the different formal models considered by the tool. In § 3 we give the principle of our translation procedure which we illustrate through experimentation in § 4 and we finally conclude in § 5 by an overview of the related and prospective works.

2   Formal Models

2.1   Conversations

We use the A&B semi-formal notation to specify WS's *conversations*. A conversation is a sequence of messages exchanged by WS's recorded in the order they are to be sent [10]. We formally define it by the following grammar:

$$
\begin{aligned}
Conversation &::= TypeDec^* \; Ik^* \; Com^* \\
TypeDec &::= \textbf{Type} \; Msg : Typ \\
Ik &::= Ag \; \textbf{knows} \; Term \; (\, ,Term)^* \\
Com &::= Ag - Op \rightarrow Ag : Msg \\
Typ, Msg, Ag, Op &::= Term
\end{aligned}
$$

Each line in the conversation is either an initial knowledge declaration *ik* for a partner, a communication activity *Com* where two partners exchange a message via a given operation or a type declaration *TypeDec* binding some message to a type. We consider three basic types: *message* for general character strings, *bool* for booleans and *nat* for integers. Partners, operations and messages are represented here by the non-terminal symbol *Term* corresponding to first order terms as defined below.

Terms. We consider an infinite set of free constants C, an infinite set of variables $\mathcal{X}$ and the set of function symbols defined below:

$$\mathcal{F} = \left\{ node_l^n, child_{\overline{i}}^n \mid i \leq l \in \mathbb{N}^*, n \in C \right\}$$
$$\cup \{apply, scrypt, sdcrypt, crypt, dcrypt, inv, invtest\}$$

We denote by $T(\mathcal{F})$ (resp. $T(\mathcal{F}, \mathcal{X})$) the set of terms over $\mathcal{F} \cup C$ (resp. $\mathcal{F} \cup C \cup \mathcal{X}$). The former is called the set of ground terms (or messages) over $\mathcal{F}$, while the latter is simply called the set of terms over $\mathcal{F}$. A substitution σ is an idempotent mapping from $\mathcal{X}$ to $T(\mathcal{F}, \mathcal{X})$ such that $\{x \mid \sigma(x) \neq x\}$ is a finite set. The application of a substitution σ to a term t (resp. a set of terms E) is denoted $t\sigma$ (resp. $E\sigma$) and is equal to the term t (resp. E) where all variables x have been respectively replaced by the term $x\sigma$.

An *equational theory* $\mathcal{E}$ is defined by a set E of equations $u = v$ with $u, v \in T(\mathcal{F}, \mathcal{X})$. We write $s =_{\mathcal{E}} t$ as the congruence relation between two terms s and t. Terms are manipulated by applying *operations* on them. These operations are defined by the set $\mathcal{F}_p = \mathcal{F} \setminus \{inv\}$ called the *set of public symbols*. Their semantics are defined with the $\mathcal{E}_{XML}$ equational theory defined above:

$$\begin{cases} sdcrypt(y, scrypt(y, x)) = x & (D_s) \\ dcrypt(y, crypt(inv(y), x)) = x & (D_{as}) \\ child_{\overline{i}}^n(node_l^n(x_1, \ldots, x_l)) = x_i & (P_{\overline{i}}) \\ invtest(x, inv(x)) = \top & (I_v) \end{cases}$$

A context $C[x_1, \ldots, x_n]$ is a term in which all symbols are public and such that its nullary symbols are the variables $x_1, \ldots, x_n$. $C[x_1, \ldots, x_n]$ is also denoted C when there's no ambiguity and n is called its *length*. We define the *application* of a context C of length n over the sequence of messages $m_1, \ldots, m_n$ to be the image of $C[X_1, \ldots, X_n]$ by the substitution $\{X_j \to m_j\}_{1 \leq j \leq n}$.

XML messages. An XML node is represented by a term $node_l^n(u_1, \ldots, u_l)$ where $node_l^n$ is a function symbol of arity l, n is the tag of the node, and the u_i are terms representing the children of the node. In order to model security constraints holding over XML messages, we represent the usual cryptographic primitives with the function symbols: *scrypt*/*sdcrypt* for symmetric encryption and decryption, *crypt*/*dcrypt* for asymmetric encryption and decryption (used also to represent digital signature and its verification), *inv* to denote key inverses and *invtest* permitting to test whether a pair of terms $\{t, t'\}$ verifies $t' = inv(t)$. Finally we use the function symbol *apply* to represent the application of a given function represented by a term f to a term t by the term $apply(f, t)$.

2.2 Communication Scenarios

We now focus on the local behaviors of all partners involved in the choreography. We call such a behavior a *partner* and use *strands* [17] a standard notion in cryptographic protocol modeling to describe it. These notions are defined below.

Definition 1. *A* strand *s is a finite sequence of messages each labeled with* ! *or* ? *where messages with label* ! *(resp.* ?*) are said to be "sent" (resp. "received"). The size of the sequence is called the* length *of s and is denoted by length(s).*

Given a strand $s = {}^!_? m_1, \ldots, {}^!_? m_n$ we also denote in the following respectively by s^i and s_i the prefix of length i of s and the message m_i.

Definition 2. *A* partner *is a triplet* $(n, \mathcal{IK}, s)$ *where n is a constant called the* name, $\mathcal{IK}$ *is a set of messages called the* initial knowledge *and s is a strand called the* communication scenario.

Given a conversation we proceed by *end-point projection* [11] to collect the local behaviors of all the involved partners. This amounts to collecting first all the participating partner names and their respective initial knowledge from the conversation's *Ik* items. Then an iteration through all the *Com* items permits to build the communication scenarios as follows: if *Com* is $p_1 - o \rightarrow p_2 : m$ then append to the communication scenario of p_1 and p_2 respectively $!msg(par(p_2), opt(o), pld(m))$ and $?msg(par(p_1), opt(o), pld(m))$.

For example, given the conversation of Fig. 1, our algorithm computes a partner $P(S) = (S, \{pk[S], inv(pk[S])\}, s)$ where s is the strand:

```
1 ?msg(par(A),opt(getKey),pld(keyReq(src(A),trgt(B))))
2 !msg(par(A),opt(getKey),
3    pld({keyResp(agt(B),key(pk[B]))}-inv(pk[S])))
4 ?msg(par(B),opt(getKey),pld(keyReq(src(B),trgt(A))))
5 !msg(par(B),opt(getKey),
6    pld({keyResp(agt(A),key(pk[A]))}-inv(pk[S])))
```

2.3 The ASLan Language

ASLan [3] is a formal language for specifying security-sensitive service-oriented architectures, the associated security policies, as well as their trust and security properties. We translate partners into ASLan roles where an ASLan role is defined by a transition system and an initial state. States are sets of facts, where facts are first order terms over a given signature. By convention, some facts in the states are used to hold the knowledge of a role r: $state\_r(step, knowledge)$

whereas some others are used to signal a new message emission: $iknows$ $(scrypt(k,m))$. A transition τ is defined by two sets of facts: its left and right hand sides denoted respectively by $LHS(\tau)$ and $RHS(\tau)$. A transition τ may bring some state s to a state s', if $LHS(\tau)$ can be unified with a subset of s (via some substitution σ). Then s' is defined to be $(s\sigma \setminus LHS(\tau)\sigma) \cup RHS(\tau)\sigma$. The language allows also to guard the transitions by conditions like equality $(equal(t,t'))$ between terms (t,t').

3   Compilation Procedure

We present in the following a compilation procedure to translate partners to ASLan roles. In § 3.1 we give an execution model for partners then in § 3.2 we provide a concrete solution to generate their executable implementations and finally in § 3.3 we show how these implementations are expressed in ASLan.

3.1   Execution Model

To provide an executable implementation of a partner p we need to analyze which values can be extracted by p from her received messages and specify how these values should be processed by her to construct the next messages to be sent. Since conversations involve cryptographically-protected messages one has to take into account information asymmetries introduced by this protection. For example if two partners exchange a cipher-text $scrypt(k,t)$, they may be seeing it differently if only one of them detains the deciphering key k. Since one of our objectives is to provide an executable implementation for a given partner p this point turns out to be critical in our case. Note that this aspect was not considered by related works like [11] on end-point projection.

Our approach can be seen as an application of [15] where informally speaking an *implementation of a communication scenario* specifies the set of public symbols a partner has to apply to its current knowledge in order to construct the messages she has to send according to the scenario. A *prudent implementation* performs in addition all possible checks or security verifications by analyzing and correlating all received messages by her at that point.

We illustrate these notions by commenting a prudent implementation of the partner $P(S)$ given below (and where pi−n is a shortcut for $child^n_{\bar{i}}$):

```
1  Step.0={X0:=pk; X1:=Ks; X2:=inv(Ks)}
2  Step.1={receive(X3) on getKey;
3     X4:=p1−keyReq(X3); X5:=p1−src(X4);
4     X6:=p2−keyReq(X3); X7:=p1−trgt(X6);
5     X8:=src(X7); X9:=trgt(X5); X10:=keyReq(X8,X9); X11:=agt(X7);
6     X12:=apply(X0,X7); X13:=key(X12); X14:=keyResp(X11,X13);
7     X15:=crypt(X2,X14); X16:=agt(X5); X17:=apply(X0,X5);
8     X18:=key(X17); X19:=keyResp(X16,X18); X20:=crypt(X2,X19)}
9  Step.2={send(X15) to X5}
10 Step.3={receive(X21) on getKey; X21?=X10}
11 Step.4={send(X20) to X7}
```

For example, in Step.0, $P(S)$ initializes her knowledge by the function symbol pk and her public and private keys. Step.1 corresponds to her first reception targeting the operation getKey and where the received message is stored in the variable $X3$. Lines $3 - 4$ describe how parts are extracted from $X3$. For example in line 4, $X6$ is assigned the second child of $X3$. All the messages that could be further used by $P(S)$ are precomputed by her as soon as possible thus reducing sending steps to emitting precomputed values (like in Step.2 and Step.4). We note that $P(S)$ being in Step.1 is also able to precompute the message corresponding to her next expected reception. Then in Step.3 the received message (stored in $X21$) is compared with the precomputed expected value stored in $X10$. This check is not necessary to the execution of $P(S)$, since $X20$ the message to be sent by her before finishing her task is already precomputed. Ignoring this test we still result in an executable implementation of $P(S)$ which is not prudent *i.e.* one that does not check its input messages as thoroughly as possible.

3.2   Solution Principle

A conversation does not explicitly specify what parts of a message being received by a partner should be extracted by him and in which order. Similarly it does not give information on how a message being sent by some partner is effectively constructed given its current knowledge. The approach proposed in [15] is to extract this information from a conversation and reduces the problem to classical decision problems in protocol analysis, namely the *reachability* and the *finite basis* problems. In this approach the conversation is projected on every partner to generate her view. Then for each partner p (with s its communication scenario) the following analysis is performed:

Sending case for all sent message m_i find a *context* C, *i.e.* a sequence of operations that permit to construct m_i given all the messages received so far among $m_1, \ldots, m_{i-1}$. If such a context exists we say that m_i is *reachable* by p and we call C an *extraction context* for m_i from the communication scenario s. We then extend this definition to any subterm of s. If for all sent message m_i there exists a context C_i such that $C_i[m_1, \ldots, m_{i-1}] =_{\mathcal{E}_{XML}} m_i$, s is said *executable* and one is given an operational implementation of it, provided that all the public symbols functions are implemented.

Reception case for all message m_i compute a finite generating set of all the pairs of contexts C, C' such that the equality $C[m_1, \ldots, m_i] =_{\mathcal{E}_{XML}} C'[m_1, \ldots, m_i]$ holds. This finite set if it exists is called *the finite basis* of the communication scenario s^i. If this computation succeeds for all received messages m_i then one can obtain a prudent implementation of s by checking after each reception m_i the messages relations specified by the finite basis.

3.3   Solving the Problem

Our approach is an application of [15] to the $\mathcal{E}_{XML}$ equational theory and is summarized below. Given a communication scenario s we first look for extraction contexts for all subterms of s. Since the sent messages are particular subterms we can obtain an implementation of s. For that we first define a reachability relation.

Definition 3. *Given a term t a partner $p = (n, \mathcal{IK}, s)$ and a step i at most equal to the length of s. We consider a list $\langle m_1, \ldots, m_l \rangle$ of messages in the union of $\mathcal{IK}$ and the set of all received messages in s^l. We say that t is* reachable *by p at step i if there is a context C such that $C[m_1, \ldots, m_l] =_{\mathcal{E}_{XML}} t$ (and also that C is an* extraction context *for t from p).*

We also define the function *reach* as follows:

$$reach(p, t) = \{min(i) \mid t \text{ is reachable by } p \text{ at step } i\}$$

Given a partner p we compute all the subterms reachable by p at all steps of its communication scenario. For that we introduce the notion of sequents to store relations holding between subterms of p.

Definition 4. *Given a partner $p = (n, \mathcal{IK}, s)$ we call γ a* sequent *of p (and denote it by $t_1, \ldots, t_k \vdash_f t_0$) an equality $t_0 =_{\mathcal{E}_{XML}} f(t_1, \ldots, t_k)$ where f is a public symbol and $t_0, \ldots, t_k$ is a possibly empty sequence of subterms of s. We call respectively t_0, f and the sequence $t_1, \ldots, t_k$ the* head, *the* symbol *and the* tail *of γ and denote them respectively by $h(\gamma)$, $s(\gamma)$ and $t(\gamma)$.*

We say that γ is *valid* at some step i when for all $0 \leq j \leq k$, $reach(p, t_j) \leq i$. We denote the set of all sequents of p by $\Gamma(p)$ and the set of all valid sequents at some step i by $\Gamma_i(p)$. If a sequent γ is valid at step i then its head is also reachable at step i by taking $f(C_1, \ldots, C_k)$ as an extraction context for t_0 from p, assuming that $C_1, \ldots, C_k$ are respectively extraction contexts for $t_1, \ldots, t_k$.

We now solve the reachability and the finite basis problems for a given partner $p = (n, \mathcal{IK}, s)$. First we compute $\Gamma(p)$ by running through all the subterms of s and collecting the corresponding sequents. For example a subterm of the form $t = scrypt(k, m)$ will provide two entries: $k, m \vdash_{scrypt} t$ and $k, t \vdash_{sdrcypt} m$. For each computed sequent γ we define an integer called its *readiness* and initially set to the size of $t(\gamma)$. This integer is used to compute the validity of a sequent as explained further in this paragraph. We also define for each subterm t of s a list of sequents $sequents(t)$ which is initialized by all the sequents γ' such that t appears in the tail of γ'. The detailed solution is illustrated by Algorithm 1 which relies on Algorithm 2 and both are given below.

Algorithm 2. *deduce*

Require: $t : subterm, i : step$
1: **if** $reach(p,t) > i$ **then**
2:    $reach(p,t) \leftarrow i$
3:    **for all** $\gamma \in sequents(t)$ **do**
4:       $\gamma.readiness$ $--$
5:       **if** $\gamma.readiness = 0$ **then**
6:          $\Gamma_i(p).add(\gamma)$
7:          $deduce(h(\gamma), i)$
8:       **end if**
9:    **end for**
10: **end if**

Algorithm 1. Reachability

Require: $\mathcal{IK}, s$
1: **for all** $t \in \mathcal{IK}$ **do**
2:    $deduce(t, 0)$
3: **end for**
4: **for all** $?m_k \in s$ **do**
5:    $deduce(m_k, k)$
6: **end for**

The idea is to perform a fix-point computation per each step i corresponding to the set $\Gamma_i(p)$. We start from subterms that are trivially reachable at some given step: elements in the initial knowledge which are all reachable at the initial step 0 and all the received messages clearly reachable at their corresponding reception step and try to deduce the newly reachable ones by checking whether there exists some sequents having their tails made only of reachable subterms. The head t of such a sequent is then reachable at step i and if this was not the case for a previous step, the value of $reach(p,t)$ is then set to i (Algorithm 2, line 2). In order to select these sequents we make use of the *readiness* field attached to each sequent which is decremented each time one element in its tail is discovered to be reachable (Algorithm 2, line 4). Since the *readiness* field is initialized by the cardinality of its tail thus whenever $\gamma.readiness$ equals zero at some step then the sequent is also valid at that step.

First, Algorithm 1 solves the the reachability problem since the value of $reach(p,t)$ is computed for all subterms of s. Second the sets $\Gamma_i(p)$ computed for all $1 \le i \le length(s)$ permit one to build a finite basis for all prefixes s^j where s is the communication scenario of p, namely the sets $\{h(\gamma) \stackrel{?}{=} s(\gamma)(t(\gamma))|\gamma \in \Gamma_i(p)\}$ for all $1 \le j \le length(s)$. We emphasize here the redundancy of these finite basis, since $\Gamma_{i-1}(p) \subseteq \Gamma_i$ for all $1 \le i \le length(s)$. This means that all the checks corresponding to sequents that are valid at some step are performed again in all the subsequent steps. We let $new(p,i)$ be the subset of elements in $\Gamma_i(p) \backslash \Gamma_{i-1}(p)$ for all $1 \le i \le length(s)$. The set $new(p,i)$ contains sequents that are valid only at step i and can be used as an optimized finite basis for the prefix s^i provided that $new(p,k)$ is also used as a finite basis for s^k for all $1 \le k \le i - 1$.

Algorithm 1 runs in linear time in the size of p represented as a directed acyclic graph (DAG) since the number of instructions performed by the algorithm is proportional to the sum of the sizes of $\mathcal{IK}$ and s represented as DAGs and the length of s.

ASLan generation. Given a partner $p = (n, \mathcal{IK}, c)$ we propose to generate its corresponding ASLan role $r(p)$. We will shortly describe the procedure we use for this purpose. First we associate a unique fresh variable name X_i for each reachable subterm t_i. These variables X_i will represent the parameters of the *state_n* fact. Then we define the initial state of $r(p)$ which will contain a *state_n* fact where all the variable X_j corresponding to values in $\mathcal{IK}$ are respectively replaced by these values. Finally we compute the transition system describing the communication behavior of $r(p)$. Each step is then translated to an ASLan transition that reflects the communication activity and the partner's knowledge evolution through the use of variables X_i while being possibly guarded by equality conditions involving these variables.

4   Experimental Results

This section is organized as follows: in § 4.1 we describe the deployment target for the prudent implementations obtained in § 3.3 then in § 4.2 we explain how our solution can be adapted for a multi-session setting and finally in § 4.3 we present an application of our approach for generating runnable Java distributions for mediators leading WS's orchestrations.

4.1   From ASLan to Servlets

We propose to realize each partner by a java servlet partially described below.

```
1 class Partner extends HttpServlet{
2   String[] X; int step;
3   void dispatch(String msg){
4     if(accept(msg)){step++; sendRemaining();}
5   }
6 }
```

First the array X is a holder for all the variables X_i defining the state of the considered role and the step field is an integer pointing to the current execution step already reached by the role. The core of the servlet is the dispatch method which is the handler of the received messages. dispatch supplies the received message msg to the accept method (not represented) which returns a positive answer only when *(i)* the step field corresponds to a reception activity and *(ii)* msg matches the parsing and the possibly inherent checks for the step step. In this case accept updates the array X possibly with newly computed values before returning. Then dispatch increments the step counter and calls sendRemaining (not represented) which is in charge of sending any message required to be sent by the role till reaching the next reception step or the end of the communication scenario.

We note that the code for the accept method can be easily generated from the ASLan specification by transforming each equality condition appended to a reception transition either to the instantiation of a new variable or to the check of a certain relation between already valuated variables. For example the portion of code to be executed by the method accept at step=3 is equivalent to the following:

```
1 if(msg.equals(X[10])){X[21] = msg; return(true);}
```

4.2   Multi-session Handling

Let us remark that the servlet presented in § 4.1 is not able to handle different interleaved sessions of the corresponding role. We propose here to leverage this restriction by modifying the generated servlet which now will hold a list of pairs $(X, step)$ representing the different sessions' states. We have then to define a *dispatch strategy* telling the servlet how messages are routed to the right sessions. As discussed in [19] a naive strategy can be applied if one is assured that all messages received by a partner have a *distinguishing value* (uniquely originating nonces) that is reachable by the partner at the reception step and such that it unambiguously defines the targeted session. Given this assumption and the prudence of the implementation we provide, one can use a naive yet correct algorithm to dispatch messages: try all the sessions for consuming an incoming message. Assuming that every reception leads to computing a distinguishing value and that the implementation performs all the possible correlation checks upon receptions we can be sure that at most one session is candidate to consume an incoming message and we call this property *unique dispatch* (UD).

We finally note that the NSPK protocol does not have the UD property, since $P(S)$ receives messages that does not contain distinguishing values (even if all other partners do). Nevertheless if every partner plays his expected part in the interleaving of two sessions of the NSPK protocol then $P(S)$ still reaches a satisfactory state where she also ends up correctly her two sessions. Therefore we think our approach stays applicable and globally correct even if the distinguishing value assumption is relaxed.

4.3   Testing Benchmark

In this section we describe a direct application of our approach for generating a prudent implementation for a *mediator* leading an *orchestration* between WS's.

In previous works [14,13] we presented an automated approach for solving an orchestration problem which we informally define here as synthesizing a new service we call a *mediator* permitting to answer all the requests of a given client while relying on a community of available services. Services are represented as security protocol roles and the orchestration problem is then encoded as the reachability of a satisfying state of the client starting from a configuration containing the community of services and given Dolev-Yao intruder capabilities for the mediator. This problem can be solved by a variety of tools from the security protocol literature and we choose CL-Atse [22] (a constraint-solver) for this task. The result returned by CL-Atse contains an A&B description of the communication (the intruder acting as) the mediator has to perform with (a subset) of the community of WS's and the client to effectively answer all the requests of the latter.

We propose to reuse the approach presented in this paper to *(i)* generate an ASLan description of the mediator and *(ii)* generate the mediator's BPEL process and thus permit leading and using the newly discovered orchestration. Objective *(i)* has been already fulfilled and our approach has been implemented and integrated to the AVANTSSAR Validation Platform [5]. Concerning *(ii)* we recall that all the generated mediators could not be brought to standard implementations and we stress the fact that our approach could at least answer the problem in a standard way whenever this is possible.

We successfully assessed our tool against three case-studies inspired from the test library [4] of the AVANTSSAR platform putting the focus on those representing orchestration problems. Our tool generated and deployed all the servlet needed by all the partners involved in each case-study and we effectively observed the conversation taking place between servlets as intended by the A&B specifications.

These case-studies tackle several aspects of security (*e.g.* probative value of digitally signed documents) and interoperability concerns and are summarized below:

- *Digital Contract Signing (DCS):* DCS represents a contract signing procedure carried out by two partners through secure access to a trusted third party web site, a business portal.
- *Public Bidding (PB)*: PB illustrates a secure document exchange, and aims at providing a web portal to manage an online call for tender, and also Bidders' proposal submissions.
- *Car Registration Process (CRP):* CRP models an e-government scenario, where a citizen have a secure access point, enabling communication with government offices and service providers in an easily usable and secure way.

Table 1 illustrates the obtained results for each case-study and for our running example where CS is the name of the case-study, $SIZE$ is the the sum of the sizes of all the partners, AGT (resp. SGT) is the time needed to generate the ASLan specification (resp. the Java servlets) for the case-study and finally AET (resp. SET) is the time needed to execute the generated ASLan specification (resp. the time needed by the generated Java servlets to end up a session).

Table 1. Tool Execution Times

CS	SIZE	AGT	SGT	AET	SET
NSPK	166	163 ms	1 s	708 ms	30 s
DCS	340	659 ms	2 s	3 m	1 m
PB	596	4 s	2 s	18 m	1 m
CRP	790	3 s	3 s	4 m	2 m

We note here that AET does not exclusively depend on the size of the case-study. Indeed CL-Atse have to first guess all the possible communication interleavings between all the generated ASLan roles. This is not the case for SET since the generated servlets respect one possible communication interleaving.

5   Conclusions

We present a tool that compiles an Alice&Bob description of a WS's choreography into their formal models enabling their automatic verification and if the models are secure into a set of java servlets that real partners can use to execute securely the choreography. We also developed a web application version of the tool (available at `https://cassis.loria.fr/WrapperGeneratorServlet/`) that permits in particular to automatically deploy the servlets generated from an A&B specification provided through a web form.

5.1   Related Works

Several works in the literature addressed the problem of translating A&B specifications of security protocols to formal languages in order to enable their verification or execution.

In [12] the authors translates A&B to CKT5 [9], a modal logic of communication, knowledge and time supporting symmetric encryption and thus adapted for security protocols. This permits to obtain a complete formal specification of the protocol, describing in particular the internal actions that should be taken by the involved partners to play their respective roles while enforcing a property equivalent to prudence [15].

In [21] the author translates a variant of the A&B notation defined over an arbitrary algebraic theory to the *IF* [6] formal language which is at the basis of ASLan. Using explicit destruction symbols this translation defines unambiguously how the protocol is supposed to be executed by honest agents according to algebraic properties of the operators. In this sense, this work is very close to ours and we can reuse its results (in particular the decidability of the finite basis problem in presence of algebraic reasoning) to extend our approach to cover using the XOR operator or modular exponentiation.

In [8] the authors propose a high-level language for specifying multiparty sessions and a compiler translating these high-level specifications to the cryptographic protocols implementing them. The considered sessions specify patterns of the message exchanges between distributed partners and their data accesses to a common database while ignoring their local behaviors and internal actions. The compiler then adds custom cryptographic protections to ensure authentication, integrity and freshness of the exchanged messages and generates the (ML) code for sending and receiving messages while enforcing the required cryptographic operations and type checks against an active adversary. The main differences with our approach is that *(i)* we consider executable choreographies and generate ready to run programs implementing them and *(ii)* we do not add security protection to the messages exchanged within the choreography in order to enforce security properties but rather permit the modeler to check whether her existing message-level policies are sufficient to enforce these properties by providing a verifiable formal specification of the choreography.

In [20] the authors generate Java code to implement cryptographic network protocols specified in CAPSL [16]. The output includes code for each party and for a demonstration environment that permits user examination and control of communication. The generated code relies on Standard Java cryptographic providers (which at the time was not supporting public key cryptography).

In [19] the authors describe a compiler that uses constraint-based analysis to produce multi-session server programs from cryptographic protocols formalized in CPPL [18]. The compilation succeeds whenever each message received by an agent playing the protocol contains a distinguishing value that can be extracted by the agent at the moment of reception. We reuse their compilation success criteria to analyze whether all partners have the UDP property before safely using our naive dispatch strategy.

5.2   Future Works

We conclude by a non-exhaustive list of possible extensions of the current work which we leave for future works:

- Provide prudent implementations supporting WS standards. To be more expressive in this direction we consider also generating enhanced SOAP engines for partners that possibly mixes cryptographic treatment and XML parsing.
- Extend the notion of prudent implementation to non-linear roles, *e.g.* by allowing roles to branch on dis-equalities between subterms;
- Sharpen the cryptographic functions definitions, *e.g.* parametrize *crypt* by the algorithm used (RSA for the current version) and any other parameter like the key size (current RSA key default length is 2048);
- Support more cryptographic primitives (*e.g.* XOR).

References

1. Network of Excellence on Engineering Secure Future Internet Software Services and Systems, NESSoS project, `http://www.nessos-project.eu`
2. Automated Validation of Trust and Security of Service-Oriented Architectures, AVANTSSAR project (2008-2010), `http://www.avantssar.eu`
3. AVANTSSAR. Deliverable 2.3: ASLan final version with dynamic service and policy composition (2010),
   `http://www.avantssar.eu/pdf/deliverables/avantssar-d2-3.pdf`
4. AVANTSSAR. Deliverable 5.4: Assessment of the AVANTSSAR Validation Platform (2010), `http://www.avantssar.eu`
5. AVANTSSAR. The AVANTSSAR Validation Platform (2010),
   `http://www.avantssar.eu`
6. AVISPA. Deliverable 2.3: The Intermediate Format (2003),
   `http://www.avispa-project.org`
7. Barros, A., Dumas, M., Oaks, P.: A Critical Overview of the Web Services Choreography Description Language (WS-CDL). BPTrends (2005)
8. Bhargavan, K., Corin, R., Deniélou, P.-M., Fournet, C., Leifer, J.J.: Cryptographic protocol synthesis and verification for multiparty sessions. In: Proceedings of the 2009 22nd IEEE Computer Security Foundations Symposium, pp. 124–140. IEEE Computer Society, Washington, DC (2009)

9. Bieber, P.: A logic of communication in hostile environment. In: Proceedings of the Computer Security Foundations Workshop III, pp. 14–22 (June 1990)
10. Bultan, T., Su, J., Fu, X.: Analyzing conversations of web services. IEEE Internet Computing 10(1), 18–25 (2006)
11. Carbone, M., Honda, K., Yoshida, N.: Structured Communication-Centred Programming for Web Services. In: De Nicola, R. (ed.) ESOP 2007. LNCS, vol. 4421, pp. 2–17. Springer, Heidelberg (2007)
12. Carlsen, U.: Generating formal cryptographic protocol specifications. In: Proceedings of the 1994 IEEE Computer Society Symposium on Research in Security and Privacy, pp. 137–146 (May 1994)
13. Chevalier, Y., Mekki, M.A., Rusinowitch, M.: Orchestration under security constraints. In: Sixth International Workshop on Formal Aspects in Security and Trust (FAST 2009), Eindhoven, the Netherlands, November 5-6 (2009)
14. Chevalier, Y., Mekki, M.A., Rusinowitch, M.: Automatic composition of services with security policies. In: Proceedings of the 2008 IEEE Congress on Services - Part I, SERVICES 2008, pp. 529–537. IEEE Computer Society, Washington, DC (2008)
15. Chevalier, Y., Rusinowitch, M.: Compiling and securing cryptographic protocols. Inf. Process. Lett. 110(3), 116–122 (2010)
16. Denker, G., Millen, J.: CAPSL integrated protocol environment. In: DARPA Information Survivability Conference (DISCEX 2000), pp. 207–221. IEEE Computer Society (2000)
17. Fabrega, F.J.T., Herzog, J.C., Guttman, J.D.: Strand spaces: why is a security protocol correct? In: Proceedings of the 1998 IEEE Symposium on Security and Privacy, pp. 160–171 (May 1998)
18. Guttman, J.D., Herzog, J.C., Ramsdell, J.D., Sniffen, B.T.: Programming Cryptographic Protocols. In: De Nicola, R., Sangiorgi, D. (eds.) TGC 2005. LNCS, vol. 3705, pp. 116–145. Springer, Heidelberg (2005)
19. McCarthy, J., Krishnamurthi, S.: Trusted Multiplexing of Cryptographic Protocols. In: Degano, P., Guttman, J.D. (eds.) FAST 2009. LNCS, vol. 5983, pp. 217–232. Springer, Heidelberg (2010)
20. Millen, J., Muller, F.: Cryptographic protocol generation from CAPSL. Technical Report SRI-CSL-01-07, SRI International (December 2001)
21. Mödersheim, S.: Algebraic properties in alice and bob notation. In: ARES, pp. 433–440. IEEE Computer Society (2009)
22. Turuani, M.: The CL-Atse Protocol Analyser. In: Pfenning, F. (ed.) RTA 2006. LNCS, vol. 4098, pp. 277–286. Springer, Heidelberg (2006)
23. W3C Consortium. XML Path Language (XPath) 2.0, 2nd edn. December 14 (2010), http://www.w3.org/TR/xpath20/
24. World Wide Web Consortium. Web Services Choreography Description Language Version 1.0, November 9 (2005), http://www.w3.org/TR/ws-cdl-10/

Evolving Security Requirements in Multi-layered Service-Oriented-Architectures

Muhammad Sabir Idrees[1], Gabriel Serme[2], Yves Roudier[1],
Anderson Santana De Oliveira[2], Herve Grall[3], and Mario Südholt[3]

[1] EURECOM,
2229 Route des Crêtes, 06904 Sophia Antipolis, France
{idrees,roudier}@eurecom.fr
[2] SAP Research,
805, Avenue du Dr. Maurice Donat 06250 Mougins
{gabriel.serme,anderson.santana.de.oliveira}@sap.com
[3] ASCOLA Group; EMN-INRIA, LINA,
Dpt. Informatique. École des Mines de Nantes,
4 rue Alfred Kastler, 44307 NANTES Cedex 3, France
{herve.grall,mario.sudholt}@emn.fr

Abstract. Due to today's rapidly changing corporate environments, business processes are increasingly subject to dynamic configuration and evolution. The evolution of new deployment architectures, as illustrated by the move towards mobile platforms and the Internet Of Services, and the introduction of new security regulations (imposed by national and international regulatory bodies, such as SOX[1] or BASEL[2]) are an important constraint in the design and development of business processes. In such a context, it is not sufficient to apply the corresponding adaptations only at the service orchestration or at the choreography level; there is also the need for controlling the impact of new security requirements to several architectural layers, specially in cloud computing, where the notion of Platforms as Services and Infrastructure as Services are fundamental. In this paper we survey several research questions related to security cross-domain and cross-layer security functionality in Service Oriented Architectures, from an original point of view. We provide the first insights on how a general service model empowered with aspect oriented programming capabilities can provide clean modularization to such cross-cutting security concerns.

Keywords: SOA, Evolution, AOP, REST, Security.

1   Motivation and Outline

Service-oriented architectures (SOAs) constitute a major architectural style for large-scale heterogeneous infrastructures and applications that are built from

---

[1] Sarbanes-Oxley Act of 2002 (Pub.L. 107-204, 116 Stat. 745, enacted July 30, 2002).
[2] http://bis.org/publ/bcbsca.htm

J. Garcia-Alfaro et al. (Eds.): DPM 2011 and SETOP 2011, LNCS 7122, pp. 190–205, 2012.

loosely-coupled, well-separated services and are subject to dynamic configuration, manipulation, and evolution. Applications in service-oriented computing have traditionally been developed using composition in homogeneous and simple frameworks. However, service-oriented architectures do not only rely on the simple composition of services but on compositions involving multiple architectural layers, especially when the underlying platforms and infrastructures are also seen as services themselves, like in cloud computing. The rapidly increasing need to integrate business applications deployed across distinct administrative domains reflects the reality of how software is being consumed nowadays. Such applications must also be compliant with security requirements and regulations, which can change and/or evolve according to the business context. For instance, access control and monitoring for intrusion detection are prime examples of functionalities that are subject to this problem: they cannot be properly modularized, that is, defined in well-separated modules, especially if they cross administrative or technological boundaries.

Problem Statement: The problem we expose in this paper is to understand how an evolution can modify the existing service-oriented architecture with respect to the new functional and more specifically non-functional (security, trust, QoS) requirements. These requirements have to be applied consistently on the system architecture, thus involving complex service orchestrations and choreographies. They often involve invasive modifications, e.g., to enable new security functionalities that depend on and require modifications to low-level infrastructure functionalities. Hence, SOAs are also subject to evolution using *vertical composition*, that is, the coordination of multiple architectural layers over which the SOA is deployed, including operating systems, application servers, enterprise service buses, orchestration engines, etc. In contrast, *horizontal composition* consists in high level service compositions towards the achievement of business goals, typically expressed as orchestrations or choreographies.

Security analysts also need to consider threats to the underlying infrastructure and middleware for a particular SOA implementation. While it is easier to analyze the protection level at each separate layer in the SOA stack, the security properties expected from the software span across those layers. The assets to be protected originate both from the horizontal and vertical compositions. The security that may mitigate potential threats to these assets have to be deployed at different parts of that stack, and in a coordinated manner.

Aspect-Oriented Software Development (AOSD)[8,1] has emerged as the domain investigating and providing solutions for the systematic treatment of such cross-cutting functionalities. Here, we aim at exploring the combination of invasive aspects and black-box aspect compositions to secure service-oriented architectures.

The current state of the art does not propose a full fledged solution to manage, in a modular way, different security requirements affecting different architectural levels in SOAs. We propose an integrated approach, relying on AOSD, that will allow for eliciting security requirements, to formally reason about the interactions among requirements and the target service compositions, to implement security functionality as aspects, and to evolve these requirements in a controlled manner. We are building an aspect based service model, enabling the conception of service compositions within cross administrative domains and allowing security functionalities to be modularized. In the current paper we report on the challenges we are facing in these research directions.

The remainder of this paper is organized as follows: Section 2 describes our view of multi-layered SOA architecture with related security concerns and security requirements discussed in Section 3. Section 4 presents the aspect based service model that we propose through a use case. Section 5 reviews the capabilities of the existing approaches in terms of aspects for security and adaptation of SOA in a distributed context. Finally, a conclusion summarizes the attained results and briefly presents future work in Section 6.

2   Multi-layered Service-Oriented Architectures

Service-oriented architectures (SOAs) are considered as advanced component-based architectures for the construction of distributed systems. SOA can be seen as a continuum of different components at different levels of system abstraction, like the infrastructure, platform/middleware, and software viewpoints (cf. Figure 1). The fundamental assumption of SOA, where the service consumer needs not to worry about service implementation details and the underlying infrastructure: the availability of a software view (cf. Section 2.1 enumeration 1) to the application designer makes it possible to hide the unnecessary complexity in the implementation of business services originating from the underlying layers. Lower layers enforce different business logics, security policies, or functional constraints and have to be coordinated together with the execution of the application in order to give access to services and resources of the infrastructure. Nevertheless, as stated in [2], apart from the notion of service orientation that eases the design through loosely coupled interfaces, the service oriented architecture itself does not provide direct solutions to many of the available intricate requirements that arise while evolving such architectures.

2.1   Layering in Service-Oriented Architectures

We distinguish the following three different layers that entail three corresponding architectural views:

1. **Software View:** this layer is the most important one for the application designer. This is the place where he implements services using other services and mechanisms from lower layers. This is also the place where the application designer specifies how processes should be coordinated through the expression of orchestrations. Such a specification is generally done using a dedicated workflow languages (e.g., BPMN2.0, BPEL). In the process of orchestration the designer associates a software functionality (the services) in a non-hierarchical arrangement using a software tool (i.e., SAP Business ByDesign) that contains a complete list of all available services, their characteristics and resources, and the means to build an application utilizing

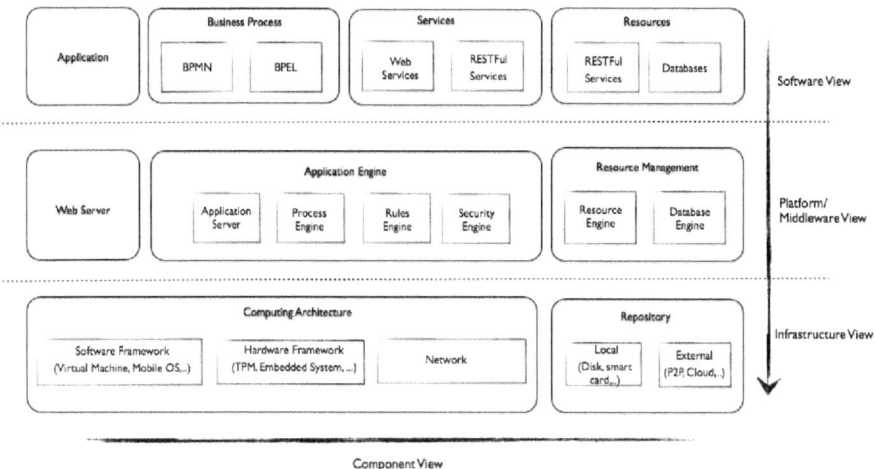

Fig. 1. A synthetic overview of Multi-layered Service-Oriented-Architecture

these sources. This specification defines how the platform layer should be configured.

Many platforms nowadays proposes Software on-demand, also known as Software as a Service (SaaS). SaaS vendors provide applications (i.e., SAP On-Demand Apps, Intalio BPM, etc.) to end users on demand. These solutions heavily rely on SOA, by abstracting every lower layer as sets of services that need to be correctly orchestrated and "consumed" by customers.

2. **Platform/Middleware View:** Service-oriented architecture middleware provides all of the facilities required to support the complete lifecycle of services. For services to operate, a middleware layer provides a collection of components (i.e., web server, application engine, or resource engine) for supporting the deployment of virtually any application. The coordination of services and the handling of the fine-grained logic of services are enforced at this layer. For instance, the definition of business rules and non functional constraints that apply to a process can be enforced by the rule engine and by the security engine components.

In order to facilitate the deployment of business applications without considering functional and non-functional constraints (i.e., cost and complexity of buying and managing the underlying hardware and software and provisioning hosting capabilities), many platforms nowadays offer the Platform as a Service (PaaS) abstraction, like Google's AppEngine, or SAP's OnDemand Platform, for application deployment and testing. PaaS provides an additional level of abstraction emulating a virtual platform on top of the infrastructure. PaaS generally features a form of mediation to the underlying services akin to middleware in traditional communication stacks.

3. **Infrastructure View:** From the infrastructure perspective, one can distinguish between the computing architecture (software framework, hardware architecture, network, etc.) and resource repository (local or distributed) components. Any of the operations related to such low-level components must be done at this layer. For instance, the secure generation/computation/storage of cryptographic keys used to secure network communication heavily depends on the software or hardware support. The use of firewalls to control communication between two organizations is also not to be handled at the service nor platform levels.

   This point of view has been conceptualized as the Infrastructure as a Service (IaaS) approach, much touted in cloud computing, and which aims at sharing the infrastructure in order to reduce the cost of operating it. Services in that case relate to the management and customization of infrastructure mechanisms. Virtualized execution environments for the deployment of applications and distributed data storage are common examples of such services. They are being supported by an increasing range of companies (Amazon, Google, SAP, etc.) and brought to the programmer through an increasing number of service oriented APIs, notably REST ones, like for instance Amazon's services EC2 for execution environments, and S3 for distributed data storage.

The research topics we expose in this paper bring to light the need to uniformly represent, to reason about, and to deploy security (but similarly other crosscutting concerns) at the different layers of the architecture. Although these software solutions are increasingly widespread, there is no support for the modular design and evolution of the corresponding security concerns.

3   SOA Security Concerns

The preoccupation in anticipating possible security flaws in the SOAs infrastructures is fundamental for increasing the reliability of e-business applications, such that it can be widely adopted, enabling the future Internet of Services. The security analysis of SOA based business process has been extensively reviewed in the literature [14,12,11,10,16]. However, it has previously been addressed mainly from an application perspective only. In comparison, not much has been done to analyze the application level impact of attacks and vulnerabilities (also extensively analyzed but in isolation of any application) at lower layers in the SOA stack.

3.1   Attacker Model

Despite the multitude of proposed attack analysis that have hitherto been described in the literature, we take the view that existing attacker models are essentially based on vulnerabilities expressed at a single layer (more frequently low-level). We have adopted a set of practices from fundamental works in attacks on

SOA and vulnerability analysis in a new combined methodology (Multi-Layered Attacker Model - MLAM) that seems to be well-adapted to SOAs layered architectures (cf. Figure 1). The perspective we have adopted for the identification of security flaws is to have a unified approach where we consider attacks/vulnerabilities at different layers of the SOA system. The essential means that we use consist in an approach for categorizing attacks and their relationships and dependencies at different levels of abstraction, and a means for specifying a range of modalities. In order to do so, we consider a layered attack view comprising the Software attack View (SaV), the Platform attack View (PaV) and the Infrastructure attack View (IaV). Due to lack of space, we only give an abstract overview of MLAM with respect to attack(s) on multilayered service-oriented architectures. However, more detailed attack analysis and threat categorization can be found in [15,7] .

At the SaV level, security flaws are mostly related to vulnerabilities in software/application/services. These attacks rely on programming mistakes (weaknesses in the application), sometimes exploiting inadequacies between the design flaw or an implementation [14]. This is the case for injections attacks, like SQL injections, which can make it possible to read and disclose confidential data to an attacker. Similarly in WSDL scanning attacks, the access information revealed about some web sites may result in more specific and more targeted attacks.

At the PaV level, attacks rely on protocol design mistakes, on weaknesses of cryptographic primitives, on weaknesses in information processing, or sometimes on the exploitation of communication and computation implicit and harmful assumptions. Furthermore, a poor configuration and the improper use of external resources (i.e., external reference attacks) may allow an attacker to perform different denial of service attacks or information theft.

At the IaV level, an attacker might target the infrastructure by abusing resources in unforeseen ways. For instance, attacks on the power consumption, computing time, or electromagnetic emissions may lead to find out what operations are performed or what is the value of some sensitive (in particular cryptographic) data. Furthermore, the possibility of a resource compromise (injecting/altering data) significantly increases in infrastructures based on decentralization (e.g., P2P, Cloud computing), due to the architecture and to the complexity or weakness of the system with respect to operations like access controls, which may require anonymous accesses, or which may be too inflexible to configure efficiently; or authentication, in particular, when the actual deployment relies on reusable tokens/passwords, or even worse on cleartext authentication and/or transmission of content.

Merging the results of these three viewpoints: SaV, PaV and IaV helps to both identify and classify attacks on different assets as well as to highlight their relationships at different layer of the service composition.

3.2   Security Requirements

The deployment of an application requires the definition of the security properties that it should meet. This is typically performed on the basis of a security policy, which aims at providing a high-level abstraction to the application developer. In the following we present the inherent complex implications of seemingly simple security properties in a multi-layered SOA system.

- **Integrity** applies to a quantum of information between two observations (defined, e.g., by a time and a location in the system). The property is satisfied when the quantum of information has not been modified between the two observations. This property should be monitored of course to check whether a message sent between services has not been altered, but also with respect to guarantee that the content of a storage facility has not been modified between two given read operations, or even to ensure that the execution of the software implementing a service is not being attacked through a modification to the execution environment or the code it runs.

- **Confidentiality** applies to a quantum of information and a set of authorized entities. The property is satisfied when the authorized entities are the only ones that can know the quantum of information. Thus, confidentiality properties defined at a high level should be translated at the resource level and will result in defensive security requirements with respect to data encryption, access control policies to data, and data placement.

- **Availability** applies to a service, platform, or a physical device providing a service. The property is satisfied when some service is operational. The property can be further detailed with the specification of a period during which the availability is required and of a set of client entities requesting the availability. Availability properties may impose requirements on the security mechanisms that can be implemented on a particular application, platform (like, availability of the specific process engine i.e., SAP Netweaver), or execution environment depending on the CPU, memory, networking capabilities of the considered environment or the availability of specific cryptographic functions (accelerated or not).

Other security properties that may be attached to services have a similar impact at the different levels of the SOA stack. In addition, due to their high level of abstraction, SOA applications often introduce new security properties that are themselves composing several primitive security properties: for instance, the concept of separation of duty may rely on the sequencing of two authentications.

4   Towards an Aspect-Based SOA Model

In the previous section, we introduced our concept of multi-layered SOA and briefly outlined how security concerns may have implications at different levels of a layered SOA stack. Evolution of services and notably their security requirements are hard to implement existing infrastructures, such as generic libraries. We claim that invasive modifications are needed to obtain an overall and consistent security across the system. In the following, we are discussing an Aspect-Oriented approach to ensure a systematic and consistent handling of security concerns. We articulate this section with an integrity-related use-case that deals with certifying the validity of different components as shown in Figure 1.

4.1 Implications of the Integrity Property on the SOA Stack

While designing one application, an architect identifies sensitive information he wants to protect from non-authorized modifications. In the following, we assume this sensitive information is a Customer object. He wants to introduce integrity mechanisms throughout the architecture to prevent attacks whenever a Customer object is used. Introduction of integrity involves different components, that depends on several layers. Modifications to enable such property are invasive and affect several modules.

To achieve the overall integrity, we envision modifications at the three views represented in Figure 1. Software view is impacted to ensure correct handling of data when the Customer object is part of a collaboration. For example, if a business process has a step that transmits Customer data over the network through a Web Service invocation. Protecting integrity at this stage can be realized with WS-Security standards that provides message integrity. Albeit the application layer is protected against alteration over communication, the Customer object can still suffer from local modifications - that occur at the Platform View. At this layer, an attacker can modify a process execution flow to extract information from the process engine, by adding one step that leaks Customer information. The Platform view is then impacted to ensure a valid execution flow that cannot be modified by external entities. The bottom layer, or the Infrastructure view is the place where we can certify the validity of the upper components. In our example, this bottom layer is used to ensure integrity of the process engine with a mechanism similar to a Trusted Platform Module.

Achieving these modifications from the bottom layer ensures that all components involved in integrity protection at higher layers cannot be further replaced and modified by unauthorized parties. We start from the infrastructure view to build trust on all layers. But the application designer who wants to implement its security property faces the complexity of modifying and configuring a huge amount of components and source code which he did not even author. Also, each layer has security concerns that differ from the other layers.

4.2 A Solution to Achieve Integrity with Aspects

A traditional approach to achieving integrity for such Customer objects requires the application designer to gather its developer team, security architects, business owners, and whoever is involved in application development, to configure and extend applications, modify programs, *etc.*. In this section, we provide some snippets of code that can, under certain conditions, make it possible to change the behavior of existing security services and components as well as business services, and also specialize services written in advance without the knowledge of a specific application through a separation of concerns between security and business requirements. This approach, which is more broadly discussed in the next section, allows a fine-grained control of the implementation of requirements of an application that relies on a multi-layer SOA.

In the following, we illustrate with different code snippets how to address integrity in the impacted views. The snippets are independent from one another, that is they represent enforcement code to achieve a higher-level purpose. This purpose is driven by the architects and security experts that specify means guaranteeing properties at different levels. This entails the instantiation of invasive modifications as discussed in the previous section. The software layer provides a signature when receiving a Customer object from a collaboration. The platform layer provides process engine integrity, such that it guarantees the execution flow of a business process and prevents anybody from injecting a new step in the process that may leak a Customer object. Finally, the infrastructure layer provides means to guarantee trusted components at the platform level, by verifying that running components are those intended.

The aspects have to obey a precise lifecycle from specification via implementation to execution. We now consider the different roles involved in the correct application of aspects at the different levels. First of all, security aspects are created to respect specifications, given by a policy or by various requirements. We expect business owners to come with requirements that are refined by security experts. The aspect development per-se is done once with a high control on the code produce, thus the correctness. The development has to be handled by trusted developers, understanding security implication of their code in base-application. The deployment can be done prior execution by owners of the application, and execution is launched by platform administrator. The platform shall prevent consumers from modifying binaries and processes.

The first snippet in Listing 1.1 represents an aspect module that can be used to track message signature upon reception. It relates to standards such as WS-Security but with adaptation: our aspect code does not look for the systematic presence of signature tokens, but rather adds this specific mechanism when a Customer object is involved. It means that the client, prior to sending, adds a signature token when involving such an object. This behavior can be represented as a policy that clients understand and apply. The code shown is executed on the server side. Line 4 shows an annotation indicating the usage of this advice code for software view integrity. The pointcut at Line 5 uses a custom token *from-message*, which binds a message received by the application to the advice code to further investigate it. Lines 6 to 8 express the advice signature, which gets a Message and Customer object. Lines 10 to 22 contain the identification extraction from the message to verify the message signature. A valid signature indicates that the message has not been tampered with and can then be processed normally by the application.

```
1  @Aspect ("perProcess", SecurityProperty.INTEGRITY)
2  class CustomerIntegrity {
3      /* (i) Retrieve and validate sign info */
4      @Coverage(Level.SOFTWARE)
```

```
5   @Around("execution (* *(Customer)) && args(c) && from-
        message(m)")
6   public Object validateCustomerSignature (JointPoint jp
7       , Customer c
8       , Message m) throws CustomerIntegrityException{
9       //get public key of issuer
10      Identity issuer = m.getIssuer(); //retrieve identity
            from msg if present
11      X509EncodedKeySpec pubKeySpec = new X509EncodedKeySpec
            (Security.getPubKey(issuer));
12      KeyFactory keyFactory = KeyFactory.getInstance("DSA",
            "SUN");
13      PublicKey pubKey = keyFactory.generatePublic(
            pubKeySpec);
14      //get message signature
15      Signature sig = Signature.getInstance("SHA1withDSA", "
            SUN");
16      sig.initVerify(pubKey);
17      sig.update(m.getData());
18      //verify
19      boolean verifies = sig.verify(m.getInlineSignature());
20      if (!verifies)
21          throw new CustomerIntegrityException (c);
22      return jp.proceed();
23  }
24 }
```

Listing 1.1. Introducing Integrity at the Software Level

The second snippet in Listing 1.2 provides process engine integrity for business processes involving Customer manipulation. The underlying engine is an orchestration engine (BPMN 2.0 or BPEL engine) that should not be modified by unauthorized parties. More precisely, we allow activity and task execution only if the issuer is authorized to do so at a given stage in a business process. Lines 4 to 8 are a specific pointcut that respects AspectJ syntax - whenever an Activity execution is detected, a check is made to know if the process definition use a Customer object, thanks to a helper class. Then, at joinpoints, the advice described in Lines 10 to 20 is triggered. The behavior introduced is to check the prior execution of the activity and whether the action is authorized or not. The overall aspect allows a cross-cutting verification that business processes manipulating Customer objects are safe with regards to the planned behavior. It does not replace the engine enforcement but add an additional layer of confidence.

```
1  @Aspect ("perProcess", SecurityProperty.INTEGRITY)
2  class ProcessEngineFlowIntegrity {
3
4      @Pointcut("call(* *.*(Activity)) && args(a) && if()")
5      public static boolean processWithCustomer (Activity a) {
```

```
6     ProcessDefinition pd = a.getProcessDefinition();
7     return Helper.processUses(pd, Customer.class);
8   }
9
10  @Coverage(Level.PLATFORM)
11  @Around("processWithCustomer(Activity)")
12  public Object validateCustomerSignature (JointPoint jp
13      , Activity a) throws ProcessIntegrityException{
14    ProcessDefinition pd = a.getProcessDefinition();
15    for (User authorizedid : pd.getAuthorizedId(a){
16      if (a.getIssuer().equals(authorizedid))
17        return jp.proceed();
18    }
19    throws new ProcessIntegrityException(a);
20  }
21 }
```

Listing 1.2. Platform Level Integrity to control business process execution

The Listing 1.3 represents the behavior to be launched once per process execution. Prior to its execution, a process performs a check to verify the integrity of all involved components running in the infrastructure. Line 4 depicts an annotation that expresses the level related to views expressed in Figure 1. It means that the given code to be executed allows integrity coverage for the infrastructure level. Line 5 contains a custom pointcut element. The *start* expresses that whenever a Platform is used, the given advice has to be executed. Lines 6 to 8 represent the advice signature. We assume that we get an object called *SecurityPlatform* representing a security instance for the running process. Then, this object is used in Lines 9 and following to verify the integrity of the given platform being started. Deploying such code assumes that a valid Trusted Platform Module is present in the infrastructure view of our application, and that all components are correctly registered. The advice code ensures then that the process engine, among other platform components, has not been tampered with.

```
1  @Aspect ("perProcess", SecurityProperty.INTEGRITY)
2  class PlatformComponentsIntegrity {
3    @Coverage(Level.INFRASTRUCTURE)
4    @Before("start(Platform) && args(p)")
5    public void testPlatformIntegrity (JointPoint jp
6        , SecurityPlatform sp
7        , Platform p) throws PlatformIntegrityException{
8      sp.getTPM().verify(p.getTPMKeys());
9
10     if (sp & SecurityPlatform.CORRUPTED)
11       throw new PlatformIntegrityException(p);
12     if (sp & (SecurityPlatform.LOADING
13         | SecurityPlatform.CHECKING))
```

```
14        p.log ("Still waiting validation");
15      else
16        sp.validate (p);
17    }
18  }
```

Listing 1.3. Introducing Integrity at the Infrastructure Level

We have highlighted how the evolution of a security requirement impacts over-all the different views involved in SOA execution. The snippets presented use AspectJ-like syntax enhanced with custom elements indicate how they are to be implemented in our framework. The pointcut language enrichment is one key to provide an easier mapping between the application execution and the over-all security wanted, this is also under study. With the case of integrity, where one can request to protect integrity of specific data, we have shown it imply invasive modifications that pervade applications and components. Furthermore, components between them have no specific relation, due to the representation at the programming level. Nevertheless, aspect definition and application re-spect a global vision controlled by architects and business owners. We propose to develop a solution based on aspects that target not only software view of an application, but also platform and infrastructure view to achieve an overall application of integrity. Therefore a major research question relies on how the service model and the aspect model need to be designed to facilitate the re-lationship of non-functional concerns to the architectural components at each layer. Another constraint is the impact on the performance of the system. One research direction is to evaluate how load-time weaving or static weaving can help to reduce the overhead.

4.3   Aspect Model Design Criteria

In order to apply AOP to the evolution of security requirements defined ac-cording to the different views we have, aspects have to meet basic properties. Generally, aspect models come in very different forms, concerning their basic concepts but also implementation strategies, suitability for the application of formal methods, etc. The proposed aspect model that is used in the previous section has different characteristics. We presented some in snippets code (List-ings 1.1,1.2,1.3) but try to formalize our contribution in this section - a work which is currently in progress.

   The aspect model we envision is based on the pointcut-advice model for as-pects, with some important extensions to be applied. The pointcut-advice model is characterized by three main abstractions: aspects, pointcuts and advice that together provide means for the concise definition and efficient implementation of so-called crosscutting functionalities of a base application, such as security, that cannot typically be modularized with existing structuring and encapsula-tion mechanisms, such as services or components. We address these requirements by the following set of major characteristics that the aspect model has to fulfill.

These characteristics are for most of them general in the sense that they apply to all three basic aspect abstractions (aspects, pointcuts and advice) - except if stated otherwise in the following:

- **Basic abstractions and relations:** The pointcut language should enable referencing all relevant abstractions of the service model and the concrete infrastructures; the advice language allows to manipulate these entities. Concrete examples for such abstractions include collaborations, processes, services and resources. Relevant relationships between them include relations between adjacent abstraction levels or the ability to protect some of them using certain security mechanisms, such as access control, while others may not be modified by that security mechanism.
- **Composition model:** The aspect model should provide a gray-box composition model, i.e., aspects may access parts of service implementations. However, such access can be restricted by explicit fine-grained conditions on the structure and behavior of the underlying base system. The aspect model will therefore provide strong control over invasive composition. Corresponding conditions will be defined as part of evolution tasks through the aspects that realize them. The conditions may then be integrated before execution in the runtime representations of aspects or the underlying infrastructure, or enforced, possibly at execution time, on service implementations.
- **Dynamic application:** Aspects should be applicable dynamically even though static application strategies may also be used, especially for the introduction of security mechanisms that would suffer from an excessive overhead. Many current aspect models only support a static or load-time application of aspects, which severely limits their applicability for many composition tasks. Our model therefore significantly broadens the use of aspects to many real-world scenarios that involve highly dynamic service applications. Another general characteristic of our model is that the model enables the aspect-based definition of service evolutions whose (security) properties can be formally analyzed.
- **Formal properties:** The aspect model should include explicit means to restrict aspects, pointcuts and advice, such that relevant formal properties of service evolutions defined using aspects can be specified precisely, formally analyzed and enforced on corresponding implementations.
- **Protocol support:** The pointcut language should include direct support for matching (parts of) protocols that govern the collaboration (choreography etc.) between entities of the service model. The advice language permits the manipulation of protocols.
- **Local state:** Aspects may contain local state that can be used to modify state of the base application. Aspect definitions may, however, restrict the kind of state that can be defined and used.

Even though our solution is not fully developed yet, we highlighted the need for a new approach to secure not only classical layers (software view) but the entire chain of components supporting service processing and coordination.

Aspect-based techniques meet our requirements to express and apply concerns that are normally difficult to address as their impact is scattered in a multi-layer SOA stack.

5   Related Work

Service-oriented systems are characterized by complex interactions among functional, management and infrastructure interfaces. Aspect-oriented approaches have been proposed to address such issues, although only in the context of existing orchestration services for SOAs.

Aspect-Oriented Software Development (AOSD) [8,1] has emerged over the previous decade as the domain of systematic exploration of crosscutting concerns and corresponding support throughout the software development process. AOSD has been applied to service-oriented systems (mainly based on web services) and also to the modularization of crosscutting security policies for sequential and distributed systems (including few work on services). However, current AOSD approaches typically target a single virtual machine or platform and the process of coordinating aspects through points of execution is centralized. Some recent approaches, such as AWED [3] and DyMac [9] support the modularization of the crosscutting functionalities of distributed applications. These systems extend basic concepts of AOSD such as pointcuts and advices to remote pointcuts and remote advices that allow concerns to be composed across different locations.

The specific case of security in service-oriented architectures has also been addressed through aspect-oriented approaches. For instance, Courbis and Finkelstein [6] proposed to weave aspects into web service orchestrations. Service orchestrations, in particular using the language BPEL, have also been extended with aspect support by Charfi and Mezini [4]. Still, not much has been done to date to provide support for multilevel horizontal and vertical service compositions or for enforcing security mechanisms at multilevel service composition in the presence of aspects. Furthermore, in a distributed context, and specifically in service-oriented computing, there are currently still very few results on the enforcement and preservation of security properties in the presence of aspects. Svirskas et al. [16] have proposed a mechanism of structured compliance proof that guarantees that these protocols are enacted in compliance with the effective policies and regulations. However, these approaches are only considering service compositions at one level.

As to the evolution of SOAs, Chen et al. [5] have proposed an extensible SOA-based platform and provided a roadmap for SOA evolution. Mingyan and Yanzhang [13] presented a service-oriented dynamic evolution model named SOEM model and gave a formal description of a series of concept in service-oriented software evolution process. Several research challenges in maintenance and evolution of SOA are also discussed in [10], like for instance multilanguage system analysis and maintenance, the reengineering of processes for migration to SOA environments and evolution patterns of Service-Oriented Systems. However, these development methods and techniques for SOA lack means to analyze and preserve properties in the presence of evolution, especially regarding security properties.

204 M. Sabir Idrees et al.

6 Conclusion and Future Work

Applications in service-oriented computing have traditionally been developed using composition in homogeneous and simple frameworks. However, the trend towards increasingly complex infrastructures indicates a need for a general service model that would make it possible to achieve a uniform approach yet to separate business process concerns from their diverse security requirements (which are even more subject to evolution over time). SOA cannot rely on the only composition of services and disregard the security of other software layers on top of which services are implemented.

We have exposed in this paper in what respect the complexity of service-oriented architectures and their evolution involve challenging research problems, in particular with respect to the understanding of security threats and even more so to the specification of security properties and mechanisms.

Research Challenges: We can summarize the major challenges we will address in the near future in the following questions:

- How to create appropriate abstractions for the different architectural layers in SOA's as to understand the impact of evolutions to the overall system security?
- How to provide support for threat analysis in cross-domain multi-layered SOAs, when moving towards to deployment models based on clouds and integration of mobile devices?
- How security concerns can be modularized and uniformly deployed in cross-domain service orchestrations using vertical and horizontal aspect orientation capabilities? We also discussed in this paper a new approach to the description of the service model relying on invasive aspects introduced at multiple levels of abstraction. This model will make it possible to develop and evolve service-oriented applications in dynamic business contexts, while keeping the complexity of managing their security manageable.
- How to manage possibly conflicting security requirements, specifically when composing distinct security aspects at a given level? We have started defining a formal model for secure services in order to deal with possibly conflicting security requirements. This specification will play a central role in the design of a flexible aspect model appropriate for dealing with multi-layer security concerns. We shall investigate how to provide security requirements specifications such that these conflicts can be detected and solved.

Acknowledgment. This work was supported by the ANR, the French National Research Organization through the project CESSA (Compositional Evolution of Secure Services with Aspects, ID.: 09-SEGI-002-01).

References

1. Akşit, M., Clarke, S., Elrad, T., Filman, R.E. (eds.): Aspect-Oriented Software Development. Addison-Wesley Professional (September 2004)

2. Bagheri, E., Ghorbani, A.: A service oriented approach to critical infrastructure modeling. In: Workshop on Service Oriented Techniques. National Research Council, Canada (2006)
3. Navarro, L.D.B., Südholt, M., Vanderperren, W., Verheecke, B.: Modularization of Distributed Web Services Using Aspects with Explicit Distribution (AWED). In: Meersman, R., Tari, Z. (eds.) OTM 2006. LNCS, vol. 4276, pp. 1449–1466. Springer, Heidelberg (2006)
4. Charfi, A., Mezini, M.: Ao4bpel: An aspect-oriented extension to bpel. World Wide Web 10(3), 309–344 (2007)
5. Chen, Q., Shen, J., Dong, Y., Dai, J., Xu, W.: Building a collaborative manufacturing system on an extensible soa-based platform. In: 10th International Conference on Computer Supported Cooperative Work in Design, CSCWD 2006, pp. 1–6 (May 2006)
6. Courbis, C., Finkelstein, A.: Weaving aspects into web service orchestrations. In: ICWS 2005: Proceedings of the IEEE International Conference on Web Services, pp. 219–226. IEEE Computer Society, Washington, DC (2005)
7. Idrees, M.S., Serme, G., Roudier, Y., et al.: State of the art and requirement analysis of security functionalities for soas. Deliverable D2.1, The CESSA project (July 2010),
   http://cessa.gforge.inria.fr/lib/exe/fetch.php?media=publications:d2-1.pdf
8. Kiczales, G.: Aspect-oriented programming. ACM Comput. Surv. 28(4es), 154 (1996)
9. Lagaisse, B., Joosen, W.: True and Transparent Distributed Composition of Aspect-Components. In: van Steen, M., Henning, M. (eds.) Middleware 2006. LNCS, vol. 4290, pp. 42–61. Springer, Heidelberg (2006)
10. Lewis, G., Smith, D.: Service-oriented architecture and its implications for software maintenance and evolution. In: Frontiers of Software Maintenance, FoSM 2008, pp. 1–10 (September 2008)
11. Lowis, L., Accorsi, R.: On a classification approach for soa vulnerabilities. In: International Computer Software and Applications Conference, pp. 439–444 (2009)
12. Lowis, L., Accorsi, R.: Vulnerability analysis in soa-based business processes. IEEE Transactions on Services Computing 99(PrePrints) (2010)
13. Mingyan, Z., Yanzhang, W., Xiaodong, C., Kai, X.: Service-oriented dynamic evolution model. In: International Symposium on Computational Intelligence and Design, ISCID 2008, vol. 1, pp. 322–326 (October 2008)
14. OWASP. Open web application security project,
   https://www.owasp.org/index.php/category:attack
15. Serme, G., Idrees, M.S., Roudier, Y., et al.: Compositional evolution of secure services using aspects. Deliverable D3.1, The CESSA project (July 2011),
   http://cessa.gforge.inria.fr/lib/exe/fetch.php?media=publications:d3-1.pdf
16. Svirskas, A., Isacenkova, J., Molva, R.: Towards secure and trusted collaboration environment for European public sector. In: 2nd International Workshop on Trusted Collaboration, TrustCol 2007, New York, USA, November 12-15 (November 2007)

Risk-Based Auto-delegation
for Probabilistic Availability [*]

Leanid Krautsevich[1], Fabio Martinelli[2],
Charles Morisset[2], and Artsiom Yautsiukhin[2]

[1] University of Pisa, Department of Computer Science,
Largo B. Pontecorvo 3, 56127 Pisa, Italy
krautsev@di.unipi.it
[2] IIT-CNR, Security Group,
Via Giuseppe Moruzzi 1, 56124 Pisa, Italy
firstname.lastname@iit.cnr.it

Abstract. Dynamic and evolving systems might require flexible access control mechanisms, in order to make sure that the unavailability of some users does not prevent the system to be functional, in particular for emergency-prone environments, such as healthcare, natural disaster response teams, or military systems. The auto-delegation mechanism, which combines the strengths of delegation systems and "break-the-glass" policies, was recently introduced to handle such situations, by stating that the most qualified available user for a resource can access this resource.

In this work we extend this mechanism by considering availability as a quantitative measure, such that each user is associated with a probability of availability. The decision to allow or deny an access is based on the utility of each outcome and on a risk strategy. We describe a generic framework allowing a system designer to define these different concepts. We also illustrate our framework with two specific use cases inspired from healthcare systems and resource management systems.

Keywords: Auto-delegation, Access control, Risk, Availability.

1 Introduction

The main function of an access control system is to intercept any access request made by an active entity (subject) to a passive entity (object) in order to decide if an access should be granted or denied. An access control system usually consists of two parts: an access control policy and a reference monitor. The access control policy explicitly defines which access requests should be allowed and which should be denied. The reference monitor is a piece of software responsible for intercepting access requests and matching them against the policy.

---

[*] Work partially supported by EU FP7-ICT project NESSoS (Network of Excellence on Engineering Secure Future Internet Software Services and Systems) under the grant agreement n. 256980 and by EU-funded project "CONNECT".

J. Garcia-Alfaro et al. (Eds.): DPM 2011 and SETOP 2011, LNCS 7122, pp. 206–220, 2012.

The problem of defining a powerful-enough access control system has been identified long time ago [21] and since then several well-known policies and systems have been proposed. Examples of access control models are the discretionary model [21,16], used, for instance, in operating systems; the Bell-LaPadula model [22], used in a military environment; the Chinese Wall model [2], used in the consulting world; and more recently-proposed the Role-Based (RBAC) model [13], used in databases and business information systems.

A common feature among these models is that they have the main focus on subjects: each policy describes which objects a subject can access. Usually, such policy defines a decision about the access for a subject independently from the other subjects. For instance, in an health-care system, a nurse cannot access a medical record regardless of the fact that a physician can or cannot access this medical record. Although this independence property makes sense in the general case, in some situations, subjects which have access to a critical object may be unavailable. In such situations the object cannot be accessed by anyone and this limitation of the access control system leads to a potentially life-threatening situation. An example could be a patient record required for curing a person who is having an heart attack or essential military intelligence report when it is unknown if the responsible officer is alive or not.

Hence, in some situations, there is a clear need to provide the access control mechanism with the possibility of granting an access that was not originally allowed. Two main approaches exist in the literature to address this need: the enforcement of delegations, and "break-the-glass" policies. A delegation mechanism [4] allows a user to delegate some of her permissions to another user. For example, a doctor delegates her right to access records of her patients to her assistant when she is not available. The main drawback of delegations is that they need to be activated beforehand, and they are not suitable in case of unexpected unavailability. Moreover, the delegatee may be also unavailable at the time of need. On the other hand, "break-the-glass" policies [1,29,3] grant access to any subject in case of emergency, usually enforcing auditing and logging mechanisms. Thus, a poorly qualified subject may get access to a critical object.

Crampton and Morisset introduced an auto-delegation mechanism [10], which tries to combine the advantages of the delegation and "break-the-glass" approaches, while limiting the drawbacks. In a system enforcing the auto-delegation mechanism, a user is associated with a level of qualification for each object. Similar to usual access control system behaviour, an access control policy in such system allows the most qualified available user for an object to access this object at any time. On the other hand, if this most qualified subject is unavailable, another, a bit less qualified user is allowed to access this object. Moreover, as for the delegation mechanism and in contrast to "break-the-glass" policies, an access is not authorised if there is a more qualified available subject.

However, Crampton and Morisset [10] define the notion of availability as a boolean notion: a user is either available or she is not. In practice, the availability of a user can depend on many parameters, such as her localisation, her level of commitment for other projects, etc. Thus, availability can be only estimated with some uncertainty, due to the *staleness* or *freshness* of the security attributes, as identified in [18].

1.1   Contributions

In the current work we assume a level of uncertainty for availability of users to be a quantitative value (probability of availability), and we propose a quantitative approach to the problem of auto-delegation. In other words, the proposed approach is capable of deciding whether an access should be granted to a user, according to the probability that a more qualified user is available. The main contribution of this paper is therefore the definition of such a policy together with the corresponding framework for the decision-making process. In this work, we provide a general mathematical model for a wide-range of situations and describe a couple of scenario-specific examples with exact equations.

This work is structured as follows. In Section 2 we describe basics of the auto-delegation mechanism and provide a high level example for finding availability probabilities required for our method. Section 3 contains the main contribution of this paper - the general approach for making decisions for auto-delegation mechanism under uncertainty. Concrete examples of application of our approach in a healthcare and in a resource-management environment are shown in Section 4. Section 5 is devoted to possible extensions of our model. Finally, we present the related work (Section 6) and we summarise results of our work (Section 7).

2   Background

2.1   Auto-delegation Mechanism

We recall in this section the auto-delegation mechanism introduced in [10]. We write $S = \{s_1, s_2, \cdots, s_n\}$ for the set of subjects, $\mathcal{O} = \{o_1, o_2, \cdots, o_m\}$ for the set of objects. An *access* is a pair (s, o), meaning that the subject s accesses the object o. Access modes are voluntarily not considered, for the sake of the exposition. However, this can be easily done by considering the set of permissions *à la* RBAC, where a permission is pair (object, access mode), instead of the set of objects. The availability of the subjects is considered to be always decidable, and, therefore, the authors introduce a set $Av(\mathcal{S}) \subseteq S$, such that a subject is available if, and only if, it belongs to $Av(\mathcal{S})$.

Each object $o \in \mathcal{O}$ is associated with a qualification hierarchy $(Q(o), \leqslant_o)$, and each subject is associated with a qualification through a function $\lambda_o : S \to Q(o)$, such that $\lambda_o(s)$ denotes the qualification level of s, with respect to o. Given two subjects s_1 and s_2, $\lambda_o(s_1) \leqslant_o \lambda_o(s_2)$ means that s_2 is more qualified than s_1 to access o. Note that the relation $\leqslant_o$ is a partial-order, and therefore two qualifications might not be comparable.

Finally, an authorization function $Auth_{adm}$ is given, such that given $\leqslant_o$, $Av(\mathcal{S})$, and an access request (s, o), $Auth_{adm}(\leqslant_o, Av(\mathcal{S}), (s, o))$ returns allow if (s, o) is authorized according to the auto-delegation mechanism, and deny otherwise. More precisely,

$$Auth_{adm}(\leqslant_o, Av(\mathcal{S}), (s, o))$$
$$= \begin{cases} \text{deny} & \text{if there exists } s' \in Av(\mathcal{S}) \text{ such that } \lambda_o(s) \leq_o \lambda_o(s'), \\ \text{allow} & \text{otherwise.} \end{cases}$$

In other words, a request by s to access o is allowed if s is one of the most qualified of the available subjects (and denied otherwise).

The auto-delegation mechanism can be either used as a standalone policy, for instance in the context of resource management, or as a combination with another policy. In the latter case, the auto-delegation mechanism is consulted only if the "normal" policy denies the access. We focus on this usage here, and we refer to [10] for a more detailed presentation.

2.2 Uncertain Availability

Usually availability of a subject is considered as a zero-one value, i.e., a subject is either available or not. But sometimes we do not have complete information about the availability of a subject and can only speak about it with some degree of certainty. For example, a doctor may be in a hospital but working on a different floor of the building. We cannot know precisely at each moment of time if the doctor is available or not for a prompt response in case of an emergency. Another example could be a person who could be currently out of her office and the only information available about her whereabouts is that 10 minutes ago the person was in some other office. Hence, it is uncertain if the person will be able to answer an urgent e-mail in the next twenty minutes. We model uncertain availability of a person as the possibility of a subject to response to the request by a certain moment of time in the future. Then we decide if another subject with certain availability but lower qualification can get an access to an object (e.g., patient medical record or a e-mail account) while the availability of more qualified subject is uncertain.

Uncertainty is usually expressed with probability. In our case, we need the probability that a person is available. Such probability could be found in very different ways. The probability could be simply assigned by an analyst, could be derived out of statistics, could be computed, etc. An example of how the probability is computed can be found in the work of Krautsevich et. al.,[19,18], though, in general, the way of acquiring the probability does not affect the following discussion.

Krautsevich *et al.*, [19,18] model position and movement of a subject with a Markov chain (assuming that Markovian property holds[1]). States (nodes) of the Markov chain represent possible spatial positions of the subject. Edges of the Markov chain represent possible transitions between the states. Transition

---

[1] In fact, the experimentation results presented in the paper prove that Markovian property does hold for such example.

probabilities, taken from the analysis of historical data, are assigned to every edge. Knowing the position of a subject at some point of time in the past the probability that the subject is in a specific location (available) at the current moment of time is computed[2].

Both discrete-time and continuous-time Markov chains may be used for the assessment of the probability. A discrete-time Markov chain is a suitable model when the number of position changes during considered time intervals is known. A continuous-time Markov chain is an appropriate model when the number of changes is not known and only the considered interval is available.

The authors also provide a decision making technique in case of uncertain position of a subject. In order to decide to grant access or to deny it a decision matrix is used with possible benefits and risks as utility. Thus, the decision is made comparing possible benefits and losses of granting access or denying it.

In the sequel, we assume that the probability of availability is known for each subject, regardless of the way of acquiring it. This assumption relies on the fact the behavior of subjects follows a predictable pattern, that can be modeled. For instance, if we do not model the possibility for a user to be hit by lightning, and if this event occurs, then we might not be able to assess that the user is not available. In other words, the accuracy of the probability of availability depends on the accuracy of the model. In the current work, we use this probability to develop a model for making a rational decision about *delegating* the right to access an object. We also use a decision matrix for the decision-making process (see Section 3.2).

3   Auto-delegation under Uncertainty

We present in this section a very abstract and general model of access control under uncertainty. We reduce an access control mechanism as a binary decision mechanism: given an access request, the access control mechanism can either allow it (positive decision) or deny it (negative decision). This decision is based on the information present in the current state of the system. When there is no uncertainty on the information, then the decision making is straight-forward.

However, when there is some uncertainty over the information present in the state, the decision process is more complex, as it is possible to make some errors. For instance, consider a simple policy when an access a is allowed if, and only if a parameter x is *true*. If we know with certainty the value of x, then the decision making simply consists in checking this value, and allowing or denying the access a accordingly. On the contrary, if there is an uncertainty over the value of x, then we can have four different decisions.

1. A *true-positive* is an access correctly allowed. For instance, we allow the access a and the value of x is *true*.

---

[2] In fact, the proposed approach computes the probability of a subject to appear in a forbidden state (be unavailable) during the considered interval. But, in order to find the probability to be in a particular state we need only slightly change the model (i.e., remove absorbing states).

2. A *true-negative* is an access correctly denied. For instance, we denied the access a and the value of x is *false*.
3. A *false-positive* is an access wrongly allowed. For instance, we allow the access a and the value of x is *false*.
4. A *false-negative* is an access wrongly denied. For instance, we deny the access a and the value of x is *true*.

In order to make a decision, the mechanism must evaluate the impact of each decision, and the corresponding probabilities. In general, specifying the actual impact of a decision is a hard task, and can depend on the request and the environment. Moreover, the impact of a false-positive might be not comparable with the impact of a false-negative. Indeed, intuitively, a false-positive can damage the system by leaking some information to non-authorised users, or allowing them to modify the system in an undesired way, while a false-negative will prevent a user to perform an access that she actually needs in order to fulfil a task, thus potentially leading to the failure of this task.

For instance, considering extreme cases, a system denying every access is clearly secure, but is of very limited interest, and does not provide any *gain*. Conversely, a system allowing every access has a high *gain*, but at the same time leads to high *damage*. The objective here is then to strike the right balance between being too strict and being too lax.

We now introduce more precisely notions of "utility", "gain", and "damage", and then we present our model to make decisions under uncertainty.

3.1   Utility, Gain and Damage

The shift from a binary viewpoint, where a state is either "good" or "bad", to a more quantitative approach, where a state is associated with a "level of goodness" and/or a "level of badness", has been undergoing in the last decade. The Computer Research Association stated it as a grand challenge to develop an accurate risk analysis for cyber-security [9], and some measures need to be defined. There have been several approaches taking advantages of such measures [8,7,6,26] or trying to calculate them using market algorithms [25].

Clearly, defining a risk measure for access control is complex [11], particularly due to the lack of a precise notion of utility (gain and/or damage), that is, a clear way to define the impact of granting or denying an access, on the contrary of, say, defining the impact of increasing the temperature of a water-heater or purchasing shares on a stock-market. Moreover, when human lives are potentially at stake, it is hard to put a number on the possible impact. However, some approximations can be done.

For instance, in an healthcare system, a situation where a patient is having a heart attack and where a medical record is unavailable might lead to a wrong or unadapted course of treatment. Such a situation might lead the patient to sue the hospital, and the financial impact on the hospital can be estimated from past similar cases. Also giving access to the medical record to unauthorised employees might lead to the divulgation of confidential information, and the patient again might sue the hospital for breach of confidentiality. In this case, gain and damages can be evaluated as financial impact over the hospital budget.

As recently stated by Kephart [17], the access control community must first establish how to measure the utility of access control decisions in order to meaningfully apply risk-based strategies. However, the objective of the work presented here is not to define what is utility, but to provide the tools to take advantage of it once it can be more precisely defined for concrete systems. Hence, we assume that there exist two general utility functions μ_g and μ_d, for the utility of granting and denying an access, respectively. More specifically, in the context of auto-delegation, for a given object o, we write $\mu_g(s_i, s_j)$ for the utility of granting the access to s_i over o while s_j is the most qualified subject available, and similarly, we write $\mu_d(s_i, s_j)$ for the utility of denying the access to s_i while s_j is the most qualified subject available.

For instance, these functions can be defined by a gain function γ and a damage function δ. Such functions can dynamically evolve, and can return complex values, such as probabilistic costs. Note that in general, the gain from allowing an access can be different from the damage of denying this access, for instance when penalties for denying accesses are involved. We provide examples of such functions in Section 4.

We assume that the domain of these utility functions is a total order, in other words, it is always possible to compare two or more different utility values and to pick the "best" value. Moreover, the qualification hierarchy for each object needs to be consistent with the utility: intuitively, if a subject s_1 is more qualified than a subject s_2 to access an object o, then the utility of the access (s_1, o) is better than the utility of (s_2, o). In practice, a good way to define the qualification hierarchy and the qualification assignment is simply to base them on the utility functions.

3.2   Mathematical Model

The question we try to answer here is when a subject s_i asks to access an object o whether the monitor should grant this access or not. In order to make such a decision, we need to determine the following points:

- the probability that a more qualified subject is available,
- the utility of granting and denying the access to s_i if such a subject exists,
- and the utility of granting and denying the access to s_i otherwise.

For the sake of exposition, we order subjects from the most qualified to the least qualified, i.e. s_1 is the most qualified subject for o and s_n is the least qualified. Thus, if qualifications of subjects relate as $\lambda_o(s_i) \leq_o \lambda_o(s_j)$ indexes relate as $i > j$. We also denote by p_j the probability that subject s_j is available.

Given the subject s_i, Table 1 describes, for a subject s_j, $i \leq j$, (first column), the probability p_a^j that s_j is the most qualified subject available (second column), and the utility in this case of granting or denying the access to s_i over o (third and fourth columns).

Table 1. Alternatives of granting or denying the access to the object o

Highest available	Probability	Utility of grant(s_i, o)	Utility of deny(s_i, o)
s_i	$(1-p_1)\cdots(1-p_{i-1})$	$\mu_g(s_i, s_i)$	$\mu_d(s_i, s_i)$
s_{i-1}	$p_{i-1}\cdot(1-p_1)\cdots(1-p_{i-2})$	$\mu_g(s_i, s_{i-1})$	$\mu_d(s_i, s_{i-1})$
$\vdots$	$\vdots$	$\vdots$	$\vdots$
s_2	$p_2\cdot(1-p_1)$	$\mu_g(s_i, s_2)$	$\mu_d(s_i, s_2)$
s_1	p_1	$\mu_g(s_i, s_1)$	$\mu_d(s_i, s_1)$

It is easy to see that when s_i is the most qualified available subject, granting the access is a true-positive while denying it leads to a false-negative. Conversely, when there exists a subject s_j available, with $j > i$, then granting the access is a false-positive while denying it creates a true-negative. We define four utility functions C^{TP}, C^{FN}, C^{FP}, and C^{TN} for these respective outcomes, such that, according to decision theory [15], the access should be granted only if Equation 1 holds.

$$C^{TP} + C^{FP} > C^{TN} + C^{FN} \tag{1}$$

In order to calculate these utility functions, we first write p_a^j for the probability of the subject j to be the most qualified subject available. Note that since s_i is asking for the access, we automatically assume that this subject is available, and it follows that the sum of p_a^j, for $j \geq i$, is equal to 1. More formally, we define $p_a^j = p_j \cdot \prod_{k>j}(1-p_k)$.

Finally, Equations 2, 3, 5, and 4 give the definition of the utility functions. For the sake of simplicity, we do not consider here any special utility or reward for the accuracy of the decision process, only the expected impact of the access, or the absence of access. However, in some situations, these utility functions might also include a mechanism to reward the fact to make good decisions, and/or to punish the fact to make bad ones.

$$C^{TP} = p_a^i \cdot \mu_g(s_i, s_i) \tag{2} \qquad C^{FN} = p_a^i \cdot \mu_d(s_i, s_i) \tag{4}$$

$$C^{FP} = \sum_{j>i} p_a^j \cdot \mu_g(s_i, s_j) \tag{3} \qquad C^{TN} = \sum_{j>i} p_a^j \cdot \mu_d(s_i, s_j) \tag{5}$$

The Equation 6 corresponds to the equation 1, after simplification, such that, if this equation holds, then the access is granted, otherwise the access is denied. We clearly focus here on the notion of expected utility, i.e., we average the utility of granting and the utility of denying, and simply pick the best option. More complex notions of risk, such as risk aggregation or worst-case scenario, could be easily included, and will be considered in future works.

$$\sum_{j\geq i} p_a^j \cdot \mu_g(s_i, s_j) > \sum_{j\geq i} p_a^j \cdot \mu_d(s_i, s_j) \tag{6}$$

The definition of the μ functions is context-dependent: for instance, granting an access over an object to a subject might prevent another, more qualified subject to access this object, in which case the maximum obtainable gain is the one from the less qualified subject. In other situations, there might be no damage associated with granting an access, thus reducing the access control mechanism to a traditional optimization problem. We define in the next section two examples of the μ functions, one in the healthcare environment, and the other one for resource management.

4   Examples

The mathematical model presented in the previous section only requires a system administrator to define the functions μ_g and μ_d for her specific environment. We consider here an healthcare system and a resource management system.

4.1   Auto-delegation for Healthcare

We consider an emergency in an hospital (*e.g.* a patient has a heart attack) when the personnel of the hospital must respond immediately. We suppose the following hierarchy of the personnel: $\lambda_o(intern) <_o \lambda_o(attending\ physician) <_o \lambda_o(senior\ attending\ physician) <_o \lambda_o(chief\ of\ medicine)$. A subject who is trying to tackle the situation needs to access the *medical record* of the patient for the selection of a proper treatment. Thus, an object o is the medical record of a patient. In this setting, the access to a resource is not exclusive: a more qualified subject can still access the resource even if a less qualified subject has already got the access. Indeed, a senior attending physician still can access the medical record of a patient during an emergency even if the record has been accessed by an intern.

The utility functions μ_g and μ_d are computed from the gain function γ and the damage function δ. Given an object o, we write γ_k for the gain obtained by the subject s_k, and δ_k for the damage caused by the same subject. We suppose that the more qualified is the subject accessing the medical record, the better the treatment the patient receives. Similarly, the more qualified is the subject accessing the resource, the lesser is the damage to the privacy of a patient.

$$\mu_g(s_i, s_j) = \begin{cases} \gamma_i - \delta_i & \text{if } s_i = s_j \\ \gamma_j - (\delta_i + \delta_j) & \text{otherwise} \end{cases}$$

$$\mu_d(s_i, s_j) = \begin{cases} -\delta_0 & \text{if } s_i = s_j \\ \gamma_j - \delta_j & \text{otherwise} \end{cases}$$

Considering the utility $\mu_g(s_i, s_i)$, we assume that the subject s_i executes her duties, however some damage δ_i is possible, e.g., the subject will corrupt the privacy of a patient. The cost $\mu_g(s_i, s_j)$ if $i \neq j$ corresponds to the case when the subject s_i accesses the resource, while one or several more qualified specialists are available, for example when an intern accesses the record while a senior attending physician is available. In this case, we assume that giving the access to the less qualified subject does not bring any gain, and therefore the gain is only the one of the most qualified available subject. However, we sum the damages caused by both subjects that access the object.

The utility $\mu_d(s_i, s_i) = -\delta_0$ stands for the damage occurring when the object is not accessed at all. The utility $\mu_d(s_i, s_j)$ if $i \neq j$ assesses the case when the access is denied to s_i and the subject s_j is available. In this case we face the gain and the damage from s_j. Table 2 illustrates the utility functions C^{TP}, C^{FP}, C^{TN} and C^{FN} with the previous definitions for the functions μ_g and μ_d.

Table 2. Utility functions C for the healthcare example

C^{TP}	C^{FP}	C^{TN}	C^{FN}
$p_a^i \cdot (\gamma_i - \delta_i)$	$\sum_{j>i} p_a^j \cdot (\gamma_j - \delta_i - \delta_j)$	$\sum_{j>i} p_a^j \cdot (\gamma_j - \delta_j)$	$p_a^i \cdot \delta_0$

We are now in position to instantiate Equation 6 with the previous definitions of μ_g and μ_d, which is given by Equation 7, and simplified in Equation 8.

$$p_a^i \cdot (\gamma_i - \delta_i) + \sum_{j>i} p_a^j \cdot (\gamma_j - (\delta_i + \delta_j)) > \sum_{j>i} p_a^j \cdot (\gamma_j - \delta_j) - p_a^i \cdot \delta_0 \qquad (7)$$

$$p_a^i \cdot \gamma_i - \delta_i > -p_a^i \cdot \delta_0 \qquad (8)$$

Equation 8 illustrates two strengths of our approach: if it is certain that s_i is not the most qualified available subject, then $p_a^i = 0$ and the access is not granted, regardless of the value of δ_i and δ_0. On the other hand, if δ_0 is important enough (*e.g.* a threat of patient death), then even if the probability that s_i is the most qualified available subject is very small, then the access can potentially be granted, thus working as a "break-the-glass" policy.

4.2 Auto-delegation for Resource Management

We illustrate here that our framework can also be used to address a typical resource management problem. We consider a channel with limited bandwidth which can be accessed by premium and regular users. A premium user pays γ^p while a regular user pays $\gamma^r < \gamma^p$, therefore, the premium user has a priority for using the channel. The resource owner delegates the right to access the resource to a regular user when the resource is not occupied by a premium user, *i.e.* the premium user is unavailable. The qualification relation is $\lambda_o(regular\ user) <_o \lambda_o(premium\ user)$. An object o is the channel and two users cannot access the channel simultaneously. Suppose that a regular user is asking for the channel and the availability of premium users is uncertain. The resource owner needs to decide what is more profitable: giving the access to the regular user or considering that a premium user is actually available and will require the channel.

$$\mu_g(s_i, s_j) = \gamma^r \qquad \mu_d(s_i, s_j) = \begin{cases} 0 & \text{if } s_i = s_j \\ \gamma^p & \text{otherwise} \end{cases}$$

Note, that since we only have two categories of users, s_j in the definition of μ_d automatically stands for a premium user. For the sake of simplicity, we consider that there is no special penalty for granting an access to a regular user while a premium user is available. There is only an implicit loss of gain, since the system could have gained more by giving the access to the premium user. The Table 3 illustrates the utility functions C^{TP}, C^{FP}, C^{TN} and C^{FN} with the previous definitions for the functions μ_g and μ_d.

Table 3. Utility functions C for resource management

C^{TP}	C^{FP}	C^{TN}	C^{FN}
$p_a^i \cdot \gamma_r$	$\sum\limits_{j>i} p_a^j \cdot \gamma_r$	$\sum\limits_{j>i} p_a^j \cdot \gamma_p$	0

Finally, we can instantiate Equation 6 with the corresponding values, and we find, after simplification, that the access to a regular user is granted if $\gamma^r > (1 - p_a^i) \cdot \gamma^p$. Clearly, this is not a surprising result, as the inequality corresponds to the intuitive decision process: the regular user can access the resource only if the expected gain is greater than the expected gain of giving the access to a premium user weighted by the probability that such a user is available. Clearly, this example illustrate that resource management can also be done within our framework.

5 Extensions

We propose here several straight-forward extensions to the model presented in the previous section.

5.1 Auto-delegation for a Dynamic System

In this extension we are going to consider the case when parameters of the systems may change over time. Parameters of the system impact the utility functions, thus re-evaluation of access decision should be done each time when parameters change. Usage control model (UCON) is based on changing attributes and allows controlling how a subject uses an object even after access is granted. We are going to propose an auto-delegation model for UCON, which should help to control the access to objects in case of dynamically changing utility. The model described in Section 3.2 assumes that the utilities for a given access is constant. However, in many situations, the utility of an access can vary over a period of time.

First, if we assume that we know the estimated time of availability of a subject, then the model can take it into account. As an example, consider the situation where a nurse needs to access a medical record for which the official physician is currently performing a surgery, and therefore unavailable for a period of n minutes. The mechanism must weight the outcomes between granting to the nurse the access now, which we denote t_0, with the potential incurred damage, thus getting the utility at t_0, or wait for n minutes and let the official physician access the medical record, and in this case getting the utility at $t_0 + n$.

Second, the probability that the subject will be available may change in time. For instance, if we have a tracing system in the hospital, we can re-evaluate the availability of more qualified subject each minute, and, on the basis of this information, grant or deny access for a less qualified subject.

5.2 Forcing Availability

In some cases, a subject unavailable in a given system can be forced to be available, at a given cost. A simple example is a physician unavailable because on leave at home, and who can be called back to the hospital, however at the cost of paying her extra hours. Another example is the unavailability of a subject due to some conflicts.

For instance, consider a subject s currently accessing a resource o_1 and being the more qualified subject for another resource o_2, although not accessing it. The policy forbids simultaneous accesses to both o_1 and o_2. If another subject s' asks to access o_2, then the mechanism has to consider two options: either granting the access to s' or releasing the access of s to o_1 so that s can be available for o_2. However, releasing the access over o_1 might incur some extra costs.

In other words, the decision mechanism might have the choice between granting the access, denying it, or forcing a more qualified subject to be available, and can choose the option with the best utility.

6   Related Work

Clearly, our approach is related to risk-based access control, as we try to make an access control decision under uncertainty. Some authors use risk as a static parameter which simply helps to assign correct privileges taking into account possible losses [23,14,28]. For example, Skalka *et al.* [28] discussed an approach for risk evaluation of authorisations, the formal approach is used to assess and combine the risks of assertions that are used in the authorisation decision. Other authors use risk as a dynamic value which depends on the current value of possible losses and benefits as well as on the probability of abusing privileges by a concrete subject [30,12,24,8]. These approaches do not cover the delegation problem, but introduce useful concepts for defining the *cost* functions.

Ni *et al.* [27] considered risk-based access control system (RAC) which assumes that the access to a resource can be granted to a risky subject if mitigation actions (post-obligations) will be applied in the future. The authors proposed an approach for the risk estimation under incomplete and imprecise data using fuzzy inferences. Similarly, Chen and Crampton propose a mitigation strategy [5] in the context of risk-based access control for RBAC models. The use of mitigations can provide the access control monitor with a wider range of possible decisions: denying a request, allowing it with some mitigations, or allowing it with no condition. Each of these decision comes with a different impact, and thus permits a finer-grained risk strategy.

Krautsevich *et al.* [20,19,18] applied risk analysis for usage control model. In [20] the authors considered the selection of the less risky data processor in service-oriented architecture. The authors indicated how risk can change after granting the access to a data processor and how the data processor can reduce its risk level to provide better service. In [19,18] authors described the approaches for risk-aware usage decision making under uncertainties caused by freshness of the policy attributes. The approaches exploits discrete-time and continuous-time Markov chains.

7   Conclusion

In this paper we have presented an access control mechanism for making delegation decisions when availability of subjects is uncertain. Our approach fits within the recent trend of tackling access and usage control issues from a risk-based viewpoint. Thus, this approach enables a finer-grained access control, but is not conservative with respect to more "traditional" approaches. Indeed, our mechanism might grant an access that should be denied (false-positive). On the contrary, a conservative approach could require to grant an access only if the system can be sure that this is the right decision. However, such a system would also deny accesses that should be allowed (false-negative), thus jeopardising the functional interest of the system. Moreover, such behaviour of the system, to some extent, encourages subjects to override the security mechanism in order to perform an access they believe they should be authorised to.

We have illustrated our framework with two simple, yet interesting examples. The first example presents the usage of the auto-delegation within an healthcare system, and the intuitive definition of the utility functions leads to the desired behaviour: as long as it is certain that a more qualified subject is available, no delegation will be given, which is consistent with the idea that an emergency situation should not automatically imply that unnecessary accesses can be granted. Hence, when there is no uncertainty, our approach is equivalent to enforcing directly the plain auto-delegation mechanism. However, if there is some uncertainty about the availability of a more qualified subjects, it is possible to grant the access to a less qualified subject, especially if the damage of not granting the access is huge. Thus, following the idea that some resources must remain accessible at all time. The second example illustrates that we can easily consider resource management problems within our framework.

The main drawback of our approach, and of most risk-based access control mechanisms, is the lack of precise utility, gain and/or damage measures for real-world applications. Concrete impact studies need to be conducted by practitioners in order to evaluate the consequences of allowing and denying accesses, beyond the usual classification between "good" and "bad" accesses. However, this lack of measures can be also understood by the relative lack of concrete risk-based tools, which creates few incentive for practitioners to perform such studies. We believe that with the growing interest of the research community for risk-based security solutions, more useful measures will be found.

Finally, the framework we have proposed is quite fertile, and paves the way for several interesting extensions, such as the introduction of time in the calculation of the utility of an access and the widening of the set of decisions to be considered. Indeed, in practice, gain and damages are time-dependent, and it might increase the accuracy of our approach if we consider whether it is more interesting for the system to grant an access now to a subject, or to wait later for another, more qualified subject to be available. Concerning the widening of the decisions set, the use of mitigations and obligations policies may lower the damage of a less qualified subject, but also lower its gain, thus requiring the monitor to use a complex risk strategy.

References

1. Ardagna, C.A., De Capitani di Vimercati, S., Grandison, T., Jajodia, S., Samarati, P.: Regulating Exceptions in Healthcare Using Policy Spaces. In: Atluri, V. (ed.) DAS 2008. LNCS, vol. 5094, pp. 254–267. Springer, Heidelberg (2008)
2. Brewer, D.F.C., Nash, M.J.: The Chinese Wall Security Policy. In: Proceedings of the IEEE Symposium on Security and Privacy, pp. 329–339 (May 1989)
3. Brucker, A.D., Petritsch, H., Schaad, A.: Delegation assistance. In: IEEE International Workshop on Policies for Distributed Systems and Networks, pp. 84–91 (2009)
4. Chander, A., Mitchell, J.C., Dean, D.: A state-transition model of trust management and access control. In: Proceedings of the 14th IEEE Computer Security Foundations Workshop, pp. 27–43. IEEE Computer Society Press (2001)
5. Chen, L., Crampton, J.: Risk-aware role-based access control. In: Proceedings of 7th International Workshop on Security and Trust Management (to appear, 2011)
6. Cheng, P.-C., Karger, P.A.: Risk modulating factors in risk-based access control for information in a manet. Technical Report RC24494, IBM T.J. Watson (2008)
7. Cheng, P.-C., Rohatgi, P.: IT security as risk management: A research perspective. Technical Report RC24529, IBM T.J. Watson (April 2008)
8. Cheng, P.-C., Rohatgi, P., Keser, C., Karger, P.A., Wagner, G.M., Reninger, A.S.: Fuzzy multi-level security: An experiment on quantified risk-adaptive access control. In: Proceedings of the IEEE Symposium on Security and Privacy, pp. 222–230 (2007)
9. Computing Research Association. Four grand challenges in trustworthy computing (November 2003)
10. Crampton, J., Morisset, C.: An Auto-delegation Mechanism for Access Control Systems. In: Cuellar, J., Lopez, J., Barthe, G., Pretschner, A. (eds.) STM 2010. LNCS, vol. 6710, pp. 1–16. Springer, Heidelberg (2011)
11. Cybenko, G.: Why johnny can't evaluate security risk. IEEE Security and Privacy 4, 5 (2006)
12. Diep, N.N., Hung, L.X., Zhung, Y., Lee, S., Lee, Y.-K., Lee, H.: Enforcing access control using risk assessment. In: Proceedings of the Fourth European Conference on Universal Multiservice Networks, Washington, DC, USA, pp. 419–424 (2007)

13. Ferraiolo, D.F., Kuhn, D.R.: Role-based access control. In: Proceedings of the 15th National Computer Security Conference, pp. 554–563 (1992)
14. Han, Y., Hori, Y., Sakurai, K.: Security policy pre-evaluation towards risk analysis. In: Proceedings of the 2008 International Conference on Information Security and Assurance, pp. 415–420. IEEE, Washington, DC (2008)
15. Hanson, S.O.: Decision theory: A brief introduction (August 1994)
16. Harrison, M.A., Ruzzo, W.L., Ullman, J.D.: Protection in operating systems. Communications of the ACM 19(8), 461–471 (1976)
17. Kephart, J.: The utility of utility: Policies for self-managing systems. In: Proceedings of Policies for Distributed Systems and Networks (to appear, 2011)
18. Krautsevich, L., Lazouski, A., Martinelli, F., Yautsiukhin, A.: Influence of Attribute Freshness on Decision Making in Usage Control. In: Cuellar, J., Lopez, J., Barthe, G., Pretschner, A. (eds.) STM 2010. LNCS, vol. 6710, pp. 35–50. Springer, Heidelberg (2011)
19. Krautsevich, L., Lazouski, A., Martinelli, F., Yautsiukhin, A.: Risk-aware usage decision making in highly dynamic systems. In: Proceedings of the Fifth International Conference on Internet Monitoring and Protection. IEEE (2010)
20. Krautsevich, L., Lazouski, A., Martinelli, F., Yautsiukhin, A.: Risk-based usage control for service oriented architecture. In: Proceedings of the 18th Euromicro International Conference on Parallel, Distributed and Network-Based Computing. IEEE (2010)
21. Lampson, B.: Protection. In: Proceedings of the 5th Annual Princeton Conference on Information Sciences and Systems, pp. 437–443. Princeton University (1971)
22. LaPadula, L.J., Bell, D.E.: Secure Computer Systems: A Mathematical Model. Journal of Computer Security 4, 239–263 (1996)
23. Li, Y., Sun, H., Chen, Z., Ren, J., Luo, H.: Using trust and risk in access control for grid environment. In: Proceedings of the 2008 International Conference on Security Technology, pp. 13–16. IEEE, Washington, DC (2008)
24. McGraw, R.W.: Risk-adaptable access control, RAdAC (2007), http://csrc.nist.gov/news_events/privilege-management-workshop/radac-Paper0001.pdf (August 16, 2009)
25. Molloy, I., Cheng, P.-C., Rohatgi, P.: Trading in risk: Using markets to improve access control. In: Proceedings of the 15th ACM New Security Paradigms Workshop, Lake TAhoe, CA, USA. ACM, New York (2008)
26. Molloy, I., Dickens, L., Morisset, C., Cheng, P.-C., Lobo, J., Russo, A.: Risk-based access control decisions under uncertainty. Technical Report RC25121, IBM T.J. Watson (September 2011)
27. Ni, Q., Bertino, E., Lobo, J.: Risk-based access control systems built on fuzzy inferences. In: Proceedings of the 5th ACM Symposium on Information, Computer and Communications Security, pp. 250–260. ACM, New York (2010)
28. Skalka, C., Wang, X.S., Chapin, P.: Risk management for distributed authorization. J. Comput. Secur. 15(4), 447–489 (2007)
29. Wainer, J., Barthelmess, P., Kumar, A.: W-RBAC - a workflow security model incorporating controlled overriding of constraints. International Journal of Cooperative Information Systems 12, 455–485 (2003)
30. Zhang, L., Brodsky, A., Jajodia, S.: Toward information sharing: Benefit and risk access control (BARAC). In: Proceedings of the 7th IEEE International Workshop on Policies for Distributed Systems and Networks, Washington, DC, USA, pp. 45–53 (2006)

Intra-role Progression in RBAC: An RPG-Like Access Control Scheme

Carles Martínez-García, Guillermo Navarro-Arribas, and Joan Borrell

Dept. of Information and Communication Engineering,
Universitat Autònoma de Barcelona
{cmartinez,gnavarro,jborrell}@deic.uab.cat

Abstract. Role-Based Access Control is an access control scheme born to accommodate organizational access control policies. Despite RBAC is widely used, it presents some handicaps when accommodating the natural user progression within a system: from low access privileges, when the user is new in the system, to higher access privileges as the user experience grows. In this paper, we build on FRBAC to propose an RBAC-like intra-role user progression scheme inspired in role playing games. User progression will result in progressive abilities acquisition and enhancing, enhancing RBAC with more expressive access control policies.

Keywords: Intra-role progression, FRBAC.

1 Introduction

Computerized role-playing games (RPG) [1] allow players to interact with a game world in a wide variety of ways offering the experience of character growing, usually from an ordinary person into a superhero with amazing powers. Multiple characters coexist in a world where every one plays several roles that can be deployed along the character life. Belonging to a role gives users the opportunity to enhance different abilities, specializing the users on some specific functions within the world. In this manner, mages are specialized to cast several spells and healers are specialists on healing themselves and other characters, in spite of mages can perform some basic cures and healers can cast some basic spells.

In RPG, players are given, gradually, additional powers every time they earn some experience. By using a fine-grained ability system, characters can experience continuous growth rather than big step jumps in power. Character progression is a learning method through a positive feedback cycle: players continually grow in power, allowing them to overcome more difficult challenges and gain even more power. While characters gain experience in the game world, they gain membership level in the roles they play. Role membership level gives a measure to determine the abilities assigned to the users playing the role. Thus, characters gaining membership level within a role, obtain new abilities and enhance the abilities that they already had, allowing them to do something that they could not do before, or to do it more effectively. Intuitively, mages of level 60

J. Garcia-Alfaro et al. (Eds.): DPM 2011 and SETOP 2011, LNCS 7122, pp. 221–234, 2012.
© Springer-Verlag Berlin Heidelberg 2012

are more powerful, in terms of number of abilities and abilities' strength, than mages of level 10.

Role-Based Access Control (RBAC) [7] is an access control model born to accommodate organizational access control systems. In RBAC, the privileges that users have are not related with the users' identity but the roles that users play. Users are granted with roles depending on their function inside the organization. Every role is assigned with different permissions which allows the role members to carry on with the functions that they are supposed to do. While the major purpose of RBAC is to facilitate authorization management and review by profiling users through roles, the ability management system of role playing games is also based on profiling characters through roles. The concept of roles represents a parallelism between RBAC and RPG being a level of indirection between users and abilities. Despite this parallelism, there are substantial differences on the understanding and purpose of roles in RBAC and RPG.

The first difference between RPG and RBAC lies on the role membership and privilege acquisition: in RBAC users are statically assigned to roles, acquiring a priori the static set of privileges associated to the roles they play, while in RPG users experiment an intra-role progression that makes them acquire privileges progressively. Another important difference lies on the understanding of roles. In RPG, roles represents limits on characters' ability to improve certain skills rather than absolute prohibitions on certain activities, while in RBAC roles are understood as a static set of privileges that users must acquire to deploy their assigned functions within the organization.

The aim of this paper is to propose an intra-role user-progression model in RBAC, inspired in role playing games, and applicable in environments where the authorization system must be aware of the progression of the users within the system. Intra-role user progression will be described in terms of leveling, which will produce progressive abilities acquisition and progressive abilities enhancing. An RPG-like user progression model would benefit RBAC with more expressive access control policies, helping on the reduction of the number of roles and permissions defined in the system. Furthermore, it will enable RBAC to accommodate a feedback-based progressive learning that will help users on the understanding of the system, acquiring more responsibility as they earn experience. The intra-role progression model could be used as a reputation system that can be used in multiple environments as QoS systems [5] and Social Networks.

However, the foundations of RBAC prevent the adoption of an RPG-like user progression model. RBAC is based on a static user-role relation which cannot represent any form of intra-role progression. When users acquire roles, they automatically acquire all the privileges assigned to these roles. Furthermore, assigning users to new roles represents a dramatic change on the users' permissions. The static permission definition and the rigid user-privilege relations make the execution of the privileges invariant along the user-privilege relation and regardless of the user's experience, thus preventing the concept of progressive abilities enhancing. To overcome the rigidity of RBAC in intra-role progression, we will base our model in FRBAC. FRBAC (Fuzzy role-based access control) [9] is a generalization of RBAC founded on fuzzy relations. The multivalued nature of the assignments in FRBAC enables intra-role progression which will be the basis of the proposed RPG-like user progression model.

The rest of the paper is organized as follows. Section 2 introduces the basic notions of FRBAC that will be necessary in Section 3 to understand the proposed intra-role user progression model. Section 4 shows an example application of the model and compares it with the implementation in RBAC to demonstrate the benefits in expressiveness terms. Section 5 provides the related work and finally Section 6 concludes the paper.

2 Background: FRBAC

FRBAC is a generalization of RBAC founded on fuzzy relations. Unlike RBAC, in FRBAC the relations between users and roles, and roles and permissions are not binary but multivalued, represented with a magnitude in the range $[0, 1]$. The user-permission relation is determined as the composition of the user-role relation and the role-permission relation and also expressed through a magnitude in the range $[0, 1]$. The magnitude of the user-permission relation determines the access degree that every user has on every permission. The access degree is used by the enforcement point of the application in order to adapt the access conditions to the authorized access degree or just determine whether the access degree is high enough to enable the access.

We use the following notation and definitions described in FRBAC:

- $USERS$ is a set of users.
- $ROLES$ is a set of roles.
- OBS is a set of resources (objects).
- OPS is a set of operations.
- $PRMS$ is a set of permissions.
- UA is a set of user-role assignments.
- PA is a set of role-permission assignments.

The user-role assignment (UA) is a fuzzy relation. UA is a set of items of the form $((u, r), \mu_{UA}(u, r))$ where $(u, r) \in USERS \times ROLES$, and $\mu_{UA}(u, r)$ is a function that returns the user-role relation strength for $u \in USERS$ and $r \in ROLES$. The strength is valued in the real unit interval $[0, 1]$. The role-permission relation or permission assignment (PA) has an analogous form: $((r, p), \mu_{PA}(r, p))$ where $(r, p) \in ROLES \times PRMS$, and $\mu_{PA}(r, p) : ROLES \times PRMS \to [0, 1]$.

3 User Progression: RPG-Like Access Control

In this section we describe a progressive abilities acquisition and enhancing model based on RBAC. We focus on FRBAC to ease the parallelism between user progression of role-playing games and user progression in an access control model.

3.1   Levels and Role Membership

Characters in a role playing game experience an evolution along their life. This progression allows players to grow a character from an ordinary person into a superhero with amazing powers. The progress is measured by counting character levels. Character levels are related to the roles they play. For instance a character can be mage of level 40, goldsmith of level 15 and level 10 gardener. Accumulating a certain amount of experience will cause the character's level to go up. This is called "leveling up", and gives players the opportunity to acquire new abilities and enhance abilities that they already had.

We define the role membership levels through the fuzzy user-role relation:

- $UA : USERS \times ROLES \to [0,1]$

Role membership levels link directly with multivalued user-role relations of FR-BAC. FRBAC allows to determine the degree in which a user plays a role through the fuzzy UA relation. Users are related with roles under a magnitude in the range $[0,1]$ which determines the user membership within a role. This magnitude is supposed to be initially low when the user is assigned to a role and increased as the user earns experience. The dynamism of the user-role relation represents the user progression and allows users to experience a continuous membership increment, which will lately result in permissions acquisition and enhancing.

The way in which the experience of the user is computed is application-dependent and it is out of the scope of this paper. Accreditation-based mechanisms, objective lists, or user seniority are just few examples.

3.2   Roles and Permissions

Abilities, in the RPG jargon, refer to the actions that a character can take within the game world. Cast a spell, market items, grow plants, are just few examples. Abilities are acquired trough the roles that the character plays. Roles in RPG do not impose absolute prohibitions on certain activities but limits on characters' ability to perform certain activities.

The role-permission relation is determined through the PA relation:

- $PA : ROLES \times PRMS \to [0,1]$

The multivalued role-permission relation (PA) of FRBAC determines the strength of the assignment of permissions to roles. It must be understood as the limits of the role members to enhance the permissions. Unlike the magnitude of the user-role assignment, whose dynamism represents the progression of the user within the role, the magnitude of the role-permission is essentially static although it can be tuned at any time if required.

3.3 Users and Permissions

As characters acquire experience in the game world, character levels are increased. Leveling up results in progressive abilities acquisition and enhancing. Abilities acquisition allow users to do things that they could not do before. Abilities enhancing allow users to do things in a more effective way that they did before. Intuitively, mages of level 60 can invoke more spells, and with more power, than mages of level 10. Progressive abilities acquisition and enhancing creates a positive-feedback cycle that is central to most role-playing games: the player grows in power, allowing them to overcome more difficult challenges, and gain even more power.

The user-permission relation (UP) determines the strength in which users are related to permissions and arises from the composition of UA and PA relations:

- $UP = UA \circ PA : USERS \times PRMS \rightarrow [0, 1]$

Where the composing operand $\circ$ stands for the standard *max-min* composition of two fuzzy relations. That is , let UA be a collection of items of the form $((u, r), \mu_{UA}(u, r))$ where $u \in USERS$, $r \in ROLES$, and $\mu_{UA}(u, r) \in [0, 1]$. Let PA be a collection of items of the form $((r, p), \mu_{PA}(r, p))$ where $r \in ROLES$, $p \in PRMS$, and $\mu_{PA}(r, p) \in [0, 1]$. The *max-min* composition $UA \circ PA : USERS \times PRMS \rightarrow [0, 1]$ is defined as follows:

$$UA \circ PA = \{((u, p), \max_r(\min(\mu_{UA}(u, r), \mu_{PA}(r, p)))) |$$
$$u \in USERS, r \in ROLES, p \in PRMS\}$$

The resulting relation UP is a collection of items of the form $((u, p), \mu_{UP}(u, p))$ where $u \in USERS$, $p \in PRMS$, and $\mu_{UP}(u, p) \in [0, 1]$. Although we use the *maximum* operand as the union and the *minimum* as the intersection of fuzzy sets, note that other *t-conorm* and *t-norm* operands could be used respectively, giving up also to another relation composition operand [8].

Note that the UA determines the membership level of users within roles, the more user-role strength, the more user-permission strength for the permissions assigned to the roles that the users play. A decreasing user-role strength will also decrease the user-permission strength. While the dynamism of the UA relation enables the progressive abilities acquisition and enhancing, the static nature of the PA relation limits the maximum strength of the UP relations by the *max-min* composition. This property links with an RPG vision of the roles, where the role membership imposes limits on characters' ability to improve certain skills rather than absolute prohibitions on certain activities.

3.4 Polymorphic Permissions

To this point we have shown how the user-permission strength is computed. In this section we will see the definition of the permissions which enable progressive abilities acquisition and enhancing.

One of the key points of user progression within a system resides on the poly-morphism of permissions. We define a polymorphic structure of permissions that differs from the definition of permissions in RBAC and FRBAC. This polymor-phism allows to condition the relation between objects and operations depending on the user ability level. The more user-permission strength, the more operations over objects will be able to execute.

Let OBS be the set of objects and OPS be the set of operations, polymorphic permissions are defined as:

- $PRMS \subseteq 2^{OBS \times OPS \rightarrow [0,1]}$

That is, the set of permissions is defined as the powerset of the fuzzy relation $OBS \times OPS \rightarrow [0,1]$. Every permission is a collection of elements of the form (obs, op, mag) where $obs \in OBS$, $op \in OPS$ and mag is a magnitude in the range $[0,1]$. The magnitude of every pair object-operation determines an order relation between them. This magnitude will be lately used to decide whether the strength of the user-permission assignment is strong enough to enable the access to the pair object-operation.

Progressive abilities acquisition. Progressive abilities acquisition in FRBAC is given by the user-permission strength and the permissions definition. On the one hand, when a user gains membership level in a role, the user automatically gains user-permission strength in all the permissions assigned to the role. On the other hand, the magnitude of every pair object-operation in the definition of permissions is related to the user-permission assignment strength in order to determine the form of the permission. Gaining user-permission strength increases the pairs object-operation that the user can execute. In other words, gaining user-permission strength increases the abilities of the user. Figure 1 illustrates an example of progressive abilities acquisition.

The *access* function determines the access degree that a user has over every pair object-operation:

- $access : USERS \times OPS \times OBS \rightarrow [0,1]$. That is, given a user u, an operation op and an object o, the *access* function returns the access degree that the user u has over the resource o through the operation op. The function is described as follows:

$$access(u, op, o) = \{\mu_{UP}(u,p) | (u, p, \mu_{UP}(u,p)) \in UP \wedge$$
$$(op, o, \mu_{OBS \times OPS}(op, o)) \in p \wedge \mu_{UP}(u,p) \geq \mu_{OBS \times OPS}(op, o)\}$$

An access degree different than 0 means that the user is related to the permission and the access must be allowed according to the access degree. The access degree is strongly related with progressive abilities enhancing and will be introduced in the following.

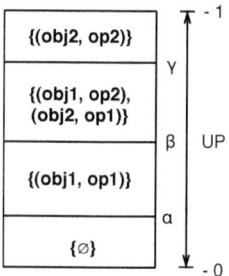

Fig. 1. The user-permission strength determines the objects and operations related by the permission. The more permission strength (UP), the more objects and operations relate the permission. In this figure, an UP in the range $[0, \alpha)$ makes the permission to relate $\emptyset$ objects and operations. An UP in the range $[\alpha, \beta)$ makes the permission to relate the $object_1$ with the $operation_1$ and so on.

Progressive abilities enhancing. As users gain experience and role levels in RPG, they also experience abilities enhancing. Abilities enhancing refers to the efficiency on doing things and it is strongly related to the ability itself. Abilities enhancing allows users to upgrade their abilities allowing, for instance, warriors to infer more damage to their enemies, mages to invoke spells with more power, gardeners to grow plants quicker, etc.

Traditionally, in the access control field, access has been seen as something binary. You can execute an operation or you cannot. You can open a door or you cannot. You can access the database or you cannot. However access may have a fractional meaning. Fractionallity on access is strongly application-dependent and refers to the efficiency, intensity or degree of execution of actions. This concept can be easily understood in systems regulated under QoS policies. The more access degree, the more resources put in the execution of the permission and, thus, improving the quality of the access/service. Although this concept easily applies to QoS, there are multiple application fields.

As the user progresses in the roles, the user-permission strength grows increasing the execution level of operations over objects, and enhancing the abilities that the user already had. The access level is determined by the returned value of the *access* function. Note that the enforcement point of the application must interpret the access level in order to constrain or adjust –if possible and required– the execution of the requested pair object-operation. This interpretation is highly application-dependent and may refer to the resources put on serving QoS-subjected services, for example.

4   Example

In this section we show an example to ease the understanding of the approach. We first describe the generic scenario and then how to implement it with FRBAC.

Finally, we discuss the implementation through RBAC to compare the user-role and role-privilege assignments of both implementations.

Imagine a social network where there are different communities. Users experience a progression in the community membership gaining and enhancing abilities as their experience grows. Every community has resources available to the community members.

Suppose that, among others, there are two communities in the social network: $Community_1$, and $Community_2$.

The resources offered by $Community_1$ are:

- Public web page.
- Member's profiles: including basic information, private information, pictures and videos.
- Storage service.

The permissions defined by the $Community_1$ are:

- Read the public web page.
- Edit the public web page.
- Read basic information on user profiles.
- Read pictures on user profiles.
- Read videos on user profiles.
- Read private information on user profiles.
- Censure user profiles.
- Access the storage service in read/write mode.

The access control policy of the $Community_1$ states:

- Public web page can be read by everybody in the social network. The web page can be edited by users of at least level 50.
- Basic information about member's profiles can be accessed by all the community members (level at least 1). Pictures can be accessed by members of level at least 20. Videos can be accessed by members of level at least 30. Private information can be accessed by members of level at least 70. Profiles can be partially or totally censured if considered inappropriate by members of level at least 100.
- Members of $Community_2$ will be able to read basic information of user profiles.
- The storage service can be accessed by members of the community. The storage space for every user is computed as the user-permission strength per 1GB.

The membership level of the community is computed taking into account the time that the user has belonged to the community and the activity of the user.

There are four users in the community. $User_1$ is member of level 70 in the $Community_2$. $User_2$ is member of level 10 in the $Community_1$. $User_3$ is member of level 50 in the $Community_1$. $User_4$ is member of level 100 in the $Community_1$.

4.1   Implementation through FRBAC

We describe the access control policies in FRBAC. We define the following two roles: `community_1_Member`, and `community_2_Member`. The user-role assignments in the social network are represented in Table 1.

Table 1. User-role assignments

	community_1_Member	community_2_Member
$User_1$	0	0.7
$User_2$	0.1	0
$User_3$	0.5	0
$User_4$	1	0

We define the following 3 polymorphic permissions: *Access_web* which according to the access control policy enables the access in read and edit mode; *Access_profiles* which enables reading basic information, pictures, videos, private information and censure profiles; and *Access_storage* that enables the access in read/write access mode. The storage space depends on the user-permission strength. The description of the permissions is shown in Figure 2.

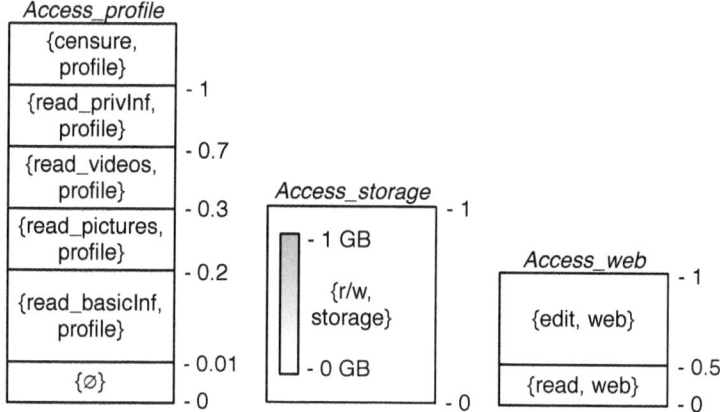

Fig. 2. Permissions

According to the access control policy, the role-permission assignments are defined in Table 2.

The user-permission assignments are computed as the composition of the user-role and role-permission assignments and are shown in Table 3.

$User_1$ is not a member of $Community_1$ and she is allowed to read the web page. Furthermore, as a member of $Community_2$, $User_1$ is allowed to access basic

Table 2. Role-permission assignments

	community_1_Member	community_2_Member
Access_web	1	0
Access_profiles	1	0.01
Access_storage	1	0

Table 3. User-permission assignments

	Access_web	*Access_profiles*	*Access_storage*
$User_1$	0	0.01	0
$User_2$	0.1	0.1	0.1
$User_3$	0.5	0.5	0.5
$User_4$	1	1	1

information on the user profiles. $User_2$ is a member of level 10 of $Community_1$. She is allowed to read the web page, read basic information of the community member's profiles, and access 100MB of storage space. $User_3$ is allowed to read and edit the web page; read basic information, pictures and videos in the member's profiles; and access 500MB of storage space. $User_4$ has the same permissions than $User_3$ and additionally can read private information and censure profiles; and access 1GB of storage space.

4.2   Comparison with RBAC

To the best of our knowledge, there is no previous work on intra-role progression models. In this section we compare the intra-role user progression model with the implicit inter-role progression of RBAC. The comparison results can be extended to RBAC reputation-based models such as [3,12].

In order to implement the example in Core RBAC [7], we need to define the following roles: $community1_1$, $community1_{20}$, $community1_{30}$, $community1_{50}$, $community1_{70}$, $community1_{100}$, and $community2_{10}$. Every role will have different associated permissions. A similar user-progression model in RBAC could be automatized conditioning the user-role assignments, making users acquire privileges progressively. Users could be assigned to the roles $community1_1$, ...,$community1_{100}$ depending on their experience. However, intra-role progression avoids the need to split the role community_1_Member.

According to the access control policy of $Community_1$, members of the role $community1_{100}$ are given with all the 8 permissions of the community. Members of the role $community1_{70}$ are given with all the permissions except the one that allows them to censure profiles. Following with the access control policy, the role $community1_{50}$ is assigned with 6 permissions, $community1_{30}$ is assigned with 5 permissions, $community1_{20}$ is assigned with 4 permissions, $community1_1$ is assigned with 3 permissions, $community2_{10}$ is assigned with 2 permissions.

Under Hierarchical RBAC [7], hierarchy relations can be defined between roles in order to reduce the number of role-privilege assignments. The role $community1_{100}$ dominates the role $community1_{70}$ which, at the same time, dominates $community1_{50}$ and so on. Senior roles inherit permissions from junior roles. $community1_{100}$ is given with the permission to censure profiles and inherits the permissions from $community1_{70}$. $community1_{70}$ is given with the permission to access private information on users' profiles. $community1_{70}$ also inherits from $community1_{50}$. The process is repeated until $community1_{1}$.

Figure 3 shows a comparison on the number of roles, user-role assignments, role-permission assignments and role hierarchies in order to implement the access control policy described in the example under Core RBAC, Hierarchical RBAC and FRBAC.

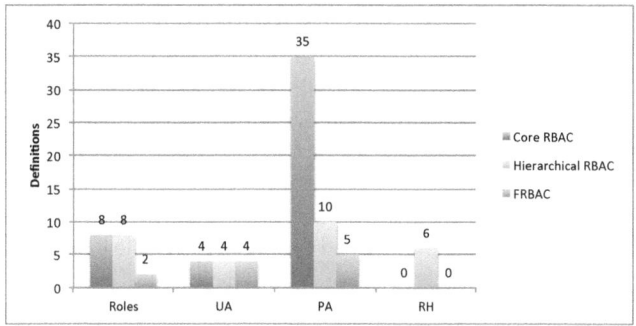

Fig. 3. Comparison between Core RBAC, Hierarchical RBAC, and FRBAC

It is noteworthy to show the impossibility to model in RBAC the variable storage space for the members of the community. RBAC considers operations as something binary, which can be executed or not. An RPG-like user progression model not only contemplates progressive abilities acquisition but progressive abilities enhancing. Progressive abilities enhancing means more efficiency on the execution of a permission. In this case, abilities enhancing refers to the increasing storage space as users seniority in the community grows.

The more granularity on the progressive abilities acquisition means more roles and more role-permission relations in RBAC. In hierarchical RBAC, the more granularity on the progressive abilities acquisition increments the role-permission and role hierarchies relations. FRBAC is able to accommodate more progressive abilities acquisition by the definition of polymorphic permissions. There is no need to split roles in FRBAC and increment the role-permission assignments.

5   Related Work

RBAC captures the organization chart of a business process through the concept of roles and role hierarchies. In that sense, RBAC is able to accommodate the natural users promotion that allow users to ascend in the organization chart. This inter-role promotion process leads to user-role assignments and can be done manually or automatizing the user-role assignments.

To the best of our knowledge, there is no prior work on user progression models dealing with intra-role progression in RBAC. Closely related, we find Trust-Based Access Control. Trust-Based Access Control aims to determine trust relations between users and service providers, based on personal experiences or inferred from third parties trust relations [2]. Trust relations will condition the interactions within principals. Intuitively, the more trust between parties, the more likely of interaction between them.

There are previous research joining Trust-Based Access Control and RBAC. TrustBAC [3] assigns users with trust levels. Then, trust levels are assigned with roles which, at the same time, are assigned with permissions. The model defines an inter-role promotion as the users earn trust in the system, rather than intra-role promotion defined in RPG. In the same direction, Takabi et al. [12] define the concept of user trustworthiness and role required trustworthiness. Users are assigned to roles if the user trustworthiness is greater or equal than the role required trustworthiness. Yong [14] determines the user reputation in order to infer automatic user-role assignments in the multi-domain environment.

Other authors have proposed the concept of trust and reputation in order to restrict RBAC. Mezzetti [10] proposes a model that enables RBAC to enforce a minimum reputation value to be maintained for users to enable user-role assignments. Woo et al. [13] propose an extension of RBAC to check if the trustworthiness of the users is greater than a given threshold in order to grant the authorization.

To the best of our knowledge, there is no previous work explicitly dealing with access level and polymorphic permissions. However, we can find in the literature marks that justify their definition. We can read in [6]:

"[...] To understand the importance of the granularity of access, consider the needs of a pharmacist to access a patient's record to check for interactions between medications and to add notes to the medication section of the patient record. Although such operations may be necessary, the pharmacist should not be able to read or alter other parts of the patient record. [...]"

The rules described in the above citation can be seen as a polymorphic permission that enables the access to different parts of the medical record through different operations. Accessing the medication section of the record is a weaker ability than reading or altering the other parts of the patient record. Pharmacists shouldn't be able to acquire the privilege in a way that enables them to access the whole records. Another mark of polymorphic permissions can be found in [4]:

"[...] We propose that the existing static access control models with binary allow/deny decisions be replaced by a dynamic multi-decision access control model based on quantified risk estimates and risk tolerance. [...] The quantifies risk estimate for any access falls into one of these risk bands. Each band is associated with a decision and an action; the decision, the action and the band boundaries

are all determined according to risk tolerance and can be changed when risk tolerance changes. The top band would be be associated with the decision deny because the risk is too high. [...]"

Risk bands fits nicely with the notion of polymorphic permissions. Moreover, risk bands also fits nicely with the concept of access level. The risk can be computed as the user-permission assignment strength. Depending on the risk involving the assignment, the access level of an operation over an object can be higher or lower. Another mark regarding to access level can be found in [11]:

"[...] consider an adult who wants to view the output of a video camera in a child's bedroom, for the purpose of checking on the child. The security policy may state that only the child's parents or babysitter can view the video. Perhaps a strong identification mechanism may provide enough authentication evidence to allow the user to see a streaming video, while a weak identification mechanism may provide only enough authentication evidence to permit the user to view a recent still image of reduced quality and definition. [...]".

The variable quality of service on accessing the web cam can be considered a form of access level.

6 Conclusions

We have described an intra-role user-progression model inspired in role-playing games for RBAC through FRBAC, and demonstrated its expressiveness in comparison with RBAC. FRBAC defines multivalued user-role and role-permission relations which allow to accommodate user progression within roles. Role progression will lately result in progressive abilities acquisition and progressive abilities enhancing. Progressive abilities acquisition and enhancing is an effective mechanism to accommodate the natural user progression within a system. It benefits RBAC with expressiveness at policy definition time. Intra-role user progression avoids the need of role splitting when the same conceptual role requires different privilege assignments related to the user experience, and thus, has clear benefit in the number of defined roles. Polymorphic privileges keep ordered the permissions and reduces the number of permissions in the system.

The model is applicable in environments where the authorization system must be aware of the progression of the users within the system, and requires a role engineering task to determine the privileges related with every access level degree. The interpretation of progressive abilities acquisition, and specially, progressive abilities enhancing is highly application-dependent.

Acknowledgments. Partial support by the Spanish MICINN (projects TIN2010-15764, TSI2007-65406-C03-02, ARES-CONSOLIDER INGENIO 2010 CSD2007-00004) and Universitat Autònoma de Barcelona (PIF 472-01-1/07) is acknowledged.

References

1. Adams, E.: Fundamentals of Game Design, 2nd edn. New Riders Publishing (2009)
2. Bonatti, P., Duma, C., Olmedilla, D., Shahmehri, N.: An integration of reputation-based and policy-based trust management. In: Semantic Web and Policy Workshop (in conjunction with 4th International Semantic Web Conference) (2005)
3. Chakraborty, S., Ray, I.: Trustbac: integrating trust relationships into the rbac model for access control in open systems. In: Proceedings of the Eleventh ACM Symposium on Access Control Models and Technologies (SACMAT 2006), pp. 49–58. ACM (2006)
4. Cheng, P.-C., Rohatgi, P., Keser, C., Karger, P.A., Wagner, G.M., Reninger, A.S.: Fuzzy multi-level security: An experiment on quantified risk-adaptive access control. In: Proceedings of the 2007 IEEE Symposium on Security and Privacy, pp. 222–230. IEEE Computer Society (2007)
5. Dovrolis, C., Ramanathan, P.: A case for relative differentiated services and the proportional differentiation model. IEEE Network 13(5), 26–34 (1999)
6. Ferraiolo, D.F., Kuhn, R.D., Chandramouli, R.: Role-Based Access Control, 2nd edn. Artech House, Inc. (2007)
7. Ferraiolo, D.F., Sandhu, R.S., Gavrila, S.I., Richard Kuhn, D., Chandramouli, R.: Proposed NIST standard for role-based access control. ACM Transactions on Information Systems Security 4(3), 224–274 (2001)
8. Klir, G.J., Yuan, B.: Fuzzy sets and fuzzy logic: theory and applications. Prentice-Hall, Inc. (1995)
9. Martínez-García, C., Navarro-Arribas, G., Borrell, J.: Fuzzy role-based access control. Information Processing Letters 111, 483–487 (2011)
10. Mezzetti, N.: A Socially Inspired Reputation Model. In: Katsikas, S.K., Gritzalis, S., López, J. (eds.) EuroPKI 2004. LNCS, vol. 3093, pp. 191–204. Springer, Heidelberg (2004)
11. Moyer, M.J., Covington, M.J., Ahamad, M.: Generalized role-based access control for securing future applications. In: 23rd National Information Systems Security Conference, NISSC 2000 (2000)
12. Takabi, H., Amini, M., Jalili, R.: Trust-based user-role assignment in role-based access control. In: ACS/IEEE International Conference on Computer Systems and Applications, pp. 807–814. IEEE Computer Society (2007)
13. Woo, J.W., Hwang, M.J., Lee, C.G., Youn, H.Y.: Dynamic role-based access control with trust-satisfaction and reputation for multi-agent system. In: 2010 IEEE 24th International Conference on Advanced Information Networking and Applications Workshops (WAINA), pp. 1121–1126 (2010)
14. Yong, H.: Reputation and role based access control model for multi-domain environments. In: 2010 International Symposium on Intelligence Information Processing and Trusted Computing (IPTC), pp. 597–600 (2010)

Distributed Orchestration of Web Services under Security Constraints[*]

Tigran Avanesov[1], Yannick Chevalier[2], Mohammed Anis Mekki[1],
Michaël Rusinowitch[1], and Mathieu Turuani[1]

[1] INRIA Nancy Grand Est,
615 allée du jardin botanique, 54000 Vandœuvre-lès-Nancy, France
{avanesot,mekkimoh,rusi,turuani}@loria.fr
[2] Université de Toulouse,
118 Route de Narbonne, F-31062 Toulouse, France
ychevali@irit.fr

Abstract. We present a novel approach to automated distributed orchestration of Web services tied with security policies. The construction of an orchestration complying with the policies is based on the resolution of deducibility constraint systems and has been implemented for the non-distributed case as part of the AVANTSSAR Validation Platform. The tool has been successfully experimented on several case-studies from industry and academia.

Keywords: Web services, automatic composition, security, distributed orchestration, formal methods.

1 Introduction

Composability, one of the basic principles and design-objectives of *Service-oriented Architecture (SOA)* expresses the need for providing simple scenarios where already available services can be reused to derive new added-value services. SOA in its SOAP Web services incarnation based on XML messaging and relying on a rich stack of related standards provides a flexible yet highly interoperable solution to describe and implement a variety of e-business scenarios involving different services possibly bound to complex security policies. Therefore automated solutions should be considered for composition to realize scalability since the composed service can be very complex either to discover or even to describe, especially if some security constraints are to be respected.

Mainly two approaches to Web service composition have been considered, namely orchestration and choreography [23]. In the former a unique business process, called a *Mediator*, aggregates the existing services, while in the latter each service is responsible for implementing its part of the composed service.

We present in this paper a scalable Web service composition approach relying on the notion of *partner* corresponding to an organization. Each partner

---

[*] This work is supported by FP7 AVANTSSAR [1] and FP7 NESSoS [2] projects.

J. Garcia-Alfaro et al. (Eds.): DPM 2011 and SETOP 2011, LNCS 7122, pp. 235–252, 2012.
© Springer-Verlag Berlin Heidelberg 2012

in a composition implements its own part of the orchestration. In this setting standard orchestration is a special case in which only one partner is involved, whereas choreography is another case in which there is one partner per available service. Several related "distributed orchestration" notions have been advocated for in the literature (e.g. [4]). However in inter-organizational business processes it is crucial to protect sensitive data of each organization providing a component service in some orchestration, and our main motivation is to advance the state of the art by taking into account the security policies while computing an orchestration.

Contributions. First, we present a formal framework to model Web services, their security policies and their intercommunication. We consider a rich structure for Web services' messages including ciphered texts to ensure non-disclosure policies. We show that in this setting the distributed orchestration problem appears to be non trivial even for linear workflows. Second, we propose an algorithm to solve the distributed orchestration problem in this setting. Our decidability result relies on advanced symbolic constraint solving techniques. Finally the paper reports a freely available prototype implementation of the automatic Web services composition approach for the non-distributed case. This prototype is one of the few automatic tools (like [27,12]) that are able to orchestrate Web services.

Related work. A common approach to *static* [8] (or *syntactic* [25]) Web services compositions is Orchestration. Web services orchestration [22] deals with a central entity called *orchestrator* or *mediator* that operates as a glue between the Client and the community of available services.

Most works on service composition rely on a *behavior model* [11], i.e. where services are considered as stateful and used by the Client according to some scenario. The behavior is usually presented as a Kripke structure, where transitions are labeled with services' operations [20]. Here we will give a small overview of related works.

A composition based on conversations (where a conversation is a sequence of messages exchanged by peers) was presented in [9]. The available services are represented by a finite set of message classes, a finite set of abstract peers (services) and a finite set of directed channels. Each channel consists of two endpoints and a set of message classes allowed to be sent over this channel. The composition problem amounts then to find a Mealy machine for each peer such that the set of possible conversations that can be seen by an external observer is equivalent to some given conversation specification.

Another work on the same lines is [7]. The authors suggest a way to synthesize and verify cryptographic protocols given a set of multiparty sessions that represent possible conversations between the participants. Given multiparty sessions represented as directed graphs whose nodes are labeled with protocol roles names and edges labeled with message descriptors and two sets of typed variables: the first one states the variables in which a role from the source node can write, and the second one — those variables from which the destination role can read. The authors propose to build first the projection for each role and then reinforce it by adding a security layer in order to guarantee integrity and secrecy properties. Moreover, a prototype of the compiler implementing this approach generates interfaces and implementations for the generated protocols in ML.

Note that these approaches aim to *generate* implementations of the participants with given behavior, while in this paper we focus on how to *compose* automatically existing ones in order to synthesize a service that is able to satisfy a given client.

In the *Roman Model* [11], the available services are specified as finite state machines. In [20] the author extends the service model from deterministic [6] to non-deterministic state machines allowing shared memory. Moreover, the approach allows one to find a *finite orchestrator generator* that can derive a set of all possible orchestrations. Note that in all these works services accept only data from a finite domain. This has motivated an extension called *COLOMBO* [5] of Web services composition which deals with messages from infinite domains. The composition problem is equivalent to finding a *Mediator* service which uses messages to interact with the available services and the Client such that the overall behavior of the mediated system faithfully simulates the behavior of given goal service. However, even in this model the Mediator is not able to handle the cryptographic primitives (e.g. decrypt an encrypted message).

In many cases a single entity (device, organization) is not able to orchestrate the Web services due to the lack of resources (e.g. absence of data requested by available services) or because of access limitations: some services are limited to a protected private network. But if partner organizations are involved in the orchestration, every party can contribute to satisfy client requests. In *distributed* or *decentralized orchestration* (e.g. [21] and [20,24] for other alternative approaches), each partner can invoke his available services and also communicate with other partners. In this way a Mediator is distributed between the partners, but still we have a dedicated one to communicate with the Client. However even in cooperation mode sensitive data should not be propagated beyond the organizational border (a company will not share secrets with partners). This is why communication between partners must be restricted. We will show below how distributed orchestration is still possible in such constrained setting. For the non-distributed case and without implementation some initial ideas were presented in [14].

Paper organization. In Section 2 we introduce some basic notions and present an example of non-distributed Web services orchestration; Section 3 starts with an example of distributed orchestration, then our formal model is explained, and ends with presenting our method for solving distributed orchestration problems. Section 4 reports our implementation for the non-distributed case.

2   The AVANTSSAR Approach

In this section we present an approach used in *AVANTSSAR Orchestrator*, a tool for automatic orchestration of Web services.

2.1   Web Service Model

Web services can be described at two levels: *(i)* The *profile*, a precise description of the interface exposed by a service in terms of a set of operations it provides, their corresponding in-bound and out-bound message patterns and possibly their security policies. From the point of view of standards, this information corresponds to the *WSDL* part of the service specification. *(ii)* The *behavior*, or the use-case scenario of the interface exposed by the service, e.g. a sequencing in the calls of the operations provided by the service. This is typically covered by the *BPEL* part of the service specification.

We use first-order terms to describe the profile of a Web service as they capture an interesting fragment of the *XML Schema* and *WS-SecurityPolicy*. On the other hand, for the behavior part of a Web service we use a transition system capturing its workflow logic. For the sake of simplicity we will assume only linear workflows (i.e. sequential workflows without branching) in this section[1].

We consider an abstraction of Web services as sequences of *actions*, where an action is either receiving or sending of a message pattern. We write $?r$ for a reception of message r, and $!s$ for an emission of message s. We call a finite sequence of actions separated with "." a *strand* [17]. To simplify we consider only *normal strands*, i.e. starting from a ? action, ending by a ! action and alternating ? with ! actions. They can be viewed as *synchronous* Web services, that is where each request implies an immediate reply[2].

The execution of consecutive receive-send actions $?r.!s$ in a normal strand together with the corresponding send and receive actions of the caller is called an *invocation* of a synchronous service. We express message patterns (like s and r) as first-order terms. More precisely, we consider an infinite set of free constants $\mathcal{C}$ and an infinite set of variables $\mathcal{X}$. Given a signature $\mathcal{F}$ (*i.e.* a set of function symbols with arities) we denote by $\mathrm{T}(\mathcal{F}, \mathcal{X})$ the set of terms over $\mathcal{F} \cup \mathcal{C} \cup \mathcal{X}$ defined recursively as follows: *(i)* $\mathcal{C} \cup \mathcal{X} \subseteq \mathrm{T}(\mathcal{F}, \mathcal{X})$ *(ii)* $\forall f \in \mathcal{F} \ \forall t_1, \ldots, t_n \in \mathrm{T}(\mathcal{F}, \mathcal{X})$ implies $f(t_1, \ldots, t_n) \in \mathrm{T}(\mathcal{F}, \mathcal{X})$, where n is the arity of f. Given a term t we denote by $\mathrm{Sub}(t)$ the set of its subterms defined recursively as follows: *(i)* $t \in \mathrm{Sub}(t)$ *(ii)* $t = f(t_1, \ldots, t_n)$ implies $\bigcup_{i=1,\ldots,n} \mathrm{Sub}(t_i) \subseteq \mathrm{Sub}(t)$. We denote by $\mathrm{Vars}(t)$ the set of variables occurring in term t, i.e. $\mathrm{Vars}(t) = \mathrm{Sub}(t) \cap \mathcal{X}$. The set of ground terms (or messages) over $\mathcal{F}$ is denoted by $\mathrm{T}(\mathcal{F})$ and defined as $\mathrm{T}(\mathcal{F}) = \{t \in \mathrm{T}(\mathcal{F}, \mathcal{X}) : \mathrm{Vars}(t) = \emptyset\}$. A substitution σ is a mapping from $\mathcal{X}$ to $\mathrm{T}(\mathcal{F}, \mathcal{X})$; a ground substitution is a mapping from $\mathcal{X}$ to $\mathrm{T}(\mathcal{F})$. The application of a substitution σ to a term t (resp. a set of terms E) is denoted $t\sigma$ (resp. $E\sigma$) and is equal to the term t (resp. E) where all variables x have been replaced by the term $x\sigma$. The list of predefined symbols and their meanings are given in Table 1.

---

[1] Taking into account branching structures of available Web services should not pose any technical problem, but would lead to some more complex notations. Moreover, the branching is allowed in the implementation.

[2] Note also that a non-normal strand can be reduced to a normal one by adding fake ? and ! actions where needed.

Distributed Orchestration of Web Services under Security Constraints   239

Table 1. Predefined functional symbols

Term	Description
$\text{enc}(t_1, t_2)$	t_1 encrypted with symmetric key t_2
$\text{aenc}(t_1, t_2)$	t_1 encrypted with asymmetric public key t_2
$\text{pair}(t_1, t_2)$	t_1 concatenated with t_2
$\text{priv}(t_2)$	corresponding private key for public key t_2
$\text{sig}(t_1, \text{priv}(t_2))$	signature of message t_1 with key $\text{priv}(t_2)$

Table 2. Dolev-Yao deduction rules

Composition rules	Decomposition rules
$t_1, t_2 \rightarrow \text{enc}(t_1, t_2)$	$\text{enc}(t_1, t_2), t_2 \rightarrow t_1$
$t_1, t_2 \rightarrow \text{aenc}(t_1, t_2)$	$\text{aenc}(t_1, t_2), \text{priv}(t_2) \rightarrow t_1$
$t_1, t_2 \rightarrow \text{pair}(t_1, t_2)$	$\text{pair}(t_1, t_2) \rightarrow t_1$
$t_1, \text{priv}(t_2) \rightarrow \text{sig}(t_1, \text{priv}(t_2))$	$\text{pair}(t_1, t_2) \rightarrow t_2$

Security policies (e.g. WS-SecurityPolicy standard's integrity or confidentiality assertions) are expressed in message patterns (e.g. integrity by a digital signature, and confidentiality by an encryption). Consider for instance a service that receives any value X and returns the result of function f on this value. This service is specified by the normal strand $?X.!f(X)$. Now if the security policy requires that incoming messages should be encrypted with the public key K_S of that service then the corresponding strand associated to the service will be $?\,\text{aenc}(X, K_S).!f(X)$ instead.

2.2 Web Service Orchestration

Following [6,5] we call a *Mediator* a service that adapts and dispatches requests from a client to the community of available services. We state the orchestration problem as follows: given a set of available services (represented as strands), a client (also represented as a strand) and an initial knowledge (represented as a finite set of terms) of a *Mediator* (a service to be composed), one must find a feasible (with regard to the elementary Dolev-Yao operations, see Table 2, that the service can execute internally) communication between the Mediator, Client and available services, such that all requests of the Client are satisfied by the Mediator service.

Orchestration example. Assume there is a demand on translating texts from French to English. It is known that the texts were obtained by automatically recognized hand-written documents and thus contain some misspells. The client's need is to send a text in French and receive back an English translation of the preliminary corrected text, i.e. the client specification is: $!t.\,?en(corr(t))$.

The available services are

1. **SpellChecker:** a service that corrects spelling (e.g. using the semantically closest word from list of possible options). Its model: $?T.!\,\text{pair}(corr(T), n(T))$,

where T is a text, $corr(T)$ is the corrected text, $n(T)$ is the number of corrections done.

2. **Translator:** a service producing an automatic translation of given text from French to English. Its security policy requires all incoming messages to be encrypted with its public key. The specification is: $?\,\mathrm{aenc}\,(M, K_{tr})\,.\,!en(M)$, where M is a text, $en(M)$ is a translation of M into English and K_{tr} is a public key of the Translator.

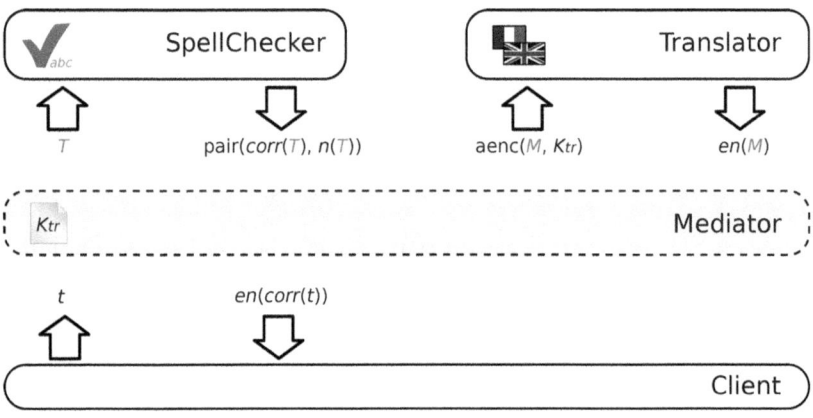

Fig. 1. Illustration for the orchestration example

We assume that the Mediator initially knows only a public key of the Translator K_{tr}. The question is how to satisfy the Client's request? The problem is illustrated in Fig. 1.

2.3   Reduction of Orchestration to Protocol State Reachability

The example shows that an orchestration problem can be reduced to checking whether there is a reachable state where the Client has received a reply on his request. Our idea is to adopt techniques from security protocol analysis, and thus to open the possibility of reusing existing tools, in order to solve the orchestration problem expressed as a reachability problem. The Mediator is a new service (that we try to generate) that organizes the communications between the given services and the Client in such a way, that the Client reaches a final acceptable state. The Mediator is conceptually similar to the Intruder [16] of the Dolev-Yao model of cryptographic protocols: the Dolev-Yao intruder tries to communicate with an honest agent, by playing some roles or faking some messages in order to reach an unsafe (or attack) state, e.g. when the honest agent sends a message from which the intruder is able to infer a secret key. We show some correspondence between entities of WS Orchestration and Protocol Analysis problem:

$$
\begin{cases}
\{K_{tr}, t\} & \triangleright & T & (1) \\
\{K_{tr}, t, \text{pair}\,(corr(T), n(T))\} & \triangleright & \text{aenc}\,(M, K_{tr}) & (2) \\
\{K_{tr}, t, \text{pair}\,(corr(T), n(T)), en(M)\} & \triangleright & en(corr(t)) & (3)
\end{cases}
$$

Fig. 2. A constraint system (T, M are variables) describing a possible orchestration

$$
Services \begin{cases}
\text{Available service/Client} & \sim & \text{Protocol role} \\
\text{Mediator} & \sim & \text{Intruder} \\
\text{Final state} & \sim & \text{Attack state}
\end{cases} Protocols
$$

Tool `CL-AtSe` [28,26] for finding attacks on protocols is placed at the core of AVANTSSAR Orchestrator. Let us survey the technique that underlies CL-AtSe on the example of § 2.2. First, the tool selects a linear order on service invocations and client calls that is compatible with their individual workflow. Suppose the following sequence has been selected:

1. Receive a request from the Client;
2. Invoke SpellChecker;
3. Invoke Translator;
4. Send a response to the Client.

Then, the tool generates a system of *deducibility constraints* from the specification of the services and the selected interleaving (see Fig. 2). A constraint is a couple denoted by $E \triangleright t$, where E is a set of terms and t is a term. A ground substitution σ is a solution of the constraint $E \triangleright t$, if $t\sigma \in \text{Der}\,(E\sigma)$, where $p \in \text{Der}\,(T)$ means that ground term p is *derivable* from set of ground terms T: formally $\text{Der}\,(T)$ is the smallest set T' containing T and such that for all $u, v \in T'$ and w such that $u, v \to w$ or $v \to w$ for some rule in Table 2 then $w \in T'$. Likewise, a ground substitution σ is a solution of a constraint system $\mathcal{S}$ iff σ is a solution of every constraint in $\mathcal{S}$.

Now we explain how the constraint system displayed in Fig. 2 is built. First the intruder receives t from the Client, i.e. his knowledge becomes $\{K_{tr}, t\}$. Second, in order to send a request to SpellChecker, the intruder must deduce some T from his knowledge (Constraint 1). Third, when he obtains the response, he adds it to his knowledge and tries to build a request acceptable by the Translator, i.e. that matches the expected pattern (Constraint 2). Finally, when he receives the response from the Translator, he tries to deduce the response for the Client (Constraint 3).

The constraint systems built by this procedure are *well-formed*, that is the sets on left-hand side of constraints are increasing (*knowledge monotonicity* property), and each variable appears first in the right-hand side of some constraint (*variable origination* property). A lot of work was done on the resolution of the constraints of this type (e.g [13,10]).

The unique solution of the constraint system in Fig. 2 is a substitution $\{T \mapsto t; M \mapsto corr(t)\}$, that can be interpreted as follows: first the Mediator sends to the SpellChecker t (text received from the Client), then he receives a response: pair $(corr(t), n(t))$. As the Mediator can decompose a pair he extracts the needed first part $(corr(t))$ and encrypt it with K_{tr}. The result is sent to the Translator that replies with $en(corr(t))$, the message expected by the Client. Thus, the Mediator can forward it and complete.

We have demonstrated some abilities of the Mediator. In this simple example it *decomposed* a concatenated message to throw away a part that is not needed (here, a number of corrections done) and *encrypted* a message with the necessary public key in order to adapt it in such way that the resulting message will be accepted by the service, since the service's policy is satisfied.

In the next example we show how *several* mediators may collaborate. In order to solve the analogous problem in these settings, a technique for resolution of well-formed constraints is not enough. Since we have to take into account knowledges of several different composers working in parallel, the constraint systems obtained in this case will probably violate the knowledge monotonicity property, and thus will not be well-formed.

3   Distributed Orchestration under Security Constraints

We extend the previous section and we show how to reduce the distributed orchestration problem to the resolution of deducibility constraints. The main difference is that the resulting constraints are not well-formed.

For the distributed orchestration we will consider multiple cooperating mediators, called *partners*. We distinguish one of them (still called Mediator) who communicates with the client, while all others do not. The partners are free to invoke available services, but the cooperation between them is restricted by communication patterns and *non-disclosure* policy conditioned by inter-organizational relationships (no sensitive data must be propagated to other organizations).

3.1   Distributed Orchestration Example

Suppose that the available services are not free and can serve only registered users (for the reason of simplicity we suppose that the Translator and the SpellChecker have a unique registered user each). Moreover, the Mediator has no credential to log in and use the Translator service, but it has an account for the SpellChecker (note that both Translator and SpellChecker are still reachable).

Fortunately, there is a partner who has an account for the Translator and can help to satisfy the client's requests (see Fig. 3), but does not want to reveal his credentials to the Mediator.

The corresponding specification of the Translator is:

$$? \, aenc \, (pair \, (pair \, (usr_{tr}, pwd_{tr}) \, , M) \, , K_{tr}) \, . \, !en(M),$$

where usr_{tr} is a login of the registered user and pwd_{tr} is the corresponding password; K_{tr} is a public key of the Translator.

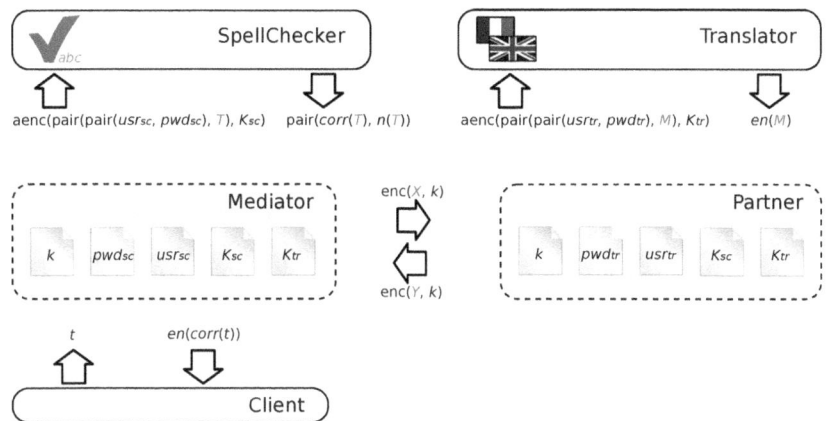

Fig. 3. Illustration for the distributed orchestration problem example

The corresponding specification of the SpellChecker is:

$$? \, \mathrm{aenc} \, (\mathrm{pair} \, (\mathrm{pair} \, (usr_{sc}, pwd_{sc}) \, , T) \, , K_{sc}) \, . \, ! \, \mathrm{pair} \, (corr(T), n(T)) \, ,$$

where usr_{sc} is a login of the registered user and pwd_{sc} is the corresponding password; K_{sc} is a public key of the SpellChecker.

We suppose that Mediator and Partner share a symmetric key k and all communications between them are encrypted with the shared key.

The problem is, again, to find a feasible communication scenario between all the parties, such that *(i)* all requests of the Client are satisfied and *(ii)* no partner can extract a sensitive data of another partner from a message received from the latter. In our example we can consider pwd_{sc} and pwd_{tr} as sensitive for the Mediator and Partner correspondingly. Later, in § 3.2 we will present a *non-disclosure condition* which is sufficient to ensure *(ii)*.

We can solve this problem if the number of *interactions* (i.e. invocations or send/receive pairs) is bounded. Suppose for simplicity that we can use every available service at most once, and that we allow one round of communication between the Mediator and the Partner (the Mediator sends request and the Partner replies).

Again, as in our previous example, we have to choose an interleaving of Client's and Partners' actions and invocations of available services (note that the number of all possible interleavings is finite).

Assume the selected interleaving is:

1. Client → Mediator
2. Mediator ↔ SpellChecker
3. Mediator → Partner
4. Partner ↔ Translator
5. Partner → Mediator
6. Mediator → Client

where $A \to B$ stands for "A sends and B receives", and $A \leftrightarrow B$ stands for "B is invoked by A". The corresponding constraint system is depicted in Fig. 4. It

$$
\left\{
\begin{array}{l}
\{K_{tr}, K_{sc}, usr_{sc}, pwd_{sc}, k, t\} \;\triangleright\; \text{aenc}\,(\text{pair}\,(\text{pair}\,(usr_{sc}, pwd_{sc})\,, T)\,, K_{sc}) \\
\{K_{tr}, K_{sc}, usr_{sc}, pwd_{sc}, k, t, \text{pair}\,(corr(T), n(T))\} \;\triangleright\; \text{enc}\,(X, k) \\
\{K_{tr}, K_{sc}, usr_{tr}, pwd_{tr}, k, \text{enc}\,(X, k)\} \;\triangleright\; \text{aenc}\,(\text{pair}\,(\text{pair}\,(usr_{tr}, pwd_{tr})\,, M)\,, K_{tr}) \\
\{K_{tr}, K_{sc}, usr_{tr}, pwd_{tr}, k, \text{enc}\,(X, k)\,, en(M)\} \;\triangleright\; \text{enc}\,(Y, k) \\
\{K_{tr}, K_{sc}, usr_{sc}, pwd_{sc}, k, t, \text{pair}\,(corr(T), n(T))\,, \text{enc}\,(Y, k)\} \;\triangleright\; en(corr(t))
\end{array}
\right\}
$$

Fig. 4. A constraint system $(T, M, X, Y$ are variables) describing a possible distributed orchestration

is built by analogy with the one in Fig. 2 (see § 2.3). For example, in the first line we have a constraint whose left-hand side represents the knowledge of the Mediator after the reception of text t from the Client (the first interaction in the selected interleaving), and its right-hand side represents the message pattern accepted by the SpellChecker, since in order to invoke the latter (see the second interaction in the selected interleaving), the Mediator needs to build a message compatible with this pattern.

We can see that the obtained constraint system is not well-formed, and thus, the existing above mentioned solving methods (except [19]) are not applicable. The reason is that the property called knowledge monotonicity does not hold. This is due to the fact that there are multiple entities (partners) whose knowledge we must take into account, while in the case of non-distributed orchestration there exists one single entity (the Mediator) whose knowledge is expressed in LHS of the constraints.

Another remark: we cannot treat the constraint system in a modular manner, i.e. consider separately a subsystem of constraints for each partner, since the obtained constraint systems are not independent as they share variables. If we do not take into account this fact and solve them separately, then we will be probably unable to join the solutions, since they can be "incompatible", i.e. a solution for one subsystem implies one value for a variable, while a solution for another may imply another value for the same variable. Moreover, these subsystems are even not well-formed, since in general they will not satisfy the variable origination property.

One of the possible solutions, that can be automatically built (§ 3.3), of this constraint system is $\sigma = \{T \mapsto t, M \mapsto corr(t), X \mapsto corr(t), Y \mapsto en(corr(t))\}$. The Mediator gets text t from the Client, sends it encrypted together with his login data to the SpellChecker, then from the reply he extracts the corrected version $corr(t)$ of the text, sends it to the Partner, who concatenates it together with his translator login/password and sends it encrypted to the Translator. Partner forwards the obtained response to the Mediator who returns it to the Client.

Note that neither $X\sigma$ nor $Y\sigma$ contains login information of the Mediator or the Partner.

3.2   Formal Model

In this section we introduce a model for the distributed orchestration. Note that the standard (non-distributed) orchestration is the special case with the unique mediator. Informally, the distributed orchestration problem is stated as follows: given a community of the available services, a Client, a set of partners each with some initial knowledge and a set of communication channels between the partners, find a feasible communication scenario between partners, available services and the Client, such that the Client reaches its final state.

In this communication scenario the circulated messages have to be sent on a set of predefined channels and they have to follow some message patterns defined per channel. Moreover some non-disclosure policies imposed on the communications are specified as a set of sensitive atomic data per partner, which should not be extractable from messages sent to other partners.

To ensure the latter we will consider a stronger property: we don't allow any occurrence of sensitive data as a subterm of these messages. Indeed, as deduction rules in Table 2 do not produce new atoms, a partner is unable to extract any sensitive data from a message that does not contain it. In this way the partners are guaranteed not to directly reveal their confidential information to other ones, but this information still can be used to invoke the available services.

Note that in order to directly solve the problem with non-disclosure policies, one should consider more complex techniques that are able to cope with satisfiability of constraint systems that includes also a negation (term t should *not* be deducible from set of terms E). Unfortunately we are not aware of any such results.

Orchestration problem input. We assume we are given:

- A set of available services $\mathbb{S} = \{S_1, \ldots, S_n\}$. An available service S_i is represented by its name and a normal (for the sake of simplicity) strand, i.e. $S_i = \langle i, A_i \rangle$, where $A_i = ?r_1.!s_1. \ldots . ?r_{e_i}.!s_{e_i}$ and $e_i \in \mathbb{N}^+$ is the number of pairs of actions in A_i.
- A client C. We can think of the client as a stand-alone available service $\langle 0, A_0 \rangle$, but A_0 is a strand which is not necessarily normal (in order to permit the client to initiate a conversation).
- A set of partners $\mathbb{P} = \{P_1, \ldots, P_k\}$ (P_1 is a Mediator) and for each partner P_i, a set of sensitive atoms N_i that he does not want to share with partners. Partner P_i is represented by its name i, his current knowledge K_i and a set of sensitive atomic values $N_i \subseteq \mathrm{Sub}\,(K_i)$, i.e. $P_i = \langle i, K_i, N_i \rangle$.
- A set of communication channels $\mathbb{C} = \{C_1, \ldots, C_u\}$ between partners. Communication channel $C \in \mathbb{C}$ is a tuple $\langle i, j, p \rangle$, where i and j are names of partners P_i and P_j correspondingly and all messages sent from P_i to P_j must match pattern p. We assume that pattern p does not contain sensitive atoms as subterms, i.e. $\mathrm{Sub}\,(p) \cap N_i = \emptyset$.
- An upper bound on the number of interactions m.

We assume that the sets of variables used to describe each available service (and in the Client) are pairwise disjoint, i.e. $\text{Vars}(S_i) \cap \text{Vars}(S_j) = \emptyset$, if $i \neq j$ and for all i, $\text{Vars}(S_i) \cap \text{Vars}(C) = \emptyset$.

Execution model. We define a *non-disclosure condition* (or *non-disclosure policy*) according to what we have already announced before: a sensitive atom of a partner never occurs as a subterm of a message emitted by him, but we will impose this policy *only* on messages emitted by one partner to another, while the communication with available services is free from this condition. We define a *non-disclosure condition* (or *non-disclosure policy*) $\mathcal{H}$ as a set of equations $\left\{ \text{Sub}(m_i) \cap N_{j_i} \stackrel{?}{=} \emptyset \right\}_{i=1,\dots,l}$, where m_i is a term and N_{j_i} is a set of sensitive atoms. We will say that a ground substitution σ is a solution of (or satisfies) $\mathcal{H}$ iff for all $i = 1, \dots, l$ an equality $\text{Sub}(m_i\sigma) \cap N_{j_i} = \emptyset$ holds.

We present a configuration as a tuple $\langle \{S_1, S_2, \dots, S_n\}, C, \{P_1, \dots, P_k\}, \mathcal{S}, \mathcal{H} \rangle$, i.e. set of available services, client, set of partners, constraint system and non-disclosure condition to be satisfied. We define a set of transitions in Fig. 5 that allow us to evolve from one configuration to another.

$$\frac{\langle \{\langle j, ?r.\,!s.\,A_j' \rangle\} \cup S', C, \{\langle i, K_i, N_i \rangle\} \cup P', \mathcal{S}, \mathcal{H} \rangle}{\langle \{\langle j, A_j' \rangle\} \cup S', C, \{\langle i, K_i \cup \{s\}, N_i \rangle\} \cup P', \mathcal{S} \cup \{K_i \triangleright r\}, \mathcal{H} \rangle} \tag{4}$$

$$\frac{\langle S, \langle 0, !s.\,A' \rangle, \{\langle 1, K_1, N_1 \rangle\} \cup P', \mathcal{S}, \mathcal{H} \rangle}{\langle S, \langle 0, A' \rangle, \{\langle 1, K_1 \cup \{s\}, N_1 \rangle\} \cup P', \mathcal{S}, \mathcal{H} \rangle} \tag{5}$$

$$\frac{\langle S, \langle 0, ?r.\,A' \rangle, \{\langle 1, K_1, N_1 \rangle\} \cup P', \mathcal{S}, \mathcal{H} \rangle}{\langle S, \langle 0, A' \rangle, \{\langle 1, K_1, N_1 \rangle\} \cup P', \mathcal{S} \cup \{K_1 \triangleright r\}, \mathcal{H} \rangle} \tag{6}$$

$$\frac{\langle S, C, \{\langle i, K_i, N_i \rangle, \langle j, K_j, N_j \rangle\} \cup P', \mathcal{S}, \mathcal{H} \rangle \qquad [\text{if } \langle i, j, p \rangle \in \mathbb{C}; \; q = \text{refresh}(p)]}{\langle S, C, \{\langle i, K_i, N_i \rangle, \langle j, K_j \cup \{q\}, N_j \rangle\} \cup P', \mathcal{S} \cup \{K_i \triangleright q\}, \mathcal{H} \cup \{\text{Sub}(q) \cap N_i \stackrel{?}{=} \emptyset\} \rangle} \tag{7}$$

where $\text{refresh}(t)$ is a term equal to t where all variables are replaced with fresh ones.

Fig. 5. Transition system

Transition 4 expresses that Partner $P_i = \langle i, K_i, N_i \rangle$ can invoke available service $S_j = \langle j, A_j \rangle$, iff he is able to build a message (ground term) that is compatible with the expected pattern. The reply of S_j will become a part of the partner's knowledge. Similarly for the message exchange of the Mediator P_1 and the Client C, except that the Client can initiate a sending (5,6). A partner $P_i = \langle i, K_i, N_i \rangle$ can send a message to a partner P_j, iff there exists a channel $C_{ij} = \langle i, j, p \rangle \in \mathbb{C}$ between them such that partner P_i can build a message compatible with pattern p and this message will not contain sensitive data from N_i as a subterm (7). Note that in this setting services cannot be reused a second time, but we are free to add several instances for services to the problem input.

A sequence of length l of configurations starting with initial one $\langle \mathbb{S}, C, \mathbb{P}, \emptyset, \emptyset \rangle$ and obtained by applying transitions from Fig. 5 is called *symbolic execution SE* of length l.

An *execution* E is a pair $\langle SE, \sigma \rangle$ of a symbolic execution SE and ground substitution σ, such that for the last configuration $\langle \mathbb{S}^l, C^l, \mathbb{P}^l, \mathcal{S}^l, \mathcal{H}^l \rangle$ of SE the $\mathcal{S}^l$ and $\mathcal{H}^l$ are satisfied by σ. We can see that an execution E defines message flow, and thus the sequence of actions performed by every Partner.

Distributed orchestration problem statement. Given a problem input as described above is there an execution $E = \langle SE, \sigma \rangle$ of length $l \leq m$ such that at the end the sequence of actions of the Client is empty, i.e. the last configuration of SE is $\langle \mathbb{S}^l, \langle 0, \emptyset \rangle, \mathbb{P}^l, \mathcal{S}^l, \mathcal{H}^l \rangle$?

3.3   Solving the Distributed Orchestration Problem

We reduce the distributed orchestration problem to the satisfiability of a deducibility constraint system under the non-disclosure of sensitive data condition and then discuss a decision procedure under the hypothesis of the bounded number of interactions.

Since one can build finitely many different symbolic executions for a fixed problem input, we can guess a symbolic execution with its final configuration $\langle \mathbb{S}^l, C^l, \mathbb{P}^l, \mathcal{S}^l, \mathcal{H}^l \rangle$ where the Client has no more actions to perform (i.e. $C^l = \langle 0, \emptyset \rangle$). Then, building the desired execution is equivalent to finding such a ground substitution σ that satisfies both $\mathcal{S}^l$ and $\mathcal{H}^l$.

We refer to [3] for the technique for solving constraint systems within the Dolev-Yao deduction system. Under non-restrictive assumption that in the problem input there exists at least one atomic value which is not sensitive to any of partners, and the assumptions stated in § 3.2 hold, we can easily adapt the mentioned technique in such way that the following theorem holds:

Theorem 1. *Satisfiability of deducibility constraint system within the Dolev-Yao deduction system under non-disclosure condition is in NP.*

And thus,

Corollary 1. *The problem of distributed orchestration is decidable and in NP.*

Note also that having a desired execution $E = \langle SE, \sigma \rangle$, and thus a sequence of actions performed by the Partners as well as their initial knowledges, we can extract a *prudent implementation* of the Partners as services (see details in [15]).

4   Implementation

We report only an implementation for the standard (non-distributed) orchestration introduced in Section 2. As mentioned above, being a special case of the distributed orchestration, the standard orchestration can be handled using

a simpler constraint solving procedure since in that case one has only to handle
well-formed constraints. To this end we use CL-AtSe tool [28]. We are not aware
of tools that can be reused to implement the distributed orchestration.

4.1   Input and Output Language

The available services, the Client and the resulting Mediator are described in
ASLan language [1], a formal language for specifying trust and security properties of services, their associated policies, and their composition into service
architectures. A service's behavior in ASLan is defined as a set of transitions,
its initial state and possibly a finite set of Horn clauses typically used to define an authorization logic; and messages to be exchanged (with applied security
policies) as first order terms.

For example, a TimeStamper service can be represented as the following transition:

```
step step_0(TS,Dummy_Time,Dummy_M,Time,M):=
  state_timestamper(TS,1,Dummy_Time,Dummy_M).
  iknows(M)
  =[exists Time]=>
  state_timestamper(TS,1,Time,M).
  iknows(pair(M, pair(Time, crypt(inv(kts), pair(apply(md5,
     M), Time)))))
```

where `state_timestamper` represents a *state* of `TimeStamper` service. The message exchange is modeled by `iknows` *facts*. The transition means that if the
`TimeStamper` being in state `state_timestamper(TS,1,Dummy_Time,Dummy_M)` receives
message M, he will generate a new Time value (`=[exists Time]=>`), pass to state
`state_timestamper(TS,1,Time,M)` and reply with message `pair(M, pair(Time,
crypt(inv(kts), pair(apply(md5, M), Time))))`. In other words, this service re-
ceives a message, stores it (encoded in his state) and reply with a time stamp of
the received message. Note that ASLan supports functional symbols equivalent
to ones from Table 1.

The global state of the transition system is given by a set of facts that are true.
A transition can fire, if it has an instance (where all the variables are replaced
with ground terms) such that all the facts of its left-hand side (LHS) are true.
As a result, the facts of the LHS are removed from the current state and the
facts of the RHS are added. The only exception is the `iknows` facts which are
considered as persistent.

Since we are looking for an orchestration, all the messages emitted by the
services or the Client or received by them should come to/from the Mediator.
Thus, every `iknows` fact (as it models the communication) once produced by
the transition comes to the knowledge of the Mediator. And vice versa, `iknows`
facts that are consumed by the services or the Client should be produced by the
Mediator.

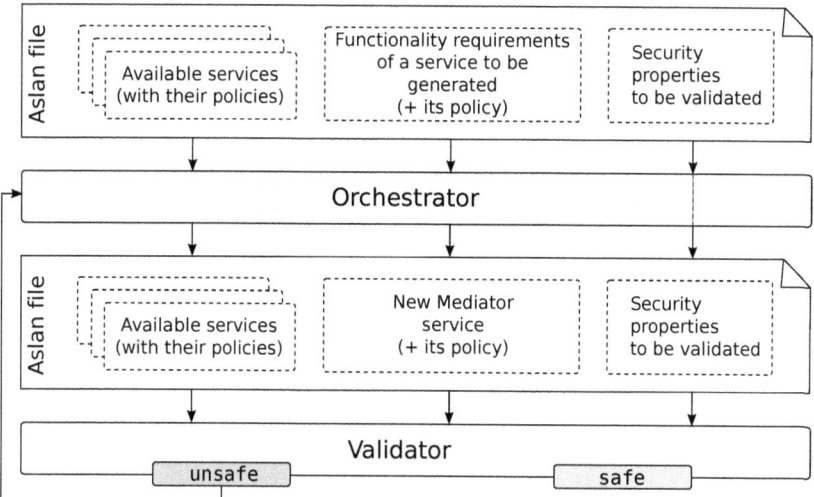

Fig. 6. The AVANTSSAR Validation platform

4.2   AVANTSSAR Platform

The Orchestrator is part of the AVANTSSAR Platform [1], an automated tool-set for validating trust and security aspects of service-oriented architectures (see Fig. 6). The overall objective of the platform is to generate from an orchestration problem a solution that meets some given security requirements (e.g., secrecy, authentication).

The AVANTSSAR platform also offers the possibility to check whether an orchestrated service (e.g. generated by the Orchestrator tool) is vulnerable to an active Dolev-Yao intruder. For that the modeler inputs some security properties, e.g. some message confidentiality requirement, before starting the orchestration generation. Though the Orchestrator does not take them into account while building an orchestration, it transfers them correctly into the generated output.

Some automatic validation tools (like [28] and others, see [1]) will check whether the property specified by the user is satisfied by the generated orchestration. The Orchestrator solves the orchestration problem, and then the solution (with the properties to be validated which are kept unchanged by the Orchestrator) are transferred to the AVANTSSAR Validator.

If the specification meets the validation goals then the orchestration solution is considered as safe *w.r.t.* the user's requirements, otherwise a verification report including the violation proof is returned. In the latter case the Orchestrator is able to backtrack and try an alternative solution. This is illustrated in Fig. 6 by the returning-arrow from the Validator to the Orchestrator.

To summarize the platform performs as follows: (*i*) it generates an orchestration (a Mediator); (*ii*) it verifies security properties on it; (*iii*) if the orchestration is vulnerable, it generates a new Mediator and jumps to (*ii*).

Table 3. AVANTSSAR Orchestrator benchmark

Input problem				Mediator generation	
Case study	Number of available services	Number of transitions	Number of Horn Clauses	Number of generated transitions	Running time
CRP	4	25	17	17	4.1 sec.
DCS	3	18	0	22	4.6 sec.
PB	2	20	2	4	1.7 sec.

Note that in general the presented tool-chain does not guarantee to return a safe orchestration (even if there exists one), since the Orchestrator is not able to produce all possible orchestrations, but only guarantees to produce one if it exists.

5   Conclusion

The automatic composition of Web services is a challenging task on the understanding that all the aspects of Web services have to be taken into account. We presented a novel approach for automatic distributed orchestration of Web services under security constraints generalizing the non-distributed case as well as tackling the Web services choreography.

Whereas there are a lot of theoretical works on the automatic composition of Web services, only a few are ended with the implementation. We described a tool that allows one to automatically orchestrate Web services taking into account in the same time their workflow, messaging and security.

We have successfully tested the tool on several industrial case studies (see Table 3), like *Digital Contract Signing* (DCS) and *Public Bidding* (PB) which are originated from commercial products of the OpenTrust company and *Car Registration Process* (CRP), a case study proposed by Siemens AG.

The Orchestrator is deployed and available at `http://avantssar.loria.fr/OrchestratorWI/`. It was implemented in OCaml and Java and its source contains of more than 20'000 lines of code.

References

1. Automated Validation of Trust and Security of Service-Oriented Architectures, AVANTSSAR project, `http://www.avantssar.eu`
2. Network of Excellence on Engineering Secure Future Internet Software Services and Systems, NESSoS project, `http://www.nessos-project.eu`
3. Avanesov, T., Chevalier, Y., Rusinowitch, M., Turuani, M.: Satisfiability of General Intruder Constraints with and without a Set Constructor. Research Report RR-7276, INRIA (May 2010), `http://hal.inria.fr/inria-00480632/en/`
4. Baresi, L., Maurino, A., Modafferi, S.: Towards distributed bpel orchestrations. ECEASST 3 (2006)

5. Berardi, D., Calvanese, D., De Giacomo, G., Hull, R., Mecella, M.: Automatic Composition of Transition-based semantic Web Services with Messaging. In: Proc. 31st Int. Conf. Very Large Data Bases, VLDB 2005, pp. 613–624 (2005)
6. Berardi, D., Calvanese, D., De Giacomo, G., Lenzerini, M., Mecella, M.: Automatic Composition of E-services That Export Their Behavior. In: Orlowska, M.E., Weerawarana, S., Papazoglou, M.P., Yang, J. (eds.) ICSOC 2003. LNCS, vol. 2910, pp. 43–58. Springer, Heidelberg (2003)
7. Bhargavan, K., Corin, R., Deniélou, P.M., Fournet, C., Leifer, J.J.: Cryptographic protocol synthesis and verification for multiparty sessions. In: 2009 22nd IEEE Computer Security Foundations Symposium, pp. 124–140. IEEE (2009)
8. Bucchiarone, A., Gnesi, S.: A survey on services composition languages and models. In: Proceedings of International Workshop on Web Services Modeling and Testing (WS-MaTe 2006), pp. 51–63 (2006)
9. Bultan, T., Fu, X., Hull, R., Su, J.: Conversation specification: a new approach to design and analysis of e-service composition. In: WWW, pp. 403–410 (2003)
10. Bursuc, S., Comon-Lundh, H., Delaune, S.: Deducibility Constraints. In: Datta, A. (ed.) ASIAN 2009. LNCS, vol. 5913, pp. 24–38. Springer, Heidelberg (2009)
11. Calvanese, D., De Giacomo, G., Lenzerini, M., Mecella, M., Patrizi, F.: Automatic service composition and synthesis: the roman model. IEEE Data Eng. Bull. 31(3), 18–22 (2008)
12. Camara, J., Martin, J.A., Salaun, G., Cubo, J., Ouederni, M., Canal, C., Pimentel, E.: Itaca: An integrated toolbox for the automatic composition and adaptation of web services. In: ICSE 2009, pp. 627–630 (2009)
13. Chevalier, Y., Küsters, R., Rusinowitch, M., Turuani, M.: An np decision procedure for protocol insecurity with xor. Theo. Comp. Sci. 338(1-3), 247–274 (2005)
14. Chevalier, Y., Mekki, M.A., Rusinowitch, M.: Automatic composition of services with security policies. In: Proceedings of the 2008 IEEE Congress on Services - Part I, SERVICES 2008, pp. 529–537. IEEE, Washington, DC (2008)
15. Chevalier, Y., Rusinowitch, M.: Compiling and securing cryptographic protocols. Inf. Process. Lett. 110(3), 116–122 (2010)
16. Dolev, D., Yao, A.: On the Security of Public-Key Protocols. IEEE Transactions on Information Theory 2(29) (1983)
17. Fabrega, F.J.T., Herzog, J.C., Guttman, J.D.: Strand spaces: why is a security protocol correct? In: Proceedings of the 1998 IEEE Symposium on Security and Privacy, pp. 160–171 (May 1998)
18. Martìn, J.A., Martinelli, F., Pimentel, E.: Synthesis of secure adaptors. Journal of Logic and Algebraic Programming 81(2), 99–126 (2012), doi:10.1016/j.jlap.2011.08.001
19. Mazaré, L.: Computational Soundness of Symbolic Models for Cryptographic Protocols. PhD thesis, Institut National Polytechnique de Grenoble (October 2006)
20. Patrizi, F.: An introduction to simulation-based techniques for automated service composition. In: YR-SOC 2009, Pisa, Italy. EPTCS, vol. 2, pp. 37–49 (June 2009)
21. Pedraza, G., Estublier, J.: Distributed Orchestration Versus Choreography: The FOCAS Approach. In: Wang, Q., Garousi, V., Madachy, R., Pfahl, D. (eds.) ICSP 2009. LNCS, vol. 5543, pp. 75–86. Springer, Heidelberg (2009)
22. Peltz, C.: Web Services Orchestration, HP white paper (2003)
23. Peltz, C.: Web services orchestration and choreography. Computer 36, 46–52 (2003)
24. Quinton, S., Ben-Hafaiedh, I., Graf, S.: From orchestration to choreography: Memoryless and distributed orchestrators. In: Proc. of FLACOS 2009 (2009)

25. ter Beek, M., Bucchiarone, A., Gnesi, S.: Web service composition approaches: From industrial standards to formal methods. In: Second International Conference on Internet and Web Applications and Services, ICIW 2007, page 15 (2007)
26. The AVISPA Project, http://www.avispa-project.org/
27. Trainotti, M., Pistore, M., Calabrese, G., Zacco, G., Lucchese, G., Barbon, F., Bertoli, P.G., Traverso, P.: ASTRO: Supporting Composition and Execution of Web Services. In: Benatallah, B., Casati, F., Traverso, P. (eds.) ICSOC 2005. LNCS, vol. 3826, pp. 495–501. Springer, Heidelberg (2005),
    http://sra.itc.it/projects/astro/
28. Turuani, M.: The CL-Atse Protocol Analyser. In: Pfenning, F. (ed.) RTA 2006. LNCS, vol. 4098, pp. 277–286. Springer, Heidelberg (2006)

On the Key Schedule Strength of PRESENT

Julio Cesar Hernandez-Castro[1], Pedro Peris-Lopez[2],
and Jean-Philippe Aumasson[3]

[1] School of Computing, Portsmouth University, UK
[2] Information Security & Privacy Lab, TU-Delft, The Netherlands
[3] NagravisionSA, Cheseaux, Switzerland

Abstract. We present here the results of a playful research on how to measure the strength of a key schedule algorithm, with applications to PRESENT, including its two variants with 80 and 128 bit keys. We do not claim to have discovered any devastating weakness, but believe that some of the results presented, albeit controversial, could be of interest for other researchers investigating this cipher, notably for those working in impossible differentials and related key or slide attacks. Furthermore, in the case of PRESENT, key schedule features shown here may be exploited to attack some of the PRESENT-based hash functions. We carried out a probabilistic metaheuristic search for semi-equivalent keys, annihilators and entropy minima, and proposed a simple way of combining these results into a single value with a straightforward mathematical expression that could help in abstracting resistance to the set of presented analysis. Surprisingly, PRESENT-128 seems weaker than PRESENT-80 in the light of this new measure.

Keywords: Key Schedule, Semi-Equivalent Keys, Annihilators, Entropy Minimization, Simulated Annealing, PRESENT.

1 Introduction

The PRESENT block cipher [7] is an ultra-lightweight substitution-permutation network aimed at extremely constrained environments such as RFID tags and sensor networks. Hardware efficiency was one of its most important design goals, and at 1570 GE it really is one of the very few realistic options in such constrained environments for providing an adequate security level. PRESENT works with two key lengths, 80 and 128 bits, and operates over 64-bit blocks with a very simple round scheme which is iterated 31 times. Each round is the composition of three operations: **addRoundKey**, **sboxLayer** and **pLayer**. The **addRoundKey** operation is simply an XOR between the 64-bit roundkey and the State; **sboxLayer** is a 64-bit nonlinear transformation which uses 16 parallel instances of a 4-to-4-bit S-box; **pLayer** is a bitwise permutation of the 64-bit internal state.

Previous works. Due to its very good performance and neat design, partly inspired by SERPENT [8], PRESENT has attracted a lot of attention from

J. Garcia-Alfaro et al. (Eds.): DPM 2011 and SETOP 2011, LNCS 7122, pp. 253–263, 2012.

cryptanalysts: Wang presented a disputed [5] differential attack [9] against a reduced 16-round variant which requires 2^{64} texts and 2^{65} memory, Albrecht and Cid [11] presented another differential attack using algebraic techniques, with a very similar complexity against 16-rounds of the 80-bit variant, and 2^{113} operations against the 128-bit version with 19 rounds. A saturation attack was presented by Collard and Standaert [12], that is able to recover the key of a 24 round variant with 2^{57} texts and 2^{57} time. Another relevant attack was proposed by Ohkuma [13], where linear approximations and a class of weak keys were used against a 24-round variant requiring $2^{63.5}$ known texts.

Contribution. The contribution of this paper is twofold: we present a number of new results on the key schedule of PRESENT, and then combine these into a single value that abstracts to some point key schedule strength and aims to be useful for other block ciphers, and specifically for comparing between them. As a side result, we conclude that PRESENT-80 seems to have a stronger key schedule than PRESENT-128.

Organization. This paper is organized as follows. In Section 2, the key schedule of PRESENT is briefly introduced. The methodology and parameters used in our experimentation are explained in Section 3. In Section 4, we describe our results regarding semi-equivalent keys, annihilators and entropy minima. Later, we propose in Section 5 a measure to evaluate the strength of a given key schedule algorithm, and provide the corresponding values for PRESENT-80 and PRESENT-128. In Section 6, we extract some conclusions and describe what we consider will be interesting future research lines.

2   The Key Schedule of PRESENT

We focus in the following on the PRESENT key schedule, first on that of its 80-bit variant, later on that of PRESENT-128.

PRESENT-80. The key is stored in a register K and represented as $k_{79}k_{78}$ $\ldots k_0$. At round i the 64-bit round key $K_i = k_{63}\, k_{62}\, \ldots\, k_0$ consists of the 64 leftmost bits of the current contents of register K:

$$K_i = k_{63}k_{62}\ldots k_0 = k_{79}k_{78}\ldots k_{16}$$

After extracting K_i, the key register $K = k_{79}k_{78}\,\ldots\,k_0$ is updated as described below:

Step 1. $[k_{79}k_{78}\ldots k_1 k_0] = [k_{18}k_{17}\ldots k_{20}k_{19}]$
Step 2. $[k_{79}k_{78}k_{77}k_{76}] = \mathrm{S}[k_{79}k_{78}k_{77}k_{76}]$
Step 3. $[k_{19}k_{18}k_{17}k_{16}k_{15}] = [k_{19}k_{18}k_{17}k_{16}k_{15}] \oplus round\_counter$

PRESENT-128 The key is stored in a register K and represented as $k_{127}k_{126}$ $\ldots k_0$. At round i the 64-bit round key $K_i = k_{63}\ k_{62}\ \ldots\ k_0$ consists of the 64 leftmost bits of the current contents of register K:

$$K_i = k_{63}k_{62}\ldots k_0 = k_{127}k_{126}\ldots k_{64}$$

After extracting K_i, the key register $K = k_{127}k_{126}\ \ldots\ k_0$ is updated (we have **two** calls to **S** in this case) as described below:

Step 1. $[k_{127}k_{126}\ldots k_1 k_0] = [k_{66}k_{65}\ldots k_{68}k_{67}]$
Step 2. $[k_{127}k_{126}k_{125}k_{124}] = S[k_{127}k_{126}k_{125}k_{124}]$
Step 3. $[k_{123}k_{122}k_{121}k_{120}] = S[k_{123}k_{122}k_{121}k_{120}]$
Step 4. $[k_{66}k_{65}k_{64}k_{63}k_{62}] = [k_{66}k_{65}k_{64}k_{63}k_{62}] \oplus round\_counter$.

3 Methodology

We have used Simulated Annealing in our search for keys with useful properties, after having a limited success in getting similarly powerful results by analytical means. For example, we found that in the case of PRESENT-80, key bits k_{76}, k_{77}, k_{78} do not enter the key schedule Sbox until round 20, and during the 20 first rounds they only appear in 15 of the round keys. Thus the Hamming weight of the differences between round keys is 15 during the first 20 rounds. However, the results we got using Simulated Annealing were way more relevant.

The main advantage of Simulated Annealing is that it allows for a black-box look-up that performs generally much better than a random search, while having very little added computational costs. In every case, we proposed fitness functions that abstracted what kind of property we were looking for, and tune parameters for trying to get the best possible results.

We used our own implementation of a Simulated Annealing algorithm in Python, and followed a bisection method to tune parameters. We ran multiple experiments, each of them taking approximately three hours in our baseline computer. The best keys found were then double tested by a different member of our team, over a different PRESENT implementation.

3.1 Simulated Annealing

Simulated Annealing [1] is a combinatorial optimization technique based on the physical annealing of molten metals. It has been quite successfully used in different cryptanalytic attacks, such as those against the Permuted Perceptron Problem (PPP) [4,3], or, more recently, Trivium [2].

We briefly describe the technique, closely following the presentation at [4] in the following:

A General Simulated Annealing Algorithm

INPUT: A temperature T, a cooling rate $\alpha \in (0,1)$, N the number of moves at each temperature, $MaxFailedCycles$ the number of consecutive unsuccessful cycles before aborting, and IC_{Max} the maximum number of temperature cycles before aborting.

ALGORITHM

Step 1.: Let T_0 be the initial temperature. Increase it until the percentage of moves accepted within an inner loop of N trials exceeds some threshold.

Step 2.: Set the iteration count IC to zero, $finished = 0$, $ILaccepted = 0$ (inner loops since last accepted move), and randomly generate a current solution V_{curr}.

Step 3.: While not($finished$) do

  Step 3.1.: Inner Loop: repeat N times

    Step 3.1.1.: V_{new}=generateMoveFrom(V_{curr})

    Step 3.1.2.: Compute cost change $\Delta_{cost} = cost(V_{new}) - cost(V_{curr})$.

    Step 3.1.3.: If $\Delta_{cost} < 0$ accept the move, so $V_{curr} = V_{new}$.

    Step 3.1.4.: Otherwise, generate a random uniform value in $(0,1) \rightarrow u$. If $e^{-\Delta_{cost}/T} > u$ accept the move, otherwise, reject it.

  Step 3.2.: If no move has been accepted after 3.1, then $ILaccepted = ILaccepted + 1$, else $ILaccepted = 0$.

  Step 3.3.: $T = \alpha * T$, $IC = IC + 1$.

  Step 3.4.: $finished = (ILaccepted > MaxFailedCycles)$ or $(IC > IC_{max})$

OUTPUT: The state V_{best} with the lowest cost obtained in the search.

We can informally say that Simulated Annealing is a type of Hill Climbing [2], that generally outperforms and has very little added cost over a random search, specially when compared with other much heavier heuristics such as Genetic Algorithms, Particle Swarm Optimization, etc. We have obtained the results presented in next Section with a standard Simulated Annealing algorithm, generally using an initial temperature of or close to $T_0 = 50$, a cooling rate $\alpha = 0.9999$, and a maximum iteration $IC_{max} = 200$.

4   Results

In this section, the strength of the PRESENT key schedule is examined in a combined search for semi-equivalent keys, annihilators, and entropy minimization.

Table 1. Semi-equivalent keys for PRESENT-80

K_1	K_2	KeySchedule Distance
0x8ba018d26545f5d34dd1	0x8ba018d26545f5d32dd1	35
0x60cf1262a6af**5d**01a7fb	0x60cf1262a6af**45**01a7fb	35
0x**83**b4d3e2f49cbd4d5e2e	0x**a3**b4d3e2f49cbd4d5e2e	35
0x8ee**b**6a18106618d098da	0x8ee**26**a18106618d098da	35
0xd0ce94581e6eda685d77	0xd0c**7**94581e6eda685d77	35
0x9f2**d**24499c081289fe11	0x9f2**8**24499c081289fe11	35
0x87668990280c70b**56**574	0x87668990280c70b**4e**574	34
0xf718fc4e**7**8a82353328a	0xf718fc4f**58**a82353328a	34
0x6c96cfd0**1**ad1a5ca7900	0x6c96cfd0**7**ad1a5ca7900	34
0xaaf6b7f4d95**26**5eb3188	0xaaf6b7f4d95**02**5eb3188	**32**
0x5a46487f**2**82a052f1b0f	0x5a46487f**8**82a052f1b0f	**32**

4.1 The Search for Semi-equivalent Keys

There are not equivalent keys for PRESENT-80 or PRESENT-128, because in both cases the PRESENT Key Schedule is an invertible mapping involving all input bits. So we started considering the search for semi-equivalent keys, that is, different keys that produce a very similar (w.r.t. the Hamming weight metric) key expansion.

The existence of semi-equivalent keys could potentially have more grievous consequences if, as it is the case of PRESENT [6], the block cipher is to be used as a hash function, because this could make finding collisions much easier.

The gap between the best pair of semi-equivalent keys we found, and the optimum value of zero (corresponding to a pair of equivalent keys) was uncomfortably close. In particular, we found key pairs (k_1, k_2) with a Hamming distance of 2 that produced very similar key expansions where all 32 round keys were at a Hamming distance of 2 bits or less, including 17 cases of distance 1 and 6 of distance zero. The total accumulated round key distance after 32 rounds of these two keys (shown in Table 1) was only 35.

We were able to obtain a lot more key pairs with these or even better characteristics, including multiple values of 34. The closest we got to a pair of equivalent keys was with key pairs

$$(0xaaf6b7f4d95265eb3188, 0xaaf6b7f4d95025eb3188)$$

and

$$(0x5a46487f282a052f1b0f, 0x5a46487f882a052f1b0f)$$

that produced very close round keys that differ only in 32 bits, that is, an average difference of a single bit for every round key.

Is this a statistically significant result? Yes, if we randomly flip one bit in the user key, this generates on average (statistics computed over 10, 000 random keys with random flips) 54.995 bits of accumulated changes in their corresponding round keys. This is relatively poor value, as in the case of a perfectly designed key expansion algorithm (i.e. a good hash function) the value should be on overage around $32 \cdot 32 = 1024$ bits. That result clearly shows that the PRESENT key schedule does not present a good degree of diffusion, and is far from having the avalanche effect.

We have found and shown in Table 1 even better results, with distances of 32, 34 and 35. The significance of our results is even clearer if we study the effect of flipping two random bits on a random key, which on average produces (statistics computed again over $10,000$ random keys with random flips but without repetition) 107.4244 bit changes. For three bit differences in the key, the average change in the sub-round keys is 157.2943, for four 204.744 bits, and 249.8925 for five bits. Values so small as 32, 34 and 35 should be considered insufficient for many applications, and too close to the optimum value of zero.

The results herein presented could be useful for other researchers of PRESENT-80 and, although by themselves do not constitute a major weakness, leave a discomforting low gap between our best findings and the global minimum that would lead to a pair of equivalent keys. Even if these pairs do not exist, our findings might easily lead to pseudo-collisions in one of the PRESENT-based hash functions. Furthermore, sparse differences in the key schedule have been successfully used before to cancel differences in the internal state [10].

Even worse results can be found for PRESENT-128, when for example the two keys

$$0x2a1145cfce0db6e38eaff175d39c90dc$$

and

$$0x2a1145cfcf0db6e38eaff175d39c90dc$$

with a difference of $0x10000000000000000000000$, generate round keys that only differ, as a whole, in 16 bits over 32 rounds. There are many other pairs with similar properties. The averages also reveal similar undesirable properties, with a random flip in a user key averaging only around 40.02 bit changes in the round keys, in contrast with the almost 55 bits modified by PRESENT-80. Worse results are also achieved by two random bit flips to PRESENT-128, with average values of 78.43 bits on the round keys, which is poor compared with the 107.42 of PRESENT-80. These results show that the 80-bit version has a stronger key schedule than the 128 bit variant – at least from the point of view of its diffusion characteristics.

4.2   Global Annihilators

We looked for keys that produced a set of round keys with a very low hamming weight. Such keys may be useful for impossible differential attacks, or for reducing the overall security of the cipher, because of course the key addition phase is way less strong under those low-hamming keys. The most interesting key we found in this regard is $0x862010e680100a028a10$, that generated an extremely low hamming weight of only 401 (for an average, for a random key, of around $32 \cdot 32 = 1024$ bits). In Table 2.A we show the round keys corresponding to this annihilator key.

Similarly, for PRESENT-128 we can obtain a value of 433.0 with key 0x484a0 4d32c22f3ae28200190103481f3 (See Table 2.B).

Table 2. Global Annihilators - PRESENT-80 (2.A) & PRESENT-128 (2.B)

Table 2.A   Table 2.B

Round	RoundKey	Hamming weight	Round	RoundKey	Hamming weight
0	0x862010e680100a02	15	0	0x484a04d32c22f3ae	27
1	0x14210c4021cd002	15	1	0x400400320206903e	15
2	0x28002842188042	11	2	0x402128134cb08bce	23
3	0x340000500050842	10	3	0x40001000c8081a40	10
4	0x20100680000a002	8	4	0xc00084a04d32c22e	20
5	0x4210040200d0002	9	5	0x4000004003202068	9
6	0x280008420080402	8	6	0xc80002128134cb09	18
7	0x400005000108402	7	7	0x60000001000c8080	7
8	0x100080000a0006	6	8	0xc22000084a04d32e	18
9	0x4210000200100005	7	9	0x4080000004003200	6
10	0x8800084200004007	9	10	0xc80880002128134e	16
11	0x1000110001084005	8	11	0x40020000001000ca	7
12	0x8100020002200027	9	12	0x82022000084a04e	12
13	0x1100102000400042	7	13	0x4000080000004000	3
14	0x82200204000f	9	14	0xc420808800021282	12
15	0x1001000010440047	9	15	0x2000000103	4
16	0x1000220020000200	5	16	0xd81082022000084e	14
17	0x5001020004400408	8	17	0x4c00000080000000	4
18	0x50080a0020400081	9	18	0xc860420808800025	13
19	0x60102a0101400401	11	19	0x8030000002000004	5
20	0xb0020c0205402022	13	20	0xe821810820220005	14
21	0x90101600418040a2	13	21	0x8600c00000080005	8
22	0x80920202c0083b	14	22	0xf8a0860420808805	17
23	0xa102801012404053	14	23	0x8618030000002005	10
24	0xd020f42050020244	16	24	0x88e2821810820226	17
25	0x31015a041e840a0c	19	25	0x4618600c00000086	12
26	0xe80906202b4083dd	23	26	0x4f238a086042080e	20
27	0x80283d0120c40565	19	27	0x4518618030000004	12
28	0x820f700507a02416	21	28	0xee3c8e2821810827	25
29	0x70159041ee00a0fa	24	29	0x1014618600c00007	14
30	0x904e02b2083dcfL	23	30	0x18b8f238a0860427	24
31	0x1283e01209c0564e	22	31	0x1c40518618030007	17

4.3 Output Entropy Minimization

When minimizing the output entropy of the key schedule, we obtained the following interesting results for PRESENT−80 (see Table 3.A), which produced an entropy of 4.006811 bits per byte for key $0x62e00e7e01030028e80$. As shown in Table 3.B, the best result we found for PRESENT−128 had a much lower entropy of 3.744336 bits per byte, for key $0x55048c3882841800b8a669e49628e086$.

It is curious that all of the experiments ran with PRESENT−80 did point towards essentially the same key, with a very high correlation between the obtained optima, but this was clearly not the case for PRESENT−128. This may have different explanations, but the simplest one is that we are much closer to the global optima in the case of PRESENT−80 than in the case of PRESENT−128, or/and that there exists a reduced number of global optima for the 80-bit version and multiple ones for the 128-bit version. In any case, all scenarios clearly favor the design of the smaller version in terms of security, at least from this test point of view. The fact that the lowest output entropy found for the key schedule of the 128-bit variant is significantly smaller than the one found for the 80-bit version, after exactly the same computational effort in the search, further strengthens this point.

Table 3. Entropy minimization - PRESENT-80 (A) & PRESENT-128 (B)

Table 3.A   Table 3.B

Round	RoundKeys		Round	RoundKeys
0	0x62e00e7e0103002		0	0x55048c3882841800
1	0x1d000c5c01cfc02		1	0x5d14cd3c92c51c10
2	0xc0003a0018b802		2	0x55541230e20a1060
3	0x3f0001800074002		3	0x55745334f24b1470
4	0x2e0007e00030002		4	0x55555048c3882840
5	0xd00005c000fc002		5	0x5555d14cd3c92c50
6	0xc0001a0000b8002		6	0x55555541230e20a0
7	0xf00018000340002		7	0x55555745334f24b0
8	0xe0001e000300002		8	0x55555555048c3880
9	0x1c0003c0002		9	0x5555555d14cd3c90
10	0x380002		10	0x55555555541230e0
11	0x2		11	0x55555555745334f0
12	0x6		12	0x55555555555048c0
13	0x4000000000000006		13	0x5555555555d14cd0
14	0x7000080000000007		14	0x5555555555554120
15	0x10000e0001000007		15	0x5555555555574530
16	0x2000020001c00028		16	0x5555555555555500
17	0xc000040000400030		17	0x5555555555555d10
18	0x5000b80000800001		18	0x5555555555555550
19	0x6000ca0017000019		19	0x5555555555555570
20	0xb0000c00194002ea		20	0x5555555555555550
21	0x9000760001800322		21	0xce55555555555550
22	0xbb2000ec0003b		22	0x5555555555555550
23	0xa00c8001764001d3		23	0x5839555555555550
24	0xd000f40190002ec4		24	0x5555555555555553
25	0x30075a001e80320c		25	0xae60e55555555553
26	0xe0bb0600eb4003dd		26	0xa555555555555553
27	0xf0c83c1760c01d65		27	0xdfb9839555555553
28	0x800f7e190782ec16		28	0xd69555555555552
29	0x40759001ecf320fe		29	0x987ee60e55555552
30	0x7bb0480eb2003df7		30	0x9b5a555555555552
31	0x1c83ef760901d64f		31	0xf61fb9839555552

5   Measuring the Strength of a Key Schedule

In the following, we propose to combine the presented results in a single measure that could give a general idea of the strength of a given key schedule algorithm, and ease analysis and comparison between different block cipher proposals. We emphasize here that this measure is completely independent of the structured used in the cipher (e.g. Feistel or SP-network) and only dependent on the key schedule function. Although we acknowledge that security is a quite complex concept that can not be fully abstracted in a single value, we however believe that this abstraction could be useful in a number of testing and designing scenarios.

The simplest and most natural way of combining these results in a single value is simply by multiplying them, like in the following formula:

$$S_{KeySchedule} = \frac{-1}{\ln(S_{Annihilators} \cdot S_{EquivalentKeys} \cdot S_{OutputEntropy})} \quad (1)$$

The above expression particularized with the results obtained over the PRESENT variants, produces the following values:

$$S_{PRESENT_{80}} = \frac{-1}{\ln(\frac{401}{1024} \cdot \frac{32}{1024} \cdot \frac{4.006811}{8})} = 0,19628$$

$$S_{PRESENT_{128}} = \frac{-1}{\ln(\frac{433}{1024} \cdot \frac{16}{1024} \cdot \frac{3.744336}{8})} = 0,17304$$

And we take $S_{KeySchedule} = 0$ if any of the $S_j = 0$.

Although this way of combining different strength results into a single value could be improved, it at least provides a simple, quick and easy way of comparing between different algorithms or variants. This is exactly our case, where contrary to our first thoughts it seems clear that the keyschedule of PRESENT−80 is, at least from the point of view of test S, more secure than that of its cousin PRESENT−128.

The overall result is consistent with the general impression extracted from the different tests, which is that the keyschedule of PRESENT−128 is less robust than that of PRESENT−80 despite the two calls to the S-box done in PRESENT−128. It seems these two lookups are not enough, and more should be allowed to offer a similarly strong key schedule.

6   Conclusions

We present a first attempt to measure the strength of a key schedule algorithm in a single and straightforward fashion, allowing meaningful comparisons between different algorithms and different variants of the same algorithm. This could potentially be useful for designing purposes, when a quick way of comparing different decisions could be handy, and for claiming and testing security properties of new block cipher proposals. Improvements to our proposed measure are possible, and we will work on then in future works, but in its current state we have proved it is good enough to analyze in some depth the key schedules of both PRESENT−80 and PRESENT−128. Our results point out to a quite good overall design that only seems slightly worrisome regarding semi-equivalent keys, specially taking into account the proposal of PRESENT as a basis for various lightweight hash functions.

We also found the slightly surprising and maybe controversial result that, in the light of these tests, the PRESENT−80 key schedule seems to be more robust than that of PRESENT−128. We think that this first attempt to measure cryptographic strength combining the results of multiple heuristic lookups opens an avenue for new kinds of more complex analysis that could help in better understanding some of the recent lightweight cryptographic primitives.

On the other hand, it will be overambitious and highly arguable to claim that this single value can be an undisputed measure of key schedule strength. Firstly, overall strength is quite tricky to define. We only aim here to have contributed a first step in this direction. Furthermore, we also acknowledge that looking at the key schedule algorithm in complete isolation as we do here could, in some cases, make little sense because a weaker key schedule does not always lead to a weaker cipher if this is properly accounted for in the design of the round function.

Apart from investigating possible improvements to the key schedule strength measure just proposed, we plan to compare that of the two key schedule algorithms explored here against that of the AES, and other lightweight algorithms like KATAN and KTANTAN [14]. We will also research for more complex ways of measuring the difficulty of the problems associated with finding keys with security-relevant properties, particularly with measures based in problem landscape complexity as in [2].

References

1. Kirkpatrick, S., Gelatt, C.D., Vecchi, M.P.: Optimization by Simulated Annealing. Science 220(4598), 671–680 (1983)
2. Borghoff, J., Knudsen, L.R., Matusiewicz, K.: Analysis of Trivium by a Simulated Annealing Variant. In: Proceedings of Ecrypt II Workshop on Tools for Cryptanalysis (2010)
3. Knudsen, L.R., Meier, W.: Cryptanalysis of an Identification Scheme Based on the Permuted Perceptron Problem. In: Stern, J. (ed.) EUROCRYPT 1999. LNCS, vol. 1592, pp. 363–374. Springer, Heidelberg (1999)
4. Clark, J.A., Jacob, J.L.: Fault Injection and a Timing Channel on an Analysis Technique. In: Knudsen, L.R. (ed.) EUROCRYPT 2002. LNCS, vol. 2332, pp. 181–196. Springer, Heidelberg (2002)
5. Kuman, M., Yadav, P., Kumari, M.: Flaws in Differential Cryptanalysis of Reduced Round PRESENT, http://eprint.iacr.org/2010/407
6. Bogdanov, A., Leander, G., Paar, C., et al.: Hash Functions and RFID Tags: Mind the Gap, pp. 283–299 (2008)
7. Bogdanov, A.A., Knudsen, L.R., Leander, G., Paar, C., Poschmann, A., Robshaw, M.J.B., Seurin, Y., Vikkelsoe, C.: PRESENT: An Ultra-Lightweight Block Cipher. In: Paillier, P., Verbauwhede, I. (eds.) CHES 2007. LNCS, vol. 4727, pp. 450–466. Springer, Heidelberg (2007),
   http://dx.doi.org/10.1007/978-3-540-74735-2_31
8. Anderson, R., Biham, E., Knudsen, L.: Serpent: A proposal for the Advanced Encryption Standard. In: First Advanced Encryption Standard (AES) Conference (1998)
9. Wang, M.: Differential Cryptanalysis of Reduced-Round PRESENT. In: Vaudenay, S. (ed.) AFRICACRYPT 2008. LNCS, vol. 5023, pp. 40–49. Springer, Heidelberg (2008)
10. Özen, O., Varıcı, K., Tezcan, C., Kocair, Ç.: Lightweight Block Ciphers Revisited: Cryptanalysis of Reduced Round PRESENT and HIGHT. In: Boyd, C., González Nieto, J. (eds.) ACISP 2009. LNCS, vol. 5594, pp. 90–107. Springer, Heidelberg (2009)
11. Albrecht, M., Cid, C.: Algebraic Techniques in Differential Cryptanalysis. In: Dunkelman, O. (ed.) FSE 2009. LNCS, vol. 5665, pp. 193–208. Springer, Heidelberg (2009)
12. Collard, B., Standaert, F.-X.: A Statistical Saturation Attack against the Block Cipher PRESENT. In: Fischlin, M. (ed.) CT-RSA 2009. LNCS, vol. 5473, pp. 195–210. Springer, Heidelberg (2009)

13. Ohkuma, K.: Weak Keys of Reduced-Round PRESENT for Linear Cryptanalysis. In: Jacobson Jr., M.J., Rijmen, V., Safavi-Naini, R. (eds.) SAC 2009. LNCS, vol. 5867, pp. 249–265. Springer, Heidelberg (2009)
14. De Cannière, C., Dunkelman, O., Knežević, M.: KATAN and KTANTAN — A Family of Small and Efficient Hardware-Oriented Block Ciphers. In: Clavier, C., Gaj, K. (eds.) CHES 2009. LNCS, vol. 5747, pp. 272–288. Springer, Heidelberg (2009)

A Traffic Regulation Method Based on MRA Signatures to Reduce Unwanted Traffic from Compromised End-User Machines

Enric Pujol-Gil and Nikolaos Chatzis

Fraunhofer Institute for Open Communication Systems,
Kaiserin-Augusta-Allee 31, 10589 Berlin, Germany

Abstract. Compromised end-user machines are an important source of the unwanted traffic that traverses the Internet. These machines have typically installed in them malicious software that misuses their network resources. Thereby, the packet streams that a compromised machine sends out consists of legitimate and unwanted packets. In this work, we present a traffic regulation method that limits the number of unwanted packets that such machines send to the Internet. The method operates on the time-series representation of a packet stream and it examines the "burstiness" instead of the rate of packets. The method filters out packets from this stream using signatures produced with wavelet-based multi-resolution analysis, along with a similarity measure. We evaluate the proposed method with real traffic traces (i.e., Domain Name System queries from legitimate end-users and e-mail worms) and compare it with a rate limiting method. We show that the method limits the amount of unwanted traffic that a compromised end-user machine sends to the Internet while it has, compared to the rate limiting method, a lower number of legitimate packet drops.

1 Introduction

A large number of Internet-connected end-user machines are misused by online criminals. This is because by misusing them, instead of deploying and using their own infrastructure, online criminals can hide the real origin of malicious activities, make more difficult the work of legal agents and increase with minimal investment the resources that they have at their disposal to carry out malicious activities. This is also related to the large number of active botnets on the Internet. Botnets are networks of compromised end-user machines (bots) that are remotely controlled by a botmaster without the consent of the legitimate end users. Current botnets usually consist of a large number of compromised end-user machines that can be remotely instructed to conduct a wide range of malicious activities. Such activities are, among others, distributing unwanted emails (spam), stealing private information, launching Distributed Denial of Service attacks (DDoS), hosting illegal content and distributing malicious software (malware). Online criminals use various techniques to turn end-user machines

J. Garcia-Alfaro et al. (Eds.): DPM 2011 and SETOP 2011, LNCS 7122, pp. 264–279, 2012.

into bots. For instance, they launch malware that can spread among Internet-connected end-user machines, they set up web sites that can exploit browser vulnerabilities and they distribute malware that can infect end-user machines. An example of malware that is very often used by botmasters to turn Internet-connected end-user machines into bots are email worms [1].

In this work, we focus on the traffic that is generated by end-user machines that are compromised (or infected) by email worms. There are two reasons for this. The first reason is that unwanted traffic is a major nuisance for service providers and end users. The second reason is that email worms continue to be a prominent medium for online criminals to reach end-user machines and remotely install on them various pieces of malware without the consent of the legitimate end users. There exist three approaches for limiting the distribution of malware in general, and email worms in particular, and thereby the unwanted traffic that malware-infected end-user machines send to the Internet. These approaches are: prevention, treatment and containment [2]. All three approaches are reactive in nature in the sense that they are intended to take effect after an infection occurs. In addition, they essentially complement each other because none of them is complete by itself and they address the same problem from different aspects. Specifically, they differ in three important ways. The first of them is the amount of time that passes before they can become operative. The second difference is that prevention and treatment methods are applicable to non-infected and infected end-user machines, respectively; whereas, containment methods operate on the traffic of possibly or actually infected end-user machines. The third difference of these approaches concerns the effect they are supposed to produce.

Specifically, prevention and treatment concentrate on limiting the number of vulnerable end-user machines that known malware can infect or reinfect. To accomplish this, prevention methods secure non-infected end-user machines so that they are protected if, or when, malware attempts to infect them. In practice, prevention is usually understood as updating the databases of signature-based detection systems after an attack signature for an emerging piece of malware has been generated and made publicly available. Treatment methods clean infected end-user machines and, subsequently, secure them against future infections by the same malware. The typical example of treatment involves removing vulnerabilities from infected end-user machines and then updating the attack signature database of the antivirus software that protects them. Instead of concentrating on limiting the number of vulnerable end-user machines that known malware can infect or reinfect, containment methods slow down the network activity of unknown (zero-day) or often even of known malware to give humans the time to adapt and apply prevention and treatment. To achieve this, containment methods prevent possibly or actually infected end-user machines from sending out or restrict the rate at which they send out suspicious traffic. Containment methods have attracted much attention because of their short reaction time and their ability to cope with threats of different nature. This work goes also in this direction and proposes a new containment method that limits the unwanted traffic malware-infected end-user machines send to the Internet.

There exist several containment methods that can effectively filter out a large amount of unwanted traffic [3,4]. Despite their effectiveness, most of these methods perform computationally expensive deep packet inspection (i.e., they operate at the application level) and are designed to be deployed topologically near the potential victims (i.e., the targeted end-user machines). This has two undesired side-effects. First, it results in a constant increase of the unwanted traffic that traverses the Internet because online criminals have to instruct compromised end-user machines to produce more traffic to reach a considerable number of potential victims [5]. Second, these methods cannot affect the communication between compromised end-user machines and online criminals. In addition, in many papers in the literature, the benefits associated with deploying containment methods topologically near the compromised end-user machines that produce unwanted traffic are pointed out (see, for instance, [2,6,7,8]). In this paper we propose a containment method that overcomes these limitations. The proposed method is designed to operate at the flow level and be deployed at common infrastructure components, such as gateway routers and local name servers, which are near compromised end-user machines.

In light of the above, the packet stream that a compromised end-user machine sends to the Internet is the result of two kinds of processes: end user-related (i.e., legitimate) and malware-related (i.e., unwanted). Hence, a packet stream consists of legitimate and unwanted packets. The proposed containment method operates on this packet stream and filters out packets with a high preference to the unwanted ones. To this end, the proposed method constructs a time series representation of packet streams and uses wavelets to analyze the burstiness of these time series. To evaluate the proposed method we conducted experiments with real traffic traces. Specifically, we evaluated the proposed method with packet streams of Domain Name System (DNS) queries. The legitimate packet streams were captured in a university network, and the unwanted packet streams were produced from a set of email worms executables. The experimental results show that the proposed method has the potential to limit the amount of unwanted traffic that compromised end-user machines send to the Internet with a minimal negative impact on the legitimate component of the packet streams.

The rest of this paper is organised as follows. In Section 2, we discuss related work. In Section 3, we explain the principle and operation of our method for limiting the unwanted traffic that compromised end-user machines send to the Internet. In Section 4, we present a set of experimental results produced by evaluating the method with real traffic traces. In Section 5, we state our conclusions and discuss our plans for future work.

2   Related Work

There exist various traffic regulation methods that are intended to operate on infrastructure components in the traffic engineering literature. These methods are usually applied to enforce Quality of Service (QoS) levels and control network congestion. These methods fall into five general categories: scheduling, queuing, dropping, policing and shaping. In this work, we concentrate on traffic regulation methods that filter out a portion of the packets in the packet streams that end-user machines send to the Internet. Such methods belong to the categories of policing and shaping and operate according to the token bucket (TB) model. According to this model, tokens are added into a bucket of limited size at a certain rate. Let B_s denote the size of the bucket, and B_r and B_u be the number of packets and the unit of time that define the rate. If n packets are to be sent in time B_u and at least n tokens exist in the bucket, then n tokens are removed from the bucket and all n packets are immediately sent. By contrast, if $k < n$ tokens are available, only the k out of the n packets are sent out. The remaining $n - k$ packets can be treated in two ways: rejecting packets that excess n or temporarily storing them and send them out in a following B_u, when sufficient tokens had been accumulated in the bucket. The methods that operate according to the first way fall into the category of policing and those that operate according to the second way fall into the category of shaping [9].

Many of the containment methods that are designed to limit the amount of unwanted traffic that traverses the Internet are based on the TB model. These methods are usually referred to as rate-limiting methods. As their name implies, to limit the potential speed at which malware can spread, the modus operandi of these methods involves limiting the rate at which an end-user machine is allowed to send traffic to the Internet. A comprehensive empirical analysis of several of these methods appears in [10]. The authors in [11] propose a method that involves maintaining a list of previously contacted IP addresses that is used to regulate the rate at which end-user machines send packets to not previously contacted IP addresses. Another method that limits the rate at which end-user machines send packets to not previously contacted IP addresses by adding and depleting tokens for each new successful and failed connection, respectively, is discussed in [12]. The method described in [13] considers the number of failed TCP connections to rate limit the outgoing traffic of an end-user machine. The method proposed in [12] controls the number of available tokens based on the number of destination IP address of TCP connection attempts and their corresponding DNS queries. The authors in [14] propose to dynamically quarantine (i.e., drop all packets from) suspiciously behaving end-user machines for a short period of time to limit the impact of quarantining on the legitimate component of the packet streams that end-user machines send to the Internet. Finally, in [15] it is proposed to rate limit packet streams in multiple time resolutions to mitigate a wider range of attacks than one-resolution rate-limiting methods.

The authors in [16] describe rate limiting as a "lenient response technique that is usually deployed when the detection mechanism has many false positives or cannot precisely characterize the attack stream". In connection with this, rate-limiting methods are intended to merely regulate the rate at which end-user machines send packets to the Internet. Thereby, they have no preference in filtering out unwanted packets. Hence, in practice, rate-limiting methods suffer from a high number of false positives (i.e., besides unwanted packets, they also filter out a high number of legitimate packets). Furthermore, they are vulnerable to intentional changes in the unwanted traffic patterns by, for instance, malware that can (be remotely instructed to) modify the rate at which it sends packets to the Internet. This vulnerability can be illustrated by the following two examples. A malware instance can (be remotely instructed to) reduce the rate at which it sends out packets to avoid that its packets are detected and filtered out. By contrast, it can (be remotely instructed to) increase the rate at which it sends out packets to produce a high number of legitimate end-user packet drops, which will force a network operator to increase the maximum allowed rate. To overcome these limitations, we propose in this work a containment method that looks at the burstiness instead of the volume of the packet streams that end-user machines send to the Internet within a given period of time.

3   Proposed Approach

In this section, we propose a traffic regulation method that limits the unwanted traffic that compromised end-user machines send to the Internet. Similar to the existing rate-limiting methods, the proposed method is designed to operate at infrastructure components topologically near compromised end-user machines. Instead of performing computationally expensive deep packet inspection (i.e., operating at the application level), the method constructs time series by counting the number of packets that end-user machines send out within a given period of time, and performs a lightweight analysis on them. Specifically, the method examines the burstiness instead of the rate of packets in a packet stream. The term burstiness refers, informally, to the statistical variability of a traffic process at a given time scale [17].

3.1   Principle

The authors in [18] introduced the wavelet-based multi-resolution analysis (MRA) to describe a signal in different time scales. This analysis is performed by applying a wavelet transform (e.g., the Discrete Wavelet Transform or DWT) to a time series, which is representation in time of the packet streams produced by a traffic process. In more detail, a time series generated by a traffic process $\{X\}$ is a set of data points, each of which represents a value at a certain period of time or time bin. In our context, a time bin $X_{j,k}$ is the number of packets generated by $\{X\}$ in the k'th interval of duration T_j. Depending on the scale of the time series (i.e., the duration of T_j), the same stream of packets can exhibit different properties. The wavelet transform decomposes a time series and produces, for each scale, a set of wavelet and scaling coefficients. In this work, we apply the DWT on the Haar basis. In this basis, the wavelet detail coefficients $W_{j,k}$ can be obtained using the formula: $W_{j,k} = \frac{1}{2}\left(V_{j-1,(2\times k)+1} - V_{j-1,2\times k}\right)$. Similarly, the wavelet scaling coefficients $V_{j,k}$ are obtained using the formula: $V_{j,k} = \frac{1}{2}\left(V_{j-1,(2\times k)+1} + V_{j-1,2\times k}\right)$. For an extensive study on Wavelet analysis we refer the reader to [19].

In [17], the authors propose to use the MRA signature of a process $\{X\}$ to characterize its burstiness. In this work we use the following definition of MRA signature: $P_{sign} = \{\varepsilon_j \mid j \in \mathbb{N}, 1 < j < N\}$, where ε_j is the energy contribution of the scale j. The energy ε_j is obtained by computing the variance of the detail coefficients or it is approximated using the following formula [19]:

$$\varepsilon_j = \frac{1}{N_j} \sum_{k=0}^{N_j} W_{j,k}^2 \tag{1}$$

In this work, we propose to use MRA signatures to filter out packets from packet streams that do not conform a given MRA signature (i.e., we regulate the burstiness of the packet stream that is being sent to the Internet). Specifically, we propose to filter out packets using a similarity measure (e.g., the Euclidean distance), along with MRA signatures. If accepting a packet decreases the similarity between the reference signature and the signature of the packet stream that is being sent out, then the packet is rejected. The main assumption in this work is that the packet streams produced by malware-related processes have different burstiness values than the packet streams that are produced by legitimate end user-related processes.

3.2 Method

As discussed in the previous section, the MRA signature of a traffic process is obtained from the set of variances of the detail coefficients produced by the Discrete Wavelet Transform. This approach is not directly applicable in our context for two reasons. The first reason is that this requires a large number of counters i.e., total number of time bins in the lowest scale. The second reason is that the DWT is applied after all the values for the time bins in the time series have been collected. We overcome these limitations by using an adaptation of the pyramid algorithm described in [20] that works sequentially on packet arrivals. The algorithm differs from the original algorithm in that the wavelet and the scaling coefficients are produced after the first packet in the next following time bin is processed. Thus, this modification makes possible to update the MRA signature of a traffic process almost on run-time (i.e., we update ε_j using Eq. 1 every time a coefficient is produced). In addition, the modified algorithm requires only $2 \times j$ counters, where j is the number of scales.

That said, in this work, we use the transient value $W'_{j,k}$ of a wavelet detail coefficient $W_{j,k}$. This value is updated every time a new packet in a time bin is observed. The reason to use this value is that it is then possible to compute, on packet arrival, the transient value of ε_j and decide immediately after whether the packet has to be filtered out. The formula to compute the transient value of ε_j is shown in Eq. 2.

$$\varepsilon'_j = \frac{1}{N_k} \left(\left(W'_{j,k} \right)^2 + \sum_{i=0}^{N_j} W_{j,i}^2 \right) \tag{2}$$

The method uses the function defined in Eq. 3 to filter out a packet p. Specifically, it uses a distance measure d, along with three MRA signatures. First, it computes the distance between a reference signature S_{ref} and a transient signature $S_{drop(p)}$, which is the MRA signature at the time p is received in the case the packet p would be dropped. Second, it computes the distance between S_{ref} and $S_{accept(p)}$. In this case, the transient signature $S_{accept(p)}$ includes the inter-arrival time of the packet p. Then, the method drops the packet p if the similarity in the first case (i.e., drop the packet) is lower than in the second case (i.e., forward the packet). Hence, the method operates using the MRA signature(s) obtained from the packet stream that is send to the Internet (i.e., it examines the packets at the egress of the infrastructure component).

$$f(p) = \begin{cases} \text{true,} & \text{if } d\left(S_{ref}, S_{drop(p)}\right) < d\left(S_{ref}, S_{accept(p)}\right) \\ \text{false,} & \text{otherwise} \end{cases} \tag{3}$$

In this operational mode the method suffers from several drawbacks. These drawbacks are caused by the functions that are used to produce the wavelet coefficients. We illustrate this problem in the Haar basis. A wavelet detail coefficient in this basis is obtained from the scaling coefficients of non-overlapping pairs of time bins: $W_{j,k} = \frac{1}{2}\left(V_{j-1,(2\times k)+1} - V_{j-1,2\times k}\right)$. Initially, when the first packets are observed during first time bin, the absolute value of the wavelet detail coefficient increases until $W_{j,k} = -\frac{1}{2}\left(V_{j-1,2\times k}\right)$. Then, if there exist further packets and these are observed during the second time bin, the absolute value of the coefficient decreases until (eventually) $W_{j,k} = 0$. In the case there are more packets, these will be observed again during the second bin. Thus, $V_{j-1,(2\times k)+1} > V_{j-1,2\times k}$ and thereby, from this point on, the absolute value of $W_{j,k}$ increases with new observations. As a consequence, the method might filter out packets prematurely if during the initial phase the value of the transient coefficient is too high. This effect can be reduced using buffers and delaying packets until the end of the time bin. However, this would introduce delays in the network and consume the valuable resources. Instead, we opt to apply the method to low scales, where this undesired effect is reduced.

In Figure 1, we show an application example for the proposed method. Assume that we deploy the proposed method at an infrastructure component like a gateway router, and that there exists a compromised end-user machine in the same network. Then, the packet stream that is sent out to the Internet is the result of two kind of processes: end user-related (i.e., legitimate) and malware-related (i.e., unwanted). In our example, both processes generate packets with the same average packet inter-arrival time (20ms). The legitimate process is a Poisson process (i.e., exponential inter-arrival times). The inter-arrival times for the packets produced by the unwanted process follow a Gamma distribution with the same rate and shape $c = 1/4$. As discussed in [17], the second process is burstier than the Poisson process.

We plot the MRA signatures for these processes in Figure 1(a). Both processes are stationary and the MRA signature of the legitimate process is known from previous observations. When the unwanted process begins its activity, the MRA signature obtained from the packet stream is modified as it is shown in Figure 1(a). In Figure 1(b) we show the effect of the method with three curves. These curves are the percentage of legitimate packet drops (false positives), the percentage of unwanted packet drops (true positives) and the expected value of the percentage of legitimate packet drops in the packet stream. This last value is obtained from the hyper-geometrical distribution that models the amount of false positives after sampling (in our case dropping) n packets from the packet stream if the sizes of both populations are known. For each scale i, we apply the method using a signature that consists of the energy contributions ε'_i for $1 \leq i \leq j$. The figure shows that the method has a preference to drop unwanted packets. For instance, at scale 4 the proposed method drops around of 22% of the legitimate packets and filters out around 48% of the unwanted packets. The expected value of the percentage of legitimate packet drops in this case is around 35%. The figure also shows that as the number of scales increases, more packets from the aggregate signal are dropped. In addition, it can be seen, as explained above, that at high scales the preference to filter out unwanted packets is drastically reduced.

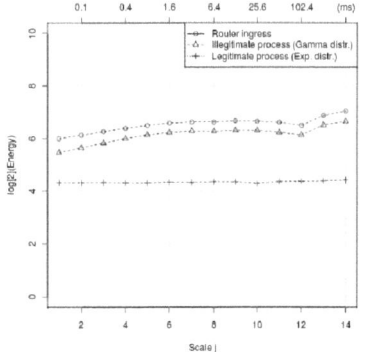

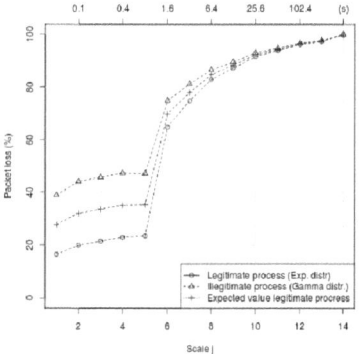

(a) MRA signatures of a legitimate and an unwanted process. The figure also shows the packet stream transmitted by a machine with these two processes as it arrives to the ingress of a router.

(b) Packet drops for unwanted and legitimate traffic and the expected value for latter. For each scale j, we show the values produced by the method using a signature formed by the energy contributions of the legitimate process until that scale.

Fig. 1. Application of the method to a packet stream that includes legitimate and unwanted packets. The legitimate process has exponentially distributed packet inter-arrival times with mean 20 ms. The inter-arrival times for the packets from the unwanted process follow a Gamma distribution with the same rate and shape c=1/4.

4   Experimental Evaluation

In this section we evaluate the proposed approach to limit unwanted traffic using real traffic traces. These traces are streams of Domain Name System (DNS) queries. We concentrate on this type of traffic for three reasons. First, because DNS queries are transmitted with a connectionless protocol i.e., UDP. Second, because limiting the number of DNS queries reduces the speed at which self-propagating code like e-mail worms propagates. [21]. Third, because it is then possible to limit the unwanted traffic produced by other families of malicious software that, as e-mail worms, use the DNS to conduct malicious activities. In the following section we show that the proposed method filters out packets from packet streams (i.e., DNS queries) and thereby it limits the amount of unwanted traffic that is send out. Furthermore, we show that the method has lower impact on the legitimate component of these streams than a rate limiting method that is based on the TB model.

4.1   Dataset Analysis

We use two sets of traces, hereafter named U-DS and W-DS. The packet streams in these traces are identified by the IP address of its host. U-DS was obtained at a university network by monitoring for approximately 13 hours the DNS queries that initiated from hosts located inside the network. It accounts for 6820 packet streams and represents legitimate traffic. W-DS was obtained from 71 different e-mail worms executables. We monitored their network activity and created a set of packet streams that represents unwanted traffic. In this dataset the activity period varies according to each worm and ranges from 11 minutes to 35 hours. The mean value for the duration of a packet stream in W-DS is 11 hours and the standard deviation 6 hours. Table 1 presents a summary of the distribution of the number of packets per packet stream in each dataset. This table suggests a heavy tail in the distribution of packets for the packet streams in U-DS, which is caused by hosts that change their IP address and by the typical usage of hosts in these type of networks. Specifically, hosts can be used by multiple users during different periods of time. Table 2 presents a summary of the distribution of packet inter-arrival times. It reveals that 25% of the inter-arrival times in the U-DS packet streams have at least an inter-arrival longer or equal than 26.2 seconds, in contrast to the 0.5 seconds in the W-DS trace. This suggests the presence of relatively long and frequent periods of inactivity in U-DS. By contrast, the inter-arrival times in W-DS are more concentrated around lower values. This is due to the functionality of worms, which are programmed to send emails with a high rate in order to increase the chances of causing an epidemic. Both tables suggest that the MRA signatures of the packet streams in these two sets of traces are different in nature. We investigate this in more depth in the following section.

Table 1. Summary statistics for the distribution of number of packets per packet stream

	Total	Mean	Min	25th Perc.	Median	75th Perc.	95th Perc	Max
U-DS	2 104 321	311	1	54	115	262	971	11 700
W-DS	2 663 557	37 514	360	6 206	26 130	46 650	114 119	251 300

Table 2. Summary statistics for the distribution of packet interarrival times (in seconds)

	Mean	Min	25th Perc.	Median	75th Perc.	90th Perc	95th Perc	Max
U-DS	97.68	0.000	0.004	0.338	26.2	290.61	599.80	43 320
W-DS	1.21	0.000	0.005	0.12	0.579	2.004	2.653	16 800

4.2 Signature Extraction

A central question to this work is if the burstiness in packet streams that are produced by legitimate end user-related processes is different than that of malware-related processes. To answer this question, we computed the MRA signatures for the packet streams in both traces. Given the nature of the network in which the traces were collected, we have divided the packet streams in the traces in sub-streams of one hour duration. In Table 3 we present the summary statistics of the energy contribution at low scales for the sub-streams produced from the packet streams in the U-DS trace. By contrast, in Table 4 we present the same statistics for the sub-streams produced from the e-mail worm traces. These two tables show that the MRA signatures of these two sets of packet streams are substantially different in this period of time. As an example, for each scale shown in the tables, around 95% of the end-user packet streams have a lower energy contribution than the 75% percent (25th percentile) of the unwanted traffic packet streams.

4.3 Experimental Results

In this section we apply to our set of traces the method proposed in Section 3, hereafter named TR-MRA. In particular, we use sub-streams of packets that are obtained by dividing the packet streams in U-DS and W-DS in periods of one hour. Later in this section we compare the results with those produced by a policing scheme based on the TB, which is explained in detail in Section 2. To set up the parameters of the TB we analyze the distribution of maximum number of packets per time unit for every packet stream. The reason why we use the maximum observed rate is to use parameters that do not cause legitimate packet

Table 3. Summary statistics of the energy distribution per scale for the packet streams in U-DS trace. Each packet stream is divided in sub-streams of one hour length.

Scale	Bin (s)	Trace (h)	Min	1st Q.	Median	Mean	3rd Q.	95th P.	Max
1	0.05	1	0	0.0001	0.0003	0.0012	0.0007	0.0040	0.3706
2	0.1	1	0	0.0001	0.0003	0.0015	0.0008	0.0048	0.6932
3	0.2	1	0	0.0001	0.0003	0.0018	0.0008	0.0054	1.0430
4	0.4	1	0	0.0001	0.0003	0.0021	0.0009	0.0061	1.0360
5	0.8	1	0	0.0001	0.0003	0.0027	0.0010	0.0066	2.0870
6	1.6	1	0	0.0001	0.0003	0.0035	0.0011	0.0071	3.0900
7	3.2	1	0	0.0001	0.0003	0.0047	0.0011	0.0080	9.2450

Table 4. Summary statistics of the energy distribution per scale for the packet streams in the W-DS trace. Each packet stream is divided in sub-streams of one hour length.

Scale	Bin (s)	Trace (h)	Min	1st Q.	Median	Mean	3rd Q.	95th P.	Max
1	0.05	1	0.0002	0.0731	0.6572	1.976	1.099	4.231	145.2
2	0.05	1	0.0002	0.0795	0.7172	2.213	1.354	4.291	163.2
3	0.05	1	0.0002	0.0745	0.7473	2.567	1.524	3.767	194.6
4	0.05	1	0.0002	0.0893	0.8249	3.038	1.748	4.985	243.8
5	0.05	1	0.0002	0.0914	1.0240	3.467	1.826	5.400	279.3
6	0.05	1	0.0002	0.0774	1.2490	4.510	2.072	6.643	381.4
7	0.05	1	0.0000	0.0888	1.3510	6.183	2.207	7.036	550.4

Table 5. Summary statistics of the packet rate at two different scales. These rates are obtained from the packet streams in the U-DS and the W-DS traces. Each packet stream is divided in sub-streams of one hour length.

Scale	Bin (s)	Duration (h)	Trace	Min	1st Q.	Median	Mean	3rd Q.	95th P.	Max
4	0.4	1	U-DS	0.00	1	2	3.27	4	9	149
			W-DS	0.00	4	10	10.5	12	18	197
7	3.2	1	U-DS	0.00	1	2	4.36	4	12	880
			W-DS	0.00	6	18	21.91	23	45	553

drops if no unwanted traffic is present in the packet stream. This configuration is shown in table 5. For space reasons, we include in there only two time resolutions i.e., 0.4 and 3.2 seconds.

A desired operational mode for containment methods is that of operating in a proactive mode. This mode eliminates the reaction time of a mitigation method because the containment method is, in this mode, applied by default i.e., before an end-user machine becomes compromised. A fundamental requirement for the methods that operate in this mode is that, in normal conditions, they produce a

Table 6. Percentile values of the legitimate packet drops due to the TB and the TR-MRA methods in proactive mode for packet streams of 1 hour length with no unwanted traffic

Scale	Bin (s)	Param.	Method	50th P.	75th P.	90th P.	95th P.	99th P.	100th P.
4	0.4	Median	TR-MRA	0.00	0.00	0.00	0.00	31.81	91.97
			TB	0.00	16.00	33.33	45.45	69.97	96.14
		95th P.	TR-MRA	0.00	0.00	0.00	0.00	31.81	91.97
			TB	0.00	0.00	0.00	0.00	19.19	85.51
7	3.2	Median	TR-MRA	0.00	0.00	0.00	0.00	31.81	91.97
			TB	0.00	25.00	42.85	57.14	80.00	98.07
		95th P	TR-MRA	0.00	0.00	0.00	0.00	31.81	91.97
			TB	0.00	2.77	20.29	33.33	66.67	96.76

very low number of false positives (i.e., legitimate packet drops). The following experiment demonstrates that the proposed method can operate in this mode. We evaluate both methods, TR-MRA and TB, using a configuration based on the median and the 95th percentile values in Tables 3 and 5 and operating at the scales presented in Table 5. In Table 6 we show the percentile values of the legitimate packet drops for these configurations. The values in the table indicate that, when there is no malicious activity, TR-MRA has in most cases a lower impact on the legitimate traffic component than the TB. For instance, for the method TR-MRA, the percentage of legitimate packet drops is 0% for 95% of the packet streams at scale 4. By contrast, for the TB method, the 95th percentile of the percentage of legitimate packet drops is 45%. The only case when the TB performs better than the TR-MRA is when it is configured with a more conservative configuration (i.e., using the 95th percentile values of the rate as parameters). The method based in the TB produces in this operational mode a higher number of false positives (i.e., when it operates at high scales) than when it operates at low scales. For our traces, the TR-MRA method is more robust than the TB as it is not affected by the scales at which it operates and produces the same results for all configurations. Hence, the TR-MRA method has the potential to be deployed in a proactive operational mode.

We here evaluate the effect of the methods on the legitimate and the unwanted components of a packet stream. We create sets of streams by aggregating pairs of legitimate and unwanted traffic traces of 1 hour length from the streams in U-DS and W-DS (i.e., packet streams produced by compromised end-user machines). In Tables 7 and 8, we present respectively the results for the false positive rate (percentage of legitimate packet drops) and the true positive rate (percentage of unwanted packet drops). We use a conservative configuration for the TB that uses the values for the 95th percentile at the 4th scale (these values appear in Table 5). For TR-MRA, we use the median values, as well conservative, that appear in Table 3 at the same scale. The values in Table 8 show that, with these configurations, both methods filter out a similar amount of unwanted traffic.

Table 7. Summary statistics on the percentage of legitimate packet drops (false positives) produced by the TB and the TR-MRA methods when they are applied to packet streams of 1 hour length that represent compromised end-user machine traffic.

Scale	Bin (s)	Method	Conf.	Mean	50th P.	75th P.	90th P.	95th P.	99th P.	100th P.
4	0.4	TR-MRA	Median	0.66	0.00	0.00	0.00	5.00	13.70	100.00
		TB	95th P.	0.84	0.00	0.00	0.00	5.12	28.67	100.00

Table 8. Summary statistics on the percentage of unwanted traffic packet drops (true positives) produced by the TB and the TR-MRA methods when they are applied to packet streams of 1 hour length that represent compromised end-user machine traffic.

Scale	Bin (s)	Method	Conf.	Mean	50th P.	75th P.	90th P.	95th P.	99th P.	100th P.
4	0.4	TR-MRA	Median	1.43	0.05	0.45	0.86	3.75	59.31	74.97
		TB	95th P.	1.43	0.05	0.45	0.86	3.75	59.31	74.89

By contrast, in Table 7 it is shown that the TR-MRA method outperforms the TB method in that it produces a lower number of legitimate packet drops. This is illustrated as follows. Both methods do not drop legitimate packets for 90% of the packet streams. The difference between the methods appears in higher percentiles than 90%. For instance, when the TR-MRA method is applied, for 99% of the packet streams the percentage of legitimate packet drops is below 13%. By contrast, for 99% of the packet streams, the percentage of legitimate packets drops produced by TB method is below 28%. These results show that the principle behind the TR-MRA method is a viable approach to limit unwanted traffic with less impact on the legitimate component of a packet stream than existing methods.

5   Conclusions and Further Work

In this paper we have presented a traffic regulation method that limits the unwanted traffic that a compromised end-user machine sends to the Internet. Instead of performing computationally expensive deep packet inspection (i.e., operating at the application level), the method constructs time series by counting the number of packets that end-user machines send out within a given period of time. Then, the method examines the burstiness instead of the rate of packets in a packet stream and produces MRA signatures produced by a wavelet transform (Haar basis). These signatures are then used to characterize the burstiness of a traffic process. The method filters out packets from packet streams that do not conform a given MRA signature (i.e., it regulates the burstiness in the packet stream that is being sent to the Internet). Specifically, it filters out packets using a similarity measure (e.g., the Euclidean distance), along with MRA signatures. We compared the method with a rate limiting method based on the Token Bucket model and show that the proposed method is more suitable to be deployed in a proactive operational mode (i.e., as a containment method) than methods that operate according to the rate of packets in a packet stream. This is because, in one hand, the proposed method limits (to a similar extent) the amount of unwanted traffic in a packet stream and, on the other hand, it produces a lower number of legitimate packet drops than the rate limiting method it is here compared to.

The proposed method has the following limitations. The first limitation, as discussed in Section 2, is that the method is limited to operate at low time scales because of the procedure applied to compute the MRA signatures. As a consequence, information on the burstiness of the packet stream at high scales is lost and thereby not exploited. Second, the method filters out packets using distance measures, along with MRA signatures, at the egress of a network infrastructure component. As a consequence, it does not take into consideration the burstiness of a packet stream as its packets arrive to the ingress of an infrastructure component. Thereby, some malicious software authors could exploit this design to limit the number of unwanted packets that the method filters out. A third limitation is that, with the actual design, it is very difficult to predict the number of legitimate packet drops.

In future work we will, in first place, investigate how to overcome the limitations described above. Second, we will extend our study to different types of packets streams and granularities e.g., legitimate and illegitimate TCP flows. Third, we will evaluate the use of MRA signatures for traffic classification systems that are based in flow-level characteristics. In connection to this, we will investigate if the method can be combined with deep packet inspection systems to exploit its ability to filter out traffic with preference towards illegitimate traffic. Finally, we envisage that the method can be applied in other contexts besides network security. Specifically, we want to investigate its application as a traffic policing scheme. The rationale behind is that, as shown in this work, the proposed method is suitable to characterize the traffic burstiness of the traffic that is forwarded by a network infrastructure component.

Acknowledgments. This work is funded by the German Federal Ministry of Education and Research within the scope of the G-Lab-Deep project[1] as part of the G-Lab project.

References

1. Kreibich, C., Kanich, C., Levchenko, K., Enright, B., Voelker, G.M., Paxson, V., Savage, S.: On the spam campaign trail. In: Proceedings of the 1st Usenix Workshop on Large-Scale Exploits and Emergent Threats (LEET 2008), pp. 1:1–1:9. USENIX Association, Berkeley (2008)

[1] http://www.g-lab-deep.de/

2. Moore, D., Shannon, C., Voelker, G.M., Savage, S.: Internet quarantine: Requirements for containing self-propagating code. In: Proceedings of the 22th International Conference on Computer Communications (INFOCOM 2003). IEEE Computer Society, Washington, DC (2003)
3. Dietrich, C., Rossow, C.: Empirical research on ip blacklisting. In: Proceedings of the 5th Conference on Email and Anti-Spam, CEAS 2008 (2008)
4. Cormack, G.V., Lynam, T.R.: Online supervised spam filter evaluation. ACM Transactions on Information Systems 25 (2007)
5. Solan, E., Reshef, E.: The effects of anti-spam methods on spam mail. In: Proceedings of the 3rd Conference on Email and Anti-Spam, CEAS 2006 (2006)
6. Weaver, N., Ellis, D.: Worms vs. perimeters: The case for hard-lans. In: Proceedings of the 12th Annual IEEE Symposium on High Performance Interconnects. IEEE Computer Society, Los Alamitos (2004)
7. Kalakota, P., Huang, C.T.: On the benefits of early filtering of botnet unwanted traffic. In: Proceedings of 18th International Conference on Computer Communications and Networks (ICCCN 2009). IEEE Computer Society, Washington, DC (2009)
8. Andersson, L., Davies, E., Zhang, L.: Report from the IAB workshop on Unwanted Traffic March 9-10, 2006. RFC 4948, Informational (2007)
9. Cisco Tech Notes: Comparing Traffic Policing and Traffic Shaping for Bandwidth Limiting. Document ID: 19645. Cisco Systems Inc.
10. Wong, C., Bielski, S., Studer, A., Wang, C.-X.: Empirical Analysis of Rate Limiting Mechanisms. In: Valdes, A., Zamboni, D. (eds.) RAID 2005. LNCS, vol. 3858, pp. 22–42. Springer, Heidelberg (2006)
11. Williamson, M.M.: Throttling viruses: Restricting propagation to defeat malicious mobile code. In: Proceedings of the 18th Annual Computer Security Applications Conference (ACSAC 2002). IEEE Computer Society, Washington, DC (2002)
12. Schechter, S.E., Jung, J., Berger, A.W.: Fast Detection of Scanning Worm Infections. In: Jonsson, E., Valdes, A., Almgren, M. (eds.) RAID 2004. LNCS, vol. 3224, pp. 59–81. Springer, Heidelberg (2004)
13. Chen, S., Tang, Y.: Slowing down internet worms. In: Proceedings of the 24th International Conference on Distributed Computing Systems (ICDCS 2004), pp. 312–319. IEEE Computer Society, Washington, DC (2004)
14. Zou, C.C., Gong, W., Towsley, D.: Worm propagation modeling and analysis under dynamic quarantine defense. In: Proceedings of the ACM Workshop on Rapid Malcode (WORM 2003), pp. 51–60. ACM, New York (2003)
15. Sekar, V., Xie, Y., Reiter, M.K., Zhang, H.: A multi-resolution approach for worm detection and containment. In: Proceedings of the International Conference on Dependable Systems and Networks (DSN 2006), pp. 189–198. IEEE Computer Society, Washington, DC (2006)
16. Mirkovic, J., Reiher, P.: A taxonomy of ddos attack and ddos defense mechanisms. ACM SIGCOMM Computer Communications Review 34, 39–53 (2004)
17. Jiang, H., Dovrolis, C.: Why is the internet traffic bursty in short time scales? In: Proceedings of the International Conference on Measurements and Modeling of Computer Systems (SIGMETRICS 2005), pp. 241–252. ACM, New York (2005)
18. Abry, P., Veitch, D.: Wavelet analysis of long-range dependent traffic. IEEE Transactions on Information Theory 44, 2–15 (1998)

19. Percival, D.B., Walden, A.T.: Wavelet Methods for Time Series Analysis. Cambridge University Press (2000)
20. Mallat, S.: A theory for multiresolution signal decomposition: the wavelet representation. IEEE Transactions on Pattern Analysis and Machine Intelligence, 674 –693 (1989)
21. Chatzis, N., Pujol, E.: Email worm mitigation by controlling the name server response rate, pp. 139–145. IEEE Computer Society, Los Alamitos (2008)

Network Securing against Threatening Requests

Yulong Fu and Ousmane Kone

University of PAU and Academy of Bordeaux
yulong.fu@etud.univ-pau.fr,
Ousmane.kone@univ-pau.fr
http://www.springer.com/lncs

Abstract. Networked systems mainly consists of autonomous components conforming to the network protocols. Those concurrent and networked components are potentially to be attacked by malicious users. They have to implement some mechanisms to avoid the possible threatening requests aimed at disrupting or crashing the system, and then provoke some denial of service attack. In this paper, we address this problem. We suggest a method to model this kind of components and we propose a robustness testing approach to evaluate the system security. A new definition of Glued_IOLTS is used to define this kind of system and an algorithm for robustness testing cases generation is given. A case study with the RADIUS protocol is presented.

1 Introduction

A central idea in systems engineering is that the complex systems are built by assembling components [1], and networked system is mainly consisted of autonomous components which conform the network protocols. These components were concurrent and networked, and are connected through some kinds of mediums to achieve some specific functions. Those concurrent and networked components are potentially to be attacked, and the network protocols have to implement some mechanisms to avoid the possible roguish requests which are aiming to disrupt or crash the system, and provoke a denial of service attack. Before deploying these components into the network, a phase of preliminary test is necessary to detect as soon as possible their capacities to resist and to be strongly secured against roguish inputs. But as the system become huge and many devices which conform different protocols were included, the principles and security issues become very complex and difficult to be analyzed. A formalist method to model the complex networks system and check the security validation base on the network protocols is strongly required. Robustness testing method considers the systems(components) work inside a complex environment, and all the normal and malicious requirements are checked to evaluate the system's robustness. Robustness testing to the network protocols can consider all the possible inputs(outputs) to the network system(devices), and check the security functions of the network protocols. We use the concurrent and networked components to model the network system, and use the robustness testing for the concurrent and networked components to check the network system's security.

J. Garcia-Alfaro et al. (Eds.): DPM 2011 and SETOP 2011, LNCS 7122, pp. 280–294, 2012.

Recently, more and more academies and researchers have mentioned this problem, and have done a lot of works on protocol conformance testing, robustness testing for the closed component, and some also considered the interoperability testing between two or more networked components. However, the robustness for the concurrent and networked systems seems be less talked about before, and we think this topic has a very realistic meaning. Because any potential risks of the concurrent components may make the system be possibly attacked and even be crashed.

The related works: In [2], the authors research on the problem of testing generation for interworking system. They generate the conformance test cases in a way of "on-the-fly", which used test propose(TP) to generate the test cases step by step to reduce the testing complexity. Although their research work is for the conformance testing, the multiple components are considered. In [3] and [4], the authors considered the interoperability testing of two concurrent components, and proposed their C-Methods to describe the concurrent system, then derive the pathes between two components to generate the interoperability test cases. In [5], the authors do well on the robustness testing for the software components, they considere the robustness problems for the closed components by experience. They give a definition of the addition set LSE (language specific error) for "dangerous" input values, and use this "error" set in their "Path generation" to generate their robustness test cases. In [6], the author presents a method to get the extended specification which include the considered "errors" to present the specification with Robustness. Our work is based on those forward works and go ahead to achieve the problem of robustness testing for the concurrent and networked components.

Our contribution is to extend the IOLTS(Input/Output Labelled Transition System) to give a definition of multiple concurrent and networked components. Then giving an approach and the algorithms to generate the robustness testing cases. This method can be used to design or examine the complex network protocol which included multiple components and different network layer protocols. The method can also be used in the software testing domain.

The following sections are organized as follows: In Section two, we introduce the general testing theories and our testing architecture. In Section three, the labelled transition system is introduced, the definitions, syntax for the LTS will be talked and our assumptions and approaches is given later. In Section four, one case study of concurrent components using RADIUS protocol is given. And the Section five is our conclusion and the future work.

2   Testing and Concurrent Components System

The Formal testing methods take the implementations as block-boxes [7], which can be only observed with inputs and outputs. In a specification based testing, a test case is a pair of input and output, which are derived from the specifications, and are executed through the implementation by the tester. The specifications are described as graphs by some kinds of modeling languages like

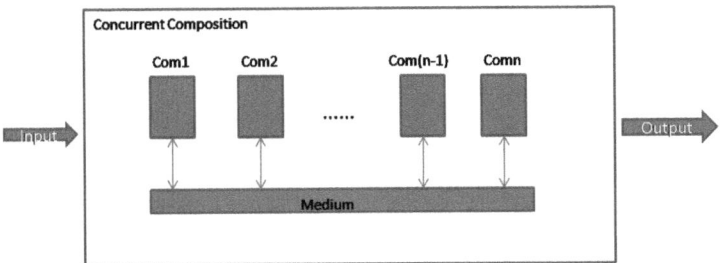

Fig. 1. Concurrent Component System

FSM, LTS ... etc. The test cases can be taken as traces of the graphs, and the testing methods are trying to see whether the traces of the specifications also exist in the implementations [8]. When running the test case through an implementation, the input sequence of the test case will cause the corresponding output sequence. If the outputs are similar to the pre-defined outputs in the test cases, we say this test case running is successful, and we note "**Pass**" to this test case. Otherwise, the test running is failed, and the test case is marked as "**Fail**" [9].

The concurrent components refers to the networked system which has many local or remote components to work together to finish some functions. Those components are connected through some materials or mediums, and exchanging messages and data through them. Fig.1 below is a brief view of concurrent components. In this example, there are n components works together, and communicated through a common Medium. Most testing methods take all the concurrent system as a black-box, which means the input and output data flows in Fig.1 become the only observable and controllable trace to the system. The processes and messages exchange inside cannot be touched by the tester.

We considered this concurrent and networked components testing from a simple instance with only two communicated components. The testing architecture is presented in Fig.2. In a concurrent components testing, each of the IUTs (implementation under test) has two kinds of interfaces. The lower interfaces LI_i are the interfaces used for the interaction of the two IUTs. These interfaces are only observable but not controllable, which means a lower tester(LT_i) connected to such interfaces can only observe the events but not send stimuli to these interfaces. The upper interfaces UI_i are the interfaces through which the IUT communicates with its environment. They are observable and also controllable by the upper tester(UT_i).

3 Robustness Testing Methods and Our Approach

Robustness is the degree to which a system or component can function correctly in the presence of invalid inputs or stressful environmental conditions [10]. Robustness testing concerns the appearance of a behavior which possibly

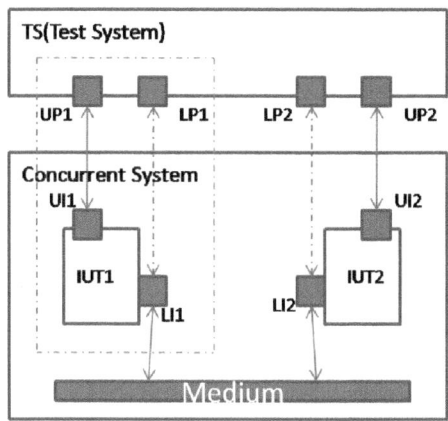

Fig. 2. Test Architecture

jeopardizes the rest of the system, especially under a wrong input. A system with robustness means it can be executed without crashing, even when it is used inappropriately [6].

We considered the specifications using IOLTS, which emphasize the input and output labels, and then we expand the IOLTS by adding the medium states and transitions into the definition to suit for the requirement of concurrent components.

3.1   Labeled Transition System

Labeled transition system is specification formalism studied in the realm of formal conformance testing, it is used for modeling the behavior of processes, and it serves as a semantic model for various formal specification languages [11].

Definition 1
A labeled transition system is a 4-tuple array $\langle S, L, T, s_0 \rangle$ where

- **S is a countable, non-empty set of states;**
- **L is a countable set of labels;**
- **T is the transition relation, which $T \subseteq S \times (L \cup \{\tau\}) \times S$**
- **s_0 is the initial state.**

The labels in L represent the observable actions which occur inside the system; the states of S are changing just cause of the actions in L. The sign τ denotes the internal and unobservable actions. The definition of T reveals the relations between states in S, for example: $(s_0, a, s_1) \in T$. A trace is a finite sequence of observable actions. The set of all traces over L is denoted by L^*, and ε denotes the empty sequence. If $\sigma_1, \sigma_2 \in L^*$, then $\sigma_1 * \sigma_2$ is the concatenation of σ_1 and σ_2. $|\sigma|$ denotes the length of trace of σ.

Definition 2

Let $P = \langle S, L, T, s_0 \rangle$ be a labeled transition system, s *and* $s' \in S$, **and let** $\mu_i \in L \cup \{\tau\}, a_i \in L$, **and** $\sigma \in L^*$, **then we have:**

$$s \xrightarrow{\mu} s' \quad =_{def} (s, \mu, s') \in T$$

$$s \xrightarrow{\mu_1 \ldots \mu_n} s' \quad =_{def} \exists s_0, \ldots, s_n : s = s_0 \xrightarrow{\mu_1} s_i \xrightarrow{\mu_2} \ldots \xrightarrow{\mu_n} s_n = s'$$

$$s \xrightarrow{\mu_1 \ldots \mu_n} \quad =_{def} \exists s' : s = s_0 \xrightarrow{\mu_1 \ldots \mu_n} s'$$

$$s \xRightarrow{\epsilon} s' \quad =_{def} s = s' \ or \ s_0 \xrightarrow{\tau \ldots \tau} s'$$

$$s \xRightarrow{a} s' \quad =_{def} \exists s_1, s_2 : s \xRightarrow{\epsilon} s_1 \xrightarrow{a} s_2 \xRightarrow{\epsilon} s'$$

$$s \xRightarrow{a_0 \ldots a_n} s' \quad =_{def} \exists s_0 \ldots s_n : s = s_0 \xRightarrow{a_0} s_1 \xRightarrow{a_1} \ldots \xRightarrow{a_n} s_n = s'$$

$$s \xRightarrow{\sigma} \quad =_{def} \exists s' : s \xRightarrow{\sigma} s'$$

$$trace(p) \quad =_{def} \{\sigma \in L^* | p \xRightarrow{\sigma}\}$$

$$init(p) \quad =_{def} \{\sigma \in L | p \xRightarrow{\sigma}\}$$

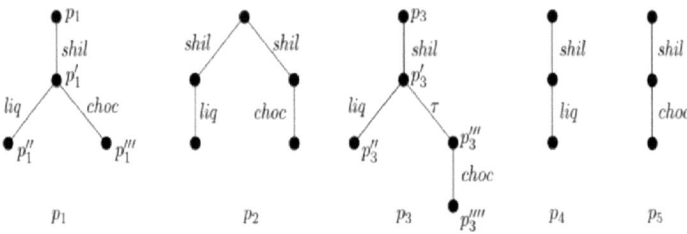

Fig. 3. Example of Candy Machine

Example 1: A normally Candy Machines can be specified by using LTS. The Candy Machine interacts with its environment by inserting shillings, and by supplying liquorice and chocolate. Fig.3 gives examples of a candy machine over the label set $L = \{shil, liq, choc\}$. P3 models a machine that accepts shilling, then either it supplies liquorice, or it makes an internal transition (τ) to offer chocolate. In this implementation of Candy Machine, $S = (p_3, p_3', p_3'', p_3''' and \ p_3'''')$, $L = (shil, liq, choc)$, $s_0 = p_3$, $\xrightarrow{choc}\}$, and $traces(p_3') = \{p_3' \xrightarrow{choc} p_3'''',$ and $p_3' \xrightarrow{liq} p_3''\}$.

Definition 3: An input-output transition system p is a labeled transition system in which the set of actions L is partitioned into input actions L_I and output action $L_U (L_I \cap L_U = \emptyset, L_I \cup L_U = L)$, and for which all input actions are always enabled in any state.

If $q \in S$, then $Out(q)$ denotes all the output labels from q, $In(q)$ denotes all the input labels to q, and $Out(S, \sigma)$ denotes the output of S after σ. $ref(q)$ represents the input actions which are not accepted by state q.

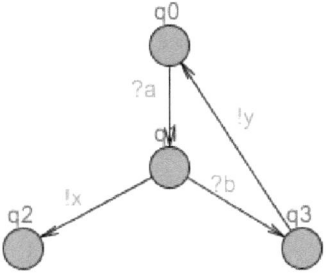

Fig. 4. Example of IOLTS

Example 2: Fig.4 is an example of Input/output labeled transition system. Comparing with LTS, it distinguishes the input labels and output labels to the system. In this example, $S = \{q_0, q_1, q_2, and\ q_3\}$, $L_I = \{a, b\}$, $L_U = \{x, y\}$, $Out(q_1) = \{x\}$, and $ref(q_1) = \{b\}$.

3.2   Our Approach

In a system with concurrent and networked components, the components need to communicate and work together like one component. These concurrent components have their own specifications, and normally, they can be tested separately. But we need a method to analyze those components together to generate the robustness testing cases.

As we described in Section 2, the concurrent components communicate each other through a common medium using their lower interfaces, and receive the messages from the environments through their upper interfaces(see Fig.2). We separated the states of each component which are directly connected to the common medium into higher_level states and low_level states, and we use the low_level states to define the common medium.

Definition 4
The states of the concurrent and networked components system have two levels:

- higher_level state s_{i_u} connects to the environment or other states of the same component.
- lower_level state s_{i_l} connects to the states of other components

A common medium is a subset of the lower_level interfaces of the states, which stimulate the messages to other components. We make S_M to denote all the states in the medium, s_i denote some state in $IOLTS_i$, s_j denote some state in $IOLTS_j$ then

$$\{\forall s \in S_M \mid \exists s_i,\ \exists s_j,\ s = s_{i\_l}, and\ Out(s_{i\_l}) \cap In(s_j) \neq \emptyset\}$$

The common medium is called "glue code" in some other articles [3], and inside the medium, it follows FIFO rules. We assume the medium' queue memory is infinite, so we do not consider the faults happened in the common medium here.

With the help of a common medium, we can glue the components together. We connect the medium states and the stimulated component's initial states with the same label as the medium state received(denoted as L_M). Then the different components are glued.

Definition 5
A Glued IOLTS. represents a set of IOLTSi (i=1,n) and a medium M, which is a 4-tuple:
$IOLTS_{glu} = \langle S_{glu}, L_{glu}, T_{glu}, s_{glu}\_0 \rangle$, which

- $S_{glu} = \langle S_1 \cup S_2 \cup ... \cup S_n \cup S_M \rangle$,
- $L_{glu} = \langle L_1 \cup L_2 \cup ... \cup L_n \rangle$,
- $s_{glu}\_0 = \langle s_1\_0, s_2\_0, ..., s_n\_0 \rangle$ is a set of initial states,
- $T_{glu} = \langle T_1 \cup T_2 \cup ... \cup T_n \cup T_M \rangle$, $T_M = \{t|t = (s_i\_l, \mu, s_j\_l), i \neq j, \mu \in Out(s_i\_l) \cap In(s_j\_l)\}$

Example 3: Fig.5 below shows a concurrent system with two components. The components' specifications can be expressed as S1 and S2. So we get the Medium states which are $S_M = \{S1_{3l}, S2_{3l}\}$. The Glued IOLTS are presented in Fig.6. The states of the medium are presented with a dual ring.

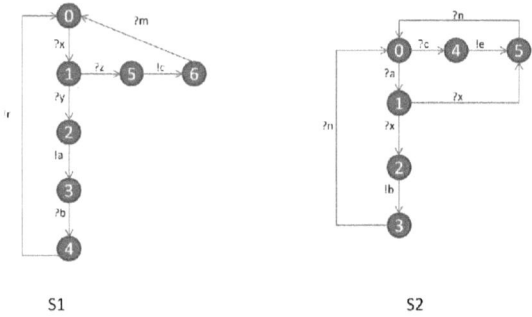

S1   S2

Fig. 5. Example of two simple components - Specification

Robustness testing needs to consider the following three kinds of possible inputs:

- Acceptable inputs, which are defined by the specifications, and sent or received inside the system, or between the components and the environment.
- Inopportune inputs, which can be taken as a subset of Acceptable inputs. But those kind of actions are sent to the wrong state of the system, and are rejected by those states.

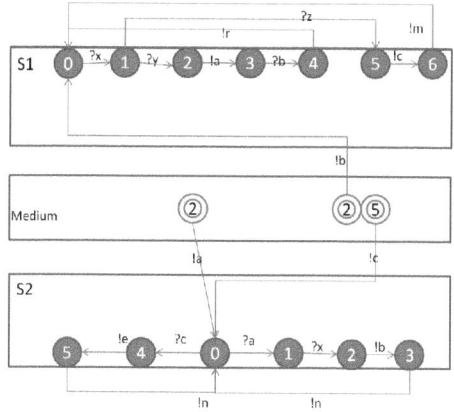

Fig. 6. Example of two simple components - Glued IOLTS

- Invalid inputs, which are out of the band of Acceptable inputs. Those invalid inputs are not acceptable to the system, and need to be tested through the robustness testing.

In order to obtain all the possible traces in the concurrent and networked components, first we need to extend the specification to include all the possible inputs actions. We use the "Meta-graph" to describe the processes of invalid inputs, and use the "Refusal Graph" to describe the inopportune inputs, then join them to one extended Glued IOLTS: S_{glu}^+ to describe all the possible pathes.

Definition 6
If the specification $S = (S^S, L^S, T^S, s_0{}^S)$ is an IOLTS, its meta-graph is a triplet $G = (V, E, L)$, where:

- $V = V_d \cup V_m$ represents the states. $V_m \subseteq 2^{Q^S}$ represents the states of S, and V_d represents the additional states to deal with the invalid inputs.
- L represents the actions of the meta-graph (the invalid inputs, outputs...).
- $E \subseteq V \times L \times V$ represents the transitions.

For example, the specification of Fig.4 has a meta-graph like Fig.7. The $?a'$ represents the invalid inputs of the specification states, $!x'$ represents the invalid outputs of specification states. The state $d1 \in V_d$, and $d2 \in V_d$ represents the states which are dealing with the invalid inputs and outputs. If the dealing state $d1$ and $d2$ receive the acceptable input $?a$, the state machine will go back to the initail state $q0$.

Definition 7
A RGraph is a bilabelled graph represented by a 5-tuple $(S, L, T, Ref, s_0)where$:

- S **is a finite set of states.**
- L **is a finite set of events.**

q0 q1 q2 q3

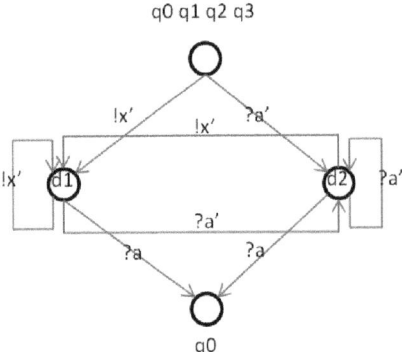

Fig. 7. an example of Meta-graph

- T **is a set of transitions.**
- Ref **is an application which defines for each state the set of events that may be refused.**
- s_0 **is an element of** S **called initial state.**

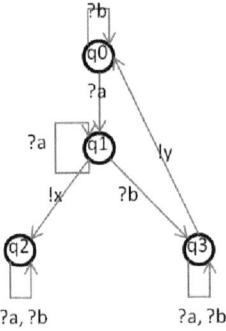

Fig. 8. an example of Refusal Graph

For example, in the specification of Fig.4. we can calculate the refusal actions for each states. $Ref(q0) = \{?b\}$, $Ref(q1) = \{?a\}$, $Ref(q2)=Ref(q3) = \{?a, ?b\}$. Then the refusal graph is like Fig.8. Each refusal labels are the inopportune inputs to the state.

Example 4: Fig.7 is the extended specification of the example 3. Here for a better understanding, we use GIB (Graph Invalid inputs Block) to describe the process of dealing with invalid inputs. By adding the elements of invalid and inopportune input actions, the S_{glu}^{+} includes all possible actions. We say the implementation of concurrent and networked components is robust if it follows the following conditions:

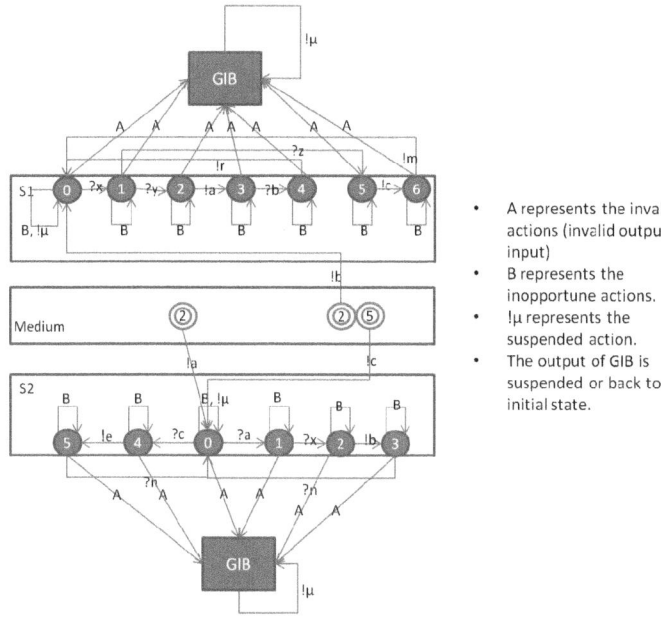

Fig. 9. Example of two simple components - Extended Specification

Definition 8
The implementations of a concurrent and networked components system are denoted as $IUTs$, S_{uni} represents the specification of the those implementations, then:

$$IUTs \ Robust \ S_{uni} \equiv_{def} \forall \sigma \in traces(S_{glu}^+) \Rightarrow Out(IUTs, \sigma) \subseteq Out(S_{glu}^+, \sigma)$$

According to Definition 6, we know that in order to check the robustness of this system, we need to see whether any traces in S_{glu}^+ can also be found in its implementation.

So the robustness test case can be generated through the following approach:

- Analyze the compositions' specifications to figure out the concurrent system described using Glued IOLTS S_{glu}.
- Calculate the S_{glu}^+
- Calculate all the possible pathes of the S_{glu}^+ to generate the test cases.
- Test Cases run on the implementation. If the implementation can pass all the test cases, the implementation is robust. If not, the implementation fail the robustness testing.

We give an algorithm in Listing 1. We believe the "initial" states are reachable, and we define the "end" states as the states which after them, the system goes back to the "initial" state or stop. The inputs of this algorithm is the Extended Glued_Specification. The pair $\langle stimulate, reponse \rangle$ denotes the actions between different systems, and the function opt() in the algorithm is to calculate the corresponding actions in this pair. The algorithm uses two recursions to trace back the specifications from the "end" states to the "initial" states. The algorithm uses an arraylist "Trace" to record all the passed labels. When the algorithm reach the "initial" state, it uses the function *Check_glue*() to detect the actions inputs from the common medium. If it find that the passed traces need the inputs from the medium, then it adds the corresponding medium label, and continue to trace back to another system. If it can not find the requirements from the passed traces, the algorithm stops this traceback, and continue to the next trace.

Listing 1. Algorithm

```
Inputs:  the states  of Glued_Specification S,
         the labels  of Glued_Specification L;
Outputs:  possible trace arraylists trace[m];
int k,m,n=0;
Arraylist trace[m], L_sti[k];
//trace[m] records the passed actions, and m represents different traces.
//L_sti[k] records the actions in one trace which will stimulate another systems.
//k represents different traces.
public main(){
    ArrayList<state> s_end;
    For (int i=0;i<S.size();i++){
        if(S.get(i).getStatus().equals("end")){
            s_end.add(S.get(i));
    }
    For (int i=0;i<s_end.size();i++){
        Traceback(s_end[i]);
        For(int j=0;j<n;j++){
            Check_glue(trace[j]);
        }
        For(int j=0;j<n;j++){
            print trace[j];
        }
    }
}
public trace Traceback(state s){
    ArrayList L= In(s);
    //arraylist L records all the input actions to state s
    If (s is initial state){
        return trace[m];
    }
    For(int i=0; i<L.size(); i++){
        trace[m+i].add(trace[m]);
        m=m+i;
        n=m;//count arraylist trace
    }
    For(int i=0;i<L.size();i++){
        trace[m].add(L.get(i));
        s=L.get(i).pre_state;
        Traceback(s);
        m=m-1;
    }
}
public void Check_glue(arraylist trace){
    For(int i=0;i<trace.size;i++){
        If (trace.get(i) in L_stiulate){
            L_sti.add(trace.get(i));
        }
    }
    If L_sti.size()=0{
        return trace;
    }
    else{
        For(int i=0;i<L_sti.size();i++){
            trace.add(opt(L_sti.get(i)));
            Traceback(opt(L_stiulate.get(i)).pre_state);
        }
        For(i=0;i<m;i++){
            Check_glue(trace[i]);
        }
    }
}
```

One possible trace for example 3 after using this algorithm is {?b !a ?y ?x !b ?x ?a !a ?y ?x}. For this trace, the algorithm begins from the end state 4 of system 1, and traces back to the initial state 0 of system 1. Then it finds the stimulate actions ?b in the trace, and adds the medium action !b to this trace and continue to trace back in system 2. When it reaches the initial state 0 of system 2, it finds another stimulate actions ?a exist in the trace, then it needs to add the medium action !a to this trace, and continue to trace back in system 1 until the initial state of system 1.

4   Experiment with RADIUS Protocol

RADIUS protocol is a network protocol between three basic components: client, NAS (network access server), and RADIUS server. The three components connected and worked together, to finish the handshaking and AAA (authentication, authorization, and accounting) security processes. This RADIUS system is a concurrent and networked components system.

Step 1. Analyze the specification and construct the Glued_IOLTS
We take the client as one part of the environment, so in the RADIUS protocol, there are two components : NAS and RADIUS server are considered. Fig.8 presents the Glued Specification of the "Authentication" processes between NAS and RADIUS server according to the standard RFC 2865 [12]. The interactions τ of RADIUS server part represent the processes of security checking. All labels' meanings can be found in Table 1.

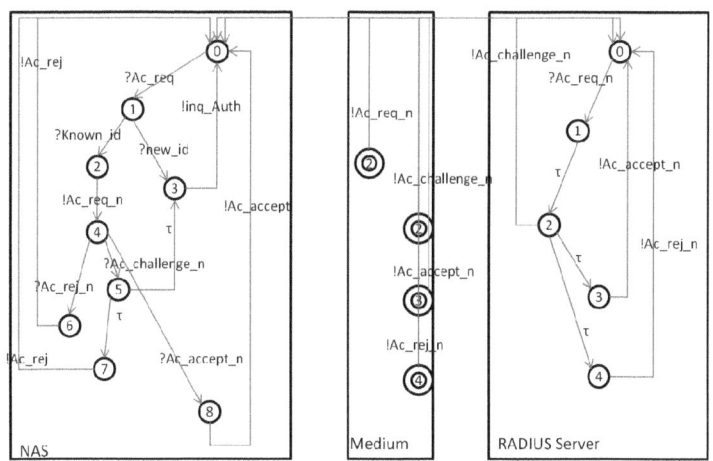

Fig. 10. RADIUS-NAS-Glued-Auth

Step 2. Calculate the S_{glu}^{+} and the possible traces
By adding the GIB and the refusal graphs at each side of Fig.8 to represent the invalid inputs and inopportune inputs, the S_{glu}^{+} can be obtained and presented in Figure 9. The Robustness Testing cases are calculated through our algorithm, it is a process of trace back. For example, one trace of Fig.9 {!Ac_rej, ?Ac_rej_n, !Ac_req_n, ?Known_id, ?Ac_req, !Ac_rej_n, *Tau*, *Tau*, ?Ac_req_n, !Ac_req_n,

Table 1. Labels and Meanings

?Ac_req	receive "Access-Request" message from Client
?Ac_req_n	receive "Access-Request" message from NAS
?Know_id	identify the client is connected before
?new_id	identify a new client
?Ac_rej_n	receive "Access-reject" message from RADIUS server
?Ac_challenge_n	receive "Access-challenge" message
?Ac_accept_n	receive "Access-accept" message from RADIUS server
!Ac_rej_n	send "Access-reject" message to NAS
!Ac_rej	send "Access-reject" message to Client
!Ac_challenge_n	send "Access-reject" message to NAS
!Ac_accept_n	send "Access-accept" message to NAS
!Ac_accept	send "Access-accept" message to Client
!inq_Auth	send "inquire username and password" message
τ	interactions (security methods, security...)

?Known_id, ?Ac_req} is one possible traceback result of our algorithm. So for this traceback, we got a robustness test case of RADIUS server protocol: {?Ac_req, ?Known_id}, and the corresponding output is {!Ac_rej}.

In this case study, we got 18 traces by considering the invalid inputs. And the results of considering the inopportune inputs are infinite. All the traceback results and the test outputs are listed in Listing 2.

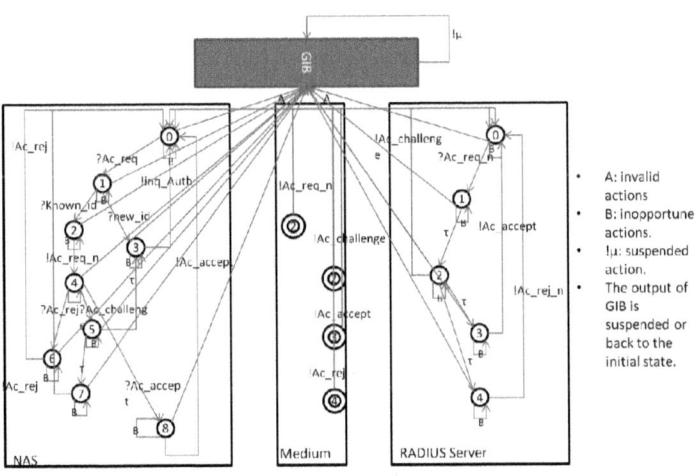

Fig. 11. RADIUS-NAS-Glued-Auth-Plus

Listing 2. Results of Trace back

```
Trace1 :  {? new_id ,? Ac_req }
Outputs :{! inq_Auth }
Trace2 :  {tau ,? Ac_challenge_n ,! Ac_req_n ,? Known_id ,
          ? Ac_req ,! Ac_challenge_n ,  tau ,? Ac_req_n ,
          ! Ac_req_n ,? Known_id ,  ? Ac_req }
Outputs :{! inq_Auth }
Trace3 :  {? Ac_rej_n ,! Ac_req_n ,? Known_id ,? Ac_req ,
          ! Ac_rej_n ,tau ,tau ,? Ac_req_n ,  ! Ac_req_n ,
          ? Known_id ,  ? Ac_req }
Outputs :{! Ac_rej }
Trace4 :  {tau ,? Ac_challenge_n ,! Ac_req_n ,? Known_id ,
          ? Ac_req ,! Ac_challenge_n ,tau ,? Ac_req_n ,
          ! Ac_req_n ,  ? Known_id ,? Ac_req }
Outputs :{! Ac_rej }
Trace5 :  {? Ac_accept_n ,! Ac_req_n ,? Known_id ,? Ac_req ,
          ! Ac_accept_n ,tau ,tau ,? Ac_req_n ,! Ac_req_n ,
          ? Known_id ,  ? Ac_req }
Outputs :{! Ac_accept }
Trace6 :  {invalidinput }
Outputs :  stop
Trace7 :  {invalidinput ,? Ac_req }
Outputs :  stop
Trace8 :  {invalidinput ,? Known_id ,? Ac_req }
Outputs :  stop
Trace9 :  {invalidinput ,? new_id ,? Ac_req }
Outputs :  stop
Trace10 :  {invalidinput ,! Ac_req_n ,? Known_id ,? Ac_req }
Outputs :  stop
Trace11 :  {invalidinput ,tau ,? Ac_challenge_n ,! Ac_req_n ,
           ? Known_id ,? Ac_req ,! Ac_challenge_n ,tau ,
           ? Ac_req_n ,! Ac_req_n ,  ? Known_id ,? Ac_req }
Outputs :  stop
Trace12 :  {invalidinput ,? Ac_challenge_n ,! Ac_req_n ,
           ? Known_id ,? Ac_req ,! Ac_challenge_n ,tau ,
           ? Ac_req_n ,! Ac_req_n ,  ? Known_id ,? Ac_req },
Outputs :  stop
Trace13 :  {invalidinput ,? Ac_rej_n ,! Ac_req_n ,? Known_id ,
           ? Ac_req ,! Ac_rej_n ,tau ,tau ,? Ac_req_n ,
           ! Ac_req_n ,? Known_id ,  ? Ac_req }
Outputs :  stop
Trace14 :  {invalidinput ,tau ,? Ac_challenge_n ,! Ac_req_n ,
           ? Known_id ,? Ac_req ,! Ac_challenge_n ,tau ,
           ? Ac_req_n ,! Ac_req_n ,  ? Known_id ,  ? Ac_req }
Outputs :  stop
Trace15 :  {invalidinput ,? Ac_accept_n ,! Ac_req_n ,
           ? Known_id ,? Ac_req ,! Ac_accept_n ,tau ,tau ,
           ? Ac_req_n ,! Ac_req_n ,? Known_id ,  ? Ac_req }
Outputs :  stop
Trace16 :  {invalidinput ,? Ac_req_n ,! Ac_req_n ,? Known_id ,
           ? Ac_req },
Outputs :  stop
Trace17 :  {invalidinput ,tau ,? Ac_req_n ,! Ac_req_n ,
           ? Known_id ,? Ac_req },
Outputs :  stop
Trace18 :  {invalidinput ,tau ,tau ,? Ac_req_n ,! Ac_req_n ,
           ? Known_id ,? Ac_req }
Outputs :  stop
```

Step 3. Assess the Robustness of the implementations

After the generations of the test cases, we need to use those test cases to test the implementations. The implementations are tested by checking the outputs with the outputs of the test cases. If the outputs of the implementations are the same as the test cases, the implementations are robust. For example, we take the trace 18 of listing 2 as a test input, which means some clients(or hackers) send a message sequence like {Access Request+Known_ID+Message for Security+Invalidinput} to the RADIUS server, the output should be "stop". If the tested system does not terminate this session, there is potential risk for the network device.

5   Conclusion

In this article, we propose a formal method to check the security of the network protocol. We believe by modeling the network system, and checking its robustness, the potential defects can be detected and then be fixed. We use the concurrent components to model and simulate the network system, and we extend the definition of Labelled Transition System to express this multiple components system. Then we give the definition, and our approach and algorithm to the robustness testing generation. We give an example of RADIUS protocol for using this method also.

For our future work, the errors which happen on the medium will be considered, and the algorithm with lower complexity will be given. The time condition also will be considered in the following research.

References

1. Bliudze, S., Sifakis, J.: A Notion of Glue Expressiveness for Component-Based Systems. In: van Breugel, F., Chechik, M. (eds.) CONCUR 2008. LNCS, vol. 5201, pp. 508–522. Springer, Heidelberg (2008)
2. Kone, O., Castanet, R.: Test generation for interworking systems. Computer Communications, 642–652 (1999)
3. Gotzhein, R., Khendek, F.: Compositional Testing of Communication Systems. In: Uyar, M.Ü., Duale, A.Y., Fecko, M.A. (eds.) TestCom 2006. LNCS, vol. 3964, pp. 227–244. Springer, Heidelberg (2006)
4. Ansay, T.: Compositional testing of communication systems-tools and case studies. Master's thesis, Concordia University (2008)
5. Lei, B., Li, X., Liu, Z.: Robustness testing for software components. Science of Computer Programming, 879–897 (2010)
6. Khorchef, S.: Un Cardre Formel pour le Test de Robustesse des Protocols de Communication. PhD thesis, University of Bordeaux 1 (2007)
7. Offutt, A.J., Liu, S., Abdurazik, A.: Geneartion testing data from state-based specification. Software Testing, Verification and Reliability, 25–53 (2003)
8. Lai, R.: A survey of communication protocol testing. The Journal of Systems and Software, 21–46 (2001)
9. Desmoulin, A., Viho, C.: Interoperability test generation: Formal definitions and algorithm. In: ARIMA-Numero Special CARI 2006, pp. 49–63 (2006)
10. Castanet, R., Kone, O., Zarkouna, K.B.: Tests de robustesse. tech. rep., LaBRI, IRIT (2003)
11. Tretmans, J.: Conformance testing with labelled transition system: Implementation relations and test generation. In: Computer Networks and ISDN Systems, pp. 49–76 (1996)
12. Rigney, C., Willens, S., Rubens, A.: Remote authentication dial in user service (radius). tech. rep., The Internet Society (2000)

A Workflow Checking Approach for Inherent Privacy Awareness in Network Monitoring

Maria N. Koukovini, Eugenia I. Papagiannakopoulou,
Georgios V. Lioudakis, Dimitra I. Kaklamani, and Iakovos S. Venieris

School of Electrical and Computer Engineering
National Technical University of Athens
Athens, Greece

Abstract. Despite the usefulness of network monitoring for the operation, maintenance, control and protection of communication networks, as well as law enforcement, network monitoring activities are surrounded by serious privacy implications. The inherent "leakage-proneness" is harshened due to the increasing complexity of the monitoring procedures and infrastructures, that include multiple traffic observation points, distributed mitigation mechanisms and even inter-operator cooperation. In this paper, an innovative approach aiming at realising the "privacy by design" principle in the area of network monitoring is presented; it relies on service-orientation primitives and abstractions, in order to verify and, when needed, to adjust network monitoring workflows, so that they become inherently privacy-aware before being deployed for execution.

Keywords: Network monitoring, privacy protection, access control, workflow verification, service decomposition.

1 Introduction

Network monitoring is very useful and important for purposes such as network operation, management, planning and maintenance, law enforcement, as well as the protection of the networks and their users from both accidental failures and malicious activities. Nevertheless, the flip side of monitoring activities is that they are natively surrounded by serious privacy implications, holding a position among the most "leakage-prone" areas of technology. Indeed, violations related to network monitoring and communications' surveillance have started hitting the headlines and feed the citizens' concerns. Moreover, the privacy domain is increasingly becoming a legislated area and legal implications surround network monitoring [19][10], whereas the underlying requirements originate not only from the data protection domain, but also from public welfare, such as public security.

In previous works (e.g., [8]), we have proposed solutions targeting privacy protection in the context of network monitoring; these works have considered the case where a single probe collects traffic data, feeding them to monitoring applications. However, monitoring infrastructures are in practice more complex, spanning across multiple traffic collection points and including distributed mitigation facilities, while involving cooperation of multiple operators.

J. Garcia-Alfaro et al. (Eds.): DPM 2011 and SETOP 2011, LNCS 7122, pp. 295–302, 2012.

The current traffic anonymisation (e.g., [14][12][7][9]) and access control (e.g., [2][6][13][17]) solutions are not suitable for such environments. The former, albeit useful as anonymisation libraries, base on "static" anonymisation patterns, while being vulnerable to attacks able to infer sensitive information [14][5]; on the other hand, the latter have not been designed for meeting the particular requirements of network monitoring [10], while they are still immature for highly dynamic environments and for automating privacy-awareness. Finally, works in the area of access control enforcement in workflow management systems (e.g., [3][4]) and Model-Driven Security (e.g., [1][11]), though important, suffer from enforcing security policies only at run-time and not during the workflow formation.

Therefore, this paper describes a work-in-progress approach aiming at introducing privacy awareness into distributed network monitoring. Considering a Service-Oriented Architecture (SOA) [16] abstraction of the network monitoring infrastructure and being centred around the concept of monitoring *workflow*, it undertakes the tasks of verifying and appropriately adjusting the workflow, so that it becomes privacy-compliant. The core ideas of this procedure are described in Section 3, while Section 2 summarises the reference architecture.

2   Reference Architecture

Our framework considers a modular, SOA-based approach for network monitoring, where the components –represented by *Agents*– are involved in *Tasks* comprising *Workflows*. As Figure 1 illustrates, a workflow's lifecycle can be roughly seen as consisting of two phases, notably *Planning* and *Execution*. The former, refers to the specification of the workflow by its designer, as well as its verification and transformation, that are the focus of this paper and described in Section 3. The Execution Phase relies on the Planning Phase's outcome and concerns the deployment of the workflow to the Agents and its execution by the underlying components; this is coordinated by entities referred to as *Orchestrators*, while the means for context and capabilities management are also provided.

Workflow verification and transformation is handled by the *Model Checker*, whereas a *Reasoner* provides the necessary intelligence, being the entity that incorporates and infers knowledge from a *Policy Model* [15]. The Policy Model consists of two basic elements: a semantically rich information model, providing abstractions of the underlying concepts, and access control rules. The latter define *permissions*, *prohibitions* and *obligations* over *Actions*, that reflect a structure similar to the *subject−verb−object* linguistic pattern and refer to situations where an *operation* op_i is performed by an *actor* a_i on a *resource* res_i, i.e., act_i = $\langle a_i,\ op_i,\ res_i \rangle$. Several types of entities may constitute actors and resources; they can be either concrete, such as *Users* and *Data*, or abstract, such as *Roles* and *Data Types*. The rules may contain additional provisions, including actions that should precede/follow the rule's enforcement, contextual conditions, as well as the –very essential for privacy– *purpose* under which the rule is applicable.

Actions are used for describing *Tasks* and *Workflows*, the definition of which is interrelated. A task t_i is an action act_i when being part of a workflow w, written

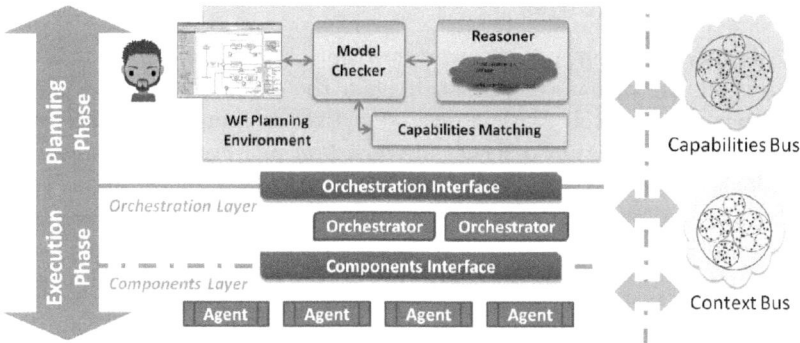

Fig. 1. Overall Architecture

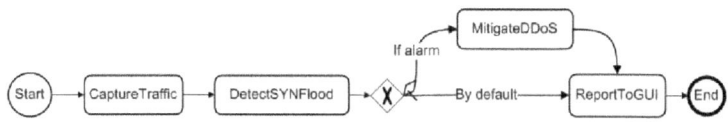

Fig. 2. The user-specified workflow

as a tuple $t_i = \langle a_i, op_i, res_i \rangle_w$. A workflow consists in a finite number of tasks, i.e., $w = \langle t_1, t_2, ..., t_n \rangle$, with control- and data-flow relationships among them. Typically, a workflow is initially specified by its designer (a user); thereupon, this workflow consisting of user-specified tasks, referred to as *skin tasks*, is subject to the workflow verification methodology, described in the following section.

3   Workflow Verification Methodology

The workflow verification procedure starts when a user u, referred to as the *initiator* and holding some role r, triggers the execution of the workflow w, declaring a purpose pu. It is worth mentioning that the initiator can also be the actor in certain tasks. This distinction serves the need to model cases where the initiator may not have access rights to a specific task himself, but can nevertheless include the task in the workflow, provided it is executed by an authorised subject. Based on the parameters $\langle w, r, pu \rangle$ and conducted by the Model Checker, the validation procedure aims at making sure that the workflow fulfils privacy and other access control requirements and includes three steps: *Purpose Verification*, *Skin Task Verification* and *Decomposition*, that are elaborated upon in the following subsections. To better illustrate, a reference network monitoring workflow example is used. In particular, we consider the scenario where a user holding the role `NetworkAdministrator` attempts to execute the workflow w depicted in Figure 2 declaring the purpose `NetworkSecurity`.

3.1 Purpose Verification

On the basis of the purpose the workflow initiator has declared, it is verified whether the initiator has the right to trigger the execution of a workflow serving this purpose, as well as that each skin task is compatible with the same purpose. The aforementioned checks are based on *role-purpose* and *task-purpose* associations, respectively, derived by the Policy Model in place. In our reference scenario, for example, it is verified that the role `NetworkAdministrator` can execute a workflow for the purpose of `NetworkSecurity` and that all tasks that appear in the workflow of Figure 2 are relevant and consistent to that purpose.

3.2 Skin Task Verification

In this step each skin task is evaluated[1], both individually and in relation to other skin tasks, regarding compliance with the policies controlling task sequence, access on operations and resources, input and output data and data flow between subsequent tasks. In that respect, requirements to be addressed include:

- The initiator must have the right to include the task in the workflow.
- The task $\langle a_i, op_i, res_i \rangle_w$ must be valid, i.e., the actor a_i must have the right to perform the operation op_i on the resource res_i.
- Each task must not conflict with precedent and subsequent tasks.
- Potentially required complementary tasks must be present.

The evaluation of each task is performed on the basis of the parameters tuple $\langle \langle a, op, res \rangle_w, r, pu \rangle$, i.e., all elements comprising the task, as well as the role of the initiator and the declared purpose. The evaluation result might be that the task is either: i) accepted, ii) conditionally accepted or iii) not accepted. Thereupon, and regarding the two latter cases, necessary modifications may need to be introduced, such as task additions, removals, substitutions, etc.

More specifically, in the case of conditional acceptance, there are two types of constraints that may arise, namely flow and real-time constraints. Flow constraints refer to the occasion where a task can be executed, provided that it is complemented with one or more certain required tasks that must precede, follow or be executed in parallel. If these tasks are not present in the workflow as required, the flow is modified accordingly. For instance, with reference to the above example, upon evaluation of the parameters $\langle \langle *, \texttt{MitigateDDoS}, * \rangle_w,$ `NetworkAdministrator, NetworkSecurity`$\rangle$ it is derived that the task `Inform-SecurityOfficer` must be executed every time `MitigateDDoS` is performed and must consequently be added to the workflow in the appropriate position.

Real-time constraints reflect the situation where, whether a task can be executed or not will eventually depend on the values of certain contextual parameters. This is addressed at design-time by ensuring that these parameters

---

[1] The skin tasks are first examined separately without considering their decomposition because, while still at the skin level, it is highly likely that not allowed task sequences are already discovered; consequently, a performance gain could be achieved by not evaluating at this step the decomposition of the tasks in question.

will indeed be evaluated at run-time and the workflow will proceed accordingly, thus specifying the differentiated behaviour of the workflow depending on real-time provisions. To this end, the task in question is replaced by a conditional branching structure, with one branch including and the other omitting the task, whereby a policy indicating the branch to be followed on occasion is attached.

Finally, a task may be not accepted because of incompatibilities identified among any of the parameters $\langle\langle a, op, res\rangle_w, r, pu\rangle$, or its relationship with other tasks; this may lead to the removal of the task, its substitution with one or more tasks in a way that the core semantics of the workflow are preserved, or even the rejection of the entire workflow. A typical case is when the type of data required as input by a task is not made available by the data flow specified. For example, upon evaluation of the parameters $\langle\langle$*, ReportToGUI, *, $\rangle_w$, NetworkAdministrator, NetworkSecurity$\rangle$, it comes out that, since the workflow has been initiated by a NetworkAdministrator, the ReportToGUI task should not have as input the detailed results of DetectSYNFlood, unless the detection task has raised an alarm; therefore, an AgggregateResults task is added before ReportToGUI in the corresponding ("by default") branch.

3.3 Decomposition

After having performed Skin Task Verification, it is determined how each higher level task is decomposed into more primitive ones (subtasks), according to the parameters $\langle\langle a, op, res\rangle_w, r, pu\rangle$. Subtask inter-relationships in resulting decompositions can have one of the following forms: *AND-decomposition*, where the execution of all subtasks is required; *XOR-decomposition*, where the execution of one of the subtasks will suffice; *Subworkflow decomposition*, meaning that the composite task is to be implemented by means of a subworkflow. Consequently, a high-level task is substituted by the corresponding AND-split/AND-join, XOR-split/XOR-join [18] or subworkflow construct, respectively. As an example, Figure 3 shows the Subworkflow decomposition of the task DetectSYNFlood.

However, task decomposition brings along implications, especially regarding the issues of workflow checking and modification. Given that each decomposition is directly derived from the Policy Model, it is valid as a stand-alone structure; still, the relationships between decomposition subtasks and the rest of workflow need to be evaluated. The procedure, which is omitted here due to lack of space, is quite similar to the one followed through Skin Task Verification in that, essentially, each subtask included in a decomposition is checked with respect to other tasks appearing in the workflow. The decomposition along with its evaluation proceed following a combined depth-first and breadth-first approach: each skin task is decomposed until no further valid decomposition can be derived or all of its subtasks are atomic tasks, and only after a skin task has been fully decomposed, the system continues with the decomposition of the next skin task (depth-first); at each level of a task's decomposition, the subtasks of this level are evaluated with respect to other tasks present in the workflow in its current status, before moving on to the next –lower– level (breadth-first). It should be mentioned that, during this procedure, not only the subtasks themselves, but also the

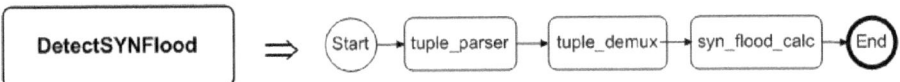

Fig. 3. The decomposition of task `DetectSYNFlood` in its subtasks

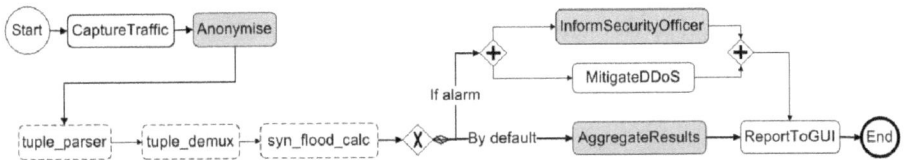

Fig. 4. The workflow as has been transformed during the verification procedure. Shaded boxes denote tasks that have been added, while dashed boxes are for tasks that appear as a result of decomposition.

type of their inter-relationships is considered: AND-decompositions imply that all subtasks must be acceptable in the current workflow, XOR-decompositions indicate that at least one of the task's descendants must be acceptable, while regarding Subworkflow decompositions, there must be at least one valid path from the subworkflow start- to end-node, in order for the task to be included.

Under this prism, decomposition relations affect conflicts detection and resolution. As can be inferred from the above, a conflict exists if all tasks participating in a XOR-decomposition or at least one task participating in an AND- or Subworkflow decomposition conflict with another task in the workflow; however, if that other task is part of a XOR-decomposition, the latter can possibly be narrowed down only to acceptable alternatives, so that finally no conflict appears. For instance, in the example workflow no conflict exists between tasks `DetectSYNFlood` and `CaptureTraffic`; during decomposition of the former, though, it is required upon evaluating the `tuple_parser` task that it must be performed only on anonymised data; this means that, in order for this task to be acceptable in the current workflow as part of the decomposition of `DetectSYNFlood`, an `Anonymise` task has to precede. Figure 4 illustrates this, along with all modifications described above for the reference workflow.

Finally, it is noted that during decomposition and skin task verification steps, each time a task is added or substituted, purpose and skin task verification are performed, while whenever a task at any decomposition level is rejected, checks must be performed up the decomposition levels, as this may result in further task rejections in higher levels, due to decomposition relationships.

4 Conclusions and Current Work

The work-in-progress presented in this paper targets at an innovative approach that aims at providing the highest possible degree of automation regarding the enhancement of network monitoring workflows with privacy features already at their specification phase. This brings along the significant advantage of maximising the chances of the workflow being executed correctly in functional (e.g., decomposition) as well as non-functional (e.g., privacy compliance) terms. Our methodology takes into account complex access control provisions (described in [15]) and enables their enforcement in the context of a distributed, SOA environment. Apparently, the concepts presented here could be applied also in other domains where privacy is a critical issue.

Current work includes the formal definition and usage, in the context of workflow verification, of more complicated concepts, such as *workflow paths* and *transformation patterns*. Furthermore, purpose is an overall complex notion and of critical importance with respect to privacy and, consequently, needs further investigation. Moreover, the effects of dynamic and contextual features on workflow evaluation and –especially– transformation include many aspects, some of which have not been yet considered; for example, in case conditional branching is specified by the workflow designer at some part of the workflow, the corresponding user-defined policies that control the flow need also to be evaluated against the Policy Model. Finally, the exact checks that need to be carried out are being further looked into. Specifically, complexity introduced as a result of task decomposition must be efficiently handled; some seemingly reasonable checks may lead to an impractical system due to performance reasons and, consequently, the underlying trade-offs need to be carefully evaluated. However, we argue that performance impact is likely of secondary importance in the proposed methodology, due to its off-line execution manner; in fact, its application at design- and not at execution-time, makes it tolerant to reasonable delays.

Acknowledgements. This research was partially supported by the European Commission, in the framework of the FP7 DEMONS project (Grant agreement no. FP7-257315). The research of M. N. Koukovini is co-financed by the European Union (European Social Fund - ESF) and Greek national funds through the Operational Program "Education and Lifelong Learning" of the National Strategic Reference Framework (NSRF) - Research Funding Program: *Heracleitus II. Investing in knowledge society through the European Social Fund.* Special thanks to our colleague Dr. Joaquin Garcia-Alfaro for the fruitful discussions and his valuable comments.

References

1. Alam, M., Hafner, M., Breu, R.: Constraint based role based access control in the sectet-framework a model-driven approach. Journal of Computer Security 16(2), 223–260 (2008)
2. Ardagna, C.A., Camenisch, J., Kohlweiss, M., Leenes, R., Neven, G., Priem, B., Samarati, P., Sommer, D., Verdicchio, M.: Exploiting cryptography for privacy-enhanced access control: A result of the prime project. Journal of Computer Security 18(1), 123–160 (2010)
3. Ayed, S., Cuppens-Boulahia, N., Cuppens, F.: Managing access and flow control requirements in distributed workflows. In: AICCSA 2008: IEEE/ACS International Conference on Computer Systems and Applications, pp. 702–710 (April 2008)

4. Ayed, S., Cuppens-Boulahia, N., Cuppens, F.: Deploying security policy in intra and inter workflow management systems. In: International Conference on Availability Reliability and Security, pp. 58–65 (2009)
5. Burkhart, M., Schatzmann, D., Trammell, B., Boschi, E., Plattner, B.: The role of network trace anonymization under attack. SIGCOMM Computer Communications Review 40(1), 5–11 (2010)
6. Cuppens, F., Cuppens-Boulahia, N.: Modeling Contextual Security Policies. International Journal of Information Security 7(4), 285–305 (2008)
7. Fan, J., Xu, J., Ammar, M.H., Moon, S.B.: Prefix-preserving IP address anonymization. Computer Networks 46(2), 253–272 (2004)
8. Gogoulos, F., Antonakopoulou, A., Lioudakis, G.V., Mousas, A.S., Kaklamani, D.I., Venieris, I.S.: Privacy-aware access control and authorization in passive network monitoring infrastructures. In: CIT 2010: Proceedings of the 10th IEEE International Conference on Computer and Information Technology (2010)
9. Koukis, D., Antonatos, S., Antoniades, D., Markatos, E., Trimintzios, P.: A generic anonymization framework for network traffic. In: IEEE International Conference on Communications, ICC 2006, vol. 5, pp. 2302–2309 (June 2006)
10. Lioudakis, G.V., Gaudino, F., Boschi, E., Bianchi, G., Kaklamani, D.I., Venieris, I.S.: Legislation-aware privacy protection in passive network monitoring. In: Portela, I.M., Cruz-Cunha, M.M. (eds.) Information Communication Technology Law, Protection and Access Rights: Global Approaches and Issues, ch. 22, pp. 363–383. IGI Global (2010)
11. Menzel, M., Meinel, C.: SecureSOA. In: IEEE International Conference on Services Computing, pp. 146–153 (2010)
12. Minshall, G.: Tcpdpriv, http://ita.ee.lbl.gov/html/contrib/tcpdpriv.html
13. Ni, Q., Bertino, E., Lobo, J., Brodie, C., Karat, C.M., Karat, J., Trombetta, A.: Privacy-aware role-based access control. ACM Transactions on Information and System Security 13(3), 1–31 (2010)
14. Pang, R., Allman, M., Paxson, V., Lee, J.: The devil and packet trace anonymization. Computer Communication Review (CCR) 36(1), 29–38 (2006)
15. Papagiannakopoulou, E.I., Koukovini, M.N., Lioudakis, G.V., Garcia-Alfaro, J., Kaklamani, D.I., Venieris, I.S.: A Contextual Privacy-Aware Access Control Model for Network Monitoring Workflows: Work in Progress. In: Garcia-Alfaro, J. (ed.) FPS 2011. LNCS, vol. 6888, pp. 208–217. Springer, Heidelberg (2011)
16. Papazoglou, M.P., Heuvel, W.J.: Service oriented architectures: approaches, technologies and research issues. The VLDB Journal 16, 389–415 (2007)
17. Preda, S., Cuppens, F., Cuppens-Boulahia, N., Garcia-Alfaro, J., Toutain, L.: Dynamic deployment of context-aware access control policies for constrained security devices. J. Syst. Softw. 84, 1144–1159 (2011)
18. Russell, N., Ter Hofstede, A.H.M., van der Aalst, W.M., Mulyar, N.: Workflow control-flow patterns: A revised view. Tech. Rep. BPM-06-22, BPM Center (2006)
19. Sicker, D.C., Ohm, P., Grunwald, D.: Legal issues surrounding monitoring during network research. In: IMC 2007: Proceedings of the 7th ACM SIGCOMM Conference on Internet Measurement, pp. 141–148. ACM, New York (2007)

Controlling Data Dissemination

Helge Janicke, Mohamed Sarrab, and Hamza Aldabbas

De Montfort University, Leicester LE19BH, UK
{heljanic,msarrab,hamza}@dmu.ac.uk

Abstract. We present a policy-based approach for the control of information flow between services. The controlled dissemination of information shared between services is achieved by the communication and enforcement of policies associated with shared information. The presented approach integrates easily as a communication middle-ware in existing service-based information systems keeping the management and distribution of policies transparent to the service implementation. This article focuses on the architecture and presents initial results that show the feasibility of the approach.

Keywords: Information Flow, Policy-Based Management, Dissemination Control, Privacy, Discretionary Access Control.

1 Introduction

Establishing private communication channels between peers in an service oriented system is well understood [11]. The confidentiality, integrity and authenticity of message exchanges from one service to another have been addressed in various research, eg. [12]. In this paper we consider the related problem of information flow and dissemination control. Given services can securely exchange messages there is an explicit need to communicate meta-information as to how a receiving service may use the information contained in a message. For example:

"Suppose Alice sends a message m to Bob via a secure channel c to prevent Eve (or any other attacker) to compromise the confidentiality of the message. Alice intention is of course to keep the information i contained in m secret from Eve. However, this intention was never communicated explicitly to Bob".

Traditional threat-models [6] assert that *Alice* and *Bob* are trusted; thus the confidentiality property of message m is preserved by the secure channel c. Consider now that the information i contained in m is processed by *Bob* (e.g. translated or fused in a mesh-up) and then retransmitted as a new message m'. Traditional approaches rely on the assumption that *Bob* is trusted not to disclose i to attackers (*Eve*), however they provide no means of communicating this requirement explicitly. The increasing openness of systems means that it becomes more difficult to develop a shared notion of an attacker and the assumption that *Bob* will not use the information is becoming unrealistic as most services today depend on the gathering and fusion of disparate information sources.

J. Garcia-Alfaro et al. (Eds.): DPM 2011 and SETOP 2011, LNCS 7122, pp. 303–309, 2012.
© Springer-Verlag Berlin Heidelberg 2012

The key contribution of this paper is a flexible policy-based mechanism that explicitly communicates the confidentiality constraints of a peer as part of information exchanges. The middle-ware approach not only provides means of automatically supplying the confidentiality constraints as part of message exchanges between peers, but also considers the flow of information at the application layer itself and is thus able to annotate the processed data with the appropriate policies to express confidentiality constraints on fused data.

2   Architecture

We take a middle-ware approach to control service's communication. Figure 1 conceptualises the architecture. The existing network stack provides secure point to point communication between peers. The policy middle-ware augments messages with meta-information describing confidentiality requirements. Between the service and the middle-ware is a sand-box. The sand-box isolates the service from the middle-ware/operating system and *traces the flow of information* through the service execution.

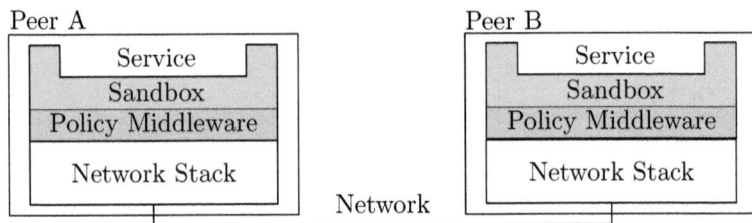

Fig. 1. Conceptual Model

3   Service

A service is a program executing on a single peer that processes information from various sources and communicates these with other services. A model of a service is a process that reads from data-sources $In = \{i_0, \ldots, i_n\}$ and writes to data-sinks $Out = \{o_0, \ldots, o_m\}$. The sandbox monitors an (in-)finite sequence of data-flows between sources In, program state S, and sinks Out. The program state is modelled as a set of memory segments s_i that can be addressed using variables. Data flow from a to b is denoted as $b \leftarrow a$, where $a, b \in In \cup Out \cup S$. The following flows are considered:

b	←	a	Description
S	←	In	input flow
Out	←	S	output flow
S	←	S	internal flow
S	←	$\emptyset$	erasure

For example the following pseudo-program can be expressed as a sequence of flows:

```
prog app:
    ds1 = read("data01.csv");
    ds2 = read("data02.csv");
    dsm = merge(ds1, ds2);
    write("146.227.68.96:2000", dsm);
end.
```

$ds1 \leftarrow \emptyset; ds1 \leftarrow data01.csv;$

$ds2 \leftarrow \emptyset; ds2 \leftarrow data02.csv;$

$dsm \leftarrow \emptyset; dsm \leftarrow ds1; dsm \leftarrow ds2;$

$stdout \leftarrow dsm$

The program reads data from two sinks (data01.csv and data02.csv) into memory. It then performs a merge on the data and keeps the result in dsm. It then writes the merged data to the address 146.227.68.96:2000. These four primitive flow operations describe the effect of the program execution rather than providing an alternative program semantics. Any service execution is described as an (in-) finite sequence of data-flows:

$$app = (s \leftarrow i_k \vee o_l \leftarrow s \vee s \leftarrow s \vee s \leftarrow \emptyset)^*$$

4   Sandbox

The sandbox isolates the service from the data-sources and data-sinks in such a way that it can intercept any input and output flow. It instruments the code such that it allows to associate with every write operation to a data-sink $o_k \in Out$ the set of data-sources $\{i_j, \ldots, i_k\}$ from which information is flowing. Based on these observation the sandbox constructs a flow-graph. For the previous example this is:

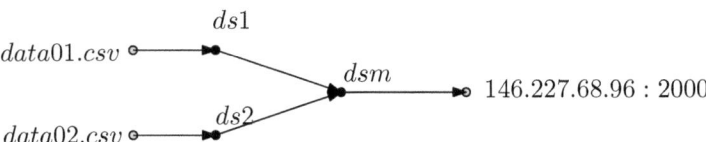

Fig. 2. Example flow within a Sandbox

We implemented a concrete sandbox for Java-Bytecode such that labels can be traced throughout the execution of a service programmed in Java. The sandbox semantics has been implemented by instrumenting the Java-Bytecode with assertions that communicate internal flows and stack-manipulations to a dedicated Runtime-Monitor. Initial performance tests show that this is a feasible approach resulting in overheads of factor 2-3 in execution time and memory usage mainly due to expanding byte-code size. Whilst this is still considerable, the prototype is not optimised and does not take advantage of static information flow analysis techniques that can reduce the overhead significantly.

5   Policy Middleware

The policy middle-ware is responsible for attaching meta-information to outgoing messages and to manage the meta-information for incoming messages. We take a discretionary approach and extract from a policy repository local to the service, a set of policy rules that reflect the confidentiality requirements of the data-sources that flow in the message exchange.

5.1   Policy

A policy is a set of rules that express how information contained in a data-source can be propagated. A key part of a policy specification is that it associates rules with user identities. For example the following rules could be present in *Alice*'s policy:

$$+ \texttt{data01.csv} \quad \rightarrow \quad \texttt{bob@example.com, eve@example.com}$$
$$+ \texttt{data02.csv} \quad \rightarrow \quad \texttt{bob@example.com}$$
$$- \texttt{data02.csv} \quad \rightarrow \quad \texttt{eve@example.com}$$

would allow information to flow from the data-sources `data01.csv` and `data02.csv` to the subject `bob@example.com`, but only allow the flow of `data01.csv` to the subject `eve@example.com`. An essential part of the middle-ware is the association of data-sinks with subjects.

The primary contribution of this paper is the linkage between policy-based dissemination control and information flow control at the service-level, we therefore use a simple policy language, but anticipate that the results are applicable to other privacy languages [7,3,1].

5.2   Middleware

The middleware intercepts all messages arriving for the application layer of the peer. Each incoming message is expected to carry a policy in addition to the application layer message. The *Ingress* Policy Enforcement Point (PEP) separates the message m from its policy p_m and queries the Policy Decision Point (PDP) whether the message should be passed to the Application Layer for Processing. This functionality is similar to a traditional firewall, if the PDP decides that the message should not be processed it returns a *DENY* to the *Ingress PEP*, if the message can be processed according to the policy it will respond *PERMIT* to the *Ingress PEP*. Depending on the policy-model used the PDP may retain or alter state information, such as attributes or history logs that can have an effect on future policy decisions. In this paper the only state retained by the PDP is the policy, which is changing based on the received messages and their dissemination policies.

The PEP passes the policy p_m to the PDP. The PDP *merges* (See Section 5.2) the policy with its own policy base and assigns a unique label l_m to the ingress message m. This label is then used by the sandbox to trace the flow of data contained in the message m using the label l_m.

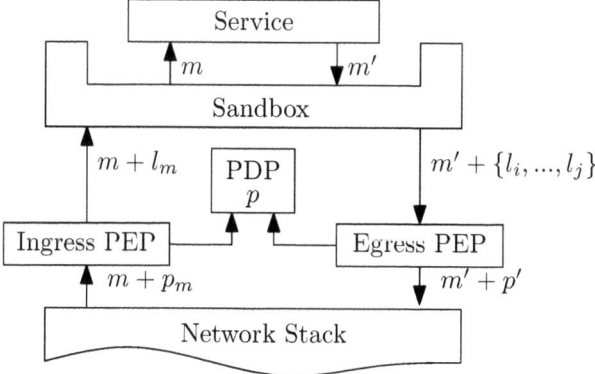

Fig. 3. Middleware Architecture

When a service is sending a message m', the sandbox will attach the set of labels $\{l_i, ..., l_j\}$ to the message before passing it on to the policy middle-ware. This set contains all labels that have been attached to data that has flown into the message. The *Egress PEP* now handles the message and queries the PDP whether the message can be send to the intended recipient. The policies that are being checked by the PDP are traditional access policies present on the peer, *as well as all policies that are matched to the labels* $\{l_i, ..., l_j\}$. If the PDP responds with *PERMIT* the message m' is augmented with a policy p' that is the combination of all policies matched to the labels $\{l_i, ..., l_j\}$ and send over the network to the intended recipient. Policies are often described as events, conditions and actions/consequence rules. Our approach requires an additional structure that maps labels to policies. A policy is therefore a set of tuples $\langle l_i, p_i \rangle$.

Ingress Policy Update. For every incoming message $m + p_m$ the PDP generates $l_m = hash(m)$ a hash (e.g. SHA2) of m as a label and update the policy p by entering a new tuple $\langle l_m, p_m \rangle$:

$$in(m, p_m) : p \leftarrow p \cup \{\langle l_m, p_m \rangle\}$$

Three cases for the update of the policy are distinguished:

1. The message m has previously been received by the peer with the same policy p_m. In this case the policy p effectively remains unchanged and the same label l_m will be traced through the sandbox.
2. The message m has previously been received by the peer with a different policy p'_m. In this case the policy p changes as the tuple $\langle l_m, p'_m \rangle$ is distinct from $\langle l_m, p_m \rangle$. The effect is that two tuples in p are indexed by the same hash l_m.
3. The message m and the policy p_m have not been received by the peer previously, hence the new tuple becomes part of p.

The hash l_m is then used by the sandbox to trace the message.

Egress Policy. For every outgoing message $m' + \{l_i, ..., l_j\}$ the PDP checks the message m' against *all* policies $\{p_i, ..., p_j\}$ for which $\langle l_i, p_i \rangle$ is in p. For the simple policy model described in Section 5.1 this is checking the recipient of the message against target flows. If a rule is matched, the rule type ($+$ or $-$) determines the decision. In our prototype simulation we take the approach that if at least one denial rule is matched the message will not be send. If the decision of the PDP is PERMIT, all policies $\{p_i, ..., p_j\}$ are attached to the outgoing message.

6 Related Work

There has been research on securing the data dissemination in peer to peer systems [2,4,5] such as message encryption, digital signature, key management etc. Traditional cryptographic solutions are using public key certificates to maintain trust, in which a Trusted Third Party (TTP) [10] or Certificate Authority (CA) certifies the identity associated with a public key of each communicated entities, therefore they can provide end-to-end secure communication channels. These approaches focus on message confidentiality, integrity and non-repudiation; they do not consider the dissemination of data between the communicating services. In [4] the confidentiality and integrity of communication to enforce access control to shared resources is addressed using PKI (Public Key Infrastructure).

More recently the focus has been on the enforcement and negotiation of privacy policies [1,3] to ensure that private identifying information (PII) is not disclosed without the consent of the individual concerned. Notably this has been applied in distributed environments that operate on low-power devices in [7]. Many challenges related to the management of data dissemination remain to be solved. One of which is the integration of such approaches into automated service-based systems – which we addressed in this paper. Trust is the important component in a security system and extensive work has been done on the negotiation of trust [13,9] within communities of peers [8]. We do not address the trust between peers in this paper, as we assume that all services are trusted in enforcing the communicated policies. We will address the integration of trust-modeling and enforcement mechanisms between services in our future work based on detected violations of policies in the system.

7 Conclusion and Future Work

We presented a framework of dissemination control for service-based distributed systems. The key contribution is the integration of runtime-monitoring techniques of application-level information flow with a policy-based mechanism to data-dissemination. Whilst most work on privacy makes the assumption that the application layer is implemented in a privacy-aware manner, the technique advocated in this paper allows for a transparent approach to dissemination control. Our framework uses a sandbox approach combined with run-time verification techniques to achieve this transparency, resulting is a much wider applicability of the underlying privacy-protection mechanisms. We provided a high-level semantic description of the sandbox and the monitoring mechanism that is able to trace flows throughout a service's execution and provided a prototype implementation for Java-based services.

We are investigating the ability of the Egress PEP to not only attach policies to the message, but to watermark the message such that a leakage of that message is attributable to the recipient. This capability would allow to integrate existing work on Trust-Management into our framework to establish the trustworthiness of recipients and adjust egress filtering rules accordingly.

References

1. Ardagna, C.A., Cremonini, M., De Capitani di Vimercati, S., Samarati, P.: A privacy-aware access control system. J. Comput. Secur. 16, 369–397 (2008)
2. Balfe, S., Lakhani, A.D., Paterson, K.G.: Trusted computing: Providing security for peer-to-peer networks. In: IEEE International Conference on Peer-to-Peer Computing, pp. 117–124 (2005)
3. Becker, M.Y., Malkis, A., Bussard, L.: A Practical Generic Privacy Language. In: Jha, S., Mathuria, A. (eds.) ICISS 2010. LNCS, vol. 6503, pp. 125–139. Springer, Heidelberg (2010)
4. Berket, K., Essiari, A., Muratas, A.: Pki-based security for peer-to-peer information sharing. In: IEEE International Conference on Peer-to-Peer Computing, pp. 45–52 (2004)
5. Damiani, E., De Capitani di Vimercati, S., Paraboschi, S., Samarati, P., Violante, F.: A reputation-based approach for choosing reliable resources in peer-to-peer networks. In: Proceedings of the 9th ACM Conference on Computer and Communications Security, CCS 2002, pp. 207–216. ACM, New York (2002)
6. Dolev, D., Yao, A.: On the security of public key protocols. IEEE Transactions on Information Theory 29(2), 198–208 (1983)
7. Gołaszewski, G., Górski, J.: Context Sensitive Privacy Management in a Distributed Environment. In: Meersman, R., Dillon, T.S., Herrero, P. (eds.) OTM 2010, Part I. LNCS, vol. 6426, pp. 639–655. Springer, Heidelberg (2010)
8. Jones, K., Janicke, H., Cau, A.: A Property based Framework for Trust and Reputation in Mobile Computing. In: Proceedings of the 2009 International Conference on Advanced Information Networking and Applications Workshops, pp. 1031–1036. IEEE Computer Society (2009)
9. Li, J., Li, N., Winsborough, W.H.: Automated trust negotiation using cryptographic credentials. ACM Trans. Inf. Syst. Secur. 13, 2:1–2:35 (2009)
10. Ooi, B., Liau, C., Tan, K.L.: Managing Trust in Peer-to-Peer Systems Using Reputation-Based Techniques. In: Dong, G., Tang, C., Wang, W. (eds.) WAIM 2003. LNCS, vol. 2762, pp. 2–12. Springer, Heidelberg (2003)
11. Stallings, W.: Cryptography and Network Security: Principles and Practice, 4th edn. Pearson Education (2005)
12. Xing, F., Wang, W.: Understanding Dynamic Denial of Service Attacks in Mobile Ad Hoc Networks. In: IEEE Military Communications Conference, MILCOM 2006, pp. 1–7. IEEE (2007)
13. Ye, S., Makedon, F., Ford, J.: Collaborative automated trust negotiation in peer-to-peer systems. In: IEEE International Conference on Peer-to-Peer Computing, pp. 108–115 (2004)

A Framework of Deployment Strategy for Hierarchical WSN Security Management

Christine Hennebert and Vincent Berg

CEA-Leti, MINATEC Campus,
Grenoble, France
{christine.hennebert,vincent.berg}@cea.fr

Abstract. The heterogeneity and relatively limited resources of the nodes deployed in hierarchical wireless sensor network (WSN) impose a new strategy to guarantee security and confidentiality. A deployment strategy is proposed and focuses on two different levels: complexity of the scheme and security requirement for the application. Three different cryptography mechanisms may be concurrently used in the same framework: PKI distribution, identity-based encryption and symmetric cryptography. As each mechanism has its advantages and disadvantages, criteria are proposed to associate each node with the most relevant security mechanism according to its capability and environment.

Keywords: WSN, Security, Cryptography, PKI, Identity-Based.

1 Introduction

The concept of the Internet of Things (IoT), a world where everything from tires to toothbrushes is connected [1], is emerging thanks to advances in low power wireless technologies, such as Low Rate Wireless Personal Area Networks (LR-WPAN IEEE 802.15.4) and Radio Frequency IDentification (RFID). The scale, heterogeneity and resource constraints of IoT devices pose new challenges, which should be addressed for their successful deployment. The European FP7 SmartSantander project proposes to deploy a scalable, heterogeneous large-scale facility composed of up to 12000 IoT devices in the city of Santander [2]. The vast majority of the IoT devices will relay information using wireless radio access. Security, privacy and trust in these new networks are key hurdles to be overcome.

The network architecture deployed in Santander is based on a hierarchical architecture with the server of the testbed at its head (Fig. 1). The server is connected through mostly wired networks to gateways that convey the information to the node either directly or using multi-hop connections. The interconnection between subnetworks employing different technologies (e.g.: IEEE 802.15.4 and RFID) is done via the server. Multiple applications with different security needs run on the testbed. This imposes different security requirements on the transiting information. Parking management, environment monitoring and WSN experimentation are examples of envisaged applications on the testbed.

This study proposes mechanisms to maintain the security for the whole network. A few key management schemes for WSN are proposed in the literature

J. Garcia-Alfaro et al. (Eds.): DPM 2011 and SETOP 2011, LNCS 7122, pp. 310–318, 2012.

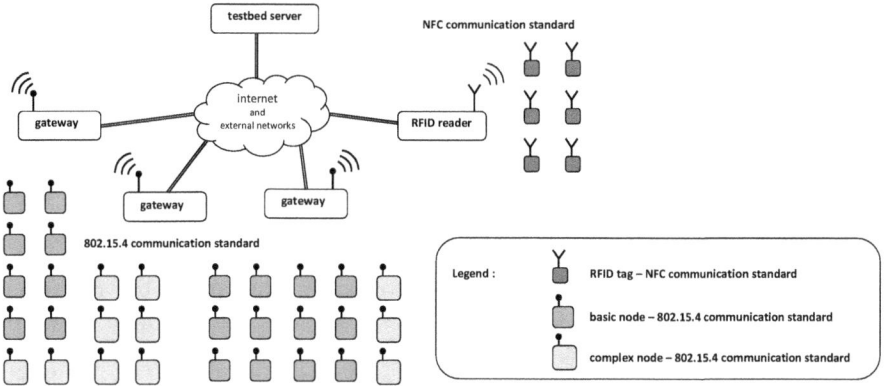

Fig. 1. Architecture of the WSN deployed in Santander

and some will be reviewed in Section 2. Most are adapted to homogenous networks and highlight the need for a security framework adapted to heterogeneous wireless sensor networks. Section 3 describes the proposed framework and introduces levels of security associated with different degrees of complexity and security needs. The advantages and disadvantages of the proposed mechanisms are then discussed in Section 4. Section 5 concludes the paper.

2   State of the Art

Most cryptography protocols described in the literature for securing a WSN rely on symmetric cryptography because of the limited resources available in the wireless sensor nodes. An initial secure channel has to be supplied to the system in order to exchange the common secret key. This may reduce its practical benefits. When a trust authority is present, in the case of hierarchical WSN architecture, these symmetric mechanisms could advantageously be completed by asymmetric cryptography techniques. Asymmetric cryptography algorithms may however lead to unreasonable complexity when systematically applied. The session key ([3] and [4]) is a practical compromise. Robust cryptography algorithms are essential to secure WSN and must be combined with relevant protocols in order to ensure the efficiency of the network security.

For some protocols, the foundation of a WSN security is based on a trust center or trust authority, which holds the secret key of the system. The ZigBee alliance for instance proposes a security extension [5] where the server keeps the master keys secret. Link and network keys are derived from the master keys to ensure the security between two entities or to broadcast a message. SPINS [6] is also built around a trust authority but distinguishes the authentication from the encryption. Each node owns a master key known to the server. All the other keys of the system are built with the help of a pseudo-random generator associated with the master key. A node receives from the server one key to use for authentication, associated with a timestamp-based protocol called SNEP, and a pairwise key to establish a secure link with each of its neighbors. The distinction between authentication and encryption reinforces the security. Alternatively, the System Manager security mechanism, introduced by Heo and Hong in 2006 [7] is based on a Public Key Infrastructure (PKI) using elliptic curve cryptography (ECC). A permanent public key and a temporary public key are defined for each node. Other protocols such as LEAP+ [8] do not require a formal trust authority also some may argue that the trust is shared as the nodes are initially pre-installed with the same master key. When the nodes are deployed to the WSN, they compute a set of keys associated to given time intervals before erasing the master key. The scheme exclusively relies on symmetric cryptography. An interesting idea is introduced: four levels of keys are built to assure node-to-node secure communications or message broadcasts. The introduction of several levels of keys brings up a scalable and efficient tool for the security needs of applications running on the WSN. If the authority holding the secret gets corrupted, the security of any element of the system is jeopardized. In his thesis published in 2009, Stenberg [9] details a technique of asymmetric key generation using ECC based on identity. Previous work [10] had established that the master key could be split into several pieces and stored in different nodes of the WSN, each piece owning a part of the secrecy. Stenberg proved that the identity key generator can be similarly split among several nodes of the WSN and proposed an elegant way to mitigate the risk of corruption of the authority center.

When using asymmetric cryptography, the emitter proves its identity with a digital signature and encryption guaranties the message confidentiality: only a legitimate receiver can then read the message. The digital signature requires a substantial amount of computational resources and leads to a significant overhead of information throughput. With symmetric cryptography, the authentication is performed using a Message Authentication Code (MAC). It is simple to compute and leads to a smaller overhead. Message broadcast authentication may be considered differently. A protocol, called TESLA [11], has been designed for message broadcasts and a lighter adaptation, called μTESLA, has been designed for WSN with limited resources [12]. A synchronization of the network entities is required for the authentication process. As for LEAP+, these protocols have been experimented in practical WSN infrastructures. Other protocols, like SPINS or System Manager, remain subjects of theoretical studies. No complete framework allowing the use of multiple protocols for a given heterogeneous WSN has been considered. Many questions raised in the SmartSantander context have been unanswered by previous work:

- How can we deploy and manage secret keys over time while maintaining a high level of security for the life duration of the system?
- How can we guarantee security of the nodes with limited resources without compromising the security of the largest nodes?
- How can we efficiently manage nodes using different communications standards?

3   Overview of the Security Framework

A common strategy is applied to deploy nodes and meet security needs over the lifespan of the WSN. It consists, for each node of the network, on the definition of a set of tasks to deploy and manage the secret keys. We propose to define 7 tasks of security management: (a) node deployment, (b) renewal of trust for one node, (c) reconnection of a node to the network, (d) resynchronization of a node, (e) maintenance or reprogramming of a node, (f) revocation of a node, (g) test of a node.

A pool of common steps are specified to realize all the tasks. For each step, a dedicated protocol should be written. It includes the messages that are sent, their content, the operations realized by each node and data that is stored permanently or temporarily in memory. Nine steps common to all the cryptography mechanisms are defined: (1) authenticate node, (2) synchronize node, (3) establish a pairwise channel, (4) broadcast the "Cluster" key, (5) broadcast the "Global" key, (6) maintain the channel between server and node, (7) revoke the node, (8) renew the trust, (9) test the node. The proposed framework supports three different cryptography mechanisms, but others could also be envisaged.

A **PKI distribution** requires a trust authority. The tesbed server takes this role, signs the node certificates using its secret master key (SMK) and manages the revocation list. The communication between the server and one node is secured using ECC-based asymmetric cryptography. Two pairs of keys secure the channel between the server and the node: one pair of secret/public keys (SK_s/PK_s) is owned by the server and another pair (SK_u/PK_u) is owned by the node. In the following protocol example, the node is initialized before deployment with its identity, ID_u, and a pair of keys, SK_u/PK_u. The "nonce" (a random number designed to avoid relay-attacks and used only once) is noted r_i and the certificate of node U is noted $Cert_u$. The meaning of the messages exchanged is marked between quotes. E indicates the encryption function and SIG is used for the digital signature. When an encryption or a decryption is realized, the key used for the operation is written in bold. The arrow indicates the way the message is exchanged between both entities.

Step 1: Addition of a node to the network with a PKI distribution mechanism

1. $U \rightarrow S$: "get_nonce", ID_u
2. $S \rightarrow U$: "send_nonce", ID_u, PK_s, r_A
3. $U \rightarrow S$: "get_cert", ID_u, PK_u, M_1 = E(m_1=("get_cert", ID_u, PK_u, r_A), **PK_s**), $Sign_1$ = SIG(Hash(m_1), **SK_u**), r_B
4. $S \rightarrow U$: "send_cert", ID_u, M_2 = E(m_2 =("send_cert", ID_u, $Cert_u$, r_B), **PK_u**), $Sign_2$ = SIG(Hash(m_2), **SK_s**), r_C
5. $U \rightarrow S$: "ack_cert", ID_u, M_3 = E(m_3=("ack_cert", ID_u, r_C), **PK_s**), $Sign_3$ = SIG(Hash(m_3), **SK_u**)

The **Identity-based encryption** mechanism uses ECC and requires a secure server. This server associates the Private Key Generator (PKG) with the node identities to build all the secret keys of the system, and delivers each key to its final owner (a node) via a pre-installed secure channel. The server may update a revocation list of the corrupted identities/nodes. The public key and identity of the node guarantees the authentication without certificate.

Symmetric cryptography is adapted to secure WSN and in the studied case, a hash chain of symmetric keys is computed for a node from a single seed.

The server holds all the keys of the hash chain for the given node and delivers successively the keys to the node after a time interval. At time interval t, the knowledge of the key $K(t)$ allows the recovery of all the previous keys according to the relation $K(t-1) = hash(K(t))$.

Security schemes using multiple levels of keys seem to be particularly adapted to the problem of SmartSantander. An analysis of the sensor network configuration leads to propose four different levels of keys: personal key, pairwise key, cluster key and global key.

Personal key: A personal key is assigned to each entity in the network and secures communications between the server and the node/gateway by providing a unique secure channel. It may be either symmetric or asymmetric and corresponds to the highest level of security at the node. A secure channel using this key may be established to transmit another key or to reprogram the node.

Pairwise key: The pairwise key secures a link between two neighboring nodes, i.e.: nodes accessible using single-hop route and supporting the same communication standard. This key uses symmetric cryptography independently from the key mechanism used by the personal key. When using asymmetric mechanisms, the pairwise key may be computed either by the server, or by the nodes using for instance Diffie-Hellman session key protocol [3]. In both cases, authentication is guaranteed by the server. The next protocol example establishes a pairwise key between two nodes for ID-based secured nodes. The pairwise key is computed by the nodes.

Step 3: Neighbor discovery for ID-based secured nodes – Pairwise key computed by the nodes

1. $U \rightarrow *$: "broadcast_hello", ID_u
2. $V \rightarrow U$: "here_neigh", ID_v, p, q, M_1 = E(m_1=(ID_v,r_A), **PK$_s$**), Sign$_1$ = SIG(Hash(m_1), **SK$_v$**)
3. $U \rightarrow S$: "check_id", ID_v, M_1, Sign$_1$, ID_u, M_2 = E(m_2=(ID_u,r_B), **PK$_s$**), Sign$_2$ = SIG(Hash(m_2), **SK$_u$**),
4. $S \rightarrow U$: "set_neigh", ID_u, M_3 = E(m_3=("set_neigh", ID_u, ID_v, r_B), **PK$_u$**), Sign$_3$ = SIG(Hash(m_3), **SK$_s$**), r_c
5. $S \rightarrow V$: "set_neigh", ID_v, M_4 = E(m_4=("set_neigh", ID_v, ID_u, r_A), **PK$_v$**), Sign$_4$ = SIG(Hash(m_4), **SK$_s$**), r_D
6. $U \rightarrow V$: "get_session_key", ID_v, ID_u, E(m_5=(ID_u, Y_a=g^{Xa} mod p),**PK$_v$**), Sign$_5$ = SIG(Hash(m_5),**SK$_u$**)
7. $V \rightarrow U$: "get_session_key", ID_u, ID_v, E(m_6=(ID_v, Y_b=g^{Xb} mod p),**PK$_u$**), Sign$_6$ = SIG(Hash(m_6),**SK$_v$**)
8. $U \rightarrow S$: "ack_neigh", ID_u, M_7 = E(m_7=(« ack_neigh », ID_u, ID_v, K_{uv}=Y$_b$^{Xa} mod p, r_c), **PK$_s$**), Sign$_7$ = SIG(Hash(m_7),**SK$_u$**)
9. $V \rightarrow S$: "ack_neigh", ID_v, M_8 = E(m_8=(« ack_neigh », ID_v, ID_u, K_{vu}=Y$_a$^{Xb} mod p, r_D), **PK$_s$**), Sign$_8$ = SIG(Hash(m_8),**SK$_v$**)

where p is a prime number and g is primitive root mod p, X_a and X_b are random numbers

---

In this other example, the pairwise key is established between two heterogeneous nodes, the first node is using a PKI-based mechanism, while the second one is secured by a symmetric cryptography. The pairwise key is generated by the server. A new notation is introduced, T_i, and indicates the type of node and its associated security mechanism.

Step 3: Neighbor discovery between PKI secured node U and symmetric secured node V

1. $U \rightarrow *$: "broadcast_hello", ID_u, T_u
2. $V \rightarrow U$: "here_neigh", ID_v, T_v, M_1 = E(m_1=(ID_v, T_v, r_A), **K$_u$(1)**), Mac$_1$ = MAC(m_1, **K$_u$(1)**)
3. $U \rightarrow S$: "check_auth", ID_v, T_v, M_1, Mac$_1$, ID_u, T_u, M_2 = E(m_2=("check_auth", ID_u, T_u, Cert$_u$, r_B), **PMK**), Sign$_2$ = SIG(Hash(m_2),**SK$_v$**)
4. $S \rightarrow U$: "set_neigh", ID_u, M_3 = E(m_3=("set_neigh", ID_u, ID_v, K_{uv}, r_B), **PK$_u$**), Sign$_3$ = SIG(Hash(m_3), **SMK**), r_c
5. $S \rightarrow V$: "set_neigh", ID_v, M_4 = E(m_4=("set_neigh", ID_v, ID_u, K_{uv}, r_A), **K$_v$(1)**), Mac$_4$ = MAC(m_4, **K$_v$(1)**), r_D
6. $U \rightarrow S$: "ack_neigh", ID_u, M_5 = E(m_5=("ack_neigh", ID_u, ID_v, r_c), **PMK**), Sign$_5$ = SIG(Hash(m_5),**SK$_u$**)
7. $V \rightarrow S$: "ack_neigh", ID_v, M_6 = E(m_6=("ack_neigh", ID_v, ID_u, r_D), **K$_v$(1)**), Mac$_6$ = MAC(m_6, **K$_v$(1)**)

Cluster key: Cluster keys are symmetric keys that are distributed to a set of nodes sharing similar interests (e.g.: geographical area, same data types or same application). These nodes may be of different technologies and a same node may belong to many clusters. The clusters may regroup nodes that are not necessarily neighbors. Communications between two subnetworks using different communication standards is achieved by the server through gateways.

In the following example, the cluster key is called K_{Cm} and it is broadcast to a subnetwork via the gateways G_1. Temporary keys K_{bc1} are used for broadcast and are disclosed with some delay to the nodes of the cluster. The cluster is identified by the tag IDC_m, while D_{UTC} and T_{UTC} are for date and time respectively. The bold arrow indicates a wired secured link.

Step 4: cluster key broadcast into a sub-network

1. $S \blacktriangleright G_1$: "broadcast_ckey_SSL", IDC_m, M_1 = E(m_1=("broadcast_ckey", IDC_m, K_{Cm}, D_{UTC},T_{UTC}), $\mathbf{K_{bc1}}$), Mac_1 = MAC(m_1,$\mathbf{K_{bc1}}$)
2. $G_1 \rightarrow *$: "broadcast_ckey", IDC_m, M_1, Mac_1
3. $U \rightarrow *$: "broadcast_ckey", IDC_m, M_1, Mac_1
4. $V \rightarrow *$: "broadcast_ckey", IDC_m, M_1, Mac_1

    ...

5. $S \blacktriangleright G_1$: "send_ckey_SSL", IDC_m, $\mathbf{K_{bc1}}$
6. $G_1 \rightarrow U$: "send_ckey", ID_u, ID_{G1}, M_2 = E(m_2=("send_ckey", ID_v, ID_{G1}, IDC_m,K_{bc1}, D_{cur}, T_{cur}),$\mathbf{K_{G1u}}$), Mac_2 = MAC(m_2,$\mathbf{K_{G1u}}$)
7. $U \rightarrow V$: "send_ckey", ID_v, ID_u, M_3 = E(m_3=("send_ckey", ID_v, ID_u, IDC_m,K_{bc1}, D_{cur}, T_{cur}),$\mathbf{K_{uv}}$), Mac_3 = MAC(m_3,$\mathbf{K_{uv}}$)

    ...

Global key: The global key is a cluster key that extends to the whole network. It uses symmetric cryptography and the size of the key is imposed by the characteristics of the smallest node of the network. It is sent to all the nodes of the network irrespective of their type.

4   Cost and Security Evaluation

To evaluate and compare the proposed security mechanisms we used the following criteria: memory cost in the nodes, complexity of the embedded functions, overhead on the throughput, ease of maintenance and management of the secret. Due to space constraints, only the results of the evaluation are presented. IEEE 802.15.4 and RFID nodes have been considered. For IEEE 802.15.4 nodes, symmetric and asymmetric keys are of size 128 bits using respectively AES-128 and ECC-based encryption. For the RFID nodes, only symmetric keys of 32 bits length are considered. The PKI distribution mechanism uses certificate of length 128 bits. Several algorithms may be employed to make the digital signature. Double encryption authentication is considered. For symmetric cryptography, the signature is achieved with a simple CBC-MAC function, producing a 32-bit overhead. The identity is encoded on 16 bits.

Memory cost: Memory space used by the node is impacted by the number of neighbors it records. We expect each node to record between 10 and 30 neighbors. PKI distribution mechanism is the greediest in terms of memory, due to the presence of the certificates. The ID-based encryption mechanism appears as an interesting compromise as it consumes hardly more memory space than symmetric cryptography while offering the benefits of an asymmetric cryptography.

Embedded complexity: Asymmetric cryptography adds a fair amount of complexity with regard to symmetric cryptography. The digital signature is the most complex function and may be replaced by a double encryption authentication using the asymmetric encryption function.

Overhead on the throughput: Symmetric cryptography leads to a small overhead as the CBC-MAC allows message authentication with only 32 bits overhead. But this advantage is limited as keys should be renewed more frequently. The overhead of the ID-based encryption mechanism is small. Although PKI distribution gives more flexibility of authentication, it comes at a significantly larger overhead in terms of throughput.

Secret management and ease of maintenance: PKI distribution mechanism offers the highest scalability thanks to the management of certificate as proof of trust according to each entity of the network. The trust is renewed without changing key or identity. Symmetric cryptography mechanism offers a good flexibility by the use of the hash key chain. The personal key is easily updated and allows renew of trust at the same time. ID-based encryption mechanism does not renew trust as well as it requires a modification of the node identity.

Table 1 reviews the advantages and disadvantages of the considered mechanisms from the point of view of the node.

Table 1. Advantages of the different schemes for the node (more ⋆ means better suited)

Criterion	PKI	ID-based	Symmetric
Memory Space	⋆	⋆⋆⋆⋆	⋆⋆⋆
Complexity	⋆⋆	⋆⋆	⋆⋆⋆⋆
Throughput Overhead	⋆⋆	⋆⋆⋆	⋆⋆
Ease of maintenance	⋆⋆⋆⋆	⋆	⋆⋆
Secret Management	⋆⋆⋆⋆	⋆⋆⋆	⋆

PKI distribution mechanism offers the best security and flexibility thanks to the management of certificate as proof of trust at the price of a higher complexity and throughput overhead. The server holds the system's secret: the "Secret Master Key" used to sign certificates. The certificate is created independently from the identity or the secret key of the node.

Symmetric cryptography mechanism requires significantly less computational complexity on the node but memory requirements should not be overlooked, as keys are stored in the node. The overall security is based on a hash chain of symmetric keys computed from a single seed. This hash chain should be managed and maintained by the server. The keys should be renewed more frequently giving a non-negligible throughput overhead. For tiny nodes the protocol may be further simplified and traded with security requirements.

ID-based encryption mechanism enjoys asymmetric cryptography but may prove more difficult to maintain as trust and identity are connected. This scheme is cost effective in terms of memory and throughput overhead. Memory space requirements are reduced as public keys are not stored but generated on the fly, throughput overhead is reduced as keys are not sent. Public and private keys are related to the identity of the node and are therefore relatively difficult to update. The trust of the system is based on the key itself, and the whole network may get corrupted when the "Secret Master Key" stored in the server is disclosed.

5   Conclusion

In this paper a framework of security management has been described: it proposes a deployment and management strategy adapted to the security of WSN composed of heterogeneous nodes. The nodes support different communication standards and have different amount of resources. A pool of security steps have been identified and each step supports three different security mechanisms which may be simultaneously deployed. The security scheme proposes 4 levels of secret keys to give flexibility to the nodes and the applications. The paper also proposed criteria to evaluate the different mechanisms as a function of the application scenario. Although based on a qualitative analysis, the tool will help to decide the mechanism to deploy according to node constraints and security objectives. Further work will involve the practical deployment in the SmartSantander infrastructure to validate the choices made in this paper. The feasibility of coexisting security mechanisms and the relevance of the strategy will be tested.

Acknowledgments. The research leading to these results was derived from the European Community's Seventh Framework Program (FP7) under Grant Agreement number 257992 (SmartSantander).

References

1. ITU Internet Reports 2005: The Internet of Things, International Telecommunications Union
2. SmartSantander Project, http://www.smartsantander.eu
3. Diffie, W., Hellmann, M.E.: New directions in cryptography. IEEE Transactions on Information Theory IT-22, 644–654 (1976)
4. El Gamal, T.: A Public Key Cryptosystem and a Signature Scheme Based on Discrete Logarithms. In: Blakely, G.R., Chaum, D. (eds.) CRYPTO 1984. LNCS, vol. 196, pp. 10–18. Springer, Heidelberg (1985)
5. Boyle, D., Newe, T.: Securing Wireless Sensor Networks: Security Architectures. Journals of Networks 3(1) (January 2008)
6. Perrig, A., Szewczyk, R., Wen, V., Culler, D., Tygar, J.D.: SPINS: Security Protocols for Sensor Networks. In: Proceedings of Seventh Annual International Conference on Mobile Computing and Networks, MOBICOM 2001 (July 2001)
7. Heo, J., Hong, C.S.: Efficient and Authenticated Key Agreement Mechanism in Low-Rate WPAN Environment. In: 1st International Symposium on Wireless Pervasive Computing, pp. 1–5 (2006)
8. Zhu, S., Setia, S., Jajodia, S.: LEAP+: Efficient Security Mechanisms for Large-Scale Distributed Sensor Networks. In: Proceedings of the 10th ACM Conference on Computer and Communication Security, CCS 2003, New York, USA (2003)
9. Stenberg, E.M.: Distributing a Private Key Generator in Ad-hoc Networks. Thesis Report, Tromsø University (May 2009)

10. Zhou, L., Haas, Z.J.: Securing ad hoc networks. IEEE Network Magazine 13(6), 24–30 (1999)
11. Perrig, A., Canetti, R., Tygar, J.D., Song, D.: The TESLA Broadcast Authentication Protocol. CryptoBytes 5(2), 2–13 (2002)
12. Liu, D., Ning, P.: Multi-Level μTESLA: Broadcast Authentication for Distributed Sensor Networks. ACM Transactions on Embedded Computing Systems (TECS) 3(4) (November 2004)

Author Index